Intelligence Support Systems

Intelligence Support Systems

Technologies for Lawful Intercepts

Paul Hoffmann and Kornel Terplan

CRC Press
Taylor & Francis Group
Boca Raton London New York

CRC Press is an imprint of the
Taylor & Francis Group, an **informa** business
AN AUERBACH BOOK

CRC Press
Taylor & Francis Group
6000 Broken Sound Parkway NW, Suite 300
Boca Raton, FL 33487-2742

First issued in paperback 2019

© 2006 by Taylor & Francis Group, LLC
CRC Press is an imprint of Taylor & Francis Group, an Informa business

No claim to original U.S. Government works

ISBN-13: 978-0-8493-2855-8 (hbk)
ISBN-13: 978-0-367-39245-1 (pbk)
Library of Congress Card Number 2005041064

Library of Congress Cataloging-in-Publication Data

Hoffmann, Paul.
    Intelligence support systems : technologies for lawful intercepts Paul Hoffmann, Kornel Terplan.
        p. cm.
    Includes bibliographical references and index.
    ISBN 0-8493-2855-1 (alk. paper)
    1. Intelligence service--Law and legislation--United States. 2. Electronic
surveillance--United States. 3. Law enforcement--United States. I. Terplan, Kornel. II.
Title.

KF4850.H64 2005
345.73'052--dc22

2005041064

Visit the Taylor & Francis Web site at
http://www.taylorandfrancis.com

and the CRC Press Web site at
http://www.crcpress.com

Contents

Preface

Telecommunications service providers are facing increased information and technical assistance requests to support law enforcement requirements, subpoenas, court orders, search warrants, and more. At the same time they are struggling with their own CapEx and OpEx reductions. On the other hand, law enforcement agencies face subpoena backlogs, expensive telecommunication interface options for data collection, and substantial resource requirements for data retention.

In this book, we will address the information and intelligence needs of wireline, wireless, cable TV, and Internet service providers; law enforcement agencies; representatives of government and international standards bodies; and product and service vendors. We will provide solutions for many technical and technological challenges, including:

- How to provide networking equipment and probes for lawful intercepts
- How to reduce performance impacts on network equipment and facilities due to lawful intercepts
- How to access, deliver, and collect information in real-time
- How to improve mediation efficiency while serving multiple functions
- How to deal with data retention and preservation issues
- How to standardize intercept technologies for various service portfolios and infrastructure components

Intelligence support systems (ISSs), the focus of this book, are about intelligence as opposed to security. Security involves providing firewalls, anti-virus protection, and intrusion detection and prevention; in other words, security is about guarding against loss. Conversely, in ISS, information is gathered about illegal activities, and that knowledge is applied to increasing security where applicable. ISSs interface with, or are part of, billing, ordering, provisioning, and authenticating systems, as well as law enforcement systems.

Chapter 1 deals with ISS basics, such as ISS application areas and positioning ISSs in the hierarchy of other support systems (OSS, BSS, and MSS). This chapter also summarizes basic requirements of law enforcement agencies. The legal background of electronic surveillance laws and duties is reviewed, with an emphasis on the basics for prerequisites of surveillance, execution rules, sanctions for noncompliance, and reimbursement strategies. Finally, a generic view of lawful intercept architectures is provided, detailing access, delivery, and collection functions.

Chapter 2 is devoted to service portfolios and networking technologies, such as circuit switching, packet switching, and wireless and cable solutions for voice, data, and video. In the case of all of these technologies, specific challenges for ISSs are outlined. Also, options for data collection and processing are reviewed.

Evolving surveillance standards are introduced in Chapter 3. Descriptions are provided of U.S. and European reference models focusing on basic lawful intercept functions and information handover interfaces.

Generic infrastructure components, such as applications, computers, storage areas, and networks, are evaluated in Chapter 4. Evaluation criteria include data-capturing options using hardware or software probes. Data collection solution architectures are also described, including probes, in-band and out-band handover, and using signaling systems as information sources. In addition, performance effects are estimated.

Chapter 5 focuses in depth on lawful intercept architectures. Access, delivery, and collection functions are discussed in regard to various service portfolios and networking infrastructure components. Particular emphasis is placed on real-time mediation as the core function of ISSs. The delivery function involves other receiver applications as well, such as fraud management, customer care, billing, capacity analysis, and prepaid credit checks. Telecommunications service providers will have to deal with large data volumes. This chapter offers solutions for data warehousing, data mining, and data retention and preservation.

Chapter 6 provides an overview of the lawful intercept frameworks and tools available from different vendors. In addition, guidelines for product evaluation and selection are addressed.

ISS solutions are addressed in Chapter 7. Multiple case studies are presented for various technologies (traditional voice, wireless, cable, IP, and Web) using different frameworks and tools vendors (e.g., SS8, Siemens, Aqsacom, and GTEN).

Operational principles are presented in Chapter 8. After technical recommendations for the United States, Europe, and Japan are outlined, the flow of lawful intercept execution is addressed in depth. Particular emphasis is placed on inventory control, order management, provisioning, fault management, and service quality in regard to the management reference model outlined in earlier chapters. Also, security frameworks are introduced as complementary solutions to ISS operations. Based on a lawful intercept model, typical job descriptions for subject matter experts are included, along with head-count estimates for various network sizes.

Financing new developments is not easy for service providers. Cost recovery solutions are rare. Chapter 9 quantifies cost components and analyzes various business models of mutual benefit to law enforcement agencies, service providers, and vendors. Also, cost reimbursement strategies are outlined for the United States, Europe, and Japan. Finally, based on one-time and recurring cost components, average expenses for lawful intercept missions are calculated.

In several cases, outsourcing models are beneficial to all parties. Chapter 10 addresses outsourcing criteria of telecommunications service providers, law enforcement agencies, application service providers, and service bureaus. In addition, the role of consulting companies is reviewed. Finally, sourcing guidelines and contract management issues are addressed.

Chapter 11 predicts trends and future directions in the areas of service, infrastructure components, frameworks, and tools supporting lawful interception. Specific expectations are outlined for the access, delivery, collection, and administration functions of lawful intercepts.

Acknowledgments

We have learned the basics about lawful intercepts from TeleStrategies, McLean, Virginia. We have used the input from TeleStrategies events and, in particular, from personal meetings with Jerry Lucas to position ISS among support systems, to define intercept access points in different networking infrastructures, and to evaluate cost-reimbursement strategies. With the study results of WIK Consult (Franz Buellingen and Annette Hillebrand), we have compared G7 countries regarding surveillance strategies, privacy policies, legal guidance for lawful interception, sanctions in cases of noncompliance, and expense reimbursement strategies. Finally, we have utilized our consulting experiences in the infrastructure sectors of telecommunications service providers in both Europe and the United States.

Framework and product suppliers provided the source to prepare the framework and product sections (Chapter 6) and the case studies (Chapter 7). Particular thanks are due to Simon Ou (Lucent Technologies); Bernd Oblinger, Joerg Axner, and Angela Timmermann (Siemens AG); Cemal Dikman (SS8 Networks); Ben Epstein (Aqsacom); Michael Ruecker (Utimaco); and Jim Hourihan (Acme Packet). Additional appreciation is due to Aqsacom and SS8 for helping with excellent acronyms and glossaries.

Also the IPDR.org (Steve Cotton and Aron Heinz) has contributed with protocol selection recommendations for the handover interface.

We would like to thank Adam Szabo for preparing the artwork and Greg Edmondson for editing the manuscript.

Special thanks are due to Richard O'Hanley (publisher), Claire Miller (managing editor and art director) and Gerry Jaffe (project editor). They were extremely helpful in every phase of this production.

Trademarks

The following list includes commercial and intellectual trademarks belonging to owners and holders whose products and services are mentioned in this book:

AcmePacket

- Net-Net Session Director™ (SD)
- Net-Net Session Router™ (SR)

Aqsacom (All Registered Trademarks)

- ALIS
- ALIS-d
- ALIS-m
- Centralized Management and Distributed Delivery (CMDD)
- Centralized Management and Centralized Delivery (CMCD)

ETI Connect

- Lawful Intercept Network Connector™ (LINC)

Forensics Explorers

- NetWitness™

GTEN (All Registered Trademarks)

- Data Collection and Filter Unit (DCFU)
- Daviath
- Amado
- Gemini
- Poseidon
- Poseidon Mobile

Siemens AG

- The Monitoring Center™

SS8 Networks (All Registered Trademarks)

- Xcipio Framework
- Xcipio for Circuit Switch Delivery Function (CSDF)
- Xcipio for Internet Access Delivery Function (IADF)
- Xcipio for Call Data Delivery Function (CDDF)
- Xcipio for CP-2300 ISP
- Xcipio for Wireless Data Delivery Function (WDDF)
- Xcipio for Softswitch Delivery Function (SSDF)

Utimaco Safeware AG

- Interception Management System™ (IMS)

About the Authors

Paul Hoffmann

Paul Hoffmann is a highly regarded telecommunications and organizational security expert with over 30 years of technical, product development, consulting, and training experiences.

After successfully completing his postgraduate studies in the field of electrical engineering and business administration, Paul worked for Phillips Germany, Litton Business Computer, Wang Computer, and Wetronic Automation before establishing Datakom Germany in 1986 and co-founding Datacom Akademie, which offers a wide variety of technical management services for global corporations throughout Europe. The primary focuses of the firm's professional activities are to address the network management, performance evaluation, and troubleshooting needs of corporations, government agencies, and telecommunications service providers.

In 2000, GTEN AG was founded and became a subsidiary of Datakom Germany. The firm uses the motto "Intelligence for a Better World" and offers cutting edge lawful interception technology products and services for carriers, ISPs, and law enforcement agencies.

Paul is a member of BAKS, the Federal College for Security Studies, and is holder of patents for lawful interception technologies. He has written over 100 articles and presented over 50 papers on national and international conferences.

Kornel Terplan

Kornel Terplan is a telecommunications expert with more than 30 years of highly successful multinational consulting and teaching experience.

He has provided consulting, training, and product development services to over 75 national and international corporations on 4 continents, while following a scholarly career that combined some 150 articles, 24 books, and 120 papers, including editorial board services.

His consulting work concentrates on network management products and services, operations support systems, traffic management, business service management, outsourcing, network management centers, strategy of network management integration, implementation of network design and planning guidelines, products comparisons, technologies for lawful interception, and benchmarking service and network management solutions.

His most important clients include AT&T, BMW, Boole & Babbage, Coca Cola, Creditanstalt Austria, Commerzbank (Germany), Ford Europe, France Telecom, Georgia Pacific Corporation, German Telekom, Groupe Bull, GTE, Hungarian Telecommunication Company, Kaiser Permanente, Salomon Brothers, Siemens, Swiss Credit, Telcel Venezuela, Union Bank of Switzerland, Unisource, and Walt Disney World.

He is Industry Professor at Brooklyn Polytechnic University in New York and at Stevens Institute of Technology in Hoboken, New Jersey.

Chapter 1

Setting the Stage

CONTENTS

The focus of intelligence support systems (ISSs) is on expanded infrastructure requirements of telecommunications service providers (TSPs), which are basically no different from the requirements of operations support systems (OSSs) and business support systems (BSSs). Intelligence plays two principal roles in this area. On one hand, it provides surveillance by collecting information on illegal activities, such as terrorism, criminal activities, fraud, and money laundering, and on the other hand, it provides the basic data that improve the bottom line of TSPs, such as revenue assurance, business intelligence (BI), and protection against telecommunications fraud. In short, ISSs are software elements or units that interface with, or are subsumed under, billing and ordering systems, provisioning and authentication systems, and outside parties such as law enforcement agencies (LEAs) (Lucas, 2003f).

TSP will be used as a generic term throughout the book for a number of different service providers, including access providers, network operators, communications service providers, electronic communications service providers, and licensed telecommunications service operators. Terms differ according to the standards for lawful interception of different countries and different LEAs.

1.1 Positioning Lawful Intercepts (LIs) and Surveillance

Information and intelligence must be differentiated from each other. Information in the context of surveillance consists of knowledge, data, objects, events, or facts that are sought or observed. It is the raw material from which intelligence is derived (Petersen, 2001).

Intelligence is information that has been processed and assessed within a given context, and it comprises many categories (Petersen, 2001). In the context of this book, communications intelligence — derived from communications that are intercepted or derived by an agent other than the expected or intended recipient or are not known by the sender to be of significance if overheard or intercepted — is the key focus. Oral or written communications, whether traditional or electronic, are the most common form of surveillance for communications intelligence, but such intelligence may broadly include letters, radio transmissions, e-mail, phone conversations, face-to-face communications, semaphore, and sign language. In practice, the original data that forms a body of communications intelligence may or may not reach the intended recipient. Data may be intercepted, it may reach the recipient at a date later than intended, or it may be intercepted, changed, and then forwarded onward. However, the process of relaying delayed or changed information is not part of the definition of communications intelligence; rather, the focus is on intelligence that can be derived from detecting, locating, processing, decrypting, translating, or interpreting information in a social, economic, defense, or other context (Petersen, 2001).

Information collection is usually used to support surveillance activities. Surveillance is defined as keeping watch over someone or something, and technological surveillance is the use of technological techniques or devices to aid in detecting attributes, activities, people, trends, or events (Petersen, 2001). Three typical types of surveillance are relevant to LIs:

1. *Covert surveillance:* surveillance that is not intended to be known to the target. Covert wiretaps, hidden cameras, cell phone intercepts, and unauthorized snooping in drawers or correspondence are examples. Most covert surveillance is unlawful; special permission, a warrant, or other authorization is required for its execution. Covert surveillance is commonly used in law enforcement, espionage, and unlawful activities.
2. *Overt surveillance:* surveillance in which the target has been informed of the nature and the scope of the surveillance activities.
3. *Clandestine surveillance:* Surveillance in which the surveilling system or its functioning is not hidden but also is not obvious to the target.

Finally, there are various categories of surveillance devices (Petersen, 2001): (1) acoustic (audio, infra and ultrasound, and sonar), (2) electromagnetic (radio, infrared, visible, ultraviolet, x-ray), (3) biochemical (chemical, biological, and biometric), and (4) miscellaneous (magnetic, cryptologic, and computer). In different contexts, including some of those described in this book, a combination of such devices might be used (e.g., a combination of acoustic, electromagnetic, and miscellaneous devices). Appropriate chapters will clearly highlight the technologies and devices in use.

1.2 ISS Basics and Application Areas

ISSs are not about security but about intelligence. Security includes providing firewalls, anti-virus protection, and intrusion detection and prevention. That is, security is about guarding against loss, whereas, in regard to an ISS, intelligence refers to gathering information about illegal activities and applying that knowledge to increasing security where applicable. In addition to interfacing with or being part of the billing, ordering, provisioning, and authentication systems, ISSs interface with or are part of law enforcement systems.

Unlike "point" intercept and security solutions that cover small portions of the networking infrastructure and are costly to implement — and may slow down the network — an ISS has low operational impact, is inexpensive to operate, and is able to proactively provide intelligence on networks of all sizes. ISSs represent a feasible option today on the basis of the communications technologies and support systems in use.

All ISS-based processes must ultimately provide comprehensive surveillance in a lawful manner. This includes comprehensive information from any type of network (e.g., wireline, wireless, access, transport, and broadband) on any scale. Moreover, the ISS-based process should provide

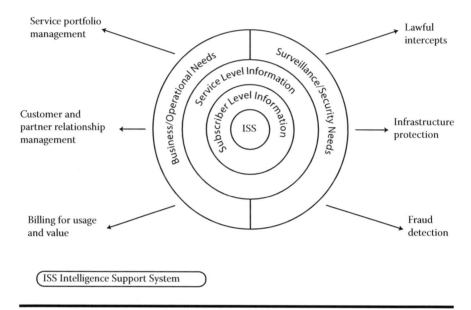

Figure 1.1 Intelligence support systems.

comprehensive information on a real-time basis; that is, it should provide proactive intelligence.

In addition to surveillance, an ISS provides differing types of general business information on networks (Cohen, 2003). The following are examples of the types of information and services provided:

- Service-usage information
- Definition and deployment of value-based services
- Subscriber-level information
- Information on network abuse or infrastructure attacks (security)
- Fraud detection
- Expansion of the mediation database by information from layer 4 to layer 7 for more accurate value- or usage-based billing
- Carrier-grade Tier-1 coverage for any network type (mobile, broadband, and backbone)
- Customer and PRM

An illustration is provided in Figure 1.1. ISS, the core, is surrounded by various layers including:

- Subscriber-level information (names, addresses, and contact numbers)
- Service-level information (metrics, compliance, and service portfolios)

- Business and operational needs (usage- and value-based billing, and relationship management)
- Surveillance and security needs (infrastructure protection and fraud detection)

Proactive intelligence requires that nationwide, even global, networks be instrumented in such a manner that all communications can be monitored on a grand scale to identify potential targets with summary intelligence while respecting privacy laws. Once these targets have been identified, further monitoring can be conducted and further intelligence obtained when lawful authorization is granted. An ISS that provides this level of information needs to capture all key summary data in a manner that is lawful and protects the rights of individuals.

Many government LEAs have developed the ability to deal with single-dimensional communication on a limited scale. Today, however, multidimensional communication on a global scale is needed if countries are to prevent terrorist attacks and other criminal acts. This can be achieved with ISSs.

Figure 1.2 shows the funnel of data capturing and processing that supports law enforcement. The top of the funnel reflects the need to provide summary intelligence information; the middle of the funnel reflects the need to provide intelligence on specific targets, and the end of the funnel represents the need to provide detailed intelligence in specific areas. The recurring elements in the process are networkwide (monitoring billions of events and thousands of targets, and summary intercept information), target specific (collecting intelligence and retargeting monitoring activities), and content specific (complete information demand for intercept, and restructuring of intelligence).

As indicated in Figure 1.2, there are three different types of intelligence (Cohen, 2003):

1. *Summary intelligence:* An ISS that provides this level of information needs to capture all key summary data in a manner that is lawful and protects the rights of individuals. For instance, an ISS may be programmed to capture information on everyone who visits a particular suspect Web site without capturing individual names. The ISS may then take this information and see if any of the IPs visiting this Web site have also been communicating via e-mail or chatting with another known target. If so, a legal authorization may be obtained to look at the individual in question in more detail.
2. *Target intelligence:* Once a target has been identified on the basis of summary intelligence or other information sources and lawful

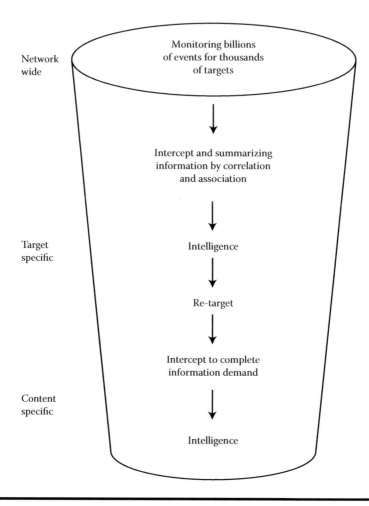

Figure 1.2 Monitoring the network for intelligence.

authorization has been received, it may be necessary to look at any and all of that particular individual's communications on all networks, including e-mail, Web sites visited, chatting, instant messaging, short message service (SMS), and multimedia messaging service (MMS) mobile phone messages, Voice-over-IP (VoIP) broadband connection calls, and so forth. Specific details can then be obtained from this information.

3. *Content intelligence:* Content intelligence may be needed to lawfully review specific content, for example, all e-mail communications of the target. The ISS should make it possible to look at this detailed content information in all forms (e.g., e-mail, VoIP, Web site replay, and chatting replay).

Figure 1.3   High-level interfaces for service providers.

1.3 The Position of ISS among Other Support and Security Systems

ISS is positioned adjacent to the OSSs and BSSs of a TSP. Figure 1.3 shows the structure and hierarchy of the most widely used support, documentation, and management systems, together with other important enterprise applications (Terplan, 2001).

These support, documentation, and management systems are not isolated from other TSP business systems. In Figure 1.3, they are positioned next to each other, illustrating the shared role of frameworks at the core that support data maintenance, workflow, messaging, and workforce management. Also, functions and services of frameworks are challenged for future applications. They are expected to add value through the following attributes:

- Flexibility to support new communication services, convergence networks, voice, and data
- Adaptability to allow implementation of new pricing schemes (e.g., new services, bundles, subscriptions, new metrics, and thresholds)
- Interoperability with numerous best-of-breed OSSs and, where applicable, existing legacy solutions
- Scalability to support rapid carrier growth
- Expediency to facilitate rapid time to market

The outside layer in Figure 1.3 represents many other enabling processes and functions of service providers that are not addressed explicitly here. These include, among others:

- *Enterprise resource planning (ERP):* A set of functions and services including asset management, maintenance, general ledger, accounts payable, procurement and purchasing, bill verification, and commissions management.
- *Customer relationship management (CRM):* Offers emerging customer-facing services including crisis management, account management, cross-selling, subscription service, bill inquiry, and bill adjustment.
- *Partner relationship management (PRM):* An emerging area focusing on well-organized collaboration between business partners. A highly flexible infrastructure is required to support mergers and acquisitions and the various depths of partnerships.
- *Sales force automation:* An emerging area involving account, sales force, opportunity, contract, and contact management.
- *Business intelligence:* Provides tailored business rules for operations metrics, service-level agreement (SLA) management, data warehousing, product management, marketing, and CRM.
- *Decision support systems (DSS):* Based on BI, business rules are implemented for a higher level of automation, in particular to operate the underlying network infrastructure.
- *Support for E-business:* This new and emerging area could play a significant role for service providers. It includes Web-based order entry and returns, Web-based problem reporting and status inquiries, electronic bill presentment and payment, and Web-based customer profile and product information. This is the basis for B2B (business to business) and B2C (business to consumer) for service providers.
- *Interconnections among multiple service providers:* All the technologies offered to enterprises, small businesses, and residential customers

may be implemented between multiple providers, retailers, and wholesalers. In addition to the traditional techniques for supporting settlements, E-commerce techniques are expected to be implemented in the future.

■ *Employee training and education:* In addition to powerful solutions designed to support workforce dispatch optimization, the training, education, and cross-education of all employees of the service provider is extremely important. This includes knowledge distribution regarding service portfolios, sales techniques, support systems, documentation systems, management systems, basic financial data, and the strategic position of the company in relation to its competitors. State-of-the-art Internet-based technologies may help to increase educational efficiency.

It is obvious that ISSs are closely connected to (1) mediation systems, (2) inventory and documentation systems, (3) provisioning solutions, and (4) billing products. These systems and products are core components of OSSs and BSSs.

Security management is considered part of a management system. Usually, TSPs structure their management solutions around FCAPS (fault, configuration, accounting, performance, and security management), and accounting and security receive special attention. With the exception of capturing raw data in networking equipment, accounting is becoming part of OSSs. Security is supported in different areas by different subject matter experts. Possible subareas may include the following:

■ Securing networking infrastructure using, among other security frameworks, intrusion detection and prevention, firewalls, and virus protection
■ Protecting customer privacy
■ Securing links to partners and other service providers
■ Authentication and authorization of their own employees for accessing and using functions and services

Chapter 8 (Operations) will address security-related questions, frameworks, and tools in more depth.

1.4 Basic Requirements for LIs

TSPs are being asked to meet LI requirements for voice, data, and video in a variety of countries worldwide. Requirements vary from country to country, but there are commonalities as well (with differences in particular details such as delivery formats). Baker (2003) provides an excellent description of streamlining requirements.

Generic strategic requirements, and objectives and goals of TSPs, government agencies, and customers are somehow contradictory when the following facts are evaluated:

- TSPs need return on investment (ROI) for their ISS deployment.
- Government agencies need information but do not have ready access to networks.
- TSPs need systems that fit business requirements without undue burden.
- Governments need cost-effective solutions with economies of scale.
- TSPs and governments need to address privacy challenges (e.g., separate content from signal).

Generic functional requirements include (1) comprehensive IP monitoring, (2) scalable, Tier-1 networks, (3) serving "any data, any network" (mobile, broadband, access, and backbone transport), (4) leveraging of commercial off-the-shelf software (COTS), (5) availability of real-time information, and (6) business or surveillance policy enforcement.

Generic legal requirements include the following, among others:

- LI must be undetectable by the intercept subject.
- Mechanisms must be in place to prevent unauthorized personnel from performing or knowing about lawfully authorized intercepts.
- If multiple LEAs are intercepting the same subject, they must not be aware of each other.
- There is often a requirement to provide intercept-related information (IRI) separately from the actual content of interest.
- If IRI is delivered separately from actual content, there must be some means of correlating the IRI and the content.
- If the information being intercepted is encrypted by the TSP and the TSP has access to the keys, then the information must be decrypted before delivery to the LEA, or the encryption keys must be passed to the LEA to allow them to decrypt the information.
- If the information being intercepted is encrypted by the intercept subject and its associate and the service provider has access to the keys, then the TSP may deliver the keys to the LEA.

In terms of requests from LEAs, there are four fundamental types (Carragher, 2003):

1. *Past billing and statistical traffic records of communications:* These records must be maintained by TSPs for a certain period of time. The duration depends on the country involved. Usually, there are

strict guidelines about storage media, with the result that TSPs may not innovate their billing systems (e.g., EBPP [electronic bill presentation and payment]) and storage devices easily without violating any data retention rules.

2. *Computer long-term storage content:* LEAs can usually search and seize computers and storage media, including damaged devices. This falls under the realm of computer forensics, an area of practice that combines science and art. LEAs today possess software tools that search PCs, servers, and networks for evidence, such as text files, images, and e-mails, that can be used to ferret out criminals. Requests from LEAs can be triggered by noncompliance issues such as violations of company policies, circulation of inappropriate content, or misappropriation of information.

3. *Current communication billing and statistical records:* This includes "pen register" and "trap-and-trace" data, usually defined under the category of IRI, and meta information about service usage.

4. *Delivery of content:* This includes collection of the full content of any type of communication offered by TSPs other than that involving information services.

1.5 Electronic Surveillance Laws

Several sets of questions need to be asked when addressing electronic surveillance laws, as given in the following text.

1.5.1 Legal Background of Surveillance

1. What segments of telecommunications acts offer the legal basis for surveillance?
2. What legal guidelines are relevant for preparing and executing surveillance actions?
3. For what products and services are surveillance laws applicable?
4. What laws are related to individual and strategic surveillance actions?

1.5.2 Duties of TSPs and Operators of Telecommunications Equipment

1. Are TSPs expected to cooperate with LEAs in regard to surveillance?
2. Who is expected to guarantee operational and technical assistance — TSPs, Internet service providers (ISPs), licensed operators, access providers, or transport providers?

3. Should this assistance be provided permanently or only on a case-to-case basis?
4. What are the exceptions to the expected support of lawful intercepts? Nonprofit providers, promotional services, and smaller providers?
5. Where and how are the technical requirements of surveillance specified?
6. Who is in charge of verifying whether requirements are being met by providers?
7. Who is in charge of approving technical surveillance devices?
8. Who is in charge of planning and installing surveillance devices?

1.5.3 Prerequisites of Surveillance

1. Under what circumstances is telecommunication surveillance requested?
2. In what cases are subpoenas and warrants required?
3. Who is in charge of supervising the legal content of surveillance requests?
4. Is real-time surveillance required, or storing, archiving, and maintaining data for future use?
5. How long should data be stored and maintained by the TSP?

1.5.4 Executing Surveillance Actions

1. Who and what are going to be under surveillance?
2. How is data handed over to LEAs?
3. What specifications are required to initiate surveillance?
4. What IDs are requested from LEAs?
5. What data is under surveillance?
6. Are only individual communications under surveillance?
7. Is only data under surveillance, or services as well?
8. What is handed over to LEAs — only IRI or communication content also?
9. What differences exist between individual and strategic surveillance?
10. Are different technical devices needed for different surveillance requests?

1.5.5 Control and Sanctions in the Area of Surveillance

1. What are reporting duties for TSPs?
2. What statistics are generated about surveillance actions, and by whom?

3. Who are the control entities that certificate equipment, facilities and procedures for supporting LIs?
4. What are the penalties for noncompliance with requested surveillance?
5. What happens if surveillance cannot be provided in a timely manner?

1.5.6 Reimbursement for Providers

1. Who covers the expenses for technical and organizational provisioning?
2. Who covers the expenses for handover of data to LEAs?
3. Does reimbursement support completed surveillance actions?
4. How are the efforts judged by TSPs?
5. Do surveillance-related expenses affect the competitiveness of providers?

Chapter 3, Chapter 8, and Chapter 9, respectively, address these issues in the case of the United States, the European Community, and Japan.

1.6 Framework of LIs

Figure 1.4 shows a generic framework of LIs (Baker, 2003) derived from a draft model commissioned by the Internet Engineering Task Force (IETF). This draft streamlines principal functions, components, and key players. This generic framework shows a high level of compliance with North American and European standards regarding lawful interception.

Several entities are included in this LI model:

- *LI administration function:* This function provides the provisioning interface for the intercept stemming from a written request by an LEA. It can involve separate provisioning interfaces for several components of the network. Because of the requirement to limit accessibility to authorized personnel, as well as the requirement that LEAs not be aware of each other, this interface must be strictly controlled. The personnel who provide the intercepts are especially authorized to do so and are often employed directly or indirectly by the TSPs whose facilities are being tapped. In many cases, the identity of the subject received from the LEA has to be translated to one that can be used by the networking infrastructure to enable the intercept.
- *Intercept access point (IAP):* An IAP is a device within the network that is used for intercepting lawfully authorized information. It may

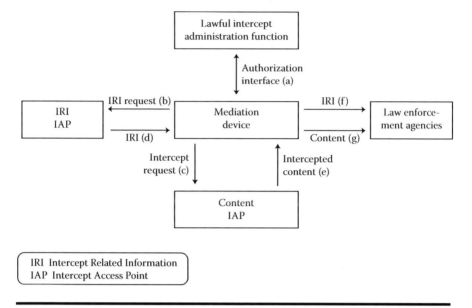

Figure 1.4   Generic framework for LIs.

be an existing device with intercept capability (e.g., a switch or router), or it may be a special device (e.g., a probe) provided for that purpose. Two types of IAPs are considered here: those providing IRI and those providing content information.

- *IRI IAP:* This type of IAP is used to provide IRI, that is, information related to the traffic of interest. There is currently no standardized definition of IRI for IP traffic. IRI is the collection of information or data associated with telecommunications services involving target identity, specifically communication-associated information or data (e.g., unsuccessful communication attempts), service-associated information or data (e.g., service profile management), and location information.

- *Content IAP:* A content IAP is one that is used to intercept the traffic of interest.

■ *LEA:* The agency requesting the intercept and to which the TSP delivers the information.

■ *Mediation device (MD):* These devices receive the data from the IAP, package it in the correct format, correlate them with LI warrants, and deliver it to the LEA. In cases in which multiple LEAs are intercepting the same subject, the MD may replicate the information multiple times.

This generic reference model contains a number of interfaces, as can be seen in Table 1.1, and it can be deployed in many different ways. More details are presented in Chapter 3.

Table 1.1   Description of Interfaces

Interface	Description
LI provisioning	LI administrative provisioning interface; parameters include target identifier, duration of intercept, type of intercept, etc.
IRI target	Specifies target identifier, duration, etc., for provision of IRI delivery
Content intercept	Provision of content intercept
IRI to MD	Internal interface between IRI IAP and MD for IRI delivery
Content to MD	Internal interface between content IAP and MD for delivery of content
IRI to LEA	Interface between MD and LEA for delivering IRI; this may vary from country to country
Content to LEA	Interface between MD and LEA for delivering content; this may vary from country to country

1.7 Challenges

Supporting lawful interception in various geographical areas is not without challenges. This concluding section concentrates on technical, economical, and privacy challenges due to lawful interception.

The technical challenges involved in surveillance for state-of-the-art networking infrastructures are enormous. Terrorists and criminals today are using not just the phone but more complex modes of communication such as e-mail, instant messaging, chat, file transfers, VoIP calls over broadband networks, and communication via Web sites. Communications devices have also increased in complexity, including new mobile data phones that combine e-mail, Web browsing, and instant messaging. But although communications networks and devices have grown exponentially more complex, they also have exponentially more potential to provide information — if this information can be obtained and synthesized with other information sources. For example, mobile phones also provide more potential intelligence, such as location information via cell IDs or triangulation of GPS (global positioning system) coordinates.

Monitoring and intercepting these new forms of communication are much more challenging than in the case of voice calls. With voice calls, technology developed over many years was used to tap a known target's voice communications based on a legal warrant. In the past few decades, intelligence gathering from targeted telephone calls has evolved to the point where virtually any information on anyone can be gathered if the target is known. In most countries, specific guidelines and legal restrictions are in place so that this information and intelligence can be collected without compromising an individual's privacy. With a legal framework in place, technology made tapping calls possible largely because voice switches were uniform around the world and most information can be directly obtained from the switch itself.

With unmanaged data networks, however, there are hundreds of different network devices and elements dispersed over global networks being accessed by a multitude of communications devices. Voice switches have been replaced by a multitude of different routers, hubs, and gateways that break up and speed communication as data packets around data networks. In these large data networks, a person's username may reside in one part of the network while his or her IP address may be literally a world away. Putting this simple information together and correlating it with other information from throughout the network to create intelligence is a difficult — almost impossible — task. Further compounding the issue is that data volumes on these new networks are thousands of times greater than the traffic on voice networks. Filtering and capturing this data involves significant scalability issues in terms of collection and processing. The amounts of data are significantly beyond what even the largest databases today can handle, so data warehousing followed by mining for later analysis is also not necessarily a viable option. In summary, the technical challenges relating to ISSs are as follows:

- Enormous volumes of dispersed data:
    - Data volumes of various services are much higher than with voice-related data.
    - Data throughout the networks (not just at the device) must be correlated.
    - Data can be missed or lost because of these huge volumes.
    - Data is too voluminous to be stored in a database without real-time processing and reduction of data.
- Need for real-time data:
    - Dispersed data requires real-time processing and correlation to produce information.
    - Network speeds make it difficult to capture and process information in real-time.

The economics of surveillance on large networks is immense as well. Today only a small portion of networks can be monitored, and this monitoring occurs reactively after a target has been identified. Costs per intercept run in the tens of thousands of dollars (Cohen, 2003). However, technologies now exist, in the form of ISSs, that can instrument entire networks economically without compromising individual freedom. This technology has been developed and deployed on the networks of many of the world's largest telecommunications carriers, which require economical application of the technology for general business purposes in this very competitive industry. These systems provide immediate ROI to the carrier through many general business applications, such as protection of network infrastructure, fraud detection, and collection of general BI on traffic patterns, services, and customers. The same technology that gathers granular information about service usage and subscriber usage for general business purposes can also — with processing modifications — provide information for surveillance.

In summary, the following are the economic challenges associated with ISSs:

- Costs of point solutions for intercepts are high.
- Scalability is not guaranteed.
- Necessary skills and procedures are lacking.
- It is difficult to guarantee ROI with surveillance only.
- Using existing technology with modifications for surveillance seems to be a viable option, but its cost justification is still difficult to support with hard numbers.

Privacy must absolutely and unconditionally be guaranteed with any system being used for surveillance according to the values and laws of the country in question. For instance, it may be legitimate to monitor a potential target and see whom they are e-mailing, but it is another thing to look inside the e-mail for content unless the appropriate legal authority has first been obtained. In the non-Internet, traditional voice world, this was not difficult to achieve because voice switches clearly separated an individual caller's identity (signal information) from what actually was said during the call (content information). With packet networks, however, signal and content information travel together over the network. As a result, it is critical that any surveillance system have the ability to collect, filter, and separate content information in a manner different from signal information. This allows the former to remain separate from the latter. It also allows signal information alone to be monitored so that intelligence can be gathered while privacy is maintained.

In summary, privacy challenges relating to ISSs are as follows:

- Legal rules differ in different countries.
- Technological issues are different for voice and data networks.
- Current technology does not support LIs and privacy laws simultaneously.

This chapter laid the groundwork for supporting lawful interception by TSPs. The chapters to follow address legal, technological, economic, and operational aspects in greater detail.

Chapter 2

Service Portfolios Overview

CONTENTS

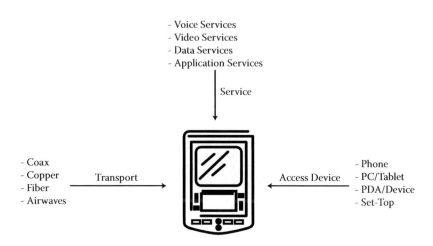

Figure 2.1 Components of products offered by service providers.

Telecommunications service providers (TSPs) usually offer a bundle of services (products) to their customers, differentiating themselves from their competitors on the basis of advanced or unique pricing structures. The more alternatives they offer, however, the more they must spend to maintain their product catalogs, train their sales force, provide their services, and offer more accurate billing.

Basically, the product offered by TSPs is a combination of multiple components: transport facilities, access devices, and various types of services. Figure 2.1 provides examples of these three basic components of the products:

1. Transport (copper, coax, fiber, airwaves, etc.)
2. Access device (phone, PC, pal digital assistant [PDA], set-top, etc.)
3. Services (voice, video, data, applications, etc.)

To provide a better understanding of the technological capabilities of lawful intercepts, basic operating principles (e.g., switching, routing, addressing, multiplexing) are explained first, followed by descriptions of typical product portfolios offered by service providers. In preparation for identifying optimal intercept access points (IAPs), four typical networking environments (wireline voice, Internet, wireless, and cable) are addressed in detail.

2.1 Basic Principles for Networking Technologies

Most emerging technologies involve basic foundation principles, which are addressed in this section. More details on the material discussed here can be found in Terplan (2001).

2.1.1 Connection-Oriented and Connectionless Communications

Communication systems that employ the concepts of circuits and virtual circuits are said to be *connection-oriented*. Such systems maintain information about users, such as their addresses and their ongoing quality-of-service (QoS) needs. Often, these types of systems use state tables that contain rules governing the manner in which the user interacts with the network. Although these state tables clarify the procedures between the user and the communication network, they add overhead to the communication process.

In contrast, communication systems that do not employ circuits and virtual circuits are said to be connectionless systems. They are also known as *datagram networks* and are widely used throughout the industry. The principal difference between connection-oriented and connectionless operations is that connectionless protocols do not establish a virtual circuit for the end-user communication process. Instead, traffic is presented to the TSP in a somewhat ad hoc fashion. Handshake arrangements and mutual confirmations of receiving traffic are minimal (and perhaps nonexistent). Network service access points (SAP) and network switching points maintain no ongoing knowledge about the traffic between the two end users. State tables are not maintained. Therefore, datagram services provide no *a priori* knowledge and no ongoing, current knowledge of user traffic. However, they involve less overhead.

2.1.2 Use of Physical and Virtual Circuits

End users operating terminals, computers, and client equipment communicate with each other through a communication channel called *physical circuit*. Physical circuits are also known by other names such as channels, links, lines, and trunks. Physical circuits can be configured wherein two users communicate directly with each other through one circuit, and no one uses this circuit except these two users. They can operate the circuit in half duplex or full duplex. This circuit is dedicated to the users. This concept is still widely used in simple networks without serious bandwidth limitations.

In more complex networks, circuits are shared by more than one user pair. Within a network, physical circuits are terminated at intermediate points via machines that provide relay services on another circuit. These machines, known variously as switches, routers, bridges, and gateways, are responsible for relaying traffic between communicating users. Because many communication channels have the capacity to support more than one user session, network devices such as switches, routers, or multiplexers are responsible for sending and receiving multiple user traffic to and from a circuit.

In an ideal arrangement, a user would not be aware that the physical circuits are being shared by other users. Indeed, the circuit provider attempts to make this sharing transparent to all users. Moreover, in such an ideal situation, users would perceive that the circuit directly connects only the two communicating parties. However, it is likely that the physical circuit is being shared by other users.

The term "virtual circuit" is used to describe a shared circuit wherein circuit users are unaware that they are sharing. This term was derived from computer architectures in which end users perceive that a computer has more memory than is actually the case. This additional virtual memory is actually stored on an external device.

There are three types of virtual circuits:

1. *Permanent virtual circuits (PVCs):* A virtual circuit may be provided to the user on a continuous basis. In this case, the user has access to the network's service at any given point in time. A PVC is established by creating entries in tables in the network nodes' databases. These entries contain a unique identifier of the user payload that is known by various names, including logical channel number (LCN), virtual channel identifier (VCI), and virtual path identifier (VPI). Network features such as throughput, delay, security, and performance indicators are also provided before the user initiates operations. If different types of services are desired and if different destination endpoints must be reached, the user must submit a different PVC identifier to the network, along with the appropriate user payload. This PVC is provisioned to a different endpoint and perhaps involves different services.

2. *Switched virtual circuits (SVCs):* An SVC is not pre-provisioned. When a user wishes to obtain network services to communicate with another user, the former must submit a connection request packet to the network. The address of the receiver must be provided, as well as the virtual circuit number to be used during the session. SVCs entail a certain amount of delay during the setup phase, but they are flexible in that they allow the user to select dynamically the receiving party and the negotiation of networking parameters on a call-by-call basis.

3. *Semipermanent virtual circuits (SPVCs):* With this approach, a user is pre-provisioned as in the case of a regular PVC. Also similar to a PVC, the network node contains information about the communicating parties and the types of services desired. But these types of virtual circuits do not guarantee that users will obtain the level

of service they request; they may be denied a particular service if the networks are congested. A more likely scenario is that continuation of a service is denied because a user has violated the rules of communication. Examples of such violations are demand for higher bandwidth and higher data rates than those outlined in the agreement with the supplier.

Dense wave division multiplexing (DWDM), which involves the use of laser technology to provide communicating parties a large number of virtual circuits, can facilitate use of physical optical channels.

2.1.3 Switching Technologies

Voice, video, and data signals are relayed in a network from one user to another through switches. This section offers an overview of prevalent switching technologies.

Circuit switching provides a direct connection between two networking components. Thus, communicating partners can utilize the facility as they see it — within bandwidth and tariff limitations. Many telephone networks use this technology. Circuit switching provides clear channels; error checking, session establishment, frame flow control, frame formatting, selection of codes, and protocols are the responsibility of the users. Today, traffic between communicating parties is usually stored in fast queues in the switch and transferred to an appropriate output line via time division multiplexing (TDM) techniques. This method is known as circuit emulation switching (CES). In summary, circuit switching offers the following attributes:

- Direct connection end-to-end
- No intermediate storage unless CES is used
- Few value-added functions
- TDM used to emulate circuit switching in modern systems

Message switching has been the dominant switching technology of the past two decades. It is still widely used in certain applications such as e-mail, but it is not employed in a backbone network. The switch is usually a specialized computer responsible for accepting traffic from attached terminals and computers. It examines the address in the header of the message and switches traffic to the receiving station. Because of the low number of switching computers, this technology suffers backup problems, performance bottlenecks, and lost messages resulting from congestion. In summary, message switching offers the following atrributes:

- Use of store-and-forward technology
- Buffers provided via disk
- Extensive value-added functions
- Star topology due to expense of switches

Innovations are being made continuously in these technologies as well. Instant messaging speeds up the information exchange between communicating parties. Also, depending on the technology, wireless data services, such as short messaging, may be included.

In packet switching, small pieces of user information are relayed to destination nodes. Packet switching has become the prevalent switching technology used with data communications networks, including such diverse systems as private branch exchanges (PBXs), LANs, and even multiplexers. Each packet occupies a transmission line only for the duration of the transmission; lines are usually fully shared with other applications. This is an ideal technology for bursty traffic. Modern packet-switching systems are designed to carry continuous, high-volume traffic as well as asynchronous, low-volume traffic, and users are given an adequate bandwidth to meet their service expectations.

The concepts of packet and cell switching are similar; each attempts to process traffic in memory as quickly as possible. However, cell switching uses much smaller protocol data units (PDUs) than those used in packet switching. In addition, PDU sizes are fixed in cell switching, whereas they may vary with packet switching. In summary, packet switching offers the following attributes:

- Hold-and-forward technology
- Buffers provided by RAM
- Extensive value-added functions for packet but not for cells

Switching will remain one of the dominating technologies in the telecommunications industry because considerable investments have been made, performance metrics have been continuously improving, and users have become very familiar with feasible applications.

Packet switching utilizes infrastructure much better than cell switching. This is the main reason for the success of IP-based services. It is expected that, in the near future, service providers will reevaluate product and service offerings that are still predominantly circuit switched. However, such a transition will be lengthy in duration because existing investments must be protected. Hybrid solutions are likely; for example, multi-protocol label switching (MPLS) applications attempt to implement packet switching via circuit-switched routes.

2.1.4 Routing Technologies

Two techniques are used to route traffic within and between networks: source routing and nonsource routing. Most of today's emerging technologies use the latter.

Source routing derives its name from the fact that the transmitting device (the source) dictates the route of the PDU through a network or networks. The source places the addresses of the "hops," the routers representing the internetworking units, in the PDU. With such an approach, there is no need for the internetworking units to perform address maintenance; they simply use an address included in the PDU to determine destinations.

In contrast, nonsource routing requires that the interconnecting devices make decisions about the route. They do not rely on the PDU to contain information about the route. Nonsource routing is usually associated with bridges and is quite prevalent in LANs. Most emerging technologies implement this approach with a VCI, which is used by the network nodes to determine where to route traffic.

The manner in which a network stores its routing information varies. Typically, routing information is stored in a software table called a directory. This table contains a list of destination nodes, which are identifiers with some type of network address. Along with the network address (or a particular type of label such as a VCI), there is an entry describing how the router is to relay the traffic. In most implementations, this entry simply lists the next node that is to receive the traffic so that the destination can be relayed.

Small networks typically provide a full routing table at each routing node. In the case of large networks, full directories require too many entries and are expensive to maintain. In addition, exchange of routing-table information can have an impact on the bandwidth available for user payload. These networks are usually subdivided into areas labeled domains. Directories of routing information are kept separately in these domains.

Broadcast networks contain no routing directories. Their approach is to send traffic to all available destinations.

Network routing control is usually categorized as centralized or distributed. In the centralized form, a network control center is used to determine routing of packets, and packet switches are limited in terms of their functions. Central control is vulnerable; a backup is absolutely necessary, but this leads to increases in operating expenses.

Distributed solutions require more intelligent switches, but they provide a more resilient solution. Each router makes its own routing decisions without regard to a centralized control center. Distributed routing is more complex than centralized routing, but for performance reasons, its advantages over the centralized approach have made it the preferred routing method in most communication networks.

2.1.5 Multiplexing Technologies

Most recently emerged and emerging technologies use some form of multiplexing. Multiplexers accept lower-speed voice or data signals from terminals, telephones, PCs, and user applications and combine them into one higher-speed stream for transmission efficiency. A receiving multiplexer demultiplexes and converts the combined stream into the original lower-speed signals. There are various multiplexing techniques, as follows:

- *Frequency division multiplexing (FDM):* This approach divides the transmission frequency range into channels — lower-frequency bands that are capable of carrying communication traffic such as voice, data, or video. FDM is widely used in telephone systems, radio systems, and cable television applications. It is also used in microwave and satellite carrier systems. Although FDM decreases the total bandwidth available to each user, this narrower bandwidth is usually sufficient for the users' applications. Isolating the bands from each other decreases bandwidth, but this disadvantage is outweighed by availability of simultaneous use.
- *Time division multiplexing (TDM):* This approach provides the full available bandwidth to the user or application but divides the channel into time slots. Each user or application is given a slot, and these slots are rotated among the attached devices. The TDM multiplexer cyclically scans the input signals from each entry point. TDMs work with digital signals. Slots are preassigned to users and applications. If there is no traffic at the entry points, the slots remain empty. This approach works well for constant bit rate applications but leads to waste of bandwidth in variable bit rate applications.
- *Statistical time division multiplexing (STDM):* This approach allocates time slots to each available port. Consequently, idle terminal time does not lead to waste in bandwidth capacity. It is not unusual for two to five times as much traffic to be accommodated on lines using STDMs than on lines using TDMs. This approach can accommodate bursty traffic very efficiently but does not perform as well with continuous, nonbursty traffic.
- *Wavelength division multiplexing (WDM):* WDM is the optical equivalent of FDM. The initial WDM systems comprised only two to four channels. In this approach, lasers operating at different

frequencies are used in the same fiber, and thus multiple communications channels are derived from a single physical path. Dense WDM goes one step further while utilizing the same physical infrastructure; in this approach, up to 32 channels may be supported. Hyperdense and ultradense WDM systems with channel densities of 40 and above and capacities of 400 Gbps are now becoming available.

2.1.6 Addressing and Identification Schemes

If user traffic is to be sent to the proper destination, it must be associated with a destination identifier. Typically, two techniques are used in this process.

An explicit address has a location associated with it. It may refer not to a specific geographical location but, rather, to the name of a network or a device attached to the network. For example, Internet Protocol (IP) addresses have a structure that permits identification of a network, a subnetwork attached to the network, and a host device attached to the subnetwork. The ITU-T X.121 address has a structure that identifies the country in question, a network within that country, and a device within the network. Other entries are used with these addresses to identify protocols and applications running on the networks. Explicit addresses are used by switches, routers, and bridges as entries in routing tables. These routing tables contain information about how to route traffic to destination nodes.

Another identifying scheme is known by the term *label*, although other terms are widely used as well, including LCN and VCI. A label contains no information about network identifiers or physical locations. It is simply a value assigned to a given user's traffic that identifies each data unit of that traffic.

Almost all connectionless systems use explicit addresses, and destination and source addresses must be provided with every PDU if it is to be routed to its proper destination.

Dynamic Host Configuration Protocols (DHCPs) help to distribute and maintain IP addresses in a dynamic manner. The major benefit of DHCPs is that they allow Internet service providers (ISPs) to more economically manage a given range of IP addresses. The disadvantage of these protocols is that it is not possible to monitor transactions on the basis of IP addresses. In such cases, the universal resource locator (URL) or authentication products are needed in addition.

The address space available with IPv4 is becoming limited, particularly outside the United States; however, it continues to be widely used. The principal benefits and shortcomings of IPv4 are as follows:

- Connectionless mechanism using hop-by-hop transmission
- No acknowledgments, fault awareness, or duplicate notification are supported, resulting in low overhead, but with unpredictable performance
- Use of variable data packet sizes between 20 and 65 KB
- Communication partners identified by destination addresses
- Lost packets retransmitted when losses are recognized, identified, and notified via higher protocol layers
- Usually best-effort type of QoS, which does not satisfy everybody
- Multicast and broadcast functions supported
- Routing supported between different networks
- Independent from physical layer
- Offers universal connectivity
- Widely used with cost-efficient software and hardware
- Future growth limited by address space of 32 bits
- Lack of support for security, auto configuration, and real-time capabilities
- Routing schemes lack efficiency
- Performance limited by fragmentation and shortage of Transmission Control Protocol (TCP) extensions

IPv6 will retain the benefits and eliminate most of the limitations of IPv4. Industry analysts predict a smooth transition from IPv4 to IPv6 over the next five to eight years.

2.1.7 Control and Congestion Management

It is very important in communication networks to control the traffic at the ingress and egress points — also known as SAPs — of the network. The operation through which user traffic is controlled by the network is called flow control. Flow control should ensure that traffic does not saturate the network or exceed the network's capacity; that is, it must manage congestion. Three flow control alternatives are used with recently emerged and emerging technologies:

1. *Explicit flow control:* This technique limits how much user traffic can enter the network. If the network issues an explicit flow control message to the user, the user has no choice but to stop sending traffic or to reduce traffic. Traffic can be sent again after the network has notified the user that the limitations have been lifted.
2. *Implicit flow control:* This technique does not restrict traffic flow absolutely. Rather, it recommends that users reduce or stop traffic they are sending to the network if network capacity situations

require limitations. Typically, the implicit flow control message is a warning to the user that the user is violating its service agreement with the internal or external supplier; the message indicates that the network is congested. In any case, if the user continues to send traffic, it risks having traffic discarded by the network.

3. *No flow control:* Flow control may also be established through not controlling traffic flow at all. Generally, an absence of flow control means that the network can discard any traffic that is creating problems. Although this approach certainly provides superior congestion management from the standpoint of the network, it may not meet users' performance expectations.

2.2 Service Portfolios

TSPs continuously review their product and service portfolios in what is expected to be a well-coordinated effort among research, design, capacity planning, and marketing functions. A common denominator should be found for customer needs, competitor portfolios, and the TSP's own technological prerequisites. Usually, there is no clear picture or documentation regarding available products, services, or available infrastructure capacity. In certain cases, sales representatives sign special agreements with their customers without checking the availability and maintainability of the service. Launching new services leads to tensions among marketing, operations, administration, and maintenance, sometimes leaving the customer unattended.

Services are grouped in accordance with wireline voice, wireline data, wireless and mobile voice and data, and integrated, cable-based, and IP-based solutions. After a brief definition of the nature of each service, critical success factors are noted.

2.2.1 *Wireline Voice Services*

This group represents both traditional and innovative voice services based on a wired physical infrastructure.

- Voice applications use telephone networks to carry human speech signals; digitalization is ongoing. Critical success factors are quality, control of congestion, and compression.
- Virtual private networks (VPNs) offer private numbering plans to businesses. Software used with VPNs assists TSPs in terms of the sharing of physical resources among multiple business subscribers. Critical success factors are quality, price, and resource sharing.

■ Intelligent networks (INs) are being used with service control points (SCPs) and service switching points (SSPs) to make immediate decisions in regard to several concurrent situations. The result is the support of many advanced features. Critical success factors are features included, speed, and quality.

■ Advanced intelligent networks (AINs) use the embedded bases of stored program-controlled switching systems and the SS7 signaling network. The result is the support of many advanced additional features. Critical success factors are features included, speed, and quality.

■ Centrex represents an alternative to PBX-based subscriber networking in which TSPs offer all available service attributes from their own location. Critical success factors are quality, price, and administration features.

Additional wireline voice services include the following:

■ Voice mail
■ Advanced voice mail
■ Automated call distributors
■ Interactive voice response
■ Advanced fax
■ Integrated computer telephony

2.2.2 Wireline Data Services

This group represents both traditional and innovative voice services based on a wired physical infrastructure. Infrastructure components may be dedicated or shared with voice services.

■ Clear channels are switched analog or digital connections using service providers' existing infrastructure. Management is the responsibility of subscribers. Critical success factors are quality, bandwidth, and provisioning of response time.

■ Managed lines are switched digital lines based on powerful TSP digital networks. Physical media can be optimally utilized via various multiplexing technologies. Critical success factors are quality, bandwidth, lack of propagation delay, provisioning leach time, and management.

■ Message switching, based on existing infrastructures and exchange of information between communicating parties, uses proprietary or standard protocols. It forms the basis for electronic data interchange and e-mail. More advanced services include unified messaging (UM) and instant messaging (IM). Critical success factors are lack of delivery delay, lack of message loss, and throughput rates.

■ Packet switching allows more efficient use of existing infrastructures. Two options are available: PVCs and SVCs. This service is widely used despite its relatively low throughput and relatively high error rates. Critical success factors are quality, control of packet loss, lack of network delay, and retransmission rate.

■ Frame relay represents the high end of fast packet switching. Recent improvements in networking technologies allow support of more bandwidth with less quality control. Critical success factors include quality, bandwidth, and bandwidth on demand.

Additional wireline data services include the following:

■ High-speed data
■ High-speed LANs
■ High-speed data transfer
■ Audio broadcasting

2.2.3 Wireless and Mobile Services

This group represents emerging voice- and data-related services that can be either complementary to or competitive with wireline services. Both TSPs and customers are waiting for advanced applications in this area. Voice-related services are addressed first.

■ Paging consists of one- or two-way alerting support for one or more persons with limited display and storage capability. This service is usually for limited coverage only. Critical success factors are coverage, storage capacity, and display capacity.

■ Cordless services are used with simple, low-power portable stations operating within a short range of a base station and providing access to fixed public or private networks. Critical success factors are coverage, applications supported, battery capacity, and compatibility among various systems.

■ Cellular services involve public land mobile radio networks for use in generally wide areas (e.g., national coverage with medium- or high-power vehicular mobiles or portable stations) and for provision of mobile access to the public switched telephone network (PSTN). Network implementations exhibit a cellular architecture enabling frequent reuse in nonadjacent cells. There are three generations of systems: (1) analog frequency-modulated systems,

(2) digital CDMA- and TDMA-based systems, and (3) multimedia integrated services. Critical success factors are coverage, roaming capabilities, quality, and compatibility among various systems.

■ Personal communication systems represent a voice-based, second- or third-generation service with smaller cells and reduced power levels. They combine wireline and wireless services and allow communication with a person regardless of his or her location. Critical success factors are quality, support of subscriber profiles, power requirements, and compatibility among various systems.

Special voice services include the following:

■ Global positioning systems (GPSs)
■ Mobile satellite systems (MSSs)
■ Universal personal communication (UPC)
■ Future public land mobile telecommunications systems (FPLMTS)

Several data-related services are available as well:

■ Cellular digital packet data (CDPD) uses existing cellular networks for the sole purpose of moving bursty data or data transmitted back and forth only occasionally and in quick, short spurts. Critical success factors are throughput rate, quality, and lack of delay.
■ General packet radio systems (GPRSs) represent the first step in GSM data solutions and in significant throughput increases. They offer up to 115-Kbps transfer rates, allow "always-on" IP connections, and do not require modifications in GSM radio systems; thus, implementation is straightforward. Critical success factors are throughput rate, quality, and lack of delay.
■ Enhanced data rates for global evolution (EDGE) constitute the next step in mobile data evolution. This service is able to provide even faster air interfaces than those supported today. EDGE is not considered the ultimate solution, because it requires expensive radio system modifications, and implementation of the target third-generation mobile networks is too close timewise to return the investment. Support data-transfer rates are in the region of 384 Kbps. Critical success factors are throughput rate, quality, and lack of delay.
■ Universal mobile telecommunications systems (UMTSs) bring multiple media together. These services differentiate vehicular, pedestrian, and indoor transfer rates, and are used in wireline and wireless network integrations. Critical success factors are features available, price, and subscriber acceptance.

- Very small aperture satellite systems (VSATs) are combined inter-active broadcast and managed fixed-connection services used by both corporate and residential subscribers. VSATs are asynchro-nous, with higher throughput rates for data receivers. Critical success factors are throughput rate, price, and quality.

- Microwave services, which support point-to-point data communi-cation, are protocol independent and bit transparent. They can be provisioned for different data transfer rates and different QoS parameters. Point-to-multipoint services involve wireless local loops (WLLs) and are designed to serve small and medium busi-nesses or households in rural areas. Operators need to obtain licenses for radio frequencies to offer this type of service. Usually, this service focuses on data communication, but sometimes oper-ators must provide voice services as well. Critical success factors are distance, geography with obstacles (e.g., mountains, high-rise buildings), and throughput rate.

- A variety of broadband wireless providers have already introduced services that use multichannel multipoint distribution services (MMDSs) and the emerging local multipoint distribution services (LMDSs). MMDSs offer broader coverage, whereas LMDSs offer greater capacity. Current service options use either the public network or a cable modem for the return path. Critical success factors are number of channels supported, service features, cover-age, and price.

- The growth of the Internet and wireless connectivity has created the possibility of accessing applications and information and con-ducting business from almost anywhere with wireless coverage. Wireless commerce (mobile commerce or M-commerce) is being driven by the move to a completely digital spectrum, with the convergence of wireless devices, mobile phones, and PDAs, and through the use of mobile data and Internet services. Critical success factors are subscriber acceptance, security, and perfor-mance.

2.2.4 Integrated Services

On the road to full convergence, integrated services target shared use of the physical infrastructure. Objectives are better quality, better perfor-mance, higher resource utilization, and better economies of scale.

- Integrated Services Digital Networks (ISDNs) provide support for all communication forms on the basis of service providers' inte-grated digital networks. There are multiple choices for bundling bandwidth. Critical success factors are bandwidth, service features available, coverage, and subscriber acceptance.

■ Asynchronous Transfer Mode (ATM) provides a high-speed, low-delay multiplexing and switching network that supports any type of user traffic, including voice, data, and video applications. ATM is one of four fast-relay services. ATM segments and multiplexes user traffic into small, fixed-length units called cells. Each cell is composed of 53 octets, with 5 octets reserved for the cell header. Cells are identified with virtual circuit identifiers contained in the cell header. An ATM network uses these identifiers to relay traffic from the equipment of the sending customer to that of the receiving customer through high-speed switches. Critical success factors are constant and variable bit rates, service features, and quality.

■ The Digital Subscriber Line (xDSL), a type of enabling technology, allows mixing of data, voice, and video over phone lines. There are different types of DSLs to choose from, each suited for different applications. All DSL technologies run on existing copper phone lines and use special and sophisticated modulations to increase transmission rates. The different types are asymmetric, rate-adaptive, high bit rate single-line, and very high bit rate. Critical success factors are throughput rates, service features, coverage, and quality.

■ Business video and multimedia take the form of desktop-based conferencing; multimedia, video-based training; PC reception of digitized broadcast video; and imaging-based document management. A few of the services identified in this subsection, including videoconferencing, multimedia, digital television, video on demand, and streaming media, might be of interest as part of service portfolios. Critical success factors are coverage, price, and quality.

2.2.5 Cable-Based Services

Cable-based services use the existing infrastructure to promote additional communication forms such as voice and data on video coax. Critical success factors are quality, power supply, maintenance of splitters, acceptance by subscribers, price, and bandwidth.

2.2.6 IP-Based Services

The basic model for IP networks assumes a clear split between service and transport layers. All service logic for user services is embedded in application programs running on hosts connected to the IP networks. IP services represent an overlay on the existing wireline and wireless infrastructure:

- In order to promote multimedia applications and reduce voice or fax expenditures, technological innovations that will allow use of the Internet and the IP protocol as the base infrastructure for voice-related services (i.e., Voice-over-IP [VoIP]) are on the horizon. Critical success factors are quality, regulation, maintenance, and management.

- IP virtual private networks (IP VPNs) are another form of VPNs. An alternative to leased/line connections, IP VPNs provide an inexpensive way to extend the corporate network to telecommuters, home workers, "day extenders," remote offices, and business partners. They are implemented by means of tunneling, in which the data to be transmitted and header information are encapsulated inside standard IP packets, usually after encryption and sometimes after compression as well. Critical success factors are acceptance by subscribers, security, handling bursty traffic, and management of firewalls.

- MPLS is a technology that can address ever-increasing network requirements. MPLS forwards information through networks by distributing and exploiting short identification markings, called labels, in packets. Use of these labels allows MPLS to forward traffic without examining a packet's IP header except when it is entering or exiting MPLS. The benefits of MPLS include improved network scalability, QoS, and traffic engineering. MPLS QoS supports sensitive data (e.g., video) by incorporating mechanisms that can provide such traffic with preferential treatment. MPLS traffic engineering allows manipulation of data flow across networks so that new services can be offered. Using this technology allows networks to be operated by combining the benefits of circuit and packet switching. Critical success factors include acceptance by subscribers, throughput rates, security, and vendor support.

- E-commerce sites on the public Internet allow large communities of buyers and suppliers to meet and trade with each other. They represent ideal structures for commercial exchange, achieving new levels of market efficiency by tightening and automating relationships between suppliers and buyers. They allow participants to access various mechanisms for buying and selling almost everything from services to materials. Critical success factors are acceptance by customers, security of trades, and handling bursty traffic.

2.3 Circuit-Switched Voice and VoIP

TSPs can be grouped on the basis of their coverage. In North America, local and interexchange service providers are differentiated. In terms of local exchange groups, incumbent local exchange carriers (ILECs) such as RBOCs and Sprint compete with competitive local exchange carriers (CLECs). CLECs include facility-based, unbundled loop and data service providers. Interexchange carriers (IXCs) include AT&T, Sprint, MCI, RBOCs, wholesale carriers, facility-based resellers, and switchless resellers. Regulatory issues in this area are still on the table, including:

- How should VoIP be regulated?
- Where is the border between information and telecommunications services?
- What are the right guidelines for lawful intercepts (LIs)?
- How should the spectrum for wireless service providers be distributed?
- How can local number portability control be established for both wireline and wireless services?
- Who is eligible for emergency service licenses?

In countries outside North America, there are other structures, but usually, old monopolies are in competition with newcomers. Owing to the declining global economy, many competitive service providers have left the market as a result of mergers and acquisitions.

Not every TSP is able to offer a complete product catalog. Providers differentiate themselves according to geographic coverage, customer demand, available infrastructure, and expected profits. Traditional telecommunications services provided include voice (facility-based and resale, long-distance and enhanced services), data and Internet (private lines, integrated services, frame relay, ATM, Internet access, IP VPNs, and Web hosting), and customer premises equipment (PBX management, data equipment management).

The profitability levels of products are continuously changing. In 2003–2004, profit margins were typically high for outsourcing, intelligent network services, Centrex, and hosted PBX; moderate for frame relay, ATM, and IP VPNs; and low for private lines, long-distance, and local service. In the case of xDSL, E911, and LIs, typically there was no profit margin, or losses were incurred (Lucas, 2003a).

The basics of traditional voice are simple, quality is excellent, services are reliable, and support is very predictable. Figure 2.2 shows a basic phone connection with three principal components:

1. *Line:* a circuit, typically two copper wires (e.g., a loop), connecting a telephone to a circuit switch
2. *Circuit switch:* a computer-controlled patch panel that can make electronic connections from lines to lines, lines to trunks, or trunks to trunks

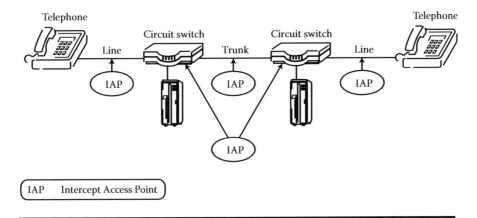

Figure 2.2 Basic wireline phone connection.

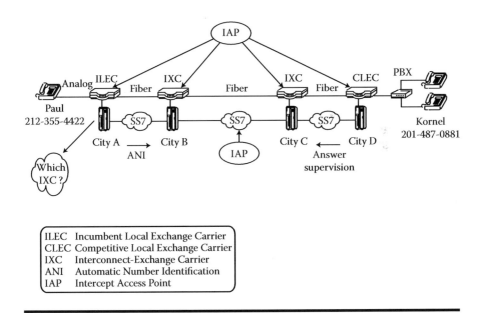

Figure 2.3 Typical long-distance phone call.

3. *Trunk:* a transmission and call setup signaling network that can send multiple calls simultaneously between switches

Figure 2.3 shows the process involved with a typical long-distance phone call. There is a second connection (signaling network) that carries call-related control information. Both networks may be utilized for LIs;

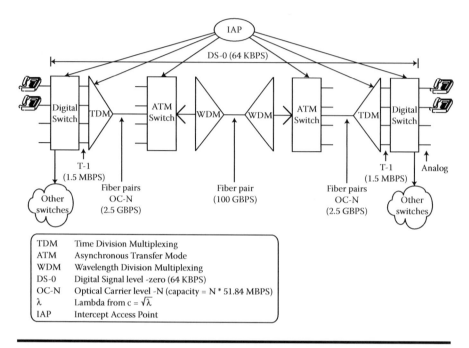

TDM	Time Division Multiplexing
ATM	Asynchronous Transfer Mode
WDM	Wavelength Division Multiplexing
DS-0	Digital Signal level -zero (64 KBPS)
OC-N	Optical Carrier level -N (capacity = N * 51.84 MBPS)
λ	Lambda from c = √λ
IAP	Intercept Access Point

Figure 2.4   Infrastructure components behind phone calls and data lines.

the decision depends on whether law enforcement agencies (LEAs) require monitoring of call-related data, call content, or both.

The physical infrastructure behind phone calls and data lines is complex. Figure 2.4 shows equipment and connections involving the use of switches and multiplexers. The bandwidth indicates the expected capacity requirements for particular geographical areas.

The Internet is making major inroads in both business and residential areas. There are, however, significant differences between typical PSTN voice and Internet data services. Table 2.1 (Lucas, 2003a) highlights the principal differences.

Communicating via packet data networks such as IP, ATM, and frame relay has become a preferred strategy of both corporate- and public-network planners. Experts predict that data traffic will soon exceed telephone traffic. At the same time, more and more companies are seeing the value of implementing VoIP networks to reduce telephone and facsimile costs and set the stage for advanced multimedia applications. Providing high-quality telephony over IP networks is one of the key steps in the convergence of voice, fax, video, and data communications services. VoIP has now been proven feasible, and the race is on to adopt standards, design terminals and gateways, and begin the rollout of services on a global scale.

Table 2.1 PSTN in Comparison with the Internet

Consideration	Voice and PSTN	Data and the Internet
Traffic type	Constant bit rate, with or without compression	Bursty; a combination of relatively small packets
Predictability	High	Low
Switch	Circuit switched (TDM)	Routers for IP packets
Hops	Few	Many
Connection type	Connection-oriented	Connectionless
Addresses	NPA-NXX-XXXX Geography-based Permanent	32 bits (8.8.8.8) NSP-based Permanent or temporary
Path during connection	Static	Dynamic
Intercarrier settlements	Yes	No
Regulation	Heavy	Unregulated, but some future regulation expected
Multimedia flexibility	No flexibility	Great flexibility

Source: From Lucas, 2003a.

However, many companies are still facing the technical challenges of transporting voice and the complexities of building commercial products. Adding voice to packet networks requires an understanding of how to deal with system-level challenges such as interoperability, packet loss, delays, density, scalability, and reliability. The Internet and corporate intranets must soon be voice-enabled if they are to make the vision of "one-stop networking" a reality.

The public telephone network and the equipment that makes it possible are taken for granted in most parts of the world. Availability of a telephone and access to national and international voice networks is considered to be essential in modern society — telephones are even expected to work when electrical power is off.

TSPs are facing a paradigm shift in that more and more communications are in digital form and transported via packet networks. Because data traffic is growing much faster than telephone traffic, there has been considerable interest in transporting voice over data networks as opposed to the more traditional practice of transporting data over voice networks.

In particular, VoIP has become attractive given the low-cost, flat-rate pricing of the public Internet. In fact, good-quality telephony over IP has now become one of the keys in the convergence of the voice, video, and data communications industries. The feasibility of carrying voice and call-signaling messages over the Internet or intranets has already been demonstrated, but efforts to deliver high-quality commercial products, establish public services, and convince users to buy into the vision are just beginning.

VoIP can be defined as the ability to make telephone calls and to send faxes over IP-based data networks (known as fax-over-IP [FoIP]) with a suitable QoS and a superior cost-to-benefit ratio. Equipment producers see VoIP or FoIP as a new opportunity to innovate and compete. The challenge is turning this vision into reality by quickly developing new VoIP-enabled equipment. For ISPs, the possibility of introducing usage-based pricing and increasing their traffic volumes is very attractive. Users are seeking new types of integrated voice and data applications as well as cost benefits.

Successfully delivering voice over packet networks represents a tremendous opportunity; however, implementing these products is not as straightforward a task as it may first appear. In the following text, product development challenges such as ensuring interoperability, scalability, and cost effectiveness are discussed, and the types of applications that will both drive the market and benefit the most from the convergence of voice and data are identified.

Figure 2.5 provides a simple overview of VoIP. This generic view is further detailed in Figure 2.6, which shows multiple service models that will be revisited in later chapters.

In terms of Internet access, there are three principal choices today: wireline, ADSL, and cable modems. These access technologies are extremely important when considering correct intercept principles, such as using hardware or software probes, implementing in-band or out-of-band data channels for intercepted data, or using embedded software for LIs.

The principal components of VoIP are displayed in Figure 2.7. Two protocols are competing for the lead position. The first is H.323, a modified ITU standard for video conferencing via ISDN, which is appropriate for VoIP enterprise networks and prepaid VoIP calling cards. However, it cannot yet be classified as carrier grade. Second, Session Initialization Protocol (SIP) represents an Internet Engineering Task Force (IETF) approach that focuses on IP-capable devices as opposed to telephones, circuit switches, and signaling networks. The addressing scheme is similar to IP addresses. Important applications may include LAN phones, global

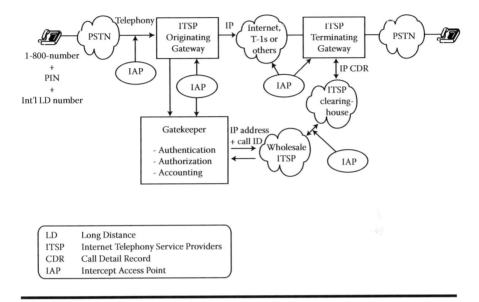

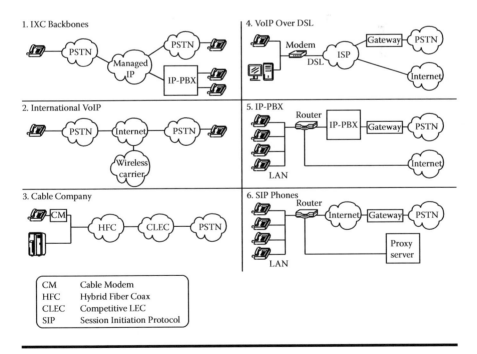

Figure 2.5   Simple overview of VoIP.

Figure 2.6   Multiple VoIP service models.

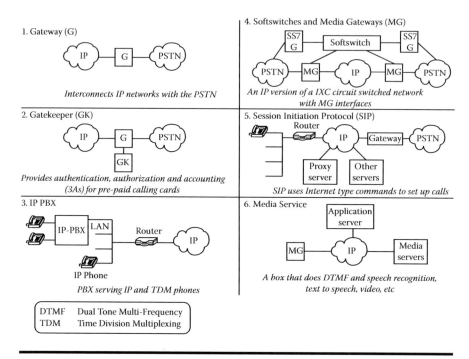

Figure 2.7   Principal VoIP components.

Centrex, and simultaneous voice and data. This protocol, which connects IP phones to SIP servers for completing a phone number to IP address conversion, connects endpoints to gateways and gatekeepers and is considered the basis for future 3G or IP-PBX solutions.

Figure 2.8 shows an SIP-call setup, including the location server and SIP server. The importance of this configuration in regard to LIs is that it indicates potential locations for IAPs.

Softswitches are assuming a central role in terms of controlling communications between calling parties. As shown in Figure 2.9, these devices are competing against circuit switches.

Table 2.2 compares the benefits and disadvantages of various VoIP technological alternatives.

Considering recent VoIP trends, issues regarding regulation, technology, and market opportunity must be evaluated carefully. More details on these issues are provided in Lucas (2003a).

Regulatory issues involved with VoIP include the following:

■ Still considered a bypass solution to traditional voice limited to certain businesses without a broad coverage by TSPs
■ Lack of regulations for (e.g., E911, Communications Assistance for Law Enforcement Act (CALEA), intercept access points)

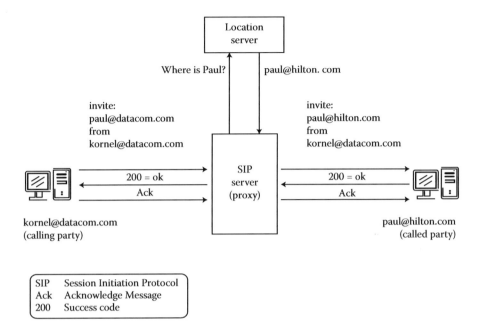

Figure 2.8 shows a SIP call setup process diagram with the following labels:

Location server

Where is Paul?   paul@hilton. com

invite:
paul@datacom.com
from
kornel@datacom.com

invite:
paul@hilton.com
from
kornel@datacom.com

SIP server (proxy)

200 = ok

Ack

200 = ok

Ack

kornel@datacom.com
(calling party)

paul@hilton.com
(called party)

SIP	Session Initiation Protocol
Ack	Acknowledge Message
200	Success code

Figure 2.8   SIP call setup process.

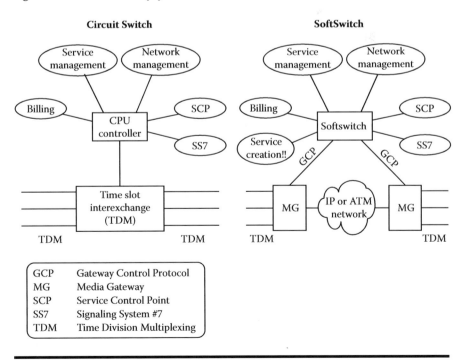

Circuit Switch

Service management   Network management

Billing

CPU controller

SCP

SS7

Time slot interexchange (TDM)

TDM   TDM

SoftSwitch

Service management   Network management

Billing

Softswitch

Service creation!!

SCP

SS7

GCP   GCP

MG   IP or ATM network   MG

TDM   TDM

GCP	Gateway Control Protocol
MG	Media Gateway
SCP	Service Control Point
SS7	Signaling System #7
TDM	Time Division Multiplexing

Figure 2.9   Comparison of circuit switches and softswitches.

Table 2.2   VoIP Technological Alternatives

VoIP Alternatives	Benefits	Disadvantages
Softswitches	Lower costs and faster deployment than circuit-switching or TDM technology	Lesser quality than PSTN while serving basically the same functions
SIP	Internet-like without central control Integrates voice and data for new services	Cannot pass through corporate firewalls/NATs SIP to PSTN phones need a proxy server and ENUM directory
IP Centrex	It needs one TSP to manage end-to-end QoS Scale economies VoIP overly complex	IP-PBXs more cost-effective due to their software architecture rather than traditional hardware Buy versus rent and more
Cable and softswitches	More efficient in regard to cable bandwidth Less costly than circuit switching	Circuit switching reliable, quality comparable to PSTN Know-how base with customers Only needs packet transmission on the cable modem side of the head end

- Lack of tax regulations on VoIP-based enhanced services
- Electronic NUMbering (ENUM) with privacy and security concerns when assigning numbers to customers

Technology issues include:

- Concerns with QoS
- Concerns with reliability, availability, and security
- Necessity for many circuit-switched service options
- Lack of clear guidelines on standards

Finally, market opportunities include:

- Convergence of voice, data, and video services
- Unified messaging
- Availability of many enterprise network opportunities
- 3G wireless and SIP deployments
- PSTN replacement

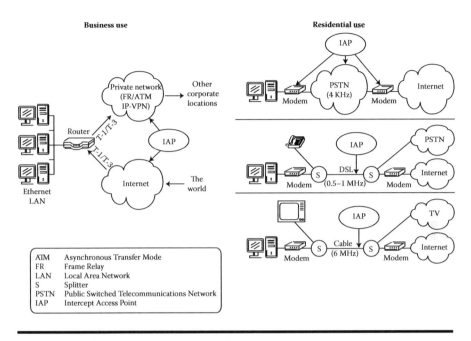

Figure 2.10   Basic configurations for business and residential use.

2.4 Internet-Related Technologies

The Internet is a public network that allows computers all over the world to communicate with each other. IP, which is associated with packet switching, routing, and LAN/WAN communications, is the global standard for exchange of data between two applications on different computers. Figure 2.10 shows typical configurations for business and residential customers. It is important to observe that there are multiple access choices for both business and residential customers, indicating the request for multiple and different IAP devices for different technologies to support LI.

If global connections are to be seamless, they must be supported by multiple ISPs and network service providers (NSPs). NSPs are IP network wholesalers that provide connectivity to retail ISPs and corporate IP networks. The prerequisite is that peering points and peering protocols are clearly defined. Figure 2.11 illustrates peering points between various service providers.

All applications are supported by a layered architecture that is simpler than the seven-layer model from Open Systems Interconnection (OSI) (Terplan, 2001). Figure 2.12 displays the layers together with their headers and trailers, which carry the control information.

The protocol suite is explained in Table 2.3.

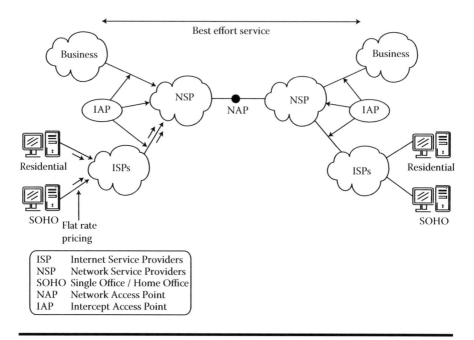

Figure 2.11   Peering points between network service providers.

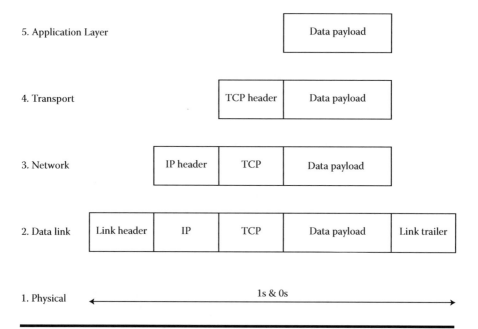

Figure 2.12   IP layers.

Table 2.3   IP Protocol Suite

Layer	Basic Functions
Applications	Web browsing, e-mail, file transfer
Transport	Support of application and reliable message delivery
Network	Use of IP addresses to ensure message reaches final destination
Link	Assembly messages along with begin and end indicators and error detection
Physical	Bits moved over wire, fiber, and radio

In particular, TCP, User Datagram Protocol (UDP), and IP play significant roles in these processes.

- *TCP:* The TCP layer and associated information served the following five functions in regard to dependable, end-to-end support of user applications (e-mail, file transfer, Web access, etc.):
    - Identifying the application being transmitted to the terminating computer
    - Segmenting and reassembling data into datagrams
    - Detecting errors in transmission at the receiving end
    - Retransmitting datagrams that have not been acknowledged
    - Slowing down the flow of packets if the IP network is congested
- *UDP:* The UDP is required for real-time applications such as voice or video conferencing. It differs from TCP in the following ways:
    - There is no retransmission of dropped or error datagrams.
    - There is no flow control.
    - QoS-enabled networks are necessary.
- *Internetworking protocol (IP):* The IP layer and associated information provide a means of ensuring that packets (application data, TCP and IP information) arrive at their intended destinations. A router is a special-purpose packet switch that routes IP packets from the source to the destination based on IP addresses encapsulated in the packets. There are two types of IP addresses: public Internet addresses and private IP addresses.

In the domain name system (DNS), words, rather than numbers, are used as identifiers. Top-level domains are as follows:

- Commercial entities (.com)
- Internet networking infrastructure (.net)

- Nonprofit organizations (.org)
- Educational institutions (.edu)
- Government (.gov)
- Military (.mil)
- International (.int)

IPv4 is the label for the current set of IP numbers used in Internet identifications. Addresses are 32 bits long and are broken down into four 8-bit octets represented by A.B.C.D. IPv6 offers a number of substantial future benefits, assuming this protocol is reaching critical mass:

- New 128-bit address format
- Greater address flexibility supporting unicast, multicast, broadcast, and "anycast"
- Auto-address configuration supporting dynamic allocation of addresses
- Routing based on recognition of address label
- Support of source routing via deep hierarchical networking structures
- Simpler and more flexible address header
- Improved QoS capabilities
- Flow labels enabling prioritization and support of various QoS alternatives
- Better security through support of authentication, data integrity, confidentiality, and privacy
- Limitation of fragmentation
- Use of anycast addresses to allow nodes to control the path along which their traffic flows
- Better performance through optional extension headers

In particular, the address format and the headers' structure will produce revolutionary changes. Source and destination addresses (using hexadecimal notation) are four times longer than in the case of IPv4, with the result that practically "anything" (e.g., household equipment, television, car electronic) can be assigned a unique IP address. This will enable LEAs to more easily identify equipment used by criminals and other individuals under surveillance. Address maintenance will not be easy, but less intensive efforts will probably be necessary for real-time correlation of multiple intelligence sources.

The new header is 40 bytes instead of 26 bytes, and the six optional headers available (hop-by-hop, routing, fragment, authentication, encapsulation security payload, and destination options) will help to optimize the use of this new protocol version. These new "outsourced" optional

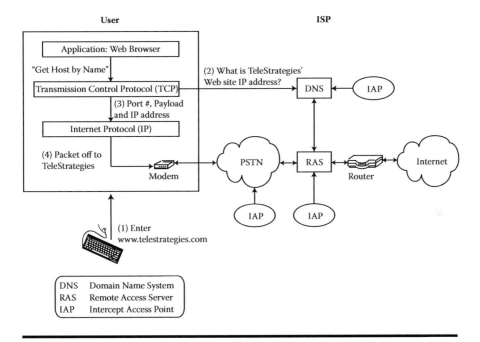

Figure 2.13   Browsing Internet home pages.

headers will enable instance routers to more easily and quickly find the optimal route, the best TSPs, and secondary destination addresses.

The WWW format is a very popular and widely used application. Individuals using Web pages in combination with interactive features, such as touchpoint phones, are frequent targets of LEA LIs. Figure 2.13 shows a typical environment of browsing Web pages of private or public companies. Pages are usually programmed in HyperText Markup Language (HTML) or eXtended Markup Language (XML). HyperText Transmission Protocol (HTTP) is the transfer protocol that carries information over an IP network.

Usage and visitor statistics are extremely helpful for strategic surveillance. Such statistics help to identify, according to geographic areas, groups interested in certain topics. It may also become the source of hidden messaging between criminals and terrorists.

In summary, generic IP benefits are as follows:

- *De facto* network protocol
- Pervasive, global reach
- Simple, inexpensive, flexible, scalable
- Open to be used by both businesses and residential users
- Compatible with any link-layer technology

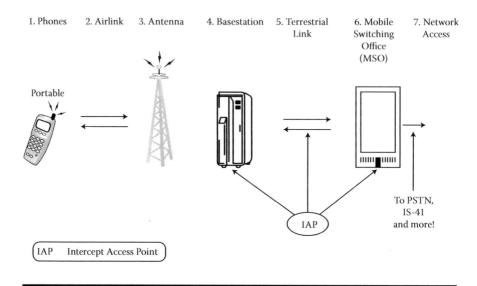

Figure 2.14   Basic configuration of wireless networks.

There are some concerns, however:

■ IPv4 address space is limited.
■ QoS and traffic management are not yet sufficiently advanced.
■ Operations support systems are not yet able to incorporate all relevant functions.
■ Security is not strong enough at present.
■ Various challenges remain in regard to LIs.

2.5 Wireless Networks

The basic configuration of wireless networks is shown in Figure 2.14. These networks comprise very different components, and each subsystem is expected to function seamlessly with each other subsystem. Solutions provided by TSPs combine wireline and wireless networks. In addition, a "second" signaling network is very helpful in terms of control.

Figure 2.15 displays principal wireless components from another perspective. SS7 has been playing a principal role in controlling the signaling in intelligent networks. This standard has been deployed globally for INs and AINs in wireline environments. Its usefulness is undisputed in other networking environments also. The SS7 signaling network is the glue between the home system and many visiting systems. As can be seen in Figure 2.15, the principal components of wireless networks are as follows:

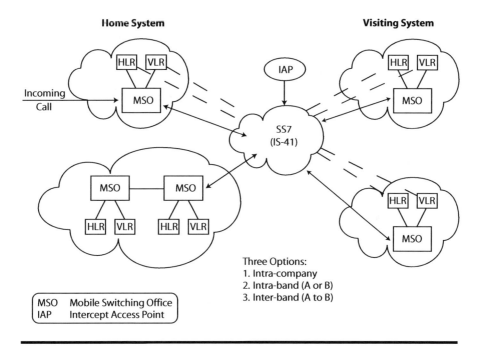

Figure 2.15   Principal components of wireless networks.

- Mobile switching office (MSO): supports distributed controlling functions
- Home location register (HLR): contains data on subscribers' home database and transient roaming information
- Visitor location register (VLR): contains information on visitors (roamers); it is in permanent contact with the HLR
- Authentication center (AUC): contains information on subscribers' encryption keys and performs clearinghouse functions
- Equipment identity register (EIR): an inventory database including information on equipment type, location, attributes, and ownership

Table 2.4 provides an overview of second- and third-generation technologies (Lucas, 2003c).

Bandwidth capabilities are displayed in Figure 2.16 (Lucas, 2003c).

Also, evolutionary steps are included for wireless technology in Figure 2.16. GPRS is the choice of many customers awaiting third-generation solutions. Figure 2.17 shows an example of a GPRS. In the case of LIs, both types of routers — SGSN (serving GPRS support node) and GGSN (gateway GPRS support node) — can be considered.

A rich application and network infrastructure allows TSPs to support infotainment, M-commerce, access, and other services. Application examples are:

Table 2.4 Overview of Second- and Third-Generation Technologies

Systems	TDMA	CDMA	GSM	IDEN
Leading North-American providers	AT&T, Cingular, Rogers	Verizon, Bell Mobility, Telus, Sprint PCS	T-Mobile, MicroCell, AT&T, Cingular	Nextel
Multiple access	TDMA	CDMA	TDMA	TDMA
Frequency band	Cellular/PCS	Cellular/PCS	PCS	SMR
Dual-mode analog (AMPS)	Supported	Supported	Not supported (spotty dual-mode GSM/AMPS and GSM/TDMA)	Not supported
2.5G systems	GPRS	cdma2000-1X	GPRS	Packet iDEN
2.75G systems	EDGE	cdma2000-1X-DO	EDGE	Not yet specified
3G systems	WCDMA	cdma2000-1XEV-DV	WCDMA	Not yet specified

Source: From Lucas, 2003c.

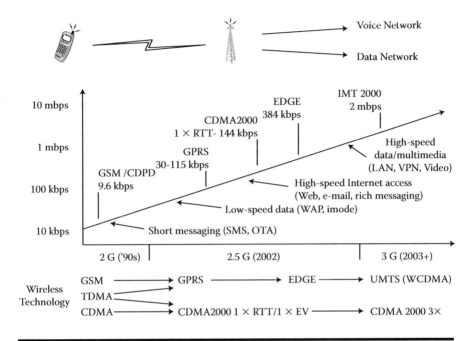

Figure 2.16   Bandwidth offers with wireless services.

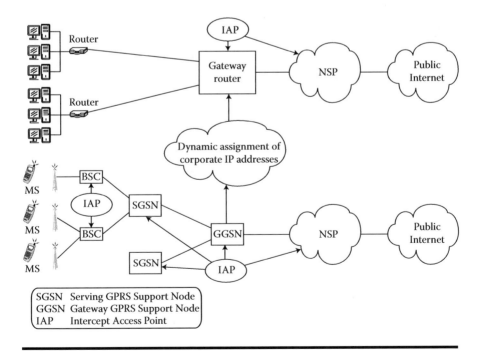

Figure 2.17   Deployment scenario for GPRS.

- *Short messaging service (SMS):* Wireless technology used to send text messages of 100 to 200 characters directly between cell phones. This is considered to be a form of IM, alerting communicating parties about unusual events. Enhanced short messaging services are also available (simple melodies, sound, animations).
- *iMode:* Wireless technology enabling users to access Internet content services using compact HTML technology. This technology was first used and has, since then, been controlled and made successful by NTT DoCoMo in Japan. It is slowly penetrating other countries as well.
- *Multimedia messaging service (MMS):* Uses the standard Internet protocol to send rich media images such as audio and video clips. Because MMS does not use the signaling channel, it can support larger message sizes.

Trends in the area of wireless networks can be summarized as follows:

- Wireless number portability is considered solved with a few exceptions in North America.
- Precise location identification will not be solved until early 2006 in North America. Other continents are even further delayed in this respect. This helps in identifying and locating criminals and terrorists within a very short period of time.
- Further decisions are expected to be made by owners — usually the government — in the area of licensing spectrums to providers.
- True third-generation solutions are expected to become available, but the time frame associated with "killing" applications is still uncertain.
- Wireless operators need operating support system/business support system (OSS/BSS) upgrades and better solutions for QoS and service-level agreements (SLAs).
- IAPs should be equipped with better products to allow better compliance with LEA requests.

2.6 Cable Networks

Two basic cable service offerings are currently available: the older analog cable systems (500 MHz bandwidth or less, 20 to 80 channels, limited set-top options, pay per view) and hybrid fiber coax (HFC) cable networks (hundreds of analog and digital channels, two-way services, HDTV, video on demand, iTV). Figure 2.18 shows a simple HFC solution. One fiber node is able to support approximately 500 homes; one headend can support approximately 20,000 homes.

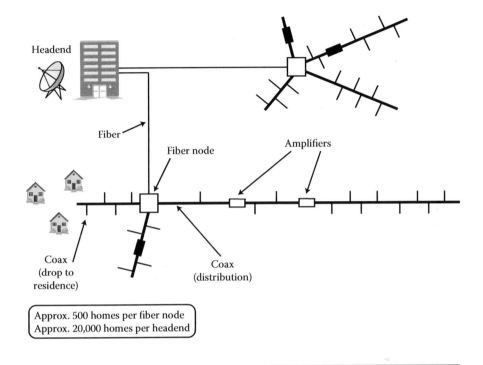

Headend

Fiber

Fiber node

Amplifiers

Coax
(drop to
residence)

Coax
(distribution)

Approx. 500 homes per fiber node
Approx. 20,000 homes per headend

Figure 2.18   Configuration of simple HFC network.

Subscribers expect at least two solutions from cable telephony: circuit-switched and VoIP. Figure 2.19 displays a typical configuration for the circuit-switched solution. Circuit switches and cable headends can encapsulate IAPs.

CableLabs is extremely helpful in terms of defining and distributing standards. In particular, PacketCable and data-over-cable service interface specifications (DOCSIS) are widely used. PacketCable involves the following attributes:

■ End-to-end system delivery specification for VoIP and other IP-based multimedia
■ Residential voice service near-term focus
■ Access network based on DOCSIS
■ Integration of three networks: HFC access, managed IP backbone, and PSTN interconnection

The architecture of PacketCable telephony networks is displayed in Figure 2.20. Key components are as follows:

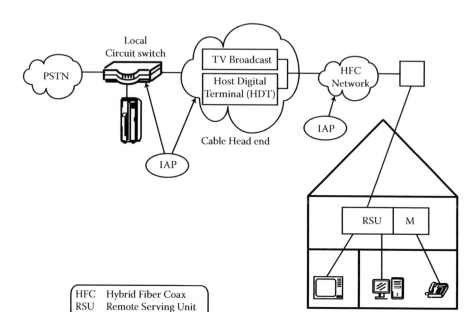

Figure 2.19 Circuit-switched solution for cable telephony.

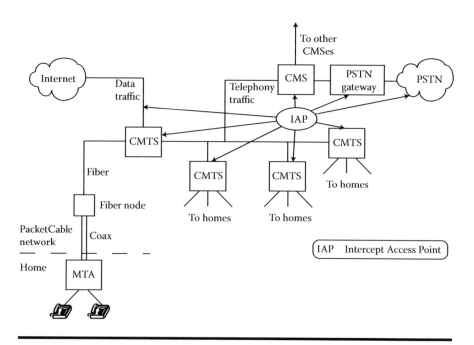

Figure 2.20 Architecture for PacketCable telephony networks.

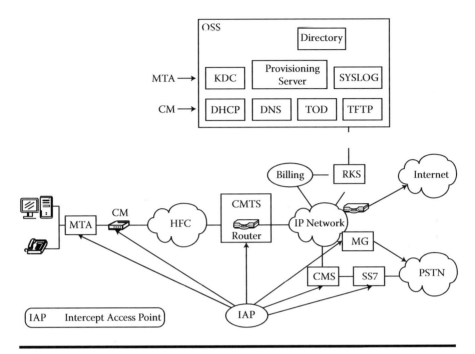

Figure 2.21 Fully equipped VoIP architecture.

- Multimedia terminal adapter (MTA): phone plug-in, connects analog to IP, can be integrated with cable modems
- Cable modem termination system (CMTS): functions in a manner similar to a DSL DSLAM, adds VoIP to Internet access functionality
- Call management system (CMS): functions in a manner similar to a softswitch, includes call agent and gate controller, performs QoS admission control
- PSTN gateway components: media gateway (MG), signaling gateway (SG), media gateway controller (MGC)

A fully equipped solution is shown in Figure 2.21. The OSS incorporates the following services (Lucas, 2003d):

- DHCP: IP addresses to modems
- DNS: Management and registration of domain names
- TFTP: Used in transferring modem configuration files
- TOD: Used for time-stamping events
- Record keeping
- Syslog: Tracking of system events
- KDC: Security support (e.g., PKI)
- Billing support

Figure 2.21 also indicates IAPs that are required for surveillance to meet intelligence demand by LEAs.

2.7 Lawful Interception Requirements for Communications Satellite Operators

Lawful interception of communications satellites at first glance may appear straight forward because at any point in the satellite coverage, footprint signals can be intercepted (Pellero, 2004). At one time, this was true; previously, long haul telecommunications channels between continental land masses were routed by means of submarine cables and satellite links. Satellite gateways located in most countries were using large dishes to convey satellite communications back and forth over cable networks. In those countries, communications were easily monitored without the very expensive exercise of trying to monitor those off-the-air communications.

However, if customers were not in one of those countries where the amount of communications made sense to build a satellite gateway, then they still had the option to spend a considerable amount of money to build their receive-only eavesdropping gateway and eventually they would succeed in their scope. Whether this is legal is not the issue here. At that time, monitoring off the air was not of interest to law enforcement because they could (and still can) monitor the same communications on the ground link at a fraction of the cost.

But then, satellite service for became available to individual users who were moving around. This is when concerns began. It happened as it die for the mobile phone and then the cellular phone market, but at a much slower pace. The first equipment was bulky and heavy, and services were expensive, requiring a "named" subscription. For these reasons, there were just a few targets. Then, technology advances made much smaller and cheaper equipment available, and satellite service providers willingly offered low air-time-rates, thus raising the interest of the potential average users.

It was at that time that TSPs and LEAs finally understood that lawful interception of such satellite traffic is not straightforward. The air interface became more complex: constellation of revolving satellites in place of the steadily positioned geosynchronous satellite, multiple access, coding, encryption, and earth station gateways located in another country created a lot of concerns in the security and law enforcement agencies, regulators, and the telecommunications industry itself around the world.

Most of the operators currently offering commercial satellite services for mobile users carefully consider, plan, and deploy security aware services and reasonable access to their telecommunications, while most of the countries interested in intercepting those communications have a different concept of reasonable access.

2.8 Summary

This chapter has summarized each of the products, services, and technologies in use today in association with LIs. The networking technology is complex; determining optimal IAPs is not a trivial endeavor. Emerging technologies such as VoIP, softswitches, wireless, and cable produce more challenges for both LEAs and TSPs than traditional solutions such as wireline voice and data intercepts.

Potential IAPs have been identified for wireline, wireless, and cable technologies. The most successful intercept solutions to date are described in detail in Chapter 4 and Chapter 5.

Chapter 3

Legal and Technical Standards for Lawful Intercepts

CONTENTS

The basic functions of lawful intercepts (LIs) are accessing data, processing data, converting data into information, delivering information to handover interfaces (HIs) with law enforcement agencies (LEAs), and securing all communications. The responsibilities of service providers and LEAs differ by country, but these generic functions seem to be valid everywhere.

On the other hand, technical and legal prerequisites of lawful interception are very different in different contexts. Basically, from a technological standpoint, all services — wireline, wireless, and Internet Protocol (IP) — can be intercepted by identifying the correct intercept access points (IAPs). However, the legal basis for LIs is a very different issue.

This chapter reviews representative geographical areas, focusing on North America, Europe, and Japan, in regard to legal and technical issues involved with LIs. Three principal groups of issues are addressed:

1. Legal background of surveillance
2. Duties of telecommunications service providers (TSPs) (along with access providers, network operators, licensed operators, communications service providers, electronic communications service providers, and telecommunications carriers)
3. Controls and sanctions for noncompliance

Unifying and simplifying the procedures involved with LIs require powerful standards. This chapter analyzes the North American (J-STD-025) and European (ETSI) standards for LIs. With a few exceptions, these standards are very similar, and most intercept technologies and tools have been designed to support both. For example, networking devices such as switches, multiplexers, and routers are intended for global use.

3.1 Principal Functions of Interception

The generic framework for LIs was introduced in Chapter 1, and service portfolios were one of the main elements described in Chapter 2. This section will summarize the principal functions of accessing, delivering, and collecting data that must be supported by all service providers. Implementation of optimal monitoring and intercepting strategies and selection of supporting tools will be addressed in Chapter 4, Chapter 5, and Chapter 6.

Identifying basic functions as early in the process as possible will facilitate allocation of functions to various standards. Two main sets of standards guidelines (J-STD-025 and ETSI) will be addressed later in this chapter.

3.1.1 Accessing Data

The following functions are important in the process of accessing data:

- Reviewing the technology to be intercepted
- Identifying network elements, such as multiplexers, switches, routers, and load balancers, with built-in capturing features
- Checking the willingness of manufacturers of network equipment and communication facilities to collaborate
- Identifying intercept-related information (IRI) and content IAPs
- Provisioning IRI and content IAPs
- Provisioning data channels to central processing (or monitoring) facilities
- Selecting and training human resources

3.1.2 Delivering Data

Several functions are important in the process of data delivery:

- Evaluating processing needs
- Evaluating mediation solutions
- Determining whether to build or purchase processing applications
- Selecting applications (if a decision to buy is made)
- Quantifying storage requirements
- Defining interfaces to data sources
- Defining interfaces to handover points
- Maintaining data, information, and intelligence
- Providing data channels from or to LEAs
- Securing data channels from or to LEAs
- Selecting and training human resources

3.1.3 Collecting Data

Finally, the following functions are important in regard to data collection:

- Defining process to authenticate requests by LEAs
- Determining the correct information and intelligence to be transferred to LEAs
- Selecting and training human resources

These principal functions should correlate closely with the LI functions defined and recommended by various standards bodies.

3.2 Surveillance Rules and Procedures in the United States

Implementations of LI technologies typically proceed at a slower-than-expected pace. The majority of TSPs take advantage of the delay in actual initiation of LIs first of all for expense and human resources reasons. No detailed regulatory guidelines are available in terms of the technologies that can be used.

3.2.1 Legal Background of Surveillance

3.2.1.1 Basics of Intercept Laws

The U.S. Criminal Code controls intercept technologies. The Federal Communications Commission (FCC) is in charge of supporting laws in this area through guidelines that meet the surveillance requirements of LEAs. The FCC established the Communications Assistance for Law Enforcement Act (CALEA) and was also involved in setting the timetable for determining the processes used by TSPs in regard to supporting LIs.

3.2.1.2 Legal Guidelines

LI procedures are based on several criminal codes, as follows (McCollum, 2003).

3.2.1.2.1 Omnibus Crime Control and Safe Streets Act of 1968 (OCCSSA)

This law is the basis of the U.S. wiretap statute. The law is clearly describing what is expected from TSPs to support LIs. TSPs are committed to supporting LEAs, and the latter gain more importance in this process by obtaining access to data. Pen register and trap-and-trace devices are also part of surveillance solutions. Title III of the wiretap statute is the part of the law applied to LIs.

3.2.1.2.2 Electronic Communications Privacy Act of 1986 (ECPA)

This legislation addresses advances in telecommunications technology not protected by the outmoded statutory language of earlier legislation (e.g., Title III). It focuses on the following emerging technologies:

■ Microwave point-to-point communications
■ Fax machines

- E-mail and voice mail
- Cellular and cordless telephones
- Data transmissions
- Remote computing services
- Paging services

In addition, it comprises electronic communications, electronic storage, procedures through which a government entity can access a telephone company's customer records, and procedures involving LEAs' use of pen registers and traps and traces.

3.2.1.2.3 CALEA

CALEA (codified, in principal part, at 47 USC 1001–1010) obliges telecommunications carriers to implement and deploy facilities that make LI expeditiously feasible. In regard to the areas of mandates and funding, CALEA:

- Obliges telecommunications carriers to ensure the ability, pursuant to lawful authorization, to isolate all electronic communications associated with a subscriber
- Obliges telecommunications carriers to ensure the ability, pursuant to lawful authorization, to isolate call-identifying information (CII) associated with a subscriber
- Obliges manufacturers of equipment for these carriers to make available associated features or modifications "on a reasonable, timely basis and [at] a reasonable charge"
- Authorizes the Department of Justice to reimburse telecommunications carriers for all reasonable costs associated with enhancement of pre-1995 equipment
- Alters the role of TSPs in court-authorized electronic surveillance activities
- Implements system security and integrity procedures

CALEA also instituted changes in Title III, codified, in principal part, at 47 USC 1001–1010. The act's punch-list items include the following:

1. Content of subject-initiated calls (conference calls)
2. Timing to associate call data to content (concurrent)
3. Notification messages (call waiting)
4. Post-cut-through dialed digits (calling cards)
5. Access to subject-initiated dialing or signaling (hook flashes)
6. Party hold, join, and drop (features)

Three additional items may be implemented at the carrier's discretion: surveillance status messages, feature status messages, and continuity checks.

The process of implementing CALEA's directives is not easy. Table 3.1 shows progress in this area from multiple perspectives.

There have been multiple postponements with CALEA; compliance dates June 30, 2002, and June 30, 2003, have been extended for various reasons. Even today, five years after publication of the punch list, intercept technologies and their implementation have not reached a satisfactory state.

3.2.1.2.4 U.S. Patriot Act

Situations in which lawful surveillance activities can take place have been significantly extended, and such extensions include wiretaps, roving wire-taps, pen registers, and trap-and-trace devices. Some of the changes occurring in this area are as follows:

- Title III and ECPA have been amended.
- Some of these amendments have created the current complexities for TSPs (e.g., how to handle new technologies and services, and draw the boundary line between information and communications services).
- LEAs can access stored voice mail with a search warrant.
- LEAs can now obtain more records with subpoenas.
- Pen/traps may be used on the Internet.
- Federal search warrants can be served nationwide.
- Electronic communication service providers have more latitude to voluntarily disclose customer records or communications in emergencies.

3.2.1.2.5 Homeland Security Act

Finally, the Homeland Security Act expanded the situations in which emergency pen/traps can be used and made it easier for electronic communication service providers to voluntarily disclose communications and records in emergencies.

Considering all acts in use today, electronic surveillance includes full wiretaps, pen registers, and trap-and-trace devices.

3.2.1.3 Services Subject to Surveillance

There are various types of wiretap surveillance services:

- *Oral surveillance:* surveillance of person-to-person communications; not relevant to the LI technologies described in this book.

Table 3.1 Progress of CALEA Implementation

Section	CALEA Implementation Section (CIS)	Industry	FCC	Other
Definitions	Provided input to FCC	Provided input to FCC	Contributed to second report and order — definition of telecommunications carrier	—
Notices of capacity requirements	Contributed to final notice of capacity for local exchange services, cellular and broadband PCS Contributed to notice of inquiry and further notice of inquiry for other technologies	Provided input to the CIS Submitted carrier statements Challenged final notice of capacity in court	—	Industry associations challenged the final notice of capacity in court
Systems security and integrity (SS&I)	Provided input to FCC	Provided input to FCC	Provided memorandum opinion and order outlining carriers' SS&I responsibilities	—
Cooperation of equipment manufacturers and providers of telecommunications support services	Consulted with individual manufacturers and providers of support services in their development of solutions	Contributed to solution developed by switch manufacturers and peripheral equipment providers	—	—

Technical requirements and standards; extension of compliance date	Consulted with the industry in developing J-STD-025 Filed deficiency petition with FCC Provided input to FCC Adopted flexible deployment initiative	Contributed to J-STD-025 for local exchange, cellular and broadband PCS Requested extension of compliance date	Contributed to third report and order determining required capabilities Granted extension	Privacy groups filed petition of deficiency with FCC
Payment of costs of telecommunications carriers to comply with capability requirements	Contributed to cost recovery regulations with definition of "installed or deployed" Reimbursed industry for a number of technical solutions	Provided input to the CIS Challenged cost recovery rules in court	—	Industry associations challenged the final notice of capacity in court
Authorization of appropriations	—	—	—	To date, Congress has appropriated $499 million
Reports	Submitted six annual reports to Congress	—	—	—

- *Wire surveillance:* surveillance of electronic human voice communications. This definition does not specify "how much wire" is required. However, it does include mobile and satellite communications with some amount of wiring in switching centers.
- *Electronic communication:* includes all other electronic communications with the exception of financial transactions.

In addition, the techniques just described include phone wire communications (all wireline and wireless phone communications), electronic wiretaps (pagers, facsimile, e-mail, and other data communication technologies), and combinations of different forms (combined or integrated services).

3.2.1.4 Objectives of Surveillance

The Omnibus Crime Control Act does not permit general surveillance of communications. However, wiretaps, pen registers, and trap and traces can be used in LIs.

3.2.1.5 Differences between Individual and Strategic Surveillance

Foreign Intelligence Surveillance Act (FISA) is the driving force behind preventive surveillance. Some of the features of FISA are as follows:

- It includes a broad definition of wire communication.
    - In limited circumstances, electronic surveillance may be conducted without a court order for up to a year.
- Court-ordered electronic surveillance activities can be conducted for up to 90 days (or more with extensions).

Under the guidance of FISA, the FBI is in charge of overseeing surveillance techniques. Carnivore — now DSC 100 — is a technical solution for intercepting packet-based applications of Internet service providers (ISPs). In particular, through this solution, e-mail and Web traffic may be filtered out and forwarded to LEAs. DSC 100 is used by the FBI in cases in which ISPs cannot, or choose not to, cooperate with LEAs.

3.2.2 Duties of TSPs and Operators of Telecommunications Equipment

3.2.2.1 Cooperation with LEAs

All TSPs are expected to cooperate with LEAs. According to the U.S. Criminal Code (18 USC 2518 (4)):

An order authorizing of a wire, oral, or electronic communication under this chapter shall, upon request of the applicant, direct that a provider of wire or electronic communication service, landlord, custodian or other person shall furnish the applicant forthwith all information, facilities, and technical assistance necessary to accomplish the interception unobtrusively and with minimum of interference with the services that such service provider, landlord, custodian or person is according the person whose communications are to be intercepted.

Duties of TSPs under CALEA include:

- Expeditiously isolating the content of targeted communications transmitted by the carrier within the carrier's service area
- Expeditiously isolating information identifying the origin and destination of targeted communications
- Providing intercepted communications and CII to LEAs so that they can be transmitted over lines or facilities leased by LEAs to a location away from the carrier's premises
- Carrying out intercepts unobtrusively so that targets are not aware of the interception and in a manner that does not compromise the privacy and security of other communications

3.2.2.2 Technical Requirements

The technical requirements for LIs are summarized in the J-STD-025-A standard, initiated in 1995 under the leadership of the Telecommunications Industry Association and Committee T1 of the Alliance for Telecommunications Industry Solutions.

3.2.2.3 Organizational Requirements

Guidelines for organizational control of LIs have been issued through the SS&I section of the USC. On this basis, the FCC has identified the following guidelines to which TSPs must adhere:

- TSPs are expected to assign LI tasks to experienced subject matter experts and to guarantee that the surveillance does not violate any laws.
- TSPs must specify rules and processes in writing. These records must include the following:
  - Clarification that surveillance by subject matter experts is executed only on the basis of legal requests

- Definition and classification of legal requests
- Description of how surveillance actions are initiated
- Description of the period during which surveillance actions are executed
- Name and contact number of subject matter expert
- Request that intercepted data not be forwarded to any other institutions
- Instruction that violations must be reported immediately to LEAs

■ TSPs must log their LI actions. These logs must contain:
- Phone numbers and other target identifications
- Date and time of surveillance
- Name of LEA requesting the surveillance
- Names of individuals signing the legal documents on behalf of the LEA
- Documentation of legal basis (e.g., FISA, Title III, and pen/trap statute)
- Name of TSP's subject matter expert

■ Protocols and surveillance logs must be signed by the TSP's subject matter experts, and they must be completed in quasi–real time. Compliance requirements must be met by the TSP when protocols and logs are signed and stored together with the legal request.

■ Protocols and logs must be saved for a reasonable duration, as determined by the TSP.

■ TSPs are expected to document and maintain materials in a faithful manner; otherwise, they may face sanctions.

3.2.2.4 Exceptions

Under CALEA, there are no exceptions for TSPs. However, exceptions may apply in the case of individual extensions for provisioning intercept technologies.

3.2.2.5 Compliance Control

No regulations are in force in terms of compliance control. Typically, however, TSPs use self-certification procedures in the area of LIs.

3.2.3 Control and Sanctions in the Area of Surveillance

3.2.3.1 Controlling Entities

According to the Omnibus Crime Control Act, the Administrative Office of the U.S. Courts is expected to prepare an annual report for Congress, outlining surveillance statistics. This wiretap report does not include information on FISA surveillance measures. Furthermore, it does not include surveillance actions in which one of the communication partners has cooperated with the surveillance.

3.2.3.2 Reporting Duties

Each federal judge and all state judges must report each warrant for surveillance to the Administrative Office of the U.S. Courts. The following information must be included in these reports:

- Name of the judge
- Reason for the warrant
- Identification of surveillance media
- Location of surveillance
- Duration of surveillance

Personal data of the target is not included. Prosecutors report directly to the administrative office in regard to all requested warrants.

3.2.3.3 Surveillance Statistics

The surveillance reports just described contain detailed statistics, including:

- Number of authorized surveillance missions
- Duration of surveillance
- Breakdown of authorized surveillance missions by state and court
- Expenses incurred
- Nature of surveillance
- Hit rates in terms of targets of surveillance
- Miss rates due to noncompliance of TSPs

In the United States, surveillance rates have increased by approximately 25 percent annually over the past five years. Surveillance activities resulting from FISA requests are not reported in detail, but the total is approaching 60 percent of non-FISA surveillance.

3.2.3.4 Sanctions for Noncompliance

TSPs must furnish applicants, such as LEAs, with all information, facilities, and technical assistance (including installation and operation of the device) necessary to accomplish the interception unobtrusively and with a minimum of interference with services. If these conditions are not met, they may face criminal or civil liability or good faith reliance defense. Sanctions are enforced on the basis of the Communication Act of 1934.

3.3 Surveillance Rules and Procedures in the European Community

Two countries are reviewed as representative examples of rules and procedures used in the European Community: France and the United Kingdom.

3.3.1 France

France regulates both LIs and data retention activities. At present, supervision of Internet-based communications is the central target of many discussions. The duties of ISPs have not yet been made available to the public. The assumption of subject matter experts is that technical prerequisites involving ISPs and LEAs have not yet been fully determined.

3.3.1.1 Legal Background of Surveillance

3.3.1.1.1 Basics of Intercept Laws

French law forms the basis for intercept regulations. Not only voice but also all other communication services may be intercepted; in addition, intercepted data may be stored.

3.3.1.1.2 Legal Guidelines

Guidelines on LIs are based on the following criminal codes:

- *Loi n0 91-636 du 10 juilliet 1991 relative au secret des correspondances èmises par la voie des telecommunications:* governs wiretaps on the basis of warrants issued by justices. Preventive security-related intercepts are included.
- *Decret n0 93-119 du 28 janvier 1993, decret relatif a la designation des agents qualifies pour la realisation des operations materielles necessaires a la mise en place des interceptions de correspondances emises par voie de telecommunications autorisee par la loi n0 91-646 du 10 juilliet 1991:* describes organizational prevention for both TSPs and LEAs. However, at present there are no technical guidelines for specifying LIs.

- *Loi sur la securite quotidienne:* advises TSPs not to delete relevant information that might be used to fight terrorism and crime.

3.3.1.1.3 Services Subject to Surveillance

All telecommunications services are subject to surveillance. There are no exceptions.

3.3.1.1.4 Objectives of Surveillance

Both targeted and preventive LIs are supported under French law. During a trial, both prosecutors and defense can review the intercepted information.

3.3.1.1.5 Differences between Individual and Strategic Surveillance

The law differentiates *ecoutes judiciaires* (LIs based on warrants) from *ecoutes administratives* and *interceptions de securite* (administrative surveillance). The latter two regulations focus more on prevention and less on use of intercepted information in trials. In addition, there are a few unique guidelines in this area:

- No overlaps between individual and strategic surveillance are permitted. The highest priority is always individual or targeted surveillance.
- The same target cannot be under surveillance by multiple LEAs at the same time.
- Intercepted data may not be distributed to other LEAs.

3.3.1.2 Duties of TSPs and Operators of Telecommunications Equipment

3.3.1.2.1 Cooperation with LEAs

According to the Autorite de Regulation des Telecommunication (ART), all TSPs as well as ISPs have compliance duties. In line with the criminal code, high-ranked LEAs are entitled to assign interception tasks to any employee of France Telecom or of other service providers. In the case of strategic surveillance, the prime minister issues a request to the service provider.

3.3.1.2.2 Technical Requirements

The goal in this area is for state-of-the-art intercept technology to be used to intercept communication data and content. All data is collected by the

Groupe Interministeriel de Controle (GIC), which in turn relays data to LEAs. To reduce resource demands, data that is not of relevance is deleted.

3.3.1.2.3 Organizational Requirements

Several organizational requirements must be met:

- Personnel with high security clearances should be considered for conducting surveillance missions.
- There must be continuity in terms of human resources (i.e., no changes in personnel within two years).
- Logs and protocols must be maintained.
- All privacy rules must be strictly followed.

3.3.1.2.4 Exceptions

There are no exceptions regarding TSPs. However, communications of doctors, lawyers, and pastors are better protected than in other countries.

3.3.1.2.5 Compliance Control

There are no specific certification procedures focusing on technical equipment and organizational prevention.

3.3.1.3 Control and Sanctions in the Area of Surveillance

3.3.1.3.1 Controlling Entities

The National Committee for Lawful Intercepts (CNCIS), which handles data regarding LIs initiated by the government, is the controlling entity. It consists of members nominated by the president, the president of the Senate, and the president of the national assembly. Their principal tasks are as follows:

- Ensuring that all warrants have been properly prepared and signed by authorized individuals
- Controlling quotas regarding forms of communication technology to be intercepted
- Supervising surveillance activities in regard to motives and nature

CNCIS members have unlimited access to information sources that include the GIC as well as all TSPs.

3.3.1.3.2 Reporting Duties

LEA members must log all their activities. Warrants are maintained locally; national statistics are not maintained.

3.3.1.3.3 Surveillance Statistics

The government maintains detailed statistics. Reported items are as follows:

- Number of LIs conducted
- Breakdowns of new, urgent, and continued surveillance activities
- Breakdowns of reasons for LIs (e.g., terrorism, national security, crime, and prevention)

3.3.1.3.4 Sanctions for Noncompliance

There are actually no formal procedures for sanctions; however, CNCIS can issue the following statements:

- Criticism of the legal background of surveillance decisions
- Violations of the telecom act by identifying illegal wiretaps and other surveillance actions

3.3.2 United Kingdom

The Regulation of Investigatory Power Act (RIPA) is the basis for LIs in the United Kingdom. The related law is still under discussion, particularly the parts regarding data retention. Critical unresolved issues include the following:

- Significant parts of the law are in use, but important guidelines, such as codes of practice and handbooks, are still lacking.
- There needs to be a law regarding governance of data retention, but it does not yet exist. Governance regarding data retention should be agreed upon between the industry and LEAs on a voluntary basis; if so, it does not comply with EU practice, which requires laws for regulating data retention.
- Data collection and access to information sources should be extended, the number of LEAs increased, and the process of LI simplified. The initial recommendations of the government have been rejected and withdrawn.

3.3.2.1 Legal Background of Surveillance

3.3.2.1.1 Basics of Intercept Laws

LIs are affected by the Telecommunication Act 1994, the Telecommunication Regulation, and various parts of the Radiocommunication Act and the Wireless Telegraphy Act 1949. RIPA involves an attempt to find the common denominator among these pieces of legislation.

3.3.2.1.2 Legal Guidelines

Legal guidelines are outlined in RIPA, which consists of the following significant parts that might be relevant in the area of LIs:

- Chapter 1 (Interception Techniques and Equipment) of Part I specifies some of the innovations included in the Interception of Communications Act 1985 (IOCA).
- Chapter 2 (Acquisition and Disclosure of Communications Data) of Part I regulates data retention.
- Part II regulates the processes associated with both individual and strategic surveillance.

All explanations in the areas of LI and duties of service providers are contained in the code of practice issued by the Home Office (HO). These explanations are considered the principal information source. In addition, the National Technical Assistance Centre (NTAC) is a consulting resource for LEAs and TSPs in the case of all questions regarding LIs.

The Antiterrorism Crime and Security Act (ACSA) regulates data retention via a set of guidelines — the *Manual of Standards for Accessing Communications Data* — issued by the Association of Chief Police Officers and HM Customs and Excise. These guidelines, which are not released to the public, deal with data collection in cases of terrorism and crime. Working agreements between LEAs and service providers are in place for executing data collection.

3.3.2.1.3 Services Subject to Surveillance

Surveillance is person based rather than based on an address or telephone number. All communications of targeted persons are included in the surveillance. The duration is usually three months; it can be extended by another three (crime) or six (national security and economy crime) months. There is no upper limit in regard to the number of extensions.

3.3.2.1.4 Objectives of Surveillance

Typically, surveillance results can be used in trials. However, there are exceptions concerning under what circumstances prosecutors, defense lawyers, and judges can review these results.

3.3.2.1.5 Differences between Individual and Strategic Surveillance

Part II of RIPA addresses both general and directed surveillance. Surveillance applications for directed surveillance are regulated. To protect privacy, application forms for LIs require detailed information:

- Names of targets
- Addresses of targets
- Birth dates of targets
- Objectives of surveillance
- Justification of surveillance activities in line with RIPA
- Details regarding surveillance techniques
- Expected surveillance results
- Law violation risks for third parties
- Dates, times, and durations of surveillance

RIPA does not provide clear guidelines on generic or strategic surveillance.

3.3.2.2 Duties of TSPs and Operators of Telecommunication Equipment

3.3.2.2.1 Cooperation with LEAs

RIPA applies to all TSPs offering public communication services and includes guidelines for data retention.

There are periodic meetings between the government and TSPs to discuss the intelligence needs of LEAs. If necessary, TSPs may seek advice from the Technical Advisory Board (TAB), which provides assistance with complicated technical requests that TSPs are unable to fulfill.

3.3.2.2.2 Technical Requirements

Technical requirements in the area of surveillance are as follows:

- Surveillance must include all communications, and intercepted data must be provided, in quasi–real time, to an interface (handover) with the LEA.

- Data transfer activities must support the simultaneous content and intercept conditions.
- The HI must support international standards (e.g., ETSI).
- Data should be filtered, and only relevant data should be forwarded to the LEA.
- Encrypted data should be decrypted before it is transferred to the HI.
- TSPs must support the simultaneous surveillance of 0.1 percent of their subscribers as targets of surveillance.
- TSPs should use reliable intercept and surveillance equipment.

TSPs may agree to requests from multiple LEAs without notifying them mutually about such multiple requests. All data is expected to be forwarded to NTAC, which is responsible for distributing data to LEAs. To reduce resource demand, data lacking in relevance is deleted.

3.3.2.2.3 Organizational Requirements

Organizational surveillance requirements are as follows:

- All equipment must be delivered within one working day.
- Surveillance equipment must be accessible for use in audits.
- Surveillance requirements must be met without notification of the target or unauthorized third parties.
- Surveillance must have minimal performance impact (e.g., delay with dialing tone and noise in conversations) in regard to the target and third parties.

3.3.2.2.4 Exceptions

The exceptions are TSPs with fewer than 10,000 subscribers and those that serve a close community, such as banks, insurance companies, or financial communities. Surveillance of certain individuals such as journalists, lawyers, pastors, and doctors requires special approval.

3.3.2.2.5 Compliance Control

The government may provide TSPs with a handbook in the near future, containing guidelines regarding all technical and organizational requests. But such a handbook is not yet available.

3.3.2.3 Control and Sanctions in the Area of Surveillance

3.3.2.3.1 Controlling Entities

The controlling entities of RIPA are as follows:

- Interception of Communications Commissioner (ICC): independent individual who issues an annual report to the prime minister, who decides about the publication of the report
- Investigatory Powers Tribunal (IPT): independent court responsible for adjudicating complaints regarding LIs

Surveillance competencies of secret services are regulated by the Institution of Surveillance Commissioner (ISC).

3.3.2.3.2 Reporting Duties

For involved parties, it is mandatory to follow the guidelines of the ICC. In addition, these parties are expected to provide the necessary data for annual reports.

3.3.2.3.3 Surveillance Statistics

Detailed statistics are expected from all entities involved in executing LIs. Data on total number of LIs is outlined in a summary report that also includes breakdowns of (1) new, urgent, and continued surveillance activities and (2) the reasons for intercepts being conducted (e.g., terrorism, national security, crime, and prevention).

Statistics regarding surveillance activities conducted in Northern Ireland are not published.

3.3.2.3.4 Sanctions for Noncompliance

The ICC evaluates all LIs. Usually, RIPA implementation errors are due to misunderstandings and misinterpretations. Intentional noncompliance is rare, but sanctions are severe. To date, no implementation of sanctions has been reported, however.

3.4 Surveillance Rules and Procedures in Japan

Japan was the last of the G7 countries to ratify legislation in the area of LIs. Domestic opinion in the country is very polarized regarding this decision: some welcome it as an absolutely necessary step to fight terrorism and crime; others are concerned about privacy issues.

3.4.1 Legal Background of Surveillance

3.4.1.1 Basics of Intercept Laws

No laws or acts focusing on LIs have been established as yet. However, telecommunications privacy is supported by a law according to which "no censorship shall be maintained, nor shall the secrecy of any means of communications be violated."

3.4.1.2 Legal Guidelines

As a result of the high priority of telecommunications privacy, the country has seen no telecommunications surveillance activity, and experts do not expect rapid changes. Related laws are the following:

- A law authorizing interceptions of telecommunications in crime investigations
- The Code of Criminal Procedure (CCP) and its extension, the Communication Interception Act

The Ministry of Justice is in charge of handling LIs. No laws or acts are in place to fight terrorism and crime, and thus international collaboration with Japan is extremely difficult.

3.4.1.3 Services Subject to Surveillance

The Communication Interception Act governs surveillance in the areas of voice telephony, facsimile, and e-mail.

3.4.1.4 Objectives of Surveillance

The overall objective of surveillance is to fight serious and organized crime. Use of LIs should result in more effective monitoring of the activities of groups such as the Yakuza mafia and the Aum sect.

3.4.1.5 Differences between Individual and Strategic Surveillance

Occasionally, the public security police initiate preventive surveillance. Japanese law does not distinguish between individual and strategic surveillance.

3.4.2 Duties of TSPs and Operators of Telecommunications Equipment

3.4.2.1 Cooperation with LEAs

All TSPs must comply with LI legislation and guidelines. The primary prerequisite is that warrants be issued by prosecutors or high-ranking police officers.

3.4.2.2 Technical Requirements

LEAs have the authority, on a case-to-case basis, to provision devices for LIs. E-mail communications are supervised via so-called temporary mailboxes, which are storage devices installed and supervised by LEAs.

Discussions regarding supervision of wireless communications are continuing. NTT DoCoMo has been approached by the National Police Agency to develop and install, without compensation, LI surveillance technologies. However, because of the high costs involved, NTT DoCoMo cannot be forced by law to initiate this project.

3.4.2.3 Organizational Requirements

Legislation requests the physical presence of a subject matter expert on behalf of the TSP for the duration of the surveillance (which can vary from 24 hours to 30 days) as a means of guaranteeing the lawfulness of surveillance activities. This request, however, has been heavily criticized by TSPs because of the high costs involved. The law allows for a backup person from the local community to occasionally replace the subject matter expert.

LEAs, including the National Police Agency and the Public Prosecutor's Office, conduct workshops with TSPs at various intervals on the topic of faithful collaboration in the area of LIs. However, a code of practice has not yet been released.

3.4.2.4 Exceptions

Some of the reasons why TSPs may choose not to cooperate with LEAs are:

- The surveillance technology is too expensive.
- The human resources required in terms of physical presence are too expensive.
- New hardware and software are required.
- The company's size does not justify the expenses involved.

3.4.2.5 Compliance Control

It is assumed that only existing networking devices and monitors are being used for LIs. As a result, special certification procedures are not required in Japan.

3.4.3 Control and Sanctions in the Area of Surveillance

3.4.3.1 Controlling Entities

As mentioned, surveillance activities are controlled via the physical presence of a subject matter expert of the TSP or a backup person from the local community. Surveillance is actually executed by members of LEAs. Individuals whose communications have been intercepted must be notified within 30 days if they have been crime targets. All intercepted communications that do not contain crime-related information must be deleted. Other parties whose communications have been intercepted are not notified.

3.4.3.2 Reporting Duties

Members of LEAs must log all surveillance actions.

3.4.3.3 Surveillance Statistics

The parliament receives an annual report from the Ministry of Justice about statistics associated with LIs. In 2002, a case regarding drug trafficking became the first successful surveillance case to be made public. Otherwise, no reported surveillance statistics are publicly available because, among other reasons, crime rates are low and the police initiate proactive searches and custodies to prevent crime and terrorism.

3.4.3.4 Sanctions for Noncompliance

Significant sanctions are in place in terms of abuse of surveillance and surveillance instruments. However, there are no known sanctions against TSPs that are unable or choose not to cooperate with LEAs.

3.5 CALEA Reference Model with the J-STD-025 Standard

The definitions contained in CALEA about information and communication services are related to the guidelines included in the Telecommunications

Act. The most important ones are as follows (for more details, see the glossary):

- *Telecommunications:* the transmission, between or among points specified by the user, of information of the user's choosing, without change in the form or content of the information as sent and received
- *Telecommunications service:* the offering of telecommunications for a fee directly to the public or to such classes of users as to be effectively available directly to the public, regardless of the facilities used
- *Information services:* the offering of capability for generating, storing, transforming, retrieving, utilizing, or making available information via telecommunications, including electronic publishing but not including the use of any such capability for the management, control, or operation of a telecommunications system or the management of a telecommunications service
- *Telecommunications carrier*:* entity engaged in the transmission or switching of wire or electronic communications as a common carrier for hire
  - Includes commercial mobile radio service
  - Includes entities engaged in the transmission or switching of wire or electronic communications to the extent that the FCC determines that such service is a replacement for a substantial portion of the local telephone exchange service and that it is in the public interest to deem it to be a telecommunications carrier for these purposes
  - Does not include entities engaged in providing information services
- *CII:* dialing or signaling information that identifies the origin, direction, destination, or termination of all communications generated by means of any equipment, facility, service, or telecommunications carrier.

3.5.1 CALEA Interfaces

The principal interfaces with the CALEA reference model are:

- Surveillance administration system (SAS): performs subject provisioning and receives alarms related to CALEA interfaces

---

* The term *telecommunications service provider* is preferred by the authors of this book.

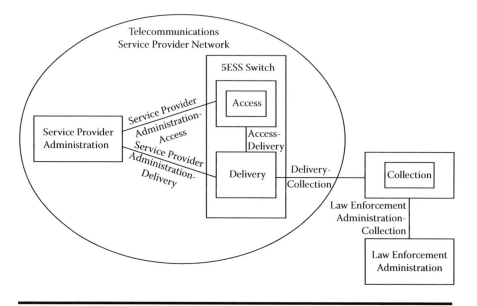

Figure 3.1   CALEA reference model.

- Call data channel (CDC): network connection reporting CII — CDC messages — from the switch to the LEA
- Call content channel (CCC): network connection delivering call content from the switch to the LEA

A reference model offering a generic view of the LI architecture (access, delivery, and collection functions) is shown in Figure 3.1.

3.5.2 CALEA Principal Functions

Basically, there are three principal CALEA functions:

1. The access functions (AFs) include network elements (CO switches, MSC, HLR, AAA, PDSN, SGSN, GGSN, routers, trunking gateways, softswitches, and CMTS) that provide access to and replication of intercepted traffic, and sniffers and splitters that can passively monitor network traffic.
2. The delivery function (DF) includes databases containing target and warrant information, provisioning interfaces, proprietary interfaces to AFs, and standards-based (J-STD-025, ETSI, TIIT, Packet-Cable) delivery of intercepted traffic to CFs. It runs on off-the-shelf UNIX-based platforms and programmable switch machines.

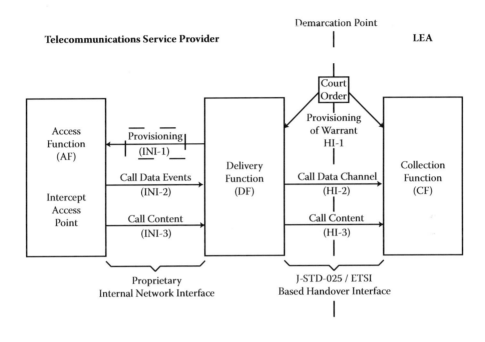

Figure 3.2 Generic view of the LI architecture.

3. The collection function (CF) collects and records lawfully authorized intercepted communications (e.g., for call content) and CII for LEAs.

Figure 3.2 shows, from another perspective, the principal functions and interfaces of the LI architecture.

3.6 European Telecommunications Standard Institute (ETSI) Reference Model for the European Community

ETSI defines lawful interception as actions, based on the law and performed by a network operator, access provider, or service provider* (NOW/AP/SvP), in which certain information is made available, and that information is provided to a law enforcement monitoring facility (LEMF).

Figure 3.3 shows the basic flow of information between service providers and LEAs.

---

* The term *telecommunications service provider* is preferred by the authors of this book.

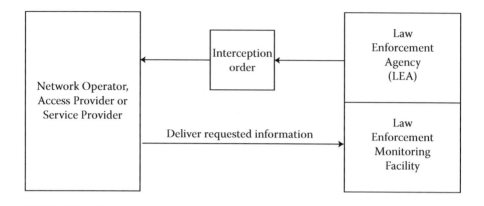

Figure 3.3   Basic information exchange.

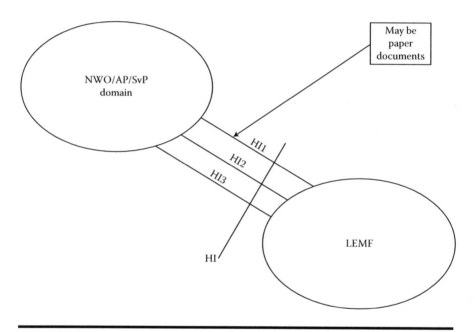

Figure 3.4   Diagram showing HIs between the NWO/AP/SvP and LEMF.

3.6.1 Basics of This Standard

The solution of choice in regard to the requirements of LEAs is a three-ported interface. Such an interface structure is shown in Figure 3.4.

The first HI port is designed to transport various kinds of administrative information from or to the LEA and NOW/AP/SvP. There must be a complete separation between the administrative interface (HI1) and the technical interfaces (HI2 and HI3) of the NOW/AP/SvP so that there is no possibility that the LEMF will establish or modify an interception without action by a mandated agent of the NOW/AP/SvP. In the case of a nonautomatic administrative interaction, this interface may be manual rather than electronic.

The functional modules include several domains.

■ TSP domain:
  – Network internal functions
  – Internal interception function (IIF)
  – Administrative function of TSPs
  – IRI mediation function
  – Content of communication (CC) mediation function for information content
■ LEA domain:
  – Law enforcement–monitoring function
  – Law enforcement–analysis function

This reference model supports various interfaces: INI (internal network interface), LI HI, HI1 (administrative information), HI2 (intercept-related information), and HI3 (CC). The HI2 and HI3 logical ports could, for example, be physically mapped to:

■ A single channel-oriented channel
■ A single packet-oriented channel
■ Several circuit-oriented channels
■ Several packet-oriented channels
■ Several circuit-oriented channels and one or more packet-oriented channels

The functional block diagram is shown in Figure 3.5. The functional components are defined in Table 3.2.

3.6.2 HIs

The three principal interfaces are described as follows.

3.6.2.1 HI1: Interface for Administrative Information

As mentioned earlier, HI1 transports administrative information from or to the LEA and NWO/AP/SvP. This port is used for the transmission of

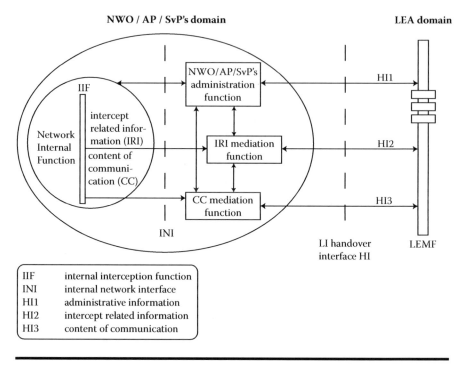

Figure 3.5 NWO/AP/SvP functional block diagram showing HIs.

the request to establish or to remove the interception action from the LEA to the NWO/AP/SvP and the acknowledgment message back to the LEA. The transmission between these parties should support manual and electronic transmissions from or to the LEMF and the NWO/AP/SvP facility.

Status reports should cover all types of alarms, reports, or information related to the intercept function. Both status reports and alarm reports are transmitted via HI1 to the LEMF or LEA if necessary. Alarms that are not specific to a certain target identity can be sent to all LEAs; other alarms (e.g., no answer from LEMF) should be transmitted only to the specific LEA to which they apply.

Typical forms of generic status reports are as follows:

- Target identity removed from service
- Change of target identity within the network
- Bulk modification of subscriber numbers
- Individual modification of subscriber numbers
- Creation of new multiple subscriber number (MSN)
- Loss of LI database (e.g., software replacement, recovery, and fallback)
- General setup failure

Table 3.2 Functional Block Diagram Components

Component	Description
IIF	Situated within the NWO/AP/SvP domain; there may be more than one IIF involved in the provision of interceptions
INI	Situated within the NWO/AP/SvP domain that exists between an IIF and the mediation function
NOW/AP/SvP administration center	Administration center, contacted via the HI1 port (which may be partly electronic and partly paper based, depending on the circumstances), used to set up the interception action according to an LEA request
Mediation function	Selects sequences and transforms information, including CC when necessary, between a number of IIFs and the HI; sometimes may be a null function (e.g., direct delivery of CC to the LEMF via HI3 with no changes)
Delivery mechanism to LEA/LEMF	Intercept requests and status and alarm reports transmitted between the administration center and the LEA/LEMF; IRI transmitted through the mediation function (may be transparent) to the LEMF; CC transmitted through the mediation function (may be transparent) to the LEMF

Examples of status reports indicating transmission problems between the NWO/AP/SvP and LEMF are transmission problems to LEMF, LEMF busy, or no answer from LEMF.

3.6.2.2 HI2: Interface for IRI

The HI2 transports all IRI. This interface is used to transmit information or data associated with the telecommunications services of the target identity apparent to the network. It includes signaling information used to establish the telecommunication service and to control its progress (e.g., target identification, identification of the other parties involved in a communication, basic services used, direction of the call or the event, answer identification and release causes, and time stamps). If available, further information such as supplementary service information or location information may be included.

In general, relaying of the IRI to the LEMF should take place as soon as possible, usually in the range of a few seconds. In exceptional cases (e.g., data link problems), the IRI may be buffered for later transmission for a specified period of time. IRI should be structured as a sequence of records:

- IRI-BEGIN record at the first occurrence of a communication attempt, opening the IRI transaction
- IRI-END record at the end of a communication or communication attempt, closing the IRI transaction
- IRI-CONTINUE record at any time during a communication or communication attempt within the IRI transaction
- IRI-REPORT record used in general cases involving non-communication-related events

IRI should be transmitted to the LEMF with no translation of information content. This process involves the following advantages:

- There is a minimum amount of translation to be kept up-to-date.
- Mediation functionalities are minimized.
- A minimal number of amendments are required when new services are introduced.

However, information may require enveloping before being passed to the LEMF.

3.6.2.3 HI3: Interface for CC

The HI3 port transports the CC of the intercepted telecommunications service to the LEMF. The CC should be presented as a transparent, clear copy of the information flow taking place during an established (frequently bidirectional) communication of the interception subject. It may contain voice as well as data.

The transmission media used to support the HI3 port will usually be those associated with a telecommunications network or its access arrangements. In cases of failure, CC is lost. The network does not provide any recording function.

3.6.2.3.1 Correlation of HI2 and HI3

When an HI3 port is established, the target's identity is passed across to enable the LEMF to correlate the CC on HI3 with the IRI on HI2. In situations in which an LEMF may be connected to more than one source as a result of interception, it is necessary to ensure a reliable correlation between the CC and IRI. Use of several simultaneous mechanisms, some of which are described in Table 3.3, will ensure correct correlation. The use of a given mechanism will be dependent on national rules and technical considerations.

Table 3.3 Possible Correlation Mechanisms

Group	CC	IRI
A	Time of arrival of call at LEMF	Time stamp in information record
B	Unique number[a] sent in an associated signaling channel	Unique number[a] in information record
B	LEMF address	LEMF address in information record
D	Particular physical channel	Particular physical channel

Note: The information provided is not exhaustive.

[a] A unique number may be devised in various ways.

3.6.3 ETSI Security Recommendations

The operations of interception facilities are generally required to be discreet, confidential, and efficient. Appropriate security features are necessary to prevent unauthorized administration as well as unauthorized use. General security requirements are as follows:

- A security management system should be established.
- There should be physical and logical access controls.
- Any necessary keys, passwords, or user identifications related to authorization and logical access to the interception function should be securely stored.
- Any transmission of passwords or user identifications for access to interception functions should be secure.
- Physical interfaces should be secured mechanically and logically to prevent unauthorized use.

Transmission of all information between the NOW/AP/SvP and LEMF across HI1, HI2, and HI3 must be confidential. During communication between systems that are not based on leased lines, appropriate mechanisms should ensure that the recipient is in a position to verify or authenticate the identity of the sender while the connection is set up. During communication between systems that are not based on leased lines, appropriate mechanisms should ensure that the sender is in a position to verify or authenticate the identity of the recipient at the time of initiation of the connection.

Only specifically authorized personnel should be able to control interceptions. In general, the LEA should not have direct access to any of the network elements.

The entire communication between the administration system and the interception function should be confidential. All internal interfaces must be secured. Interception functions should be implemented in such a manner that:

- The interception subject and his or her correspondents are unaware that a lawful interception is active.
- During the intercepted communication itself, the quality of the communication remains the same as usual and the service is unchanged, including all supplementary services (e.g., call forwarding).
- When there is no intercepted communication, communication quality remains the same and the service is unchanged, such that there is no modification to services supplied or information received either by the interception subject or another party.

An NWO/AP/SvP employee who has been duly authorized may be permitted to know that an interception is in progress or that a subscriber is an interception target. However, this is not the case for NWO/AP/SvP employees who have not been duly authorized.

3.7 Summary

In this chapter, we have outlined LI functions. These functions will be streamlined and matched with standardization results from North America and Europe later in this book. As a consequence of recent technological progress, all communication services can be intercepted. Either networking equipment (e.g., switches, multiplexers, routers, modems, firewalls, and load balancers) or communication facilities can offer low-overhead interception access points (IAPs).

However, legal requirements differ greatly from technological requirements. Here we have provided a short overview of the wiretap and content interception laws in force in North America, Europe, and Japan. Criminal codes are different in each country, but the situation is the same everywhere: LI proponents and privacy protectors are fighting against each other.

Chapter 4

Intercept Access Points in Infrastructure Components

CONTENTS

Telecommunications service providers (TSPs) are expected to expand their service portfolios at intervals, to reduce capital and operational expenses, to optimize pricing strategies, to innovate their infrastructures, to acquire new customers, and to make profits. Many TSPs have added another element to this list: supporting lawful intercepts (LIs).

The components of the infrastructure in the area of LIs include applications, computers, storage areas, networks, and network equipment. There is typically debate on the part of subscribers as to where services end and applications begin and who should be in charge of developing and deploying applications. Applications are on top of the products offered by TSPs. Currently, this application layer is thin. But TSPs are always interested in increasing their service portfolios by offering packaged applications. It is expected that, over time, the degree of service intelligence will grow, with the result that development of applications by subscribers will become unnecessary and redundant.

This chapter begins by discussing three standard approaches that streamline TSP business processes, followed by a short generic review of infrastructure components. Particular emphasis will be placed on monitoring principles in association with LIs. Also, signaling systems will be addressed as a source of intercept information. Finally, the effects of LI activities on resources of TSPs will be assessed.

4.1 Blueprints and Guidelines for TSPs

The time for proprietary solutions is over. TSPs can no longer afford to maintain numerous and different support, documentation, and management systems. Standards bodies and industry associations can provide help in streamlining processes and organizational structures.

Three applicable solutions — the enhanced telecommunications operations map (eTOM), the telecommunications management network (TMN), and the control objectives for information and related technology (CobiT)

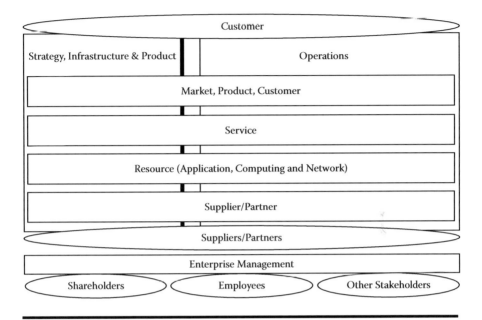

Figure 4.1 eTOM business process framework: Level-0 processes.

— are addressed in this section. IT infrastructure libraries (ITILs), another solution for enterprise IT departments and, in some cases, TSPs, are not addressed in detail in this book.

4.1.1 eTOM

The eTOM business process framework serves as the starting point for development and integration of business and operations support systems (OSS), and it helps drive the TeleManagement Forum (TMF) members' work in developing next-generation OSS (NGOSS) solutions. In the case of service providers (SPs), it provides a neutral reference point as they consider internal process reengineering needs, partnerships, alliances, and general working agreements with other providers. For suppliers, the eTOM framework outlines potential boundaries of software components and the required functions, inputs, and outputs that must be supported by products.

The eTOM framework includes the enterprise processes required by SPs. It is not an SP business model, however; it does not address strategic issues or questions of who an SP's target customers should be, what market segments the provider should serve, and so forth. A business process framework represents one part of an SP's strategic business model and plan.

Figure 4.1 shows the highest conceptual view of the eTOM business process framework (Level-0 Processes). This view provides an overall

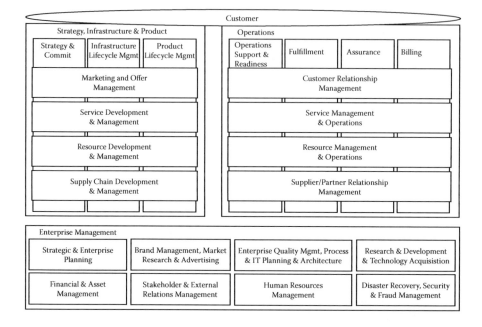

Figure 4.2   eTOM business process framework: Level-1 processes (Level-0 view).

context differentiating strategy and life-cycle processes from operations processes in two large groupings, shown as two separate boxes. It also differentiates key functional areas in five horizontal layers and illustrates the interacting internal and external entities within a given enterprise.

Figure 4.2 shows the Level-0 view of Level-1 processes. This detail is needed to position and analyze business processes. Seven vertical process groups — representing the end-to-end processes required to support customers and manage a business — are presented. The eTOM focuses on the core customer operation processes of fulfillment, assurance, and billing (FAB). Operations support and readiness is differentiated from FAB real-time processes to increase the focus on enabling support and auto-mation in FAB (i.e., online, immediate support of customers). The strategy and commit vertical, and the two life-cycle management verticals, are also differentiated because, unlike operations processes, they do not directly support the customer, and they adhere to different business time cycles.

The horizontal process groupings shown in Figure 4.2 distinguish functional operations processes and other types of business functional processes (e.g., marketing versus selling and service development versus service configuration). The functional processes shown at left (within the strategy and commit, infrastructure life-cycle management, and product life-cycle management vertical process groupings) enable, support, and direct work in the operations verticals.

In summary, eTOM involves a number of improvements relative to the earlier TOM:

- It expands the scope of operations to all enterprise processes.
- It distinctly identifies marketing processes due to their heightened importance in today's E-business world.
- It identifies enterprise management processes so that everyone involved is aware of his or her critical tasks, thereby enabling process framework acceptance across the enterprise.
- It moves FAB to the high-level framework to emphasize that customer priority processes are the focus of the enterprise.
- It defines an operations support and readiness vertical process grouping applicable to all functional layers other than enterprise management. To integrate E-business and make customer self-management a reality, there must be an understanding within the enterprise regarding the processes needed to allow increasing amounts of direct, online customer operations support and customer self-management.
- It recognizes three enterprise process groupings that are distinctly different from operations processes: strategy and commit, infrastructure life-cycle management, and product life-cycle management.
- It recognizes the different cycle times of strategy and life-cycle management processes and the need to separate these processes from those involving customer priority operations, in which automation is most critical. It does so by decoupling the strategy and commit process and the two life-cycle management processes from the day-to-day, minute-to-minute cycle times of customer operations processes.
- It moves from a customer care or service orientation to a customer relationship management (CRM) orientation that emphasizes customer self-management and control, increasing the value customers contribute to the enterprise and the use of information to customize and personalize individual customer needs. Elements are added to this customer operations functional layer to represent better selling processes and to integrate marketing fulfillment within CRM.
- It acknowledges the need to manage resources across technologies (i.e., application, computing, and network) by integrating the network and systems management functional process into the resource management and operations area. Also, it situates IT management in this functional layer as opposed to an outbound process layer.

4.1.2 TMN

This is a special network implemented to help manage an TSP's overall telecommunications network. As such, it interfaces with one or more individual networks at several points to exchange information. It is logically separate from the networks it manages, and it may be physically separate as well. However, a TMN may use part of the telecommunications network for its own communications.

The TMN effort is chartered by the Telecommunications Standardization Sector of the International Telecommunications Union. Its development began in 1988 and has concentrated primarily on the network's overall architecture, using the Synchronous Digital Hierarchy (the international version of the North American Synchronous Optical Network, or SONET) technology as a target. However, TMN techniques are applicable to a broad range of technologies and services.

TMN is an extension of the Open Systems Interconnection (OSI) standardization process. It attempts to standardize some of the functionality, and many of the interfaces, of managed networks. When a TMN is fully implemented, the result will be a higher level of integration. TMNs are usually described as involving three different types of architectures:

1. The functional architecture describes the appropriate distribution of functionality within TMN, in the sense of allowing for the creation of function blocks from which a TMN of any complexity can be implemented. Requirements for TMN-recommended interface specifications are based on the definitions of function blocks and the reference points between them.
2. The information architecture, based on an object-oriented approach, provides the rationale for application of OSI systems management principles to TMN principles. The OSI principles are mapped to the TMN principles and, as necessary, expanded to fit the TMN environment.
3. The physical architecture describes interfaces that can actually be implemented, together with examples of the physical components that make up the TMN.

Management functions are grouped into the five areas identified as part of the OSI model. Examples are as follows:

1. Fault management (alarm surveillance, testing, and problem administration)
2. Configuration management (provisioning and rating)

3. Performance management (monitoring of service quality and traffic control)
4. Security management (management of access and authentication)
5. Accounting management (rating and billing)

The management requirements that helped shape the TMN specifications address planning, provisioning, installing, maintaining, operating, and administering communications networks and services.

TMN specifications use standard Common Management Information Protocol (CMIP) application services when appropriate. However, one of the key concepts of the TMN specifications is their introduction of "technology-independent" management, which is based on an abstract view of managed network elements. This abstract view and a single communication interface allow diverse equipment to be managed. Thus, TMN-managed networks can consist of both TMN-conforming and nonconforming devices.

TMN specifications define an intended direction, but many smaller details involved in the process must be determined. Published TMN specifications address the overall architecture, the generic information model, management services and functions, management and transmission protocols, and an alarm surveillance function. Future areas of focus will be the service layer, traffic (i.e., congestion), and network-level management.

The relatively slow pace of TMN specification development has not prevented companies from recognizing the benefits of the TMN approach to management. The TMF is incorporating TMN into its specifications, and many companies are beginning to build, or specify, management systems and components that comply with TMN principles. Systems that comply with these principles reduce costs and improve services due to several reasons (Terplan, 2001):

■ Standard interfaces and objects make it possible to rapidly and economically deploy new services.
■ Distributed management intelligence minimizes management reaction time to network events.
■ Mediation makes it possible to handle similar devices in an identical manner, leading to more generic operation systems and vendor independence.
■ Mediation allows management and transparent upgrading of existing device inventories.
■ Distributed management functions increase scalability, isolate and contain network faults, and reduce network management traffic and the load on operations systems.

Many of the benefits that accrue from the TMN principles are due directly to the distributed architecture and its mediation function. The TMN architecture addresses communications networks and services as collections of cooperating systems. By managing individual systems, TMN has a coordinated effect on the overall network.

This coordination can be illustrated through a simple example. Within an enterprise, one operations system may deal with network-element inventory, another may deal with traffic planning, and several element managers may deal with network elements of various types. When a customer requires a circuit of a specific bandwidth and quality, all these systems must be coordinated to meet the customer's needs. The TMN architecture not only facilitates this effort, it allows for this function to be distributed among several systems. Such a distribution allows a TMN-based system to handle global networks by enabling workloads to be spread across multiple systems.

This ability to subdivide and distribute the total management effort requires clear definitions of functions, interfaces, and the information model. These topics, defined in the TMN specifications, are outlined subsequently.

The TMN architecture identifies specific functions and their interfaces. These functions are what allow a TMN to perform its management activities. The architecture also provides flexibility in terms of building a management system by allowing certain functions to be combined within a physical entity. The function blocks described subsequently, along with typical methods of their physical realization, are defined according to the TMN specifications (Terplan, 2001).

4.1.2.1 Operations Systems Function (OSF)

This function, in the form of a TMN-compliant management system or set of management applications, monitors, coordinates, and controls TMN entities. The OSF makes it possible for general activities such as management of performance, faults, configuration, accounting, and security to be performed. In addition, specific capabilities in regard to planning of operations, administration, maintenance, and provisioning of communications networks and systems should be available. These capabilities are realized through an operations system that can be implemented in many different ways. An example would be a descending abstraction system (e.g., business, service, and network) wherein the overall business needs of the enterprise are met by coordinating the underlying services. In turn, individual services are realized through coordination of network resources.

4.1.2.2 Work Station Function (WSF)

The WSF provides the TMN information, such as access control, topological map displays, and graphical interfaces, to the user. These functions are realized through a workstation.

4.1.2.3 Mediation Function (MF)

This function acts on information passing between an OSF and a network element function (NEF) or Q adapter function (QAF) to ensure that the data produced through the MF complies with the needs and capabilities of the receiver. MFs can store, adapt, filter, threshold, and condense information. In addition to providing the abstract view necessary to treat dissimilar elements in a similar manner, MFs may also help local management in regard to their associated NEFs (in other words, MFs may include element managers).

The MF is realized through a mediation device. Mediation can be implemented as a hierarchy of cascaded devices, using standard interfaces. This cascading of mediation devices and the various interconnections to network elements provide TMNs with a great deal of flexibility, as well as allowing for future design of new equipment to support a higher level of processing within the network element, without the need to redesign an existing TMN.

4.1.2.4 QAF

This function is used to connect non-TMN-compliant NEFs to the TMN environment and is realized in a Q adapter, which allows legacy devices (i.e., those that do not support TMN management protocols, including Simple Network Management Protocol [SNMP] devices) to be accommodated within a TMN. A Q adapter typically performs interface conversion functions (i.e., it acts as a proxy).

4.1.2.5 NEF

This function is realized through the network elements themselves, which can present a TMN-compliant or noncompliant interface. Such elements include physical elements (switches), logical elements (virtual circuit connections), and services (operations systems software applications). Figure 4.3 illustrates the functions occurring within a TMN environment. The portions falling outside the TMN environment are not subject to standardization. For example, the human interface portion of the WSF is not specified in the TMN standard.

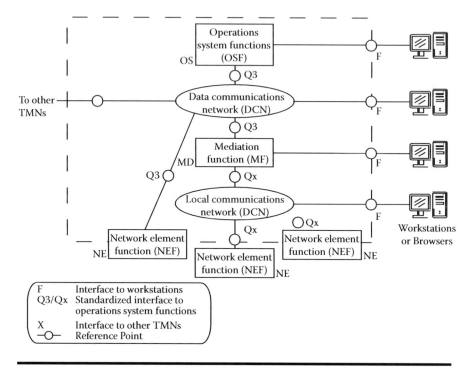

Figure 4.3 Functions within the TMN architecture.

Within the TMN specification are well-defined reference points iden-tifying the characteristics of the interfaces between function blocks. The reference points identify the information that passes between the function blocks. The function blocks exchange information using the data commu-nications function (DCF). The DCF may perform routing, relaying, and internetworking actions at OSI layers 1 to 3 (i.e., physical, data link, and network) or their equivalents. These functions are performed in the data communications network. Figure 4.3 also shows the reference points (F, G, M, Qx, Q3, and X) defined in the TMN specifications. These reference points are characterized by the information shared between their end-points, and they can be further explained as follows:

- F is the interface between a workstation, an operations system, and a mediation device.
- G is the interface between a workstation and a human user. The specification of this interface is outside the scope of TMN.
- M is the interface between a Q adapter and a non-TMN-compliant network element. This interface, not specified in TMN, is actually one of the most important, given that today's networks consist primarily of devices that do not comply with the TMN standard.

- Qx refers to the interface between a Q adapter and a mediation device, a TMN-compliant element and a mediation device, and between two mediation devices.
- Q3 refers to the interface between a TMN-compliant element and an operations system, a Q adapter and a mediation device, a mediation device and an operations system, and between two operations systems.
- X is the interface between operations systems in different TMNs. The operations system outside the X interface may be part of either a TMN or a non-TMN environment. This interface may require increased security relative to the level required by Q interfaces. In addition, access limitations may be imposed.

At present, only the Q3 interface has been specified to any detailed degree. The definition outlined includes the Q3's management protocol (CMIP), alarm surveillance capabilities, and operations in the generic model used to describe the network. Alarm surveillance refers to a set of functions that enable monitoring and polling the network concerning alarm-related events or conditions.

The TMN information model, which focuses on the management-protocol object classes required to manage such a network, includes an abstraction of the management aspects of network resources and related support management activities. Information about objects is exchanged across TMN-standard interfaces.

The TMN specifications make up a generic information model that is technology independent. This independence allows management of diverse equipment in a common manner, through an abstract view of network elements. This concept is vital if a TMN is to achieve its goals. The generic information model also serves as a basis for defining technology-specific object classes. These classes support a technology-independent view while enabling more precise management.

For example, a switch used to perform common management activities, such as provisioning or performance gathering, could be defined according to TMN specifications. In addition, this generic switch definition could be extended to cover the peculiarities of a particular vendor's switch. The extended definition could be used for such specialized activities as controlling the execution of diagnostic routines. TMN generic modeling techniques can be used by resource providers or management system providers to define their own objects.

The TMN specification includes an information model that is common to managed communications networks. This model can be used to generically define the resources, actions, and events that exist in a particular network.

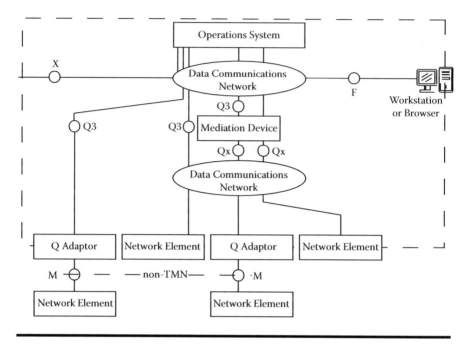

Figure 4.4   Sample TMN physical architecture and interfaces.

The TMN architecture is an excellent means of visualizing network and service management solutions. Figure 4.4 shows a simple solution (Terplan, 2001) representing a typical network management system (NMS) layer integrating various element management systems (EMSs). Additional management applications help support service management layer (SML) and business management layer (BML).

The visualization technology may be used to support various regional network management systems. On top of these network management systems, service-oriented messages, events, and alarms may be extracted and displayed in various service centers.

4.1.3 Control Objectives for Information and Related Technology (CobiT)

CobiT is an IT governance, control framework, and maturity model. Its purpose is to ensure that IT resources are aligned with an enterprise's business objectives so that services and information, when delivered, meet quality, fiduciary, and security needs. It is also intended to provide a mechanism to balance IT risks and returns. CobiT defines 34 significant processes, links 318 tasks and activities to them, and defines an internal control framework for them all.

CobiT can be used by business or IT management, but its origins are in auditing. It was developed by the Information Systems Audit and Control Association, which is an international organization based in the United States. More recently, the IT Governance Institute has made some contributions. CobiT is often introduced in an enterprise via the audit route. As a result, IT managers often view CobiT as a threat to their positions rather than as a useful and powerful framework for communicating effectiveness and value to their companies.

CobiT processes and control objectives are segmented into four domains: (Gartner, 2002)

1. Planning and Organization (PO)
    P01 Define a strategic IT plan
    P02 Define the information architecture
    P03 Determine the technological direction
    P04 Define the IT organization and relationships
    P05 Manage the IT investment
    P06 Communicate management aims and directions
    P07 Manage human resources
    P09 Assess risks
    P10 Manage projects
    P11 Manage quality
2. Acquisition and Implementation (AI)
    AI1 Identify automated solutions
    AI2 Acquire and maintain application software
    AI3 Acquire and maintain technology infrastructure
    AI4 Develop and maintain IT procedures
    AI5 Install and accredit systems
    AI6 Manage changes
3. Delivery and Support (DS)
    DS1 Define and manage service levels
    DS2 Manage third-party services
    DS3 Manage performance and capacity
    DS4 Ensure continuous service
    DS5 Ensure system security
    DS6 Identify and allocate cost
    DS7 Educate and train users
    DS8 Assist and advise customers
    DS9 Manage problems and incidents
    DS10 Manage problems and incidents
    DS11 Manage data
    DS12 Manage facilities
    DS13 Manage operations

4. Monitoring (M)
   M1 Monitor the processes
   M2 Assess internal control adequacy
   M3 Obtain independent assurance
   M4 Provide for independent audit

CobiT is based on established frameworks, such as the Software Engineering Institute's Capability Maturity Model, ISO 9000, and Infrastructure Library (ITIL). However, CobiT does not include control guidelines or practices, which are the next level of detail. Unlike ITIL, CobiT does not include process steps and tasks because it is a control framework rather than a process framework. CobiT focuses on what an enterprise needs to do, not how it needs to do it, and the target audience is auditors, senior business management and senior IT management.

4.1.4 The Infrastructure Library (ITIL) Processes

ITIL is based on delivering best-practice processes for IT service delivery and support, rather than defining a broad-based control framework. It focuses on the method. ITIL has a much narrower scope than CobiT because of its own focus on IT service management, but it defines a more comprehensive set of processes within that narrower field of service delivery and support. ITIL is more prescriptive about the tasks involved in those processes and, as such, its primary target audience is IT and service management. Some enterprises have combined CobiT and ITIL to provide a more comprehensive IT governance and operations framework.

The principles behind the CobiT and ITIL frameworks are consistent. Auditors often use CobiT in combination with the ITIL self-assessment workbook to assess the service management environment. CobiT provides a set of key goal and performance indicators, and critical success factors for each of its processes. These add value to ITIL because they establish the basis for managing.

The development processes of the two frameworks are not linked to each other, and both would benefit from closer collaboration. However, they are unlikely to contradict each other in any substantive way.

4.2 Reference Model of the Infrastructure

The infrastructure of a TSP consists basically of three components:

1. Applications and services
2. Computers
3. Networks and network equipment

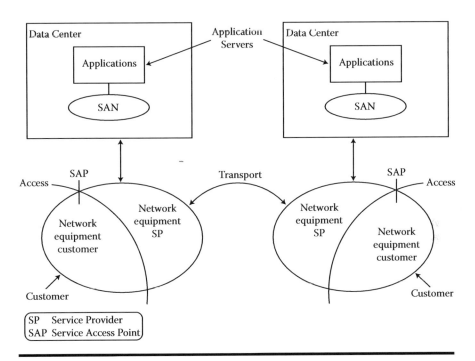

Figure 4.5 Generic infrastructure of an SP.

Figure 4.5 shows a simple diagram that includes all the principal components. The layers of Figure 4.3 can be recognized here: network equipment, networks (access and transport), services between service access points (SAPs), and business-related applications.

In terms of intercept access points (IAPs), literally any of the system segments may serve as sources of information and intelligence.

4.2.1 Applications and Services

The concepts of application and service are not yet clearly separated from each other. The following differentiations are recommended:

- *Business applications of SPs* refer to applications in the BML of the network architecture, including
  - OSSs
  - Business support systems (BSSs)
  - Marketing support systems (MSSs)
  - CRM
  - Partner relationship management (PRM)
  - Sales force automation (SFA)
  - Enterprise resource planning (ERP)

- Business intelligence (BI)
- Decision support systems (DSSs)

From the perspective of SPs, these are the core functions in regard to conducting business. The intelligence support system (ISS) will join this group and serve as the focal point for providing intelligence to law enforcement agencies (LEAs).

■ *Services and products* are sold to customers with guaranteed quality of service (QoS) and service-level agreements (SLAs) measured and reported between SAPs. Depending on the products offered, TSPs can be classified into one (or more) of the following groups:
  - Incumbent local exchange carrier (ILEC): Strong provider that owns a considerable number of telecommunications facilities and does not want to relinquish this position easily. Typically, ILECs will possess legacy support systems allowing minimal interoperability or integration. The result is high operating costs.
  - Competitive local exchange carrier (CLEC): Smaller, flexible provider that owns few or no telecommunications facilities. By offering excellent customer care and new services, CLECs attempt to build their support structure step by step. Their support systems are typically state-of-the-art, lightweight, and inexpensive to operate. In certain cases, they use service bureaus for billing and provisioning.
  - Internet service provider (ISP): Provides Internet access to business and residential customers. ISPs vary widely in size. Major challenges include access control, eligibility control, peering to each other and to other carriers, managing quality, and maintaining acceptable performance levels.
  - Application services provider (ASP): Emerging SP that must combine application, systems, and network management. Service-level expectations are extremely high; customers may rely on ASPs for all their business operations.
  - Inter exchange carrier (IEX): Primarily responsible for long-distance services with stepwise penetration of the local exchange area. IEXs can be both incumbent and competitive providers, leading to the need for heterogeneous support systems.
  - Post, telegraphy, and telephone (PTT): Strong provider, similar to an ILEC, that owns a considerable number of telecommunications facilities but possesses limited-capacity support systems.
  - Competitive access provider (CAP): Facility-based or non-facility-based, CAPs are similar to ILECs but offer carefully selected local loops to high-profit commercial customers.

- Integration communications provider (ICP): Emerging provider with integrated service offerings concentrating on next-generation high-speed data and wireless services, particularly for business users. There is expected to be a high level of acceptance of ICPs in the market space. In terms of support systems, they buy instead of build; occasionally, they use service bureaus for billing and provisioning. They take advantage of the fact that intranet, extranet, virtual private networks, E-commerce, and multimedia applications require more bandwidth than is available over traditional circuit-switched voice networks.
- Cable services provider (CSP): Emerging SP that offers access networks. CSPs face technological challenges that must be overcome; for example, they buy instead of build support systems, and these systems are typically extremely limited. Occasionally, they use service bureaus for billing and provisioning.
- Content services providers (CSP): Emerging E-commerce SPs that concentrate on value, quality, and timeliness of content. Their main competition is ISPs and ASPs.
- Network services provider (NSP): Responsible for providing a reliable networking infrastructure consisting of both equipment and facilities. Typically, the responsibilities of NSPs are limited to the physical network. However, EMSs are usually included in their offerings. Wireless carriers provide cellular, personal, and mobile communications services.
- Enterprise services provider (ESP): Emerging SP from the enterprise environment. ESPs offer services for limited user communities with particular attributes. They use and customize their own existing support systems.

■ *Business applications of customers* refer to applications typical for the enterprise under consideration. They are extended or integrated with each other using communications-related appliances, such as e-mail, chat, instant messaging, unified messaging, file transfers, Web services, short message services (SMSs) and multimedia message services.

In several cases, services are identical to targeted applications. This is the case, for instance, with e-mail and instant messaging.

In general, service intelligence levels are increasing, with the result that customers do not need to engage in a significant amount of in-house development. Communications-related services can be customized and extended to satisfy user needs.

4.2.2 Computers

This group of components contains all the computing resources associated with SPs' data centers. Application hosts and storage area resources, as well as demilitarized zone (DMZ) firewalls, are typical components. Of course, there are many more processors, but they are traditionally assigned to network equipment. Further differentiation will assist in the process of subdividing infrastructure components into software and hardware categories.

The software infrastructure comprises application- and process-independent software components and basic services. These services are also called horizontal services. This software, built on the hardware and network infrastructure, is the basis for applications. Examples are:

- Office components and services
- Location and directory services
- Data management services
- Data interchange services

Operating systems and operating-system extensions are seen as part of the hardware infrastructure.

In contrast to the logical tiers of the software infrastructure, the hardware infrastructure is divided into physical tiers: (1) client systems, (2) server systems, and (3) storage systems. In addition, each of these tiers is divided into hardware, operating system, and operating-system extensions.

It is getting more and more difficult to draw the line between computers and networks. Due to distributed processing capabilities, grid computing, on-demand computing, adaptive computing, virtualization of computing resources and utility computing, networks are practically becoming the "computer."

4.2.3 Networks and Network Equipment

Chapter 2 offered a number of examples regarding network architectures. This subsection differentiates between transport and access networks. The media are identical in both cases: wire, coax, fiber, and airwaves.

Typical examples of transport network equipment are:

- Switches
- Bridges
- Multiplexers
- Routers

- Amplifiers
- Activators
- Fault diagnostic tools
- Element managers

The access segment consists of two principal groups: provider equipment and customer equipment. The line of demarcation is usually drawn by ownership. Often, customer premises equipments (CPEs) are managed by TSPs.

On the provider side, the following equipment is common:

- Edge routers
- Traffic shapers
- Load balancers
- Gatekeepers
- Gateways
- Firewalls
- Web switches

4.2.4 Reference Management Architecture

The infrastructure reference model includes the comprehensive logical architecture commonly used by TSPs in operating their networks (Figure 4.6). The intent of this architecture is to provide a framework for identifying automation flows between the network, network-facing systems, and back-office OSSs, BSSs, and ISSs. The following are some important points regarding this architecture that TSPs should keep in mind:

- The framework encompasses multiple layers of the TMN stack.
- The networks shown may encompass multiple access and transport providers (combination of wireline and wireless providers).
- Underlying systems, such as data warehouses and other applications, are not included.
- There may be functional overlaps between systems.
- TSPs will typically deploy a subset of these systems and may not want to integrate all systems.
- An integration engine involving a "message bus" can be used, but this not the only integration option.

Each principal component of the reference model will be briefly described by grouping business applications into customer-facing and network-facing solutions.

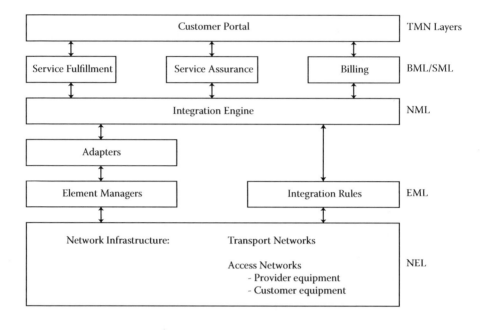

Figure 4.6 Reference management architecture for SPs.

4.2.4.1 Customer-Facing Solutions

4.2.4.1.1 Service Fulfillment Systems

Service fulfillment systems are used to receive and handle orders, provision service, and create/update information for customer billing.

Order-management and provisioning processes begin with order entry, through SFA tools or Web-based customer order-entry portals. Either way, orders must be entered, validated, and inserted into order-management workflows. The representation of this system in Figure 4.6 encompasses this functionality. CRM is frequently connected with order management. External and internal orders for LIs follow the usual or expedited order-management process flows.

The design and assign function is the part of the provisioning process in which circuits and services are designed and assigned to available physical/logical inventory. These systems typically interact with network inventory systems. Support for LIs requires additional design and assign functions because IAPs must be defined, and capacity for collecting, storing, and processing intercept- and content-related information must be ensured.

The primary engineering system that most carriers employ is a network inventory system. These systems support inventory entry and tracking of both physical and logical inventory. An ideal inventory system also integrates tightly with design and assign systems, as well as producing capacity threshold events and detailed inventory-tracking reports. Other engineering-related systems include traffic analysis and planning systems, which provide network engineering with software tools allowing sophisticated trend analyses to be performed and forecasting capacity requirements to be met.

Workforce management (WFM) systems are used in the service fulfillment process for scheduling and routing field technicians to perform physical provisioning activities such as cross-connecting subnetworks at peering points, installing CPEs, and deploying probes for surveillance. The primary areas on which these systems focus are work orders, skills of technicians, truck inventory, and schedules. It is important to note that WFM systems have a role in service assurance as well; technicians are dispatched to repair network problems that cannot be solved via the network operating center (NOC). Gateway systems are used for two primary purposes: to order resources on a trading partner's network and to provision non-network resources from third-party providers.

4.2.4.1.2 Service Assurance Systems

Once a service is operational, the TSP's primary responsibilities are to ensure that the service remains operational, to provide data to the customer on the performance of the service, and to provide customer support in the use of the service.

The key system in this area of provider business processes is CRM. This system is the source of records for all customer and service data, and it often plays a dominant role in service delivery processes such as order management. Also, it frequently houses workflow data for customer support processes, such as trouble ticketing and change requests. CRM systems are most commonly used by customer support representatives (CSRs) in call centers; however, Web-based front ends that allow customer self-service may also be in place.

Often, separate systems are used for customer-originated and NOC-originated trouble tickets. Both network and customer trouble ticketing play a key role in service assurance processes. Automation of these processes invariably involves automated creation, tracking, and closure of trouble tickets, along with appropriate customer and field personnel notifications throughout the ticketing workflow.

SLA-reporting systems require that providers be able to collect detailed performance statistics from the network, as well as aggregate and summarize these statistics for the customer. These systems must support high transaction volumes in regard to accumulation of network statistics. It is important to note that the same systems used in SLA statistics provision and collection are often used with the overall network performance statistics through which the network engineering organization optimizes the network and identifies capacity problems.

In the case of LIs, subject matter experts should observe and evaluate performance effects stemming from surveillance. These effects may include the following:

- Additional bandwidth demand to transfer intercept- and content-related data from IAPs (hardware or software probes) to management stations
- Overhead in network equipment (switch/router) due to collection software
- Storage requirements of TSPs or LEAs

Surveillance-related law regarding gathering intercept and content intelligence requires that customers not experience any negative service quality or service performance effects as a result of LI activity.

4.2.4.1.3 Billing Systems

Billing systems can be simple enough to handle flat-rate monthly billing or complex enough to compute and present bills for usage-based or value-based services. They are usually the final workflow destination in customer-facing processes. At the point at which an order is fully provisioned, tested, and sent to billing, it is considered a revenue-generating service. Support of LIs is not considered a revenue-generating service.

To successfully automate various business processes, it is critical that both engineering and traffic analysis/planning systems be tightly coupled with logical and physical inventory events and queries across EMS interface boundaries. LIs require additional inventory that may be maintained in securely partitioned segments or as part of the master system.

4.2.4.2 Network-Facing Solutions

4.2.4.2.1 Network Management Systems

Suppliers do not always implement the NEL, EML, and NML interfaces of TMN. Often, NMSs are implemented that use SNMP, TL1, or CORBA protocol stacks. Leading management applications are as follows:

- Incident management
- Fault isolation and correlation
- Problem management
- Activation of network components
- Mediation of collected data
- Performance optimization

4.2.4.2.2 EMSs

These manage and administer a homogeneous family of managed objects using a unified graphical user interface (GUI) in the case of users or a standardized interface in the case of management frameworks. Management frameworks are connected with legacy OSSs and BSSs and with emerging ISSs.

The infrastructure components connect all the systems together. These components are coordinated by a message bus through which all messages are published and exchanged. In addition to the message bus, integration rules are also used, including rules for routing, conversion, and basic data for workflow support.

Many vendors in the area of mediation devices implement universal adapters to translate EIA (Enterprise Integration Architecture) messages. Such adapters are provided by IGS, IBM, and CORBA developers.

4.2.4.3 Role of Multitechnology Network Management

Figure 4.7 shows a simple architecture involving five technologies: asynchronous transfer mode (ATM), SDH/Sonet, dense wave division multiplexing (DWDM), wireless, and cable.

At present, TMF Recommendation 513 is considered the standard in regard to the compatibility of different technologies. This recommendation focuses on robust capabilities in the following areas:

- Notification: alarms, managed-object creation/deletion, state changes, and protection switches
- Topology: subnetworks, topological links, and protection management
- Inventory: hierarchical equipment management and managed-element information
- Performance: query/notification configuration and threshold-crossing alarms
- Provisioning: subnetwork connections and traffic descriptors
- Administration: EMS, and GUI cut-through

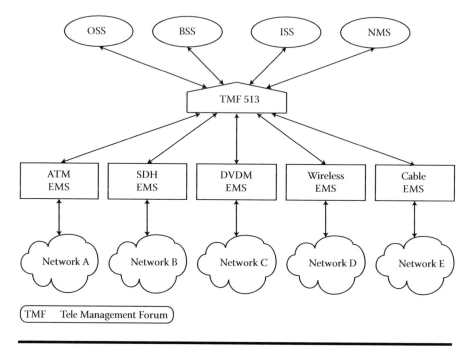

Figure 4.7   Management of heterogeneous multilayer, multiprovider networks.

4.2.5 Overlaying Infrastructure Components

In some cases, architectural components stretch across several layers, tiers, and levels. These components, which form the overlaying building blocks, are security infrastructure and systems management infrastructure.

4.2.5.1 Security Infrastructure

The security infrastructure comprises all architectures, components, and services that provide basic security functions in line with international standards. Both session and transactional security concepts are important in supporting LIs. Session security includes:

- Authentication
- Access control and authorization
- Confidentiality
- Data integrity

Transactional security focuses on the following:

- Proof of source
- Non-repudiation
- Digital signature
- Key management
- Audits

The amount of security achievable is only as strong as the weakest link in a chain of various components and products distributed over all the functions involved in LIs. The principal security target is the handover interface, along with the overall communication between TSPs and LEAs.

4.2.5.2 Systems Management Infrastructure

The systems management infrastructure comprises architectures, components, and services that support several principal functions, including:

- Availability management
- Performance management
- Delivery management
- Remote management
- Configuration management

Systems management can become quite complex because it involves the use of multiple hardware platforms, operating systems, and storage concepts. Systems management is delivered through various elements of each layer of the hardware/software infrastructure. In the case of LIs, additional components must be considered, for example:

- Hardware and software extensions (plug-ins) of network equipment (e.g., switches and routers)
- Monitoring software in SS7 nodes (e.g., SCP and STP)
- Hardware or software probes
- Management stations (MSs) for controlling probes
- External monitoring devices
- Access, delivery, and collection applications
- Dedicated database servers
- Document managers
- Reporting applications

Systems management solutions are available from various suppliers such as Hewlett Packard, Computer Associates, IBM, and BMC.

4.3 Principles of Monitoring and Intercepts (Hardware and Software Probes)

Today's state-of-the-art technology allows all facets of networking infrastructures to be monitored. However, everything has a price tag. In making decisions in this area, both TSPs and LEAs must address the following issues:

- How to identify dynamic targets
- How to deal with roaming subscribers
- How to intercept compressed and encrypted traffic
- How to capture call-in-progress
- How to meet real-time constraints
- How to deal with identity management
- How to identify locations of targets
- How to identify prepaid targets

LIs require full network-monitoring capabilities, which has led to the following concerns, among others, on the part of TSPs:

- How can the combination of internal and external LI capabilities be optimized?
- Does the capability exist to handle the growing level of data throughput, which will require monitoring of high-bandwidth channels?
- How can it be ensured that the packets to be monitored, as well as intelligence packets, are not lost?
- Are highly distributing IAPs too expensive?
- When multiple sources must be considered, does the necessary high-speed processing power exist to handle real-time data association?

4.3.1 Internal and External Lawful Interception

Depending on accessibility to network system components, LEAs request Internet Protocol (IP) interception through processes internal or external to the networks that presumably support the traffic and applications of a target under surveillance.

Internal interception enables the LEA, via the mediation platform and handover interfaces, to extract interception-related information (IRI, otherwise known as call data) and the target's content data directly from application servers (e.g., e-mail, Web, and chat), network access systems (e.g., RADIUS), DSL/cable modem termination points, routers, switches, and so forth, which are all part of the infrastructure of the network operator (NWO) or SP. Internal interception of application platforms has the obvious advantage of *directly* delivering target data to the mediation platform, in that the application is inherently known and the interception data is explicitly provided.

Interception of internal network transport elements also narrows the network traffic originating from or traveling to specific targets. Common Wi-Fi network "sniffing" is, in effect, a form of internal interception, because it focuses on a specific wireless LAN with highly localized targets — namely, the targeted users contained within the coverage zone of the wireless base station.

Nevertheless, internal interception involves two strong assumptions that might not be valid. First, it is assumed that targeted IRI and content data from selected network and applications systems are available to the LEA, perhaps through mandates associated with local or national regulations. Second, the network and applications systems must support secure data paths to the mediation platform (e.g., mail servers must output targeted header and content information directly to the interception mediation platform). However, such assumptions may not hold. In many developed countries, ISPs are often reluctant to open their networks to LEAs without a considerable legal battle; hence, their operations are not readily adaptable to systematic lawful interception.

Perhaps even more problematic are the current applications systems in place, which, as a result of their design and implementation, are not readily conducive to interception. For example, most servers designed to handle large volumes of e-mail must still be modified if they are to provide systematic delivery of targeted IRI and content through purpose-built ports dedicated to interception data conveyance. This is not a trivial undertaking, especially when interception ports have to also accommodate requisite network security to protect the transport of interception data and prevent "back door" attacks on the system. Finally, mechanisms must be in place to prevent targets from detecting that their data flows are being intercepted; this implies the need for secure application designs.

When internal interception is not available, or when LEAs request that surveillance be conducted in a clandestine manner, interception needs to take place at network levels outside the realm of the target's immediate application service or network provider. In other words, external interception — performed on Internet circuits outside the target's immediate network, typically in adjacent networks or at major public network concentration points — is necessary.

The core equipment usually consists of a probe made of a physical tap or a router with filtering capabilities. This probe typically replicates traffic flow through a network point at the physical layer; the filter targets packets containing specified IP addresses or IP-address ranges and routes them to a port dedicated to interception.

From there, packets are routed to the mediation platform and, ultimately, to the LEA for analysis of datagram headers and content. Systems that perform external interceptions tend to be sophisticated and are not officially publicized. In instances in which traffic is light, open source programs can assist in analyzing the protocols and content of data traversing a given path.

Targets must not be aware that they are the subject of surveillance. Even minimally sophisticated targets may suspect that interception of some kind is taking place if they detect the following:

- *Trace route commands:* These commands display the router hops that a subject's Internet traffic traverses in moving to or from a given destination. Any changes from ordinary patterns could imply the introduction of an interception router or other device. However, proper use of interception probes can avoid the introduction of new router hops.
- *Unusual signaling activity in their modem, Voice-over-IP (VoIP) interface box, or other hardware:* These devices carry important identification and traffic information associated with the interception target, but they can also reveal interception activity to the target. Therefore, it is not recommended that CPE be probed; this process poses risks for LEAs, especially when the devices are tampered with by users.
- *Degradation of or interruptions in service:* These are obvious factors in arousing suspicion on the part of targets that surveillance might be taking place.

4.3.2 Access Function (AF) Implementation Approaches

The basic choices in regard to AFs (data sources) are network or service elements and probes. If network or service elements are the choice, several issues associated with these elements should be addressed in detail:

- They are restricted in terms of the part of the network in which access, routing, or service is performed.
- They may be able to handle only compressed/encrypted traffic.
- They may require interception of multiple elements.
- They may require sophisticated data exchanges.
- Provisioning and delivery require a number of different interfaces.

Furthermore, any additional function, either hardware or software, may affect the ability of the network or service element to deliver the degree of performance expected. Observations have shown that when data collection functions involving usage-based billing are incorporated into routers, performance is significantly affected.

Relevant issues associated with probes include the potential for reuse in other applications, use of an additional nonservice element, and increased flexibility in regard to compliance with future requirements.

4.3.3 Use of Probes

When the decision is made to use a probe, providers must determine whether they want to use active or passive probes, software or hardware probes, dedicated or shared probes, or flow-based analysis probes.

4.3.3.1 Active versus Passive Probes

An active probe becomes part of the network, and thus it will capture all the traffic that flows through it. However, such probes are costly to deploy because they must be engineered in such a way that they do not have an impact on the network (e.g., by affecting reliability or latency).

A passive probe refers to a probe in which traffic is only monitored. Even in this passive situation, sufficient processing speed is required. A benefit of this method is that there is no impact on the service network or consumers; a drawback is that statistical methods are required to prove reliability.

4.3.3.2 Software versus Hardware Probes

In general, as well as in this case, software is more flexible than hardware but involves some overhead, whereas hardware is faster and does not involve overhead. Software is easier to reconfigure and allows easier addition of new capabilities (e.g., extraction of content intercept information, decoding of tunnels, and new protocol metadata); there is also the potential for recycling. Hardware involves limited upgrade paths but has the potential for better availability/reliability and scalability, and it is the only viable solution in terms of active monitoring.

SMON is a simple way of standardizing the controlling of port mirroring sessions in a switched environment. In the hub environment, port mirroring is not necessary, because every LAN connection receives all data. In switched environments, however, switch vendors have implemented port mirroring, which allows the switch to copy all the data from specific ports to a monitoring device in addition to forwarding data to the targeted destination.

Control of port mirroring is mostly vendor specific. SMON provides a standard, SNMP-based method for setting up and clearing port mirroring sessions. Although this method has been implemented by various vendors to support SNMP-based port-mirroring on the switch and SMON-based port mirroring control from the MS, the generic monitoring market has not changed significantly.

4.3.3.3 Dedicated versus Shared Probes

Dedicated probes involving only a single function have an excellent performance record, and will effectively fulfill LI requirements. However, it remains difficult to justify the high costs of these types of probes.

When probes are shared among multiple functionalities toward a "mediation" probe, issues that must be addressed are leverage of investment, the high risk of effects on cross-application boundaries, and security risks. However, ISS requires sharing up to a certain extent, and priorities must be set by TSPs.

4.3.3.4 Flow-Based Analysis Probes

Flow-based analysis is an interesting alternative or complementary solution to probe-based network analysis. Although flow-based analysis typically lacks the granularity of potential deep packet analyses in probe-based solutions, it can cover a much larger infrastructure at a lower cost.

One could argue that, in a highly meshed networking environment, probe-based traffic analysis is prohibitively expensive, and flow-based analysis can perform much better at more reasonable costs. Networking hardware vendors can present the statistics any way they prefer; probe vendors can offer vendor-independent traffic statistics.

Probe vendors often attempt to integrate flow-based solutions into their products to provide a combined solution and to avoid being forced out of the monitoring market. Some vendors go as far as claiming that a large number of probes are necessary to allow efficient processing of a large amount of traffic-flow information.

It has been proven that flow-based statistics produce large amounts of data — approximately 20 GB per month on a 100,000-port network — but still less than the amount of data generated by NetFlow for the same environment. The expected ratio is 50 to 1. In the case of large networking infrastructures, collection of flow statistics may require a distributed management architecture. Nonprobe vendors have shown that flow-based statistics can be collected and presented using one collection station for up to 500 router/switch interfaces. Probe vendors usually work with one probe for up to 16 such interfaces.

The most prominent management software vendor in regard to sFlow is InMon. The most prominent hardware vendor supporting sFlow is Foundry, in cooperation with Hewlett Packard. NetFlow is implemented and maintained by Cisco.

The IPFIX protocol is a template-based flow-reporting method that supports flow aggregation, QoS, BGP nexthop, VLANs, multicast, network address translation (NAT), Multi-Protocol Label Switching (MPLS), and IPv6, among others. The IETF is moving closer to ratifying IPFIX as a new standard for flow reporting. This standardization process is highly supported and driven by Cisco owing to the fact that IPFIX is based on a high NetFlow version.

The most significant challenge with all flow-based solutions is reporting — assuming that data can be collected without affecting performance. In regard to LIs, it will be the key to determining the optimal data reduction and information-reporting solutions.

Although the IETF sFlow draft standard has been available for some time, few vendors have implemented it. However, as network traffic speeds grow to a gigabit and to 10 GB in some infrastructures, sFlow will become a more important technology for tracking network performance and providing network security.

The sFlow technology uses random sampling of LAN and WAN data packet flows across an entire network to allow users a detailed, real-time view of network traffic performance, trends, and problems. sFlow is deployed through network management information bases (MIBs) — either hardware- or software-based agents — running on the actual switches and routers present in the network. This allows for a broader picture of network performance.

According to sFlow proponents, monitoring takes place on every port of every sFlow-enabled switch, rather than on only the port or segment to which a probe is attached. Proponents also argue that the technology allows for more widespread network monitoring in that mirroring every port would be difficult and expensive in terms of both network staffing and LAN bandwidth. Up to one half of a switch or router would have to be dedicated to port mirroring to achieve this mirroring level (Hochmuth, 2004).

Figure 4.8 shows the principal components of sFlow solutions. The most important functions are as follows (Hochmuth, 2004):

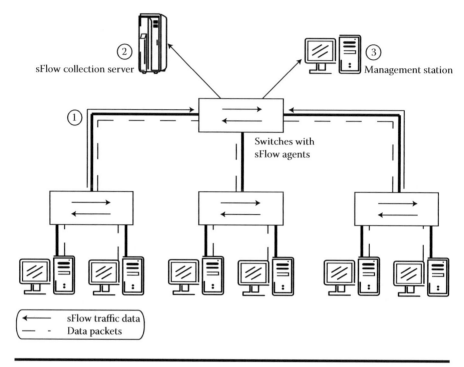

Figure 4.8   Functional overview of sFlow.

- Switches with sFlow agents use random samples of traffic from all ports on the switch.
- Sample data is sent to an sFlow collection server, in which sFlow samples from the network are calculated.
- Management workstations can tap the sFlow server to view an overall picture.

Instead of capturing and logging every packet on a switch or router port, sFlow MIBs take random samples of packets traveling through ports. These so-called sFlow datagrams are forwarded to an sFlow collection server on a network — the data communications network (DCN) or the production network of the SP. On this box, the datagrams are run through an algorithm that generates a complete model of network traffic based on the sampled data.

The technology behind sFlow was developed jointly by engineers at InMon, a manufacturer of switch-monitoring software, and developers at HP and Foundry Networks. Support of sFlow is included in products such as HP OpenView, nGenius Performance Manager from NetScout, and Traffic Server from InMon.

In addition to providing real-time snapshots of network performance, sFlow can be used as a network security tool. An example can be seen in the case of unauthorized network devices acting as NAT boxes, including commodity NAT-enabled wireless routers. Although NAT devices attached to a network might be in the form of legitimate end nodes, they can also serve as back doors allowing access to unauthorized connections from wired or wireless users. Because sFlow samples traffic from every port in a network, sFlow data analyzers can identify nodes that are acting as NAT devices on a network by comparing subnet data among switches/routers and NAT devices.

LI requires more granularity than sFlow-based techniques may provide. However, particularly in the case of strategic surveillance, statistical techniques are very useful. If suspicious traffic flows are detected, on-the-fly provisioning may help to activate monitoring solutions that are able to provide both intercept-related and content-related data for LEAs.

Before determining the optimal solution in regard to conducting LIs, providers should answer the following questions:

■ Does the network/service element actually complete its functions, or are they delegated to a probe?
■ Does the support available in the network/service element meet all legal requirements?
■ Does the (active) solution affect QoS for all users?
■ Does the solution prevent packet loss?
■ Is security maintained across application boundaries in multiuse deployments?
■ Can a software solution ultimately compete with a hardware-centric solution?
■ Can multiple users really use the IAP, or will there be unintentional adverse effects on other applications? Can this situation be avoided?

4.3.4 Intelligence Transmission

TSPs usually operate a separate DCN. In such cases, intelligence data may be routed to this network and relayed to handover LEA interfaces. This out-of-band solution, sometimes preferred in situations involving operational isolation, involves the following benefits:

■ Implementation of out-of-band infrastructure with signal splitters
■ Improved selectivity in terms of dynamic address changes and multicast
■ Support of heterogeneous vendor environments

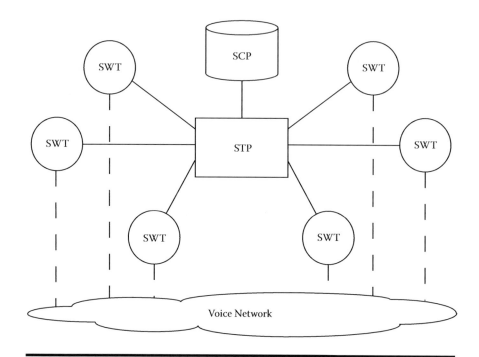

Figure 4.9 Signaling network example.

If no DCN is available, traffic sharing cannot be avoided. This in-band solution is beneficial in that it uses existing network elements, is independent of link-access technology (e.g., plain old telephone services (POTS), ISDN, xDSL, cable, and wireless), and reduces costs. It is preferred when the independence from access technology and cost reduction criteria are relevant.

In the case of all in-band solutions, traffic separation should be supported. Traffic shapers could perform this function. A dedicated band is always preferable in that better security solutions are provided.

4.4 Use of Signaling Systems for LIs

Signaling networks, such as SS7, offer an alternative source of intelligence collection. Figure 4.9 shows a signaling example in which the signaling network is separate from the voice network. This network system can be centrally controlled or fully meshed, and IAPs can be implemented on selected links or integrated into service control points (SCPs), SWTs, or STPs (Figure 4.10).

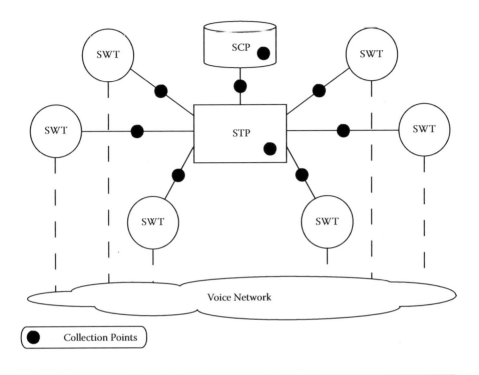

Figure 4.10   Collection points in SS7 networks.

Signaling is an excellent intelligence source for several reasons:

■ Calls rely on signaling (switches sometimes do not produce records, and call-tracing capability must be preconfigured for a line in switches but not for signaling networks).
■ Much more data is provided than in the case of a switch (network views of calls, rather than switch views, can follow calls throughout the network).
■ Support is provided for real-time data in the areas of access and delivery.
■ SS7 is an international standard used throughout the world.
■ Issues regarding the "3 Ws" — Who uses the network? When are they using the network? What are they using the network for? — are addressed.

The principal application areas are real-time and historical call traces, suspect-call profiles, and call patterns and associations.

4.5 Resource Planning for LIs

From the perspective of resource utilization, the generic technical requirements for LI may be summarized as follows:

- *Low latency:* As a result of the additional access, distribution, and collection functions available, customer service does not suffer, and performance effects should be kept to a minimum. In certain cases, additional latency times must not exceed 3 ms.
- *Deployment:* The provisioning, configuration, and administrative functions should enable TSPs and LEAs to immediately deploy traces from servers to listeners. However, this process might require a sophisticated switching fabric controlled by a central console.
- *High availability and scalability:* Solutions under consideration must handle current network speeds as well as the increasing speeds that will be available in the future. In other words, the LI framework selected must survive technological changes that occur in the access and transport networks of TSPs.
- *Graphical user interface:* These interfaces are expected to help subject matter experts operate rapidly and efficiently by entering trace information, starting and stopping sessions, and generating and distributing reports and statistics.
- *Degradation:* Routers are very sensitive to additional load, and performance impacts due to data collection and data storage problems can be considerable. Listeners/probes must run at 98 percent of router speed.
- *Central server and distributed listeners/probes:* Servers must be capable of handling multiple listeners. This function depends on the architecture of the LI platform and on the networking alternative (in-band or out-of-band) connecting the central server with the probes.
- *Capability of monitoring multiple sessions:* Whether listeners can monitor multiple sessions depends on their capacity and capability and how much data they are able to maintain before transfer to the LEA.
- *Reporting:* Formats must be configurable with a few canned reports and a larger number of report templates.

Additional capacity is required for both networking facilities and communication equipment if detrimental performance effects are to be avoided. The sizing of additional resources is usually supported through analytical and simulation tools. Before use of these tools, however, capacity must be aggregated according to:

- Communication forms such as voice, data, and video
- TSP networking sites that are part of the surveillance architecture
- Access networks
- Transport networks
- Principal network equipment, such as switches, routers, gateways, load balancers, traffic shapers, and firewalls
- Principal servers that are part of the front-office architecture of TSPs
- Principal storage devices, such as DAS, NAS, and SAN, that support the data retention policies of both TSPs and LEAs

Computing required network capacities is not an exact science, but modeling and simulation tools are available that allow one to evaluate multiple alternatives regarding data input and configuration. After a finite number of iterations, capacity planners know the limits of their proposed physical configuration.

Sizing is one part of a process that consists of several steps. The first step is to define the requirements that the network must satisfy. This involves collecting information on anticipated traffic loads, traffic types, and sources and destination of traffic. This information is used, in turn, to estimate the network capacity needed. The design process includes various design techniques and algorithms allowing evaluation and quantification of various network topologies. It also includes link and node placements, traffic-routing paths, and equipment sizing. After a candidate network solution has been developed, it must be analyzed to determine its cost, reliability, and delay characteristics. This step is referred to as performance analysis. After this step, the first design iteration is complete.

The entire process may be repeated, either with revised input data or a new design approach. The basic idea of this iterative process is to produce a variety of networks from which to choose. In the case of most realistic design and sizing problems, it is not possible, from a mathematical viewpoint, to know how the optimal network supporting LIs should appear. To compensate for this inability to derive an analytically perfect sizing solution, network designers must use trial-and-error techniques to determine the best options. After surveying a variety of designs, they can select the one that appears to provide the best performance at the lowest cost.

Because network design and sizing involve exploring as many alternatives as possible, automated heuristic design tools are often used to produce quick, approximate solutions. Once the overall topology and major design aspects have been determined, it may be appropriate to use additional, more exact solution techniques to refine the details of the network design.

4.6 Summary

Each TSP needs a blueprint detailing services, technology, infrastructure, and organization. Standards organizations attempt to provide assistance in terms of developing generic architectures and guidelines. In particular, the ITU and TMF are dealing with such blueprints and guidelines. This chapter has introduced TMN, CobiT, and eTOM as the basis of streamlining business processes, support tools, and allocation of human resources to processes and tools. Doing so, LIs can be supported more easily. Almost all infrastructure components offer options for IAPs. The challenge is to find the optimal solution, one involving low provisioning costs, low overhead, and a high level of performance. This chapter has reviewed a number of strategic options for probes versus embedded data-capturing solutions. The next two chapters will address concrete solution architectures for multiple infrastructure components.

Chapter 5

Extended Functions for Lawful Intercepts

CONTENTS

The basic architecture for lawful intercepts (LIs) was briefly discussed in Chapter 1, North American and European standards for lawful interception were addressed in Chapter 3, and Chapter 4 focused on intercept access points (the entry points for accessing intelligence-related raw data) in the networking infrastructures of telecommunications service providers (TSPs). In this chapter, we continue our discussion by focusing on three major areas associated with LI actions:

1. The central role of mediation in accessing, formatting, correlating, and transforming data into actionable information that serves various applications
2. The use of data warehousing to deal with the large volumes of intelligence-related data that are handed over to law enforcement agencies (LEAs)
3. Applications based on intelligence relayed to LEAs by TSPs or outsourcers

We also address in some detail protocols for handover, feasible data formats, storage concepts, and document management solutions.

5.1 Principal Functions of LIs

The principal functions of lawful interception activities include both core functionality (access, delivery, and collection functions) and extension targets (mediation, data warehousing, and retention- and intelligence-related special applications). Figure 5.1 displays these extended principal functions.

Brief definitions of these principal functions are as follows:

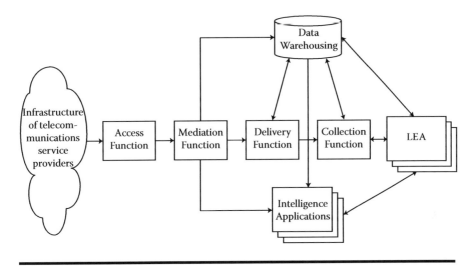

Figure 5.1   Principal functions of lawful interception.

- *Access function:* coordination of data capturing in the infrastructure components of TSPs
- *Delivery function:* processing of LI-related and content-related data
- *Collection function:* collection and recording of lawfully intercepted communications by LEAs
- *Mediation function:* single point of contact for all raw data collected in infrastructure components that might be used in various intelligence support system applications (e.g., LIs, billing, fraud protection, and traffic pattern recognition)
- *Data warehousing and retention functions:* database containing LI-related and content-related information
- *Intelligence applications:* form of innovative software dealing with strategic surveillance designed to support prosecution of criminals and avoidance of future crimes

The basic requirements associated with these functions have been covered in previous chapters.

5.2 Role of Mediation

Mediation is a growing field of specialty in the telecommunications industry that rests on the foundation of complex hybrid network architectures. As new services are deployed, their network structures are built on top of, or alongside, the existing infrastructure. It is not realistic to expect the new infrastructure to replace the old, because older systems are well established and have been a source of significant amounts of capital investment. Rather, such an evolution takes the form of incremental changes over time; in most cases, the existing system is not replaced but enhanced. This creates an environment that demands the coexistence of different protocols, different data rates, and different device types from a variety of vendors. A single approach to managing these ever-changing networks is impossible, given that new services create new and often incompatible network demands. The first basic need in terms of mediation is to manage this diversity.

Bandwidth issues and the addition of new services demanded by customers — without increases in price — result in network costs rising faster than revenues. Adding services becomes a race for market domination as competitors enter the field and new offerings become commodities. Price pressures highlight the second basic need associated with mediation: to lessen the impact of the introduction of new technologies and services by creating a layer of abstraction for back-office systems such as billing, customer care, and fraud management.

Data and packet networks represent the third general type of infrastructure. These networks are meshed, particularly in the case of IP, but they do not monitor the content or usage data of the traffic they carry. Service providers use hybrid approaches to offer voice, private line, and other enhanced services, including packet data services, over a mixed-network infrastructure. This exemplifies the third basic need for mediation, which focuses on back-office systems coping with the networks used in both new and traditional circuit-switched voice services — in other words, using one back-office system for multiple services. The only alternative is to build individual back-office systems for each type of network technology, a very expensive proposition.

As telecommunications assumes an increasingly important role in the delivery of commercial content, a new type of network interconnection point will be introduced by TSPs. Similar to the multiplication of interconnects that came with telecom deregulation and competition, content delivery will increase the need for traffic measurement at network interfaces. Each content provider will want its share of the revenue, and thus traffic flows will need to be monitored. This represents the fourth basic need for mediation: traffic flow analysis.

Traffic flow analysis is most efficient when it is performed closest to the network elements the traffic is flowing through. Traffic flow analysis is recommended to be implemented as a separate function. It would not be cost-effective for billing or other back-office systems to cope with the intricacies of the network interconnections and process the usage data, primarily because of the bulk of the data to be analyzed. Mediation systems

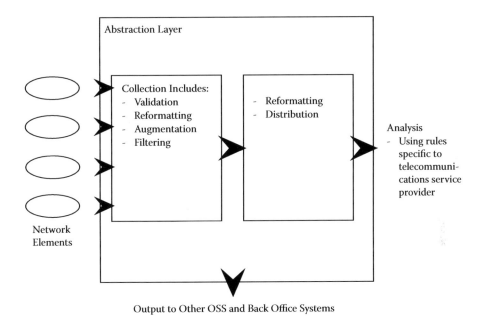

Figure 5.2 Typical mediation system.

are most efficient in performing this function because they are specifically designed to do so.

On the basis of raw data, intelligence may be derived through the use of processing and analysis techniques. The fifth basic need for mediation is that of providing intelligence in complex, interconnected networks in real-time. Traffic analysis may be utilized for either strategic or preventive surveillance. Figure 5.2 shows a typical mediation system.

The mediation process is initiated with the collection of usage data from network elements. Data is usually produced in native or proprietary formats. Mediation systems convert this data into protocols that are supported by downstream systems. This process involves validation, reformatting, augmentation, filtering, aggregation, and correlation of raw data. These functions reduce the burden on downstream systems by creating a layer of abstraction from the complexity of the network infrastructure. True mediation spans all network types, offering a convergent approach to the process of merging different technologies.

In converged networks, mediation offers data correction, sophisticated error analysis, and revenue assurance, all in the context of real-time or near-real-time processing. Its value resides in its ability to provide current analyses — vital in areas such as prepaid services, traffic analysis decisions, cost decisions, and LI intelligence — rather than analyses delayed by time. In addition to near-real-time processing, the mediation system provides

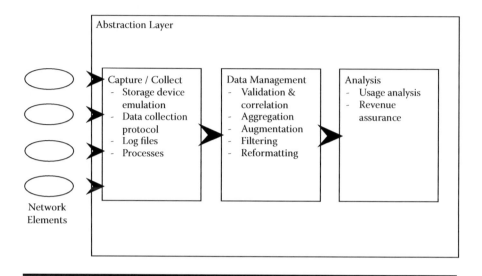

Figure 5.3 Typical mediation steps.

an environment for analyzing network usage via a generic perspective. This may be used as input for preventive surveillance as well.

The mediation process encompasses several logical steps (see Figure 5.3). The first step is data collection. Historically, mediation was synonymous with, and limited to, data collection, but today the concept stretches further. The most common form of data collection relies on information collected directly from network elements. This can occur either through storage device emulation — generally referred to as magnetic tape emulation — or by implementing a specific data collection protocol. Protocol implementation can involve either proprietary or standard protocols, and data can be collected via record-by-record modes or file modes, in which records are assembled into files before being collected.

A second type of network element collection involves log files that assemble information from network elements and then store the data for later retrieval. The disadvantage of this method is that it results in an extra level of complexity in the installation of additional network elements to ensure that all key data items are retained. Log files can be very large, and these file sizes do not lend themselves to near-real-time processing. To circumvent this problem, some switch vendors have implemented streaming protocols or have allowed users to reduce the file creation and collection intervals, thus allowing near-real-time processing. Log files have the greatest advantage in deployments in which data collection involves traditional call detail records (CDRs). Vendors with experience in telecommunications systems include log-file collection to expand their coverage of circuit-switched systems.

The other method for collecting usage information from a telecommunications network is that of using probes, which gather data through packet headers. Probes are used in legacy environments to collect signaling information; in IP networks, probes gather usage information. When used in large network deployments, this approach requires a robust system owing to the wide variety of protocol types and the large volumes of data. Essential in some next-generation and converged networks, probe use ensures sophisticated analyses based on packet data but does not offer a total solution. Experienced vendors offer both network element collection and probe collection.

The next step in the mediation process involves data management functions. Some vendors provide a full spectrum of such functions, which can be deployed in a variety of networks. Validation and correction are examples of data management functions that precede actual data analysis. These operations enable one-time record collection and processing, which saves on the processing costs associated with the downstream billing system and ensures that only valid data is processed and distributed. Once the data has been structurally validated, it can be standardized to simplify further processing.

In the case of some types of usage data, multiple events need to be aggregated to provide a single overall record. For example, a streaming IP service may create multiple event records for the delivery of a single content item. In such a case, the aggregated record is the input for the next process — which is more efficient than sending a multitude of event records. In other instances involving multiple network elements, correlation can be used to create a network perspective of the transaction. In other words, the record of an event is implied through the correlation of records from a number of different network elements. Also, usage data can be aggregated into a less granular form when detailed information is not necessary. Wholesale environments often use less granular data in instances in which processing detailed records is expensive. Aggregation is possible for strategic surveillance, but not for individual surveillance.

The next step in the mediation process is augmentation, which is based on business rules defined by the TSP. The purpose of augmentation is to preprocess billing data, which simplifies downstream processing. Parameters such as destination, service type, and customer information can be analyzed for inconsistencies and corrected. Downstream billing systems operate more efficiently in the absence of these inconsistencies.

TSP-defined business rules also help in filtering and consolidating usage records, ensuring that appropriate, clean records are distributed to the billing system or to other consumers of usage data. Filtered and consolidated records are transferred in bulk from a single system, which prevents duplication and inconsistencies, and reduces processing costs.

Finally, data is reformatted and distributed to other systems. The mediation system replicates detailed or aggregated usage records to meet the service expectations of every consumer, converting the data into the formats needed by them.

Analysis of usage data is a critical process. Several operations support system/business support system/intelligence support system (OSS/BSS/ISS) vendors offer additional analytical systems in areas such as churn management, network usage analysis, and revenue assurance. Mediation vendors can prepare the required data for these systems and, in some cases, offer tools to be used in performing the analyses. Such tools create a specialized network usage data warehouse in parallel with the data management function.

As the mediation market develops, vendors are expanding their product suites to offer greater product capabilities. At present, mediation vendors operate in the following three segments:

1. Single system mediation, IP-focused: Vendors using this approach are new entrants to the market hoping to obtain a market share through restricted product capability. Products in this segment offer specialized capability focused only on IP-based services or networks.

2. Complex mediation, circuit-switched and packet-capable: Vendors with more experience usually offer product suites capable of mediating complex mixes of protocols. Often these vendors begin by offering legacy-based mediation and then expand their product suites as providers roll out enhanced services.

3. Complex mediation with other OSS functions: As vendors gain experience, product extensions enable links with other OSS functions. Some of these vendors offer mediation systems to supplement their billing systems. Experienced vendors also find that their products can be deployed in other industries as well, dividing their products into telecom and enterprise segments.

Since there are no IP CDRs that can be used for ISS mediation, vendors cobble together usage data from a variety of sources, including remote monitoring (RMON) probes, Remote Authentication Dial-In User Service (RADIUS) servers, Web server log files, and router software agents.

Any company that wants to implement pay-to-pay content or services will rely heavily on the visitor activity data captured by its site. These "clicks" are already used extensively for assessing effectiveness of site design, as well as for other business purposes such as advertising and referral fees. However, simple capture of universal resource locator (URL) data is insufficient for effective Web billing, because the different elements of a URL can have very different meanings in a billing or business context. Data sources in this area that might also be used for LIs are as follows:

- *Domain names:* This first rung in the URL ladder is obviously critical in determining that a user has accessed a given site. For Web hosting services, the domain name indicates which hosted customers' billing meters are running. Some E-business sites also create separate domain names for individual services or content areas.
- *File names and extensions:* In contrast to domain names, file names and extensions allow providers to bill for specific content or types of content (e.g., streams, MP3s, PDF files). Each file type may carry a different price tag. Individual files of the same type may even be processed differently from each other.
- *Variables:* Many sites give users the ability to enter some type of variable as part of their service or content request. A site offering information about various geographic areas, for example, may have "city" as one of its variables. Each time a new city is entered, there may be another click on the billing meter, or a user may be allowed to check several cities for one price. In addition, users may be allowed to search cities in their own state at no charge. Regardless of how charges are specifically structured, such variables are distinct elements of utilization and billing formulas.
- *Universal resource identifier (URI) substrings:* When the domain name, file name and extension, and any variables from a URL are eliminated, the URI is still available. This substring may also help define the type of content or service a user has accessed. Again, this URI may be important to a hosting service that is billing customers separately for different content or service areas. In addition, it may be used by the site's owner to differentiate a premium server or other value-added feature.

Networked infrastructures are built with a variety of devices, such as routers, switches, firewalls, load balancers, and so forth. In addition to performing operational and transport functions, these devices also generate highly valuable site activity data. Examples are as follows:

- NetFlow records network and application resource utilization.
- RADIUS log files provide access to information on a continuous basis.
- RMON data adapters provide utilization data for various network layers.
- Proprietary or device-specific protocols provide additional information in their headers and trailers.

This data is extremely useful in determining who accessed what, for how long, or how much. Many device vendors and third-party developers are introducing powerful application-aware monitoring tools that can help value-added content and service providers to more accurately track consumption of infrastructure resources. An effective rating system must be able to tap into all these various data types and flexibly translate them into the specific types of utilization parameters required by each particular rating formula.

These types of data are most often used by TSPs and hosting services, although they may also be applied to a variety of Web business models. In addition, a given network service may be running on a specific User Datagram Protocol (UDP) port number, or a certain protocol may have a specific UDP port number or a specific utilization charge attached to it. In such cases, basic network-level data will also have to be captured and incorporated into the service rating formula. To support a particular business objective, these diverse activity metrics may have to be aggregated with a great deal of flexibility, precision, and speed.

With so many different information sources available, the location from which a mediation system obtains its data is crucial. For instance, because RADIUS servers track who accessed a particular Web host and for how long, their log files can be valuable for billing, especially in the process of tallying up charges for Web server space. However, RADIUS servers disclose only a portion of the picture; they can track access to Web servers but cannot report on network utilization: how much bandwidth on a given IP connection was consumed by a particular application or end user. This type of information is becoming important to providers as they begin to offer multiple IP services.

Network probes and monitors are another excellent source of utilization data. RMON1 and RMON2 probes can be in the form of stand-alone, embedded hardware, or software. These probes continuously measure LAN segments and end-user- and application-specific bandwidth utilization. They can report metrics at Layers 2 and 3 as well as higher levels. Often, the large amount of captured data results in processing problems. Also, the bandwidth requirements to transfer data from probes to the centrally located processing facility may cause overhead and generate additional resource demand.

Web servers maintain logs that may be utilized to determine applications and end-user-related metrics. Examples of such metrics are visitor identifications, duration of visits, frequency of visits, and resource demand. Most of these metrics can be utilized as bases for IP billing.

Routers and switches are also valuable sources for accounting information. Routers and switches offered by Cisco Systems, for instance, run

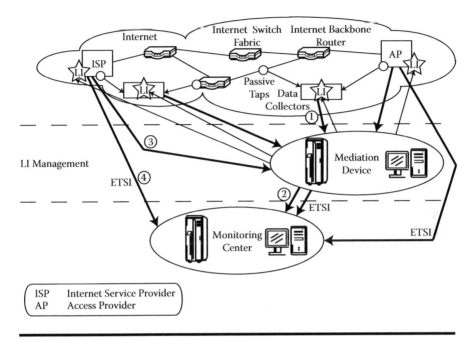

Figure 5.4   Role of mediation for lawful interception.

NetFlow, a proprietary flow-monitoring utility that keeps tabs on packet activity. Most mediation and billing vendors can tap directly into NetFlow — module under international operation system (IOS) — data. Vendors offering IP mediation packages should consider other vendors for capturing data, as well. The principle of data gathering will be the same, but application programming interface (API) support on behalf of the vendor is necessary.

The key role of mediation devices for LIs can be demonstrated with the Monitoring Center (MC) solution from Siemens (Axland, 2004). Figure 5.4 displays how the mediation device collects and consolidates LI-related data from various sources, such as ISPs, passive taps, access providers, switches, and routers. The steps are as follows:

1. Siemens data collector relays pre-ETSI to mediation device.
2. Mediation device delivers ETSI to MC.
3. Network-integrated functions relay pre-ETSI to mediation device.
4. Network-integrated functions relay ETSI to MC.

Figure 5.5 goes one step further and includes third-party mediation devices and the operations support system (OSS) for lawful interception. The interfaces are identified as follows:

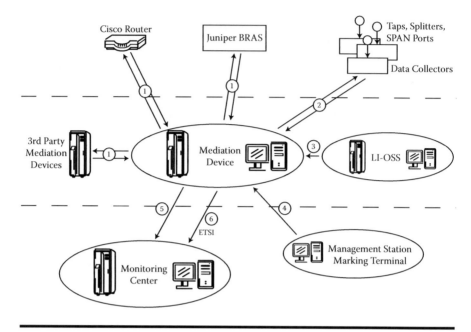

Figure 5.5   Front-office and back-office solutions in combination.

- Vendor interfaces specified or to be defined
- Siemens proprietary interfaces
- LI-OS interface (in development)
- Siemens proprietary interface for marking entities
- Intermediate Siemens proprietary interface
- ETSI interface

As can be seen in Figure 5.4 and Figure 5.5, standard and proprietary interfaces are deployed in combination.

5.3 Handover Interfaces (HIs)

Chapter 3 summarized the standards for handover of intelligence-related information to LEAs. However, these standards do not specify the format of the content, the handover protocol, or the physical facilities for the handover.

The HI is the peering point between TSPs and LEAs. This interface must be standardized in terms of format, protocol, and physical connections. In addition to reductions in costs and delays, the main reasons for standardizing this HI are as follows (Rutkowsky, 2003):

- Business record exchange: Standardization assists in the creation and management of subscriber data, a fundamental component of business operations and a source of revenue.
- Compliance with laws and regulations: Most national and local jurisdictions require generation, retention, preservation, protection, and sharing of various subscriber data (e.g., Intelligent Network ONA).
- Maintenance of investigative capabilities: Such standardization allows all types of access (e.g., wireless and Internet environments); it also facilitates investigation and prosecution of criminal and terrorist activities.
- Compliance with international treaties and requirements: Standardization allows cybercrime treaty and international law enforcement user requirements to be met.
- Judicial orders or warrants: Most legal systems provide for search, and production, of subscriber data in response to subpoenas.
- Reduction of costs and delays for each participating entity.

Data volumes flowing through this interface must be carefully estimated to allow proper sizing of the physical infrastructure of the peering point. Two types of data must be clearly separated from each other: intercept-related data (real-time IRI and content relayed from TSPs to LEAs) and subscriber- or customer-related data (generic customer information and retained or preserved IRI and content). Both the frequency and data volumes of each handover action are important in these estimations. Typically, the frequency of real-time IRI is much higher than the real-time content. However, content volumes are usually significant.

Generic subscriber information volumes can become large when all details are handed over. The amount of retained or preserved IRI, or content, depends on the length of the surveillance period, the number of targets, and individual volumes. TSPs, LEAs, and outsourcers all have an interest in collecting and maintaining statistics regarding these volumes, given that the results are valuable in regard to costing, charging, and reimbursing LI missions.

5.3.1 Formatting Handover Data

The various markup languages offer an excellent basis for entry into the documentation standardization process. The following subsections summarize the present status and future trends regarding these markup languages; more attention is devoted to eXtensible Markup Language (XML), considered today to be the de facto documentation standard (Terplan, 2003).

5.3.1.1 HyperText Markup Language (HTML)

HTML is easy to understand, and can be written by hand or generated from other text formats by translators. HTML is actually a simple document type of Standard Generalized Markup Language (SGML).

HTML is simpler than NROFF and other document languages in that it is not programmable. As a result, the descriptive capabilities of HTML are limited to low-level constructs, such as emphasis or indented lists. However, because HTML parsers are rather forgiving of HTML coding violations, many Web pages contain coding mistakes incorporated purposely to achieve particular layout effects on popular browsers.

HTML is optimized for display rather than printing or storage. It has no notion of pages, making formatted printing difficult. HTML involves serious limitations. For example, it does not provide the flexibility Web publishers need to create home pages. HTML pages are static, and dynamic updates are essentially not supported. If Web technology is to be successfully implemented for network and systems management, then, attributes, flexibility, and dynamics are absolutely necessary. In the past, most technologies added interactivity to pages by using server-based CGI programs, Java applets, browser plug-ins, ActiveX controls, and scripting languages, which had little to do with HTML. Now, however, with Dynamic HTML (DHTML), new client-side technologies, combined with scripting languages such as JavaScript, may solve many of HTML's problems.

5.3.1.2 Dynamic HyperText Markup Language

DHTML extends the current set of HTML elements and a few other elements, such as style sheet properties, by allowing them to be accessed and modified by scripting languages. Dynamic features that make pages come alive with movement and interactivity can be added by exposing tags to scripts written in a language such as JavaScript or VBScript (Terplan, 2001).

Tags are accessed through the document object model (DOM), which describes each document as a collection of individual objects such as images, paragraphs, and forms down to individual characters. The document object model of DHTML can be complex, but there are ways to get around this complexity. Developers may use the DOM to find an image on a page and replace it with another when a user rolls a cursor over it. Such rollovers or animated buttons are common. DHTML can also animate a page by moving objects around, build an expanding tree structure to navigate a site, or create a complex application such as a database front end.

The common language denominator is expected to be the DOM, which is the basis for DHTML. This platform- and language-neutral interface will allow programs and scripts to dynamically access and update the content, structure, and style of documents.

DOM is being used by both of the leading suppliers, Microsoft and Netscape. Their DOM implementations are currently very similar; in the future, however, differences will be seen with such features as positioning, dynamic fonts, and multimedia controls. With support for CSS (cascading style sheet) and absolute positioning, advanced layouts can be made to work under each browser. With DHTML and absolute positioning, it is possible to create sophisticated multimedia applications that can avoid frequent dialogues with the Web server. However, building DHTML-based pages is still about programming. Including dynamic elements on a page is a major step away from a static page paradigm and toward the idea of Web pages as programs.

5.3.1.3 Extensible MarkUp Language (XML)

The DOM sets out the methods by which Web developers can access elements of HTML and XML documents to manipulate page elements and create dynamic effects, and it serves as the key enabling technology for DHTML. Three principal areas of use are associated with XML applications:

1. High-end publishing, in which XML and SGML are viewed as highly structured document languages
2. Use of the extensible nature of XML by Web developers to create application-specific markup tags
3. Use of XML as a data exchange format for distributed Web applications

With XML and DHTML, it is relatively easy to share user interfaces and information on the Web.

XML can help to eliminate the major limitations of HTML; for example, it can facilitate Web searches, foster interindustry communication, and enable new forms of distributed Web-based applications. However, XML will not solve everything, and it will not result in HTML becoming obsolete.

Both HTML and XML are subsets of SGML, but XML could define HTML as a DTD (document type definition) of its own. They intersect again only with regard to DHTML in which both require the use of a DOM.

While the core syntax of XML is fairly well defined, many other areas need to be addressed. For example, XML includes no presentation services;

another technology must be deployed to present XML data within a Web browser. Eventual use of a style sheet language such as CSS or XSL (eXtensible Style Language) seems likely. Many users implement HTML as the presentation language for XML. To support presentation, Java applets may be downloaded to allow even complex data forms. XML mirrors SGML in that it lacks linking capabilities. To eliminate this weakness, the eXtensible Linking Language (XLL) is being added to XML. There is also a need to connect XML with DOM to support scripting capabilities.

Without presentation, scripting, and linking, XML is limited to being a data format. However, some applications are defined as either vertical (supporting specific industries) or horizontal (for generic use). Microsoft has defined CDF (Channel Definition Format) to push content to selected targets. Open Software Description (OSD) has been defined in XML to support software installation procedures. Synchronized Multimedia Integration Language (SMIL) is used to define multimedia presentations for Web delivery. Also, meta-languages, such as the Resource Definition Framework (RDF), will be defined in the future.

XML involves a simple premise — describing data elements and their properties in plain text and providing a hierarchical framework for representing structured data for any domain, in a language that allows for transmission of this encoded information across any interface. XML is optimized for data exchange with the following attributes:

- Because XML easily transforms to the data exchange requirements of multiple parties, it enhances a communication provider's ability to expand its trading partner web. By using XML, a communication provider has more opportunities to interpret and process information with partners and across systems.
- The XML architecture of an OSS is easy to incorporate into an overall solution architecture, since its translatable nature does not mandate a delivery method. In this way, it also addresses the fundamental business problem of what delivery vehicle to use as the landscape of downstream partner systems evolves.
- XML is easy to use and tool-enabled, so users are not required to go to great lengths to find developers schooled in XML. Additionally, XML is applicable across multiple computing platforms, laying the groundwork for a provider to develop seamless integrations throughout the enterprise.

XML can provide solutions to business-to-business (B2B) problems. As service providers compete for position in the changing communications marketplace, more emphasis is being placed on how customer and partner relationships are managed. XML, and its integration into the fiber of a provider's business, is allowing some companies to pull away from their competitors.

However, there are still a few areas where more work is needed, including standardization of many of the accompanying technologies, such as XSL and XML schemas. Even more important, different industries need to standardize XML schemas for B2B transactions to better facilitate integration. Though the amount of work involved is significant, many organizations are dedicated to ensuring that it is completed; they realize that there is no future in being an "island" in an interconnected business world.

The challenges facing XML are significant. Specifications regarding associated technologies, such as style sheets and linking, are not yet complete. XML style sheets, which are based on DSSSL (Document Style and Semantics Specification Language), will most likely compete against CSS. The linking model of XML is more advanced than HTML, but it is incomplete and overly complex. The nature of the interaction between XML and DOM needs further clarification.

Industry analysts assume that XML will be used together with HTML. HTML is widely used and is becoming more powerful with CSS and DOM. XML may add formality and extensibility. Formality allows for guaranteed structure, exchange, and machine readability, which are difficult (though not impossible) with HTML. Extensibility refers to the opportunity to create specialized languages for specific applications. Such languages may have significant power within particular intranets or in the area of managing networks and systems.

Microsoft has rapidly implemented its XML Data Reduced (XDR) schema, which may be on its way to becoming a *de facto* standard. The number of industry groups designing their own DTDs or schemas is increasing significantly.

To carry out business processes, many transaction units must be assembled in real-time. These units are usually maintained in directories. Directories are now being enabled to operate across corporate boundaries, pointing users to services wherever they exist. To accomplish this work, directories need to be able to speak a common language. The Directory Services Markup Language (DSML) is the emerging standard for expressing directory content in XML.

Directories typically store and manage information about each user in an enterprise; this includes names, addresses, phone numbers, and access rights. In addition, directories are increasingly storing metadata about available Web services: what they do, what they require as inputs, how they are executed, what the results will be, who wrote them, and how to pay for them. Combined with the power of XML, this information allows the emergence of entire new classes of individually tailored applications for E-commerce.

Applications consume DSML documents as they would XML documents because DSML is a subset of XML. Applications can transmit DSML documents to other DSML-enabled applications on the Internet. This process effectively extends the Lightweight Directory Access Protocol (LDAP) across firewalls to any Internet transport protocol, such as HTTP, FTP, or SMTP. This is a major benefit for B2B commercial processes, which are one of the primary targets of EBPP. Standard tags defined by DSML include object class, entry, attribute, and name, referring to well-established directory analogs.

LDAP, other directories, and vendor APIs will remain in place, and directories will continue to operate in their traditional manner. However, new B2B E-commerce capabilities are now available.

XML, considered the language of the future for the Internet, is designed to solve many of the problems that occur in existing Internet applications, most specifically those involving standardized description and interchange of data. XML is intended to provide a single technical standard for describing documents such as bills.

When XML documents are used, a new type of data store is needed: the XML database. Software supporting this new database is designed to effectively store and manage the increasing number of XML documents. XML is typically used for data exchange, but the growing numbers of documents (in many cases, bills) justify special repositories. The benefits of this database are as follows:

- Efficient storage of XML documents
- Rapid search and retrieval of documents
- Ease of application development
- Allows changes to documents without changes in underlying data structures
- Ease of manipulation of document collections

However, there are some weaknesses as well:

- Inefficiency in handling structured data
- Underdeveloped query language standards
- Lack of tools for integration with existing relational data
- Possibility of data integrity problems
- Performance effects caused by conversion to underlying objects or relational structures
- Volume problems associated with large numbers of XML documents

As of yet, no formal standards are in place for such an XML database. Database providers are taking the initial steps by changing or extending their product offers to include XML database capability.

5.3.2 *Handover Protocols*

There are many standards to be considered in the data handover process. Examples include the following:

- Standard SNMP MIBs
- RADIUS
- ASN.1
- AMA/AMADNS
- GTP
- RMON1 and RMON2
- Java messaging service
- IPDR NDM-U
- CORBA

But standards and practical deployments are very different. In common use are the following handover alternatives:

- Log files
- FTP and TFTP
- Enterprise SNMP MIBs
- NetFlow, cFlow, sFlow
- TCP/IP
- Syslog
- EAI buses (e.g., from Vitria and Tibco)
- MQSeries from IBM
- Databases from various suppliers
- Proprietary APIs
- Command list interfaces

As is often the case, however, there are problems with these approaches. The most important drawbacks are as follows:

- Lack of carrier-grade reliability
- Difficulty in introducing new services and new attributes
- No backward compatibility
- Inflexibility
- Insufficient granularity
- Too much granularity
- Negative performance effects
- Usually not real-time based
- Restrictions in functionality

There are several common requirements for an efficient handover protocol:

- Reliability and fault tolerance (no loss of valuable intercept data, compliance with regulatory requirements, negotiated SLA)
- Flexibility (e.g., avoidance of constraints on data models)
- Scalability (e.g., operates over WANs, supports multiple intercept access points [IAPs] simultaneously)
- End-to-end (TSP to LEA) real-time operations with minimum latency
- Efficiency and minimum impact on service element and network
- Ease of implementation
- Open interface to many IAPs or mediation systems

IPDR Streaming Protocol is a new, reliable, real-time protocol that (1) leverages IPDR foundations, (2) uses XDR-based compact binary encoding and TCP/IP transport, (3) is applicable to a broad set of services and domains, and (4) is specifically designed to address requirements for data exchange applicable to the area of LIs. The attributes of this protocol are its reliability, flexibility, efficiency, and manageability; the fact that it provides real-time streaming; and the fact that it leverages overall IPDR technology benefits.

5.3.2.1 Reliability

Why is reliability important?

- Support of critical applications
- Avoidance, through high availability, of additional availability costs
- Compliance with regulatory requirements

How can reliability be increased?

- Use of data-capturing systems that provide scalable availability
- Use of application-level acknowledgment for information exchange
- Use of reliable transport, such as TCP/IP
- Use of built-in fallover and fallback mechanisms
- Use of redundant probes and hot standby support
- Use of cost-effective deduplication mechanism
- Use of tunable keep-alive messages

5.3.2.2 Flexibility

Why is flexibility important?

- All services are supported, including emergency services
- Reductions in proliferation of other surveillance-related protocols
- Support of a wide range of LI models
- Support of a variety of OSSs/BSSs, including billing, fraud, performance management, and fault management
- Investment protection

How can flexibility be increased?

- Use of readable XML schema definitions of record structures
- Negotiation of upgrades ("future-friendly")
- Specified transformations to and from XML or XDR IPDR files

5.3.2.3 Efficiency

Why is efficiency important?

- Minimizes effects on network and service elements, on the network itself, and on data-capturing systems
- Reduces costs
- Allows large amounts of data to be handled

How can efficiency be increased?

- Compute and export only the data requested by collectors (e.g., LEAs)
- Export data only with collector subscription
- Use entire bandwidth via windowed application-level acknowledgment
- Minimize fall-over times by keeping hot standby ready with "keep-alives"
- Compact (XDR) data representation

5.3.2.4 Manageability

Why is manageability important?

- Supports a global, heterogeneous environment
- Supports plug-and-play for large multivendor deployments

How can manageability be increased?

■ Built-in negotiation of protocol version, data capturer and exporter capabilities, templates, and fields
■ Support by exporter and collector of one or multiple versions of protocols
■ Use of back-end-friendly interfaces

5.3.2.5 Real-Time Streaming

Why is real-time streaming important?

■ Allows hot surveillance-related applications
■ Allows real-time reaction to activity (e.g., target identification, fraud, and security breaches)
■ Supports other real-time applications

How can real-time streaming be implemented?

■ Immediate transmission of intercepted data with minimal latency and avoidance of periodic batch closes
■ Continuous stream of events sent from IAPs
■ Presence of hot backup allowing a secondary option to receive data in the case of configurably defined criteria

5.3.2.6 Leverage of Overall IPDR Technology Benefits

IPDR technology benefits are leveraged via the following:

■ Use of information model-based service descriptions, applicable regardless of encoding or transport method
■ Availability of open source implementations without the need to pay royalties
■ Uniform applicability in network data collection
■ Open standards-based format
■ Availability of certified products

The IPDR protocol is broadly applicable to Voice-over-IP (VoIP), CPEs, data over cable, media and application servers, and traffic analyzers.

5.3.3 Physical Handover Interfaces (HIs)

Transport of information between the TSPs and the LEA must ensure a secure data flow encompassing the following features:

- *Authentication:* This is designed to ensure that the LEAs are who they say they are when they are attempting to gain access to the interception network and data. This prevents a rogue organization, disguised as an LEA, from engaging in intercept activities.
- *Confidentiality:* This ensures that no third parties can eavesdrop on the transmitted data.
- *Integrity:* This ensures that the data has not been corrupted through deliberate modification or transmission error.
- *Non-repudiation:* The TSP cannot deny having received the interception from, or having sent it to, the LEA.

Of course, protective measures on the part of TSPs must be in place at the edge of, and within, their respective networks and systems. In addition, the data flow cannot be interrupted and dropped, and there must be sufficient buffering in the event of a transmission disruption between the LEA and the network or service.

Interception data is delivered from the TSP to the LEA via a number of means, including:

- *Dial-up connections:* These connections support ad hoc connections between LEAs and TSPs to outsourcers. All security tools can be implemented, but, as a result of the urgent need for rapid connectivity, usually they are not. Speed and performance are limited. Considering the high-tech solutions available in the area of LIs, this physical interface should be used only occasionally or as a backup.
- *Private dedicated circuits:* This provides the most secure method of delivery, but it has the drawback of higher costs for the LEA, which usually must pay for the dedicated line. On the other hand, this type of service can, in certain configurations, bring revenue to the TSP and thereby help offset the cost of the interception.
- *Integrated Services Digital Network (ISDN):* Basically, all communication forms can be supported by the ISDN. The important advantage is that the existing physical infrastructure may be reused by a more state-of-the-art signaling technology. Bandwidth is easily bundled according to the needs of the communicating partners.

■ *Secure circuits over a public network:* These networks include VPNs (virtual private networks) running over the public Internet but with the necessary encryption and authentication control to ensure confidential data delivery. Also included in this class are X.25 packet networks.

■ *Public networks:* In this case, interception information is delivered via an Internet connection, and there is no inherent protection of the data. If data traffic is light, stand-alone encryption can be applied for a semisecure solution.

■ *3G wireless services:* These services enable flexible, ad hoc connections between all communicating partners (e.g., LEAs, TSPs, MCs, and outsourcers). Data rates are acceptable and enable LEAs to narrow in on targets very rapidly, practically while moving toward those targets. It is not recommended, however, that large data volumes be transmitted to back-office applications.

■ *Partner-ready connectivity between LEAs, TSPs, MCs, and outsourcers:* Different solutions may be considered, depending on the actual security requirements in place. LEAs may be included, via extranets, in the networking infrastructures of providers. In such cases, information exchange is supported in so-called "partner rooms." If the collaboration is expected to be deeper, LEAs may become part of providers' intranets. Networks of LEAs may even be connected directly to the networking infrastructure of providers using various peering-point alternatives such as message buses, middleware, CORBA, Distributed Component Object Model (DCOM), and others. Most likely, however, Web services will standardize collaboration between partners.

5.4 Data Retention and Data Preservation Solutions

A data warehouse is a database created specifically for the purpose of business analysis, traffic analysis, and strategic surveillance, in contrast to online transaction processing systems established for automating business operations. Data warehouses contain data extracted from various TSP support, surveillance documentation, financial, marketing, and management systems. Data can be moved and altered, or transformed, so that they are consistent and accessible for analysis by LEAs. They can be used by service providers of all sizes, with all types of hardware, software, and networking infrastructures. Figure 5.6 shows the generic structure of a TSP data warehouse solution.

Data is extracted from the support, surveillance-related documentation, marketing, financial, and management systems. After proper formatting,

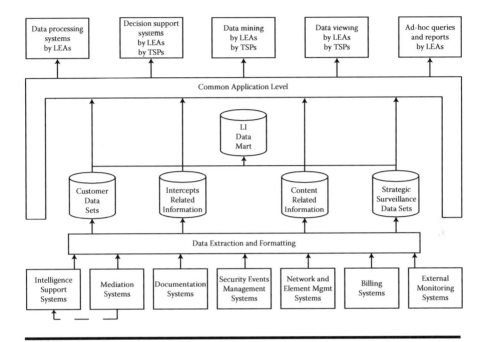

Figure 5.6 Architecture of a telecommunications service provider data warehouse.

various data sets can be partitioned. These data sets feed data to an LI data mart, as well as a common application interface, to serve various end-user applications:

- Consolidation of multiple data sources into one database
- TSP marketing research and marketing support
- LEA strategic surveillance
- LEA data mining
- Maintenance of product portfolios
- Consolidation of knowledge packs to support reactive fault management
- Maintenance of history trouble tickets

Data warehouses are integrated and contain data from diverse legacy applications. This data is historical and represents both summary and detailed data. Information contained in the warehouse is subject oriented, time variant, and nonvolatile. "Subject oriented" refers to the fact that the data warehouse has been designed and organized by the major subjects of the corporation (e.g., customer, vendor, activity, etc.).

In contrast, the legacy environment is organized according to functional applications. The data warehouse is integrated because it contains data that has been transformed into a state of uniformity. For instance, gender can be considered a data element. One application may encode gender as male or female, another as 1 or 0, and a third as x or y. As data is placed in the data warehouse, it is converted to a uniform classification; that is, gender will be encoded in only one way. As a data element passes into the warehouse from applications where it is not encoded yet for this uniform classification, it is converted to create consistency.

Internally coding data is only one aspect of integration, however; representation of data should be considered as well. For example, in one application a data element is measured in yards, whereas in another it is measured in inches or centimeters. As this data element is placed in the data warehouse, it is converted into a single uniform state of representation.

A third characteristic of a data warehouse is that it is time variant. Each unit of data can be considered to be a snapshot, and each snapshot has one moment of time at which it was created. The values are dependent on the time of the snapshot (i.e., they are time invariant). Unlike time-variant warehouse data, operational data is updated as business conditions change. Operational data represents values that are updated whenever the real-world objects that they represent change. In the data warehouse, each time a change occurs, a new snapshot is created that marks that change. The time-variant characteristic of the data warehouse is the feature that allows so much data to be stored there.

Finally, data warehouses are nonvolatile; they generally involve "load-and-access" environments. After the data has been transformed and integrated, it is loaded en masse into the warehouse, from which it is accessed by end users. In contrast, data in the operational environment is updated on a record-by-record basis. This volatility requires considerable overhead to ensure the integrity and consistency of the database for such activities as rollback, recovery, commits, and locking.

The basic technology of the data warehouse does not require the underlying integrity component of transaction-oriented database management systems. Because of its nonvolatility, it permits design practices that are in many ways unacceptable in the operational environment, and vice versa. Figure 5.7 shows a typical data warehouse structure.

Typically, data warehouses have a four-level structure. The bulk of the data resides in the current level of detail, where it is accessed by end-user analysts. From this level, a lightly summarized level of detail is created, which serves midlevel management. Next comes the highly summarized level of data for the benefit of top management. Beneath these three levels resides the older level of detail, data that is at least two or three years old.

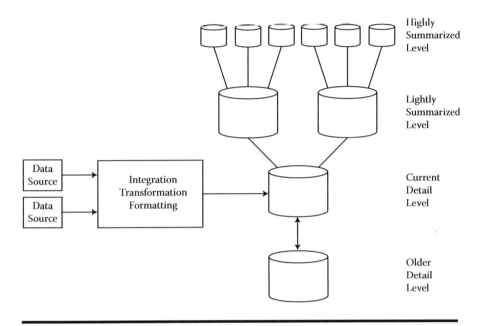

Figure 5.7   Structure of the data warehouse.

There is a predictable flow of data into and through the data warehouse. Data enters into the current level of detail of the warehouse from the integration and transformation processes, which, in turn, have been provided with data by the legacy applications. As it ages, the data then flows into the older level of detail. As the data is summarized, it flows into the lightly summarized level of data, and then again into the highly summarized level.

Finally, perhaps the most important component in the data warehouse architecture is the metadata. End users cannot efficiently access the data in the warehouse unless they have a way of knowing what data is stored there and where it is located. Metadata refers to data about data, a catalog of what data is in the warehouse and pointers to this data.

Users must not only be able to locate data in the warehouse, but they must also be able to manage this data. For this reason, metadata not only needs to describe the structure of the data in the warehouse, but it must contain data modeling information, including data extraction and transformation histories and data summarization algorithms. This information is essential if end users are to trace the data back to operational sources. The metadata may also contain data usage statistics. The availability and increasing maturity of extraction and transformation tools, combined with powerful features for creating and managing metadata, are key drivers behind the rapidly increasing number of data warehouse implementations.

Data warehouses can reside on a variety of platforms, depending on the level of detail and summarization. Frequently, data warehouses are physically distributed but logically unified. Typical solutions are as follows:

- Highly summarized data typically resides on PC workstations.
- Lightly summarized data typically resides in C/S structures.
- Current data typically resides on mainframes or in C/S structures.
- Older detail-level data is expected to reside on bulk storage devices.

State-of-the-art data warehouses offer Web access, in combination with the following benefits for LEAs as well as TSPs:

- *Infrastructure:* Using Web access shifts the burden of platform compatibility to the browser and presentation vendors.
- *Access:* Both internal and external users have easy access via the Internet, eliminating the need to extend the corporate network.
- *Cost:* Web browsers represent a fraction of the cost of online analytical processing (OLAP) and other client tools. They also involve shorter learning curves.
- *Leverage:* The Web browser can be used in every application that provides a Web gateway.
- *Control:* Maintenance can be isolated to a centralized point.
- *Independence:* Web access allows wide choices in terms of hardware and operating systems.

5.5 Document Management and Document-Related Technology (DRT)

Document management is gaining in importance, leaving behind its isolation as a niche and ad hoc solution for various TSP processes. DRS is increasingly assuming the role of an integration aid, gluing together multiple documentation products. Document management refers to a set of technologies used to incorporate and manage existing, and new, documents within an enterprise for the purposes of wider distribution and easier access.

Each document is considered a file or part of a file, which may be structured or unstructured, and stored in a computer system. It can be considered as an authentic and ambiguous unit of information that can be retrieved at any point of time. A document is composed of any collection of information in any format (video, audio, text, Web pages, CD, paper, images, schematics, drawings, spreadsheets, etc.) and can be located anywhere within the company. Such documents might or might not have any construct, but they are structured in the way they are captured or validated to be an enterprise document.

As a result of the current opportunities available in terms of modifying, adding, and changing data in computer systems, there are strict requirements regarding maintenance of electronic documents. These requirements are centered around the following:

- Retrieval of status, composition, form, and content of documents at the point of their creation
- Maintenance of dynamic links between document units
- Automatic updates of documents
- Changes in relationships
- Structuring documents of individual components
- Dependency of formats and runtime environments
- Other document maintenance guidelines

The principal application areas of DRS include imaging, workflow support, repository, and retrieval. Implementation frequency depends on the industry; TSPs concentrate on all these areas, with a slight emphasis on workflow. Each phase of the service cycle includes one or another form of DRS.

Document management helps to integrate various technological and organizational solutions for TSPs. Figure 5.8 shows a simplified structure of this integration.

Today, DRS penetrates almost all processes and functions supported by TSPs. Good practical examples can be seen in cases of enterprise resource planning (ERP) and IP-related integration. There are two types of documents in this category:

1. *Collaboration documents:* These are short, unstructured documents such as e-mails, notes, messages, postings, and memos. They assist in group work and are characterized as immediate posting, minimal audit, and history tracking or revision tracking. They do not need to be validated because the collaboration in which they appear is itself being subjected to the validation process.
2. *Enterprise documents:* These documents help drive business operations. They include manufacturing procedures, product design specifications, marketing requirements of products, business transactions, and escalation procedures. They need to be validated, tracked, monitored, and widely distributed if they are to support operations.

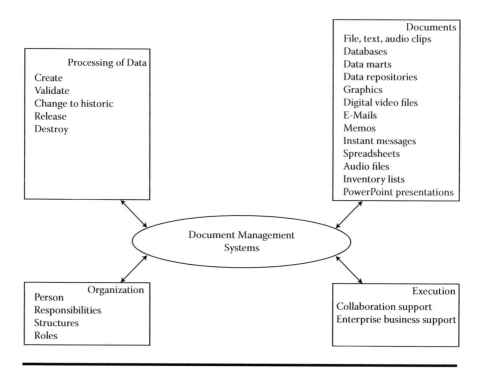

Figure 5.8   Integration capabilities of document management.

Document management systems should ensure that the contents of the documents they contain are current, accurate, and approved. "Current" means that the document is in effect at the time of publishing. Often, within organizations there are many revisions and changes to enterprise documents; knowing which one is current and approved is crucial to operations. "Accurate" means ensuring an enforced review of each document. Enforcement steps are determined by the implementers and users of the system. Once defined, they provide accuracy to a document within the enterprise. "Approved" means that the document can be used. This feature is critical to service providers' departments (that collaborate with the LEA) when services are subject to constraints such as legal, contractual, ethical, or moral guidelines; it is also important for market positioning. The following areas are considered the primary targets of DRS penetration:

- Internet, intranet, and extranet documentation
- Document, workflow, and knowledge management
- E-commerce and the use of digital signatures
- Document input, distribution, and storage
- OCR, ICR, and pattern recognition

- Databases, data warehouses, data marts, and retrieval engines
- Imaging and multimedia applications
- Archival and record management
- Secure communication and unified messaging
- Groupware and office solutions
- Forms, templates, and output management
- Content management and content distribution

TSPs can gain several key benefits from using DMS. These benefits include the following:

- *Manageable and scalable information:* The instrumental benefit in using DMS is that of being able to control all existing enterprise documents for the purpose of tracking and reuse. Without such a system, it is extremely difficult for a TSP to fully understand, and have a complete picture of, its intellectual property and operations. Furthermore, such information is often reused or reformatted as changes occur. According to estimates made by industry experts, as much as 60 percent of white-collar employees' time is spent recreating documents from existing ones. The ability to reuse documents in a different format and context is a highly scalable corporate competitive advantage.
- *Higher productivity:* DMS helps those in all branches and groups within the TSP's organization to know exactly what to do by providing them with current, accurate, and approved information. This represents the highest form of a productivity tool, short of human effort itself.
- *Faster time to market:* One of the advantages of this high-productivity tool is the ability it provides a company to run its operations as effectively as possible. The result is faster time to market for products and services.
- *Accurate and effective execution:* By its nature, a DMS ensures that information content is current, accurate, and approved. The contents of the DMS are usually procedures, processes, or operational flows of an organization, as well as other documents, detailing how the organization functions.
- *Compliance with regulatory requirements:* Because the DMS manages all the required data, information demands (e.g., Sarbanes–Oxley Act, LIs for LEAs) can be met in a timely manner without additional expense.

A DMS requires a several-step approach for proper deployment. These steps are as follows:

1. Analysis of the documents to be managed: Not all documents need to be managed in the DMS.
2. Determination of the purpose of management: After Step 1, a clear objective of such a system must be defined. For example, this objective could be information exchange with other providers and LEAs.
3. Selection of the appropriate technology: Since DMSs offer a wide selection of technologies, users can narrow down the technology segment for quick and easy implementation and focus on project planning.
4. Planning for implementation: To effectively implement a DMS, several key players should buy in before initiation of the project. Because a DMS is mainly designed for enterprise documents, the support of senior management is necessary before even a feasibility study can begin. DMS represents a cultural change more than a technology change. Although DMSs utilize the latest options in network, storage, security, distributed objects, and other enabling technologies, their true impact is on the operational process, which all the individuals involved must buy into.

Thus, not only must the implementation plan clearly detail the benefits of using such a system instead of the old filing cabinets, but it must also provide immediate benefits because the goal of each of the major milestones — that is, capture; validation; status change to historical; release; and destruction — is to encourage wide usage and employee participation. The principal phases are as follows:

- *Capture:* Documents are created by word processing software, imaging, graphics software, and spreadsheets. A key point in this phase is not only the creation of new documents in a standard format that allows ease of scalable distribution and access, but also the conversion of legacy documents to the same standard. Most DMS vendors offer software that accepts documents in multiple formats prior to populating their information repository. Integration of multiple formats is important, and integration of multiple identities of documents is critical. Many documents are re-creations of other documents that are quite large. Thus, users need to capture or create a new document that is a structured tree of other documents that might not be in the same physical storage location or same format. Such a system would then maintain a dynamic linkage throughout the life of a particular document to allow distribution of the document anywhere on the network without any loss of integrity.

- *Validation:* This phase includes several key operations. First, the document has to be verified to determine its accuracy. Verification can be accomplished by having a work management technology enforce review and approve steps before classifying a particular document as accurate. Second, all revision control and management must be in place to ensure that such documents indeed represent the latest official information on which to act. Third, security and ownership rules are assigned so that document control and auditing can be accomplished.
- *Status change to historical:* After about 120 to 180 days, the document is no longer subject to audits and revision, and it becomes an actual record.
- *Release:* This phase includes distribution, ownership, access, and archiving. Within each of these operations, a strong backbone network with sufficient security is required. Back-end archiving can be accomplished through information repository, ownership, or access rules, all of which are part of standard DMS software offerings from major vendors.
- *Destruction:* The document is no longer needed, and it is erased from the document management system entirely and securely.

5.6 Information Life-Cycle Management

Information life-cycle management (ILM) is a process that enables TSPs, LEAs, and outsourcers to move surveillance-related data down the path of storage resources, from a high-performance, high-capacity filer or disk array to a lower-end disk array, to a tape silo, so that it is near-line, and then finally to a permanent archival media.

As did hierarchical storage management (HSM) before it, ILM uses a tiered approach. However, HSM moves data based on age alone, whereas ILM determines tiers on the basis of business value. Business value is determined jointly by TSPs and LEAs. As can be seen in Figure 5.9, there are three major storage architectures in use today: direct attached storage (DAS), network attached storage (NAS), and storage area networks (SANs).

An example of a DAS is a RAID system connected directly to a server. An SAN is a network, and the NAS device is a turnkey file server. Both architectures externalize the server-storage connection and provide the benefits of networked storage. However, in their current formats, the NAS solution serves files over regular messaging networks or a dedicated NAS network, whereas the SAN solution moves block data over a separate, dedicated network. The key difference is that, in an SAN, the file system is on the server side of the network, whereas in NAS architecture the

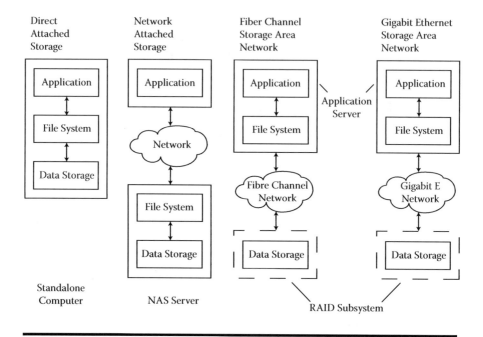

Figure 5.9 Storage architectures.

network is located between the server and the file system. Depending on the network, SANs can be divided in two subcategories: Ethernet SANs and Fiber Channel SANs.

In addition to new storage devices, there are different technological approaches available to assist in the organization, handling, and management of the growing amount of data; these are as follows:

- The rapid and rather unruly explosion of LI-related data calls for a storage resource management (SRM) framework. A technical solution for easing storage management is storage virtualization: abstraction of storage whereby the underlying storage device is masked from the host server accessing the data. All the data needed by the host server or the application is available on a single virtual device, and from the standpoint of the application, it does not matter which disk or tape system holds the data.
- Storage virtualization will permit database administrators to manage far more storage than would otherwise be possible. Virtualization can transform physical storage into a utility pool that is available to all, resulting in significant cost reductions. Balancing load, adding storage, and migrating data can be handled through policy-based management software.

- Bandwidth outside computers has far exceeded bandwidth inside them. While network speeds increase by leaps and bounds, the weakest link in the data delivery chain — the file server or the NAS device — reduces system throughput. Some vendors are attempting to overcome these limitations with new system architectures for storage servers.
- Two technologies that are blurring the distinction between NAS and SANs and could provide a significant boost to NAS performance are the virtual interface (VI) architecture and the direct access file system (DAFS).

5.7 Receiver Applications

LEAs or outsourcers, as the receivers of collected data, are expected to take advantage of this data. It is assumed that they can access all necessary data, collected and maintained by TSPs. The nature of the applications under consideration, the times at which data is activated, executed, and evaluated, and interpretation of results are very different. Both targeted surveillance and strategic observations are supported. This is a dynamically changing area with many new applications. In most cases, however, suppliers of such applications do not market them aggressively; rather, they are interested in playing the role of a professional outsourcer to LEAs.

5.7.1 Support for Recognizing Criminal Activities

5.7.1.1 Search for Criminal Activities

This area falls under strategic surveillance owing to the fact that there are no specific targets at the initiation of the process. Observation of communication directions and paths, and evaluation of the contents of various applications, may help narrow lists of potential targets. However, large amounts of data must be evaluated, filtered, analyzed, sorted, classified, and selected to reach conclusions regarding individuals, groups, locations, or suspect activities.

5.7.1.2 Communication Analysis

Collection of actionable intelligence requires in-depth analysis of communication activities. This process involves correlation of time stamps, locations, communication relationships, authentications, directions, and communications forms and volumes. Location tracking, geographical information systems, and data mining are some of the methods under consideration to support such analyses.

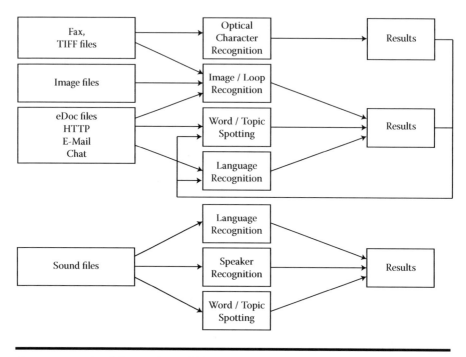

Figure 5.10 Applying and combining automated intelligence support.

5.7.1.3 Content Analysis

In-depth analysis of communicated content is necessary as well. This involves analyzing and correlating application identifications, language recognition, speaker recognition and identification, word spotting, topic recognition, optical character recognition, logo recognition, and image recognition. Both text-based and audio-based analyses are frequently used.

5.7.1.4 Automated Intelligence Support

Content is created from text- and audio-based documentation elements. Results are generated by combining and correlating multiple inputs, including faxes, TIFF files, image files, eDoc files, HTTP, e-mail, chat, and sound files. Figure 5.10 shows an example of such a combination and correlation (Axland, 2004). In a further step, languages and speakers may be recognized by using combined forms of intelligence.

5.7.2 Analysis Procedures and Tools

Intercepting and collecting communications is just the initial step. This raw information must be analyzed and transformed into actionable intelligence, which can be used to further the investigation and seek conviction of the offenders. Intelligent analysis tools assist both TSPs and LEAs in extracting important information from the intercepted data, determining patterns and relationships, and applying the information more effectively to decisions affecting the case. The following types of tools are important with regard to intelligent analysis of intercepted data.

5.7.2.1 Free Search

Free search tools reduce costs and conserve time by determining the significance of huge amounts of information derived from e-mail, chat, instant messaging, Web sites, and transferred files. Advanced call data searches can find specific information such as a person's name or a specific telephone number. Sophisticated text searches, according to call content, allow service providers and LEAs to search all locations and all forms of information with simply a keyword, phrase, or synonym. Fuzzy searches are used to improve the effectiveness of search activities by shortcuts based on previous experiences. Reports of call details can also provide investigators with important information.

5.7.2.2 Visual Analysis

Visual analysis tools represent another category of tools that provide assistance to service providers and LEAs. These tools help to combine all the intercepted data into graphic presentations, pictures, and charts so that otherwise hidden patterns and relationships can be identified.

5.7.2.3 Location Tracking

Knowing the criminal's location, even as the call is being intercepted, can be as important as the call itself. Location-tracking solutions (e.g., Verint's RELIANT) can provide a graphic positioning of a target using a cell phone, drawing the route and direction of the target directly onto maps of the geographical area.

5.7.2.4 Voice Verification

Verifying the identity of a speaker in a particular conversation can be accomplished through a voice verification solution. A voice bank stores voice samples so that the user can compare the intercepted caller's voice to these samples. This helps ensure accuracy of evidence, in addition to enhancing the effectiveness of the investigation.

5.7.2.5 Court Evidence

Successful prosecutions require comprehensive collection and strict adherence to the rules of evidence handling. Intelligent analysis tools provide LEAs and prosecutors with the basis to develop and manage intercepted communications throughout the process, from collection to prosecution.

Storage and archiving, which are critical parts of the process, are expected to be automated to a certain extent to prevent errors and reduce labor expenses. A portable player could replay the original evidence for courtroom presentations.

5.7.3 Use of Geographical Information Systems (GISs)

The MC from Siemens is an advanced, flexible, yet complex collection of software modules and hardware components that operate together to perform monitoring tasks in an auditable, secure, and reliable manner. The MC handles intercepts of voice and data in fixed and mobile networks, as well as the Internet and other IP networks.

When a PSTN fixed-line network is in place, LEAs can, in most cases, determine the physical address of the target subscriber based on the telephone number used. The network service provider can match the subscriber number to an exchange and, further, to the address of the line to the subscriber. As a result of the mobility of the device used in GSM/GPRS/UMTS systems, this location information is not available for these systems.

What is available to the network service provider is a discrete identifier of the cell from which the mobile device receives its signal. Using an MC add-on application called MC-GIS, this information can be transposed to a physical map showing the current location of the mobile device. Further extrapolations to the incoming information can indicate the direction of travel of the mobile device. This add-on is discussed in more detail next.

5.7.3.1 Use of Cell Identifiers

A GSM/GPRS/UMTS mobile device communicates via a cell transmitter and receiver. In any given region, there may be multiple cells whose footprints overlap. Cell transmitters and receivers are controlled by a base station controller (BSC) (Figure 5.11). The base station controller decides which cell of an overlapping group will manage the mobile device based on the reported signal strength of the device. Each cell has a unique identifier within a network. This cell identifier is provided, in adherence to LI standards, to the MC as a parameter of the call-related data, more strictly known as intercept-related information.

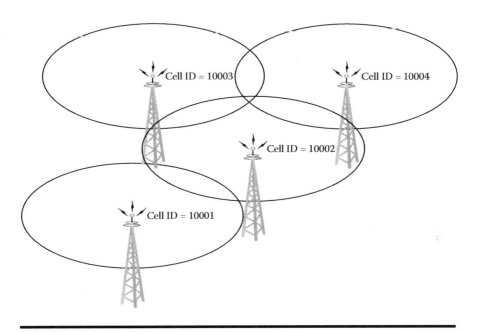

Figure 5.11   GSM/GPRS/UMTS network cells.

Table 5.1   GSM/GPRS/UMTS Network Cells

Cell ID	Longitude	Latitude	Geo-Accuracy
10001	W83.56.42.19	N48.17.23.04	300
10002	W83.56.52.16	N48.17.31.16	350
10003	W83.56.43.54	N48.17.38.27	320
10004	W83.57.03.35	N48.17.39.34	350

The network provider has a table of cell identifiers and the physical location of the cell antenna. Each cell antenna is tuned to a known radius of effective transmission called *geo-accuracy*. This information is configured in the MC's GIS server. The MC-GIS client is integrated with the Unified User Station (UUS) of the MC and uses the IRI cell identifier parameter to locate the mobile device on a map.

The geo-accuracy of the indicated cell is used to illustrate the level of accuracy of the mobile device's location. The UUS user is shown a circle around the antenna on the physical map, and the user knows that the mobile device is somewhere in the circular region. Corresponding data is summarized in Table 5.1.

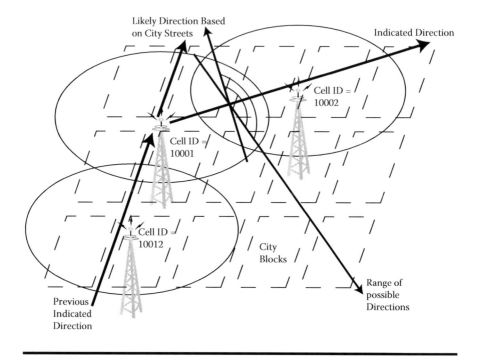

Figure 5.12   Network cells overlapping footprints.

5.7.3.2 Use of Location and Movement Indications

As the mobile device moves, crossing from one cell footprint to another, the mobile system "hands off" control of the device from one cell to another (Figure 5.12). The mobile device is now handled by another cell with a different cell identifier. While the mobile device is in the process of an active call, this new cell identifier is passed on to the MC in IRI records.

The new location of the mobile device is shown on the physical map, and a line is drawn on the screen connecting the new location and the previous location. The new location may have the same level of accuracy associated with it, or it may be greater or smaller depending on the geo-accuracy of the new cell.

Whatever the level of accuracy of the new mobile device location, it gives the user a better idea of where the mobile device is, where it has been, and the direction in which it is moving. Perceived accuracy is improved if the physical map shows that the mobile device more than likely has to travel on a particular road, footpath, alley, or other route.

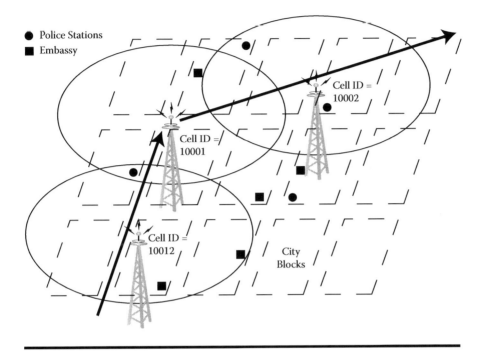

Figure 5.13   Mobility profiles.

5.7.3.3 MC-GIS Client

The MC-GIS client is launched from the UUS and depicts the location and movements of a mobile device, overlaid on a physical map. If the mobile device is in a call while moving, the location points are joined by a solid black line. If the mobile device moves between calls, the location points between calls are joined by a dotted line.

There are a number of possibilities with regard to enhancing the information showing the location of the mobile device. For example, a *mobility profile* for multiple targets may be displayed simultaneously. A mobility profile (Figure 5.13) is a graphical semitransparent layer of information that can be overlaid on maps and other layers. An example of a mobility profile would be a graphical location representation of all the embassies located in the map region. One layer per target can be shown, and layers can be switched on or off by checking off their tick box in the top left-hand panel (Figure 5.13). Using mobility profiles, the MC-GIS client user can build an enhanced understanding of what the mobile device user is doing.

There are further enhancements, under study by switch manufacturers, to improve upon the level of location information currently provided from the switch.

5.8 Summary

In this chapter, we have introduced extended key functions of intelligence support systems (ISSs). In combination with the access, delivery, and collection functions that are at the core of LIs, mediation, data warehousing, and intelligence applications are important in ensuring the rich functionality of ISSs. As mentioned in previous chapters, lawful interception is an important part of an ISS, but not the only one. Core and extended functionality, together, give TSPs the basis for justifying LI-related investments. The next chapter describes solution architectures for both core and extended functions from various suppliers.

Chapter 6

Lawful Intercept Solution Architectures

CONTENTS

Frameworks and tools play a central role in lawful intercepts (LIs). Frameworks are the basis for a suite of products supporting various technologies. Point products represent best-of-breed solutions addressing specific areas of LIs that might be used together with frameworks. This chapter concentrates exclusively on representative samples. After introducing three framework alternatives, we discuss various tools used in LIs.

Positioning products is relatively easy, because Communications Assistance for Law Enforcement Act (CALEA) and European Telecommunications Standard Institute (ETSI) offer streamlining standards. This is not the only way to categorize products, however; they can also be grouped according to front-end or back-end functions and features. Most products support the access and delivery functions associated with lawful interception.

Support of the collection function is always subject to agreements between telecommunications service providers (TSPs) and law enforcement agency (LEAs). Unfortunately, there are very few known products on the market that support data mining, evidence finding, and correlation functions. Mediation systems will not be addressed in detail here; mediation functionality is usually part of LI frameworks.

6.1 Frameworks for LIs

Frameworks offer the basis for LI-related applications that support standard functions such as access, delivery, and collection. They typically include recommended hardware, a recommended operating system, security features, database links, a graphical user interface (GUI), and generic housekeeping functions. Usually, suppliers also offer multiple applications for various telecommunications services and products.

6.1.1 Xcipio from SS8 Networks

SS8 Networks developed Xcipio™, an open-architecture, real-time, scalable LI platform (available on Sun's Solaris UNIX operating system and industry-standard Sun Microsystems servers), as a cost-effective solution for the provisioning, access, delivery, and recording activities involved in LIs. The LI market is a dynamic one, with TSPs constantly adding new switch releases, switch types, edge devices and technologies, and so forth to their networks. In addition, LI standards evolve as technology and government requirements change. Recognizing this rapidly changing environment, SS8 designed Xcipio to easily accommodate such changes.

The ultimate goal is to meet customers' needs with high-quality products and highly skilled professionals. SS8 often acts as a bridge between the TSP and network equipment manufacturers, providing expertise in legal intercept technology so that the end solution fits customers' needs. In addition to partner relationships with network equipment providers, SS8 has close ties with LEAs and works with them on a regular basis, exchanging ideas for new solutions, explaining aspects of existing solutions, and ensuring that SS8 products meet current requirements.

Xcipio leverages all principal technologies and supports LI requirements of both domestic and international markets as well as multiple delivery standards for traditional circuit-switched (wireless and wireline), next-generation packet, Internet service provider (ISP), and 2G/3G wireless data and hybrid networks.

Xcipio's modular architecture supports multivendor switch environments with a common interface that increases ease of setup and operation. Xcipio complies with the following standards: TIA J-STD-025, ETSI ES-201-671, TIIT in the Netherlands, and PacketCable. Xcipio also complies with the International Softswitch Consortium (ISC) requirements.

SS8 has extensive experience in the LI market. It was one of the first companies to deploy a CALEA-compliant solution, boasts a list of customers that include the top wireless and wireline service providers, partners with top equipment vendors, actively participates in standards committees, and focuses on establishing close working relationships with customers.

6.1.1.1 Features of the Framework

Xcipio is a complete LI solution that provides state-of-the-art intercept capability for the provisioning, access, delivery, and recording of authorized communications. Xcipio supports the following:

■ Legacy wireless and wireline networks as well as newly deployed technologies such as Voice-over-IP (VoIP) and 2G/3G wireless data networks
■ Multiple network elements, such as time division multiplexing (TDM) switches, softswitches, media gateway controllers, call agents, routers, trunking gateways, cable modem termination systems (CMTS), and so forth, from a central location

Xcipio provides a future-proof path to expanding LI capabilities throughout current and future networks. Its scalable architecture lends itself to entry-level implementations and can easily be upgraded or modified to meet growth requirements resulting from network expansions, increases in subscriber populations or intercept volumes, changes in monitoring patterns, and new monitoring requirements. Through its modular architecture, Xcipio also supports collocated, regional, or centralized deployment models and provides configurations for country-specific regulations.

Xcipio allows centralized operational management for TSPs and ensures single administration and access points for LEAs. Thus, it enables TSPs to more efficiently manage LI operations located at multiple sites or distributed over multiple networks.

Attributes of the Xcipio solution include the following:

■ All access methods and log-ins through Xcipio are documented and intended for authorized system users.
■ SS8 does not provide access to its systems by any means other than those that are fully documented.
■ Information contained in Xcipio cannot be distributed or transferred to other systems except by means of documented methodologies. No other form of automatic data extraction or transfer exists.
■ Xcipio only permits capture and delivery of call information and voice communications related to the entity listed on the warrant.
■ The functionality of Xcipio is partitioned according to specified user log-in types and passwords.
■ Physical access to Xcipio is restricted to either network connectivity via the Ethernet card or a direct connection through the RS232 port.

Additional security measures provided by Xcipio are:

- RADIUS log-in authentication
- Secure shell communication
- Optional encryption methods for delivery of data and content
- Isolated delivery (fan-out) of data and content to different agencies
- Filters addressing the needs of different types of warrants
- Centralized operational management of call data delivery
- Security platform scans
- Encrypted database
- Logging of all administrative/user activities on the system
- Restricted access to system error logs and alarms
- Quarterly testing of the latest security patches from Sun Microsystems to ensure the operating system remains secure

Xcipio reduces switching equipment costs in that features can be provisioned on the switch as the single virtual LEA, eliminating the need for additional physical interfaces from each switch. By providing a single point of access to the network environment, Xcipio enables carriers to centralize their surveillance operations in a more controlled, cost-effective, and secure way. This reduces overall administration costs for service providers and simplifies the LEA's job by providing a single interface into a carrier's multiswitch, multivendor network.

A crucial part of the SS8 services package is training and knowledge transfer to the system administrators who install and maintain the Xcipio system as well as to the operators and agents who use the intercept platform. SS8 provides structured training courses on either its own premises or the customer's site. Figure 6.1 shows the principal components of Xcipio.

6.1.1.2 Applications of Xcipio

Xcipio comprises six applications designed to meet the specific needs of different networks (circuit switch, call data delivery, Internet, softswitch, wireless data, and recording equipment). These applications operate on a common service layer with four modules that provide provisioning, call data processing, call-content routing, and recording functionality. The service modules use common operations, administration and management (OA&M) and protocol layers that operate on Sun servers and interface with proprietary call-content routing devices. The applications are as follows:

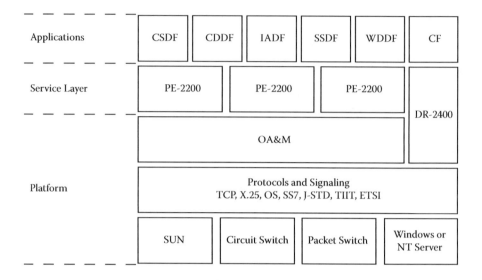

Figure 6.1 Components of Xcipio.

- *Circuit switch delivery function (CSDF)* for traditional wireline and wireless networks. CSDF is an off-switch LI application that is compatible with inputs from a variety of switching vendors and supports both wireless and wireline networks. The CSDF collects, secures, and distributes to authorized LEAs (using national standards) pertinent call information and voice communications from network switches.
- *Call data delivery function (CDDF)* for centralized delivery of J-STD call data. This application provides a single point in the network to control the delivery of call data from wireless and wireline switches to LEAs.
- *Internet access delivery function (IADF)* for ISP networks. The IADF is a delivery function that enables ISPs to deliver session-identifying information and communications content to LEAs using standard protocols, transmission media, and delivery standards. It supports access to Ethernet and Asynchronous Transfer Mode (ATM) sessions and works at full line rate.
- *Softswitch delivery function (SSDF)* for next-generation packet-switched networks. The SSDF provisions, communicates with, and collects call data information from the softswitches in the network. From this information, the SSDF can identify and communicate with the edge devices (routers, trunking gateways, CMTS) handling the call and request a replicated voice stream from them. The SSDF then processes the call data and content so that they conform to

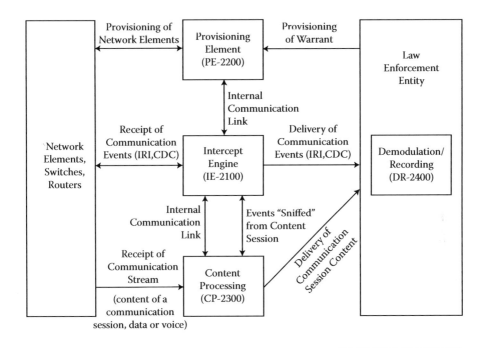

Figure 6.2 Supporting-service modules of Xcipio.

the requirements of the applicable LI standard and distributes them to the authorized LEA collection facilities.

- *Wireless data delivery function (WDDF)* for centralized delivery of 2G data and 3G wireless data. This application allows a single point in the network to provision, control, format, and deliver wireless data from 2G interworking functions and emerging 3G technologies such as general packet radio service (GPRS), 1 x radio transmission technology (1xRtt), wideband code division multiple access (WCDMA), and enhanced data rates for global evolution (EDGE).
- *Collection function (CF)* for recording and storage of intercepted information. This application provides physical connectivity to receive data and content from the delivery applications and stores it for use by the LEA. It provides mechanisms for producing media copies of the information.

6.1.1.3 Service Layer Modules

Xcipio's applications operate on a common service layer with four supporting modules, as shown in Figure 6.2. These modules are briefly described in the following subsections.

6.1.1.3.1 PE-2200 Provisioning Element

This module is responsible for provisioning the elements of Xcipio (IE-2100 and CP-2300) as well as network devices (switches, softswitches, call agents, trunking gateways, etc.). The PE-2200 supports local and remote GUIs via a Web-based browser. In addition, it maintains a database of provisioned target subscriber information including target identities, case identities, monitoring start and stop dates, and the law enforcement destinations that need to receive the monitored call data/content. This module can run on the same server as the intercept engine (described in the following subsection) or on a separate stand-alone server for larger configurations.

6.1.1.3.2 IE-2100 Intercept Engine

This module is responsible for operating the switch engines and OA&M, managing intercept access points, processing all data packets and messages, and transmitting them to the LEA. It receives call events from the network elements (switches, softswitches, trunking gateways, call agents, etc.), maps them to appropriate case identities from the provisioning database, filters them according to court order criteria, converts them to a standard format, appends case identity information, and routes them to the appropriate LEA.

6.1.1.3.3 CP-2300 Content Processing

This module is responsible for processing, routing, replicating, identifying, encapsulating, encrypting, and delivering of content (packet or TDM voice) to LEAs. In the case of voice interception (TDM or Voice-over-Packet [VoP]), the CP-2300 is controlled by the IE-2100 as it delivers voice streams to the LEA. In an ISP network, the CP-2300 is first provisioned with target-identifying information by the PE-2200. This information is then used to identify and filter out packets belonging to the target subscriber. From these packets, "event" messages are identified and sent to the IE-2100 for further processing and delivery to the LEA.

6.1.1.3.4 DR-2400 Demodulation/Recording

This module is responsible for receipt, storage, analysis, and playback of intercepted communications. It is typically owned and maintained by the LEA, although in some cases it is situated on the premises of the TSP.

Xcipio operates on a globally proven OA&M platform that has been deployed in more than 50 countries. Xcipio implements a generic managed object server (GMOS) that is responsible for maintaining and administering the delivery function configuration and databases. It protects (e.g., prevents unauthorized access, manipulation, and disclosure) intercept controls, intercepted call content, and call-identifying information in a manner consistent with the security policies and practices of TSPs. Xcipio offers:

- ITU-standard MML support
- GUI for surveillance provisioning
- Built-in test tools for remote testing
- Full SS7-compliant management systems
- Alarm reporting and error logging
- Automatic software fault recovery
- Automatic or manual disk backup

Xcipio supports interface specifications regarding delivery of multimedia services over two-way cable in real-time (PacketCable™ standards PKT-SP-ESP-I01, PKT-SP-EM-I02, and PKT-TR-ESCF-V01-991229). It runs on industry-standard Sun Microsystems servers and proprietary TDM/IP switching devices. Xcipio supports X.25, TCP/IP, 10/100BaseT, GigE, ATM, and SS7 interfaces.

6.1.2 Aqsacom ALIS

The Aqsacom lawful interception management solution (ALIS) operates as a real-time mediation platform intended to satisfy a variety of LI requests. It ensures an interception implementation that is nonintrusive, completely transparent, and independent of the underlying connectivity technology.

The system's client/server (CS)-layered architecture comprises two functional entities: ALIS-m for target provisioning and central system management and ALIS-d for mediation and delivery of interception content. Figure 6.3 shows the functional structure of the ALIS.

6.1.2.1 Features of the Aqsacom Solution

Several principal features, described in the following subsections, are addressed by the ALIS framework.

6.1.2.1.1 Provisioning

The management and provisioning entity, ALIS-m, holds the intelligence of the system and is responsible for provisioning, workflow synchronization, and confidentiality and security of access to the data. Multi-administration support (in which a single target can be subject to interception

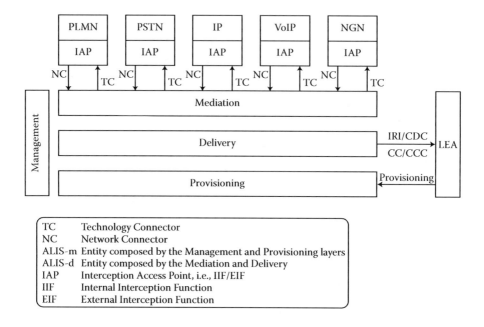

Figure 6.3 Functional structure of ALIS.

activities on behalf of different LEAs) and provisioning features provide the user optimal flexibility and security to start, stop, query, and modify LI operations.

An array of interception criteria are supported, including mobile subscriber ISDN number (MSISDN), international mobile subscriber identity (IMSI), international mobile station equipment identity (IMEI), IP address, MAC address, user id, and geographical criteria such as origin, destination, and cell. The friendly GUI allows many operational tasks to be automated (e.g., automatic triggering or stopping of an interception operation at a predefined date and time).

Consistency checks are used to guarantee coherence between the data housed in the network's internal interception functions and the interception specifications of the ALIS database. Consistency checks can be initiated either manually or automatically. Because historical data is of paramount importance in the activities of LEAs, consistency check operations are systematically logged in the activity log.

Also, electronic provisioning processing capabilities for third-party applications are supported to allow provisioning operations to be performed via such applications.

6.1.2.1.2 Mediation

ALIS-d supports the mediation aspects of lawful interception operations. Aqsacom's patented network connectors and technology connectors ensure total network and vendor transparency. Mediation operations are performed on interception content (intercept-related information [IRI]/call data channel [CDC], content of communication [CC]/call content channel [CCC]) to match the format constraints imposed by different regulatory bodies and standards organizations (e.g., ETSI, CALEA, and ETSI-NL) or other country-specific requirements. Some of the technological areas covered through ALIS's comprehensive mediation capabilities are as follows:

- TDM-coded voice for both public switched telephone networks [PSTNs] and public land mobile networks [PLMNs], with support for the leading industry codecs (e.g., G711, G723.1, and G729)
- VoIP-coded voice with support for the leading industry codecs (e.g., G711, G723.1, and G729)
- E-mail
- IP data streams (e.g., Web pages)

6.1.2.1.3 Delivery

ALIS-d supports the delivery aspects of lawful interception operations. Intercepted content is delivered to the concerned LEA/monitoring center (MC) via secure data links. Delivery of IRI/call identifying information (CII) can also be carried out through short message services (SMSs) or via fax. If required, interception content can be buffered for a predefined period of time.

In addition, transfer to an external medium such as a DAT tape or a CD-ROM is possible under special circumstances. Delivery mechanisms based on open standards such as remote operation service element (ROSE) or file transfer protocol (FTP) are used to communicate with the other components that are part of the lawful interception chain. The security of the connections between the different elements is guaranteed by using trusted paths with support for open standards (e.g., IPSecurity [IPSec] or Secure Socket Layers [SSL]).

6.1.2.1.4 Management

The management layer is responsible for all systems-critical security administration actions involving both system and user (e.g., intercepting operator) data. Trusted paths are used to guarantee data confidentiality, and the user is kept informed with regard to logs, statistics, results, and alarm messages.

6.1.2.1.5 Interception Access Points (IAPs)

IAPs are the logical points within the TSP's network at which capture of interception content takes place. They are supported by either internal interception functions (IIFs) or external interception functions (EIFs).

In cases in which no IIF is available in the network, ALIS can be enhanced with interception function capabilities so that it acts as a passive, nonintrusive information "sniffer." In terms of EIFs, the following are part of the ALIS suite:

- ALIS SS7-enabled EIF
- ALIS GPRS-enabled EIF
- ALIS SMS-enabled EIF
- ALIS e-mail-enabled EIF
- ALIS IP-enabled EIF
- ALIS VoIP-enabled EIF

6.1.2.1.6 Authentication, Access Methods, and Security

Stringent system access control rules apply. Access can occur locally (e.g., through a LAN), remotely (via a WAN), or through remote access using a secure dial-up connection with a user-identity exchange and a call-back procedure.

User authentication is performed over trusted paths and can take multiple forms ranging from entry of a userid–complex password combination to authentication based on biometrics. A complex password is a mix of alphabetic, numeric, and special characters. ALIS supports biometrics access control technologies such as finger- and eye-print reading.

Access attempts and data regarding the target and operator responsible for provisioning are systematically time-tamped and logged. Access to this data is subject to stringent authentication and authorization procedures, including biometrics access control and encryption algorithms.

To allow for optimal security, the information exchange between the access point (e.g., eye-print reading device) and the user authentication entity takes place over a secure link with encryption capabilities. Unlike password entry, it is not possible to "borrow" a fingerprint to log onto the system. Thus, biometrics access control is a means of clearly identifying who does what on the system.

6.1.2.1.7 Billing

ALIS's billing capabilities offer added value to TSPs. Billing can be based on criteria such as length of interception period, number of IRI/CDCs handled, or number of events treated (calls, e-mail, or FTP sessions).

Because ALIS is a multi-administration solution, different billing criteria can be used in different administrations. To comply with stringent confidentiality requirements, target identity and LEA access number can be hidden in billing reports. Invoices can be delivered in formats and frequencies conforming to the requirements of LEAs.

The ALIS billing system also enables a communications services firm or other independent agency to offer outsourcing of lawful interception services (when regulations allow) and thereby generate new revenue streams.

6.1.2.1.8 Alarms and Statistics

A reliable series of alarms and statistics are produced and logged by ALIS. Alarms can be sent to the global alarm management center of the network through protocols such as SNMP. If required, they can also be sent to the LEA. Export of alarm information via file or removable media is supported.

6.1.2.1.9 Activity Logging

ALIS produces a series of system logs and interception operation logs. Because the information contained in these logs is critical to law enforcement authorities, only users with the appropriate credentials are given access and authorization to manipulate this sensitive data.

6.1.2.2 Physical Architecture and Deployment Alternatives

The modular architecture of ALIS supports a series of possible configurations to optimally address the operational requirements of a communications services provider, an LEA, or a particular interception order.

6.1.2.2.1 All-in-One Box

"All-in-one box" is a turnkey, portable solution in which all functional components (provisioning, mediation, and delivery) are located within a transportable system. Provisioning is performed over trusted paths and can be done either locally or remotely. To allow for provisioning operations to be performed via third-party applications, electronic provisioning processing capabilities for such applications are also supported.

In addition, this solution supports multiple interceptions of the same target and delivery of intercepted content to multiple LEAs. Figure 6.4 shows the all-in-one-box deployment alternative.

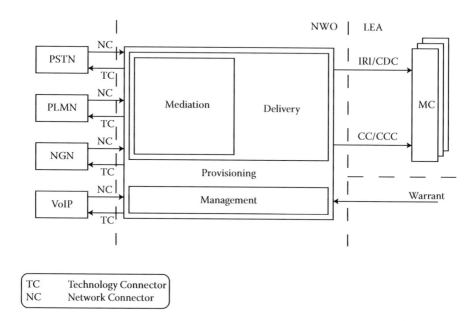

Figure 6.4 All-in-one-box deployment alternative of ALIS.

6.1.2.2.2 Centralized Management and Distributed Delivery (CMDD)

The CMDD configuration separates system administrative and legal responsibilities from technical responsibilities. This configuration allows for a joint approach: Because data collection and data delivery capabilities are colocated but dissociated from provisioning capabilities, they can be shared among multiple networks and network operators. Also, the configuration accommodates a number of interception practices while working with one or many operators over a given network or group of interconnected networks.

Provisioning is performed over trusted paths and can be done either locally or remotely, and electronic provisioning processing capabilities for third-party applications are supported. Again, multiple interceptions of the same target and delivery of intercepted content to LEAs is supported. Figure 6.5 shows the ALIS CMDD alternative.

6.1.2.2.3 Centralized Management and Centralized Delivery (CMCD)

The CMCD alternative is a high-end, permanent, and centralized solution. This configuration allows different operators to carry out data mediation,

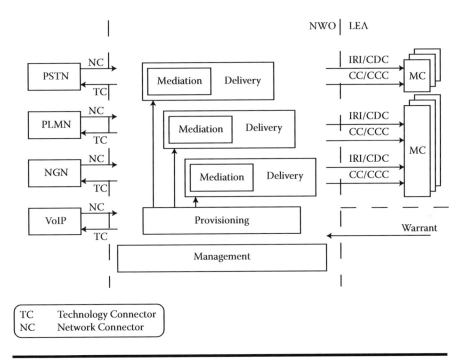

Figure 6.5 Centralized management and distributed delivery alternative of ALIS.

while a single legal entity (e.g., a designated government agency) carries out the centralized functions of provisioning and delivery. CMCD allows for high flexibility in terms of performance and scalability and is cost-effective in that each functional module can evolve independently.

Provisioning is performed over trusted paths and can be done either locally or remotely, and electronic provisioning processing capabilities are available for third-party applications. Multiple interceptions of the same target and delivery of intercepted content to LEAs is supported. Figure 6.6 shows the CMCD solution.

6.1.2.3 Additional Framework Features of ALIS

6.1.2.3.1 Regulatory and Standards Compliance

To preserve its customers' investments and keep its solutions open for future evolution, Aqsacom is an active member of 3GPP and ETSI, and it closely monitors the developments suggested by the leading regulatory and standardization bodies. ALIS is compliant with recommendations of 3GPP, ETSI, and CALEA and supports several other national lawful interception requirements (e.g., those of Australia, Belgium, France, Norway, Sweden, Germany, and the Netherlands).

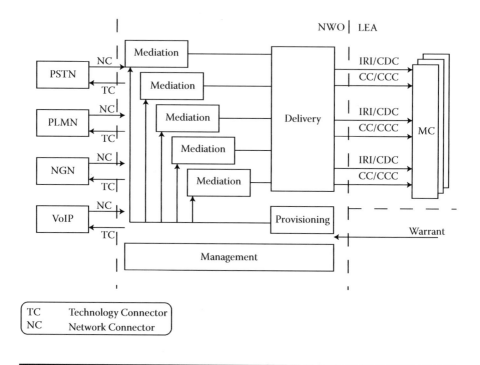

Figure 6.6   Centralized management and centralized delivery alternative of ALIS.

6.1.2.3.2 Vendor Compliance

Aqsacom's solutions comply with the specifications of the vast majority of telecommunications and IP equipment manufacturers, including Alcatel, Cisco, Ericsson, Juniper, Lucent, Motorola, Nokia, Nortel, and Siemens.

6.1.2.3.3 Characteristics

Aqsacom orders and deploys hardware locally to fully comply with local technical, safety, security, and environmental requirements. ALIS runs on standard Intel-based hardware. The underlying operating system is either Microsoft Windows (NT and 2000), UNIX, or Linux.

6.1.3 GTEN AG Framework

GTEN AG partners with network providers and providers of telecommunication services to address their legal obligations concerning monitoring of voice and data communications. GTEN develops technical facilities that fulfill the requirements involved in implementing legal surveillance actions for monitoring telecommunications. The GTEN solution is not dependent on network components provided by various manufacturers; thus, the company can offer effective alternatives with regard to efficiency as the technical basis of service concepts in combination with implementation of monitoring missions.

GTEN offers its customers a complete overall concept with regard to implementing monitoring missions, including all necessary activities, services, and systems. The solution is based on technology developed in strict compliance with legal requirements, guidelines, and regulations, and a corresponding framework concept.

The GTEN framework concept has been certified by the German Federal Ministry of Economics and Technology (BMWi). The existing license (e.g., for packet switching networks such as X.25 and frame relay) has been expanded to include xDSL, Ethernet, ATM, and EDSA technologies.

Benefits of GTEN framework solutions can be summarized as follows:

■ Monitoring technology (monitor server/data collection and filter unit [DCFU] and monitor client) is provided in the form of an integrated framework. This technology is continuously adapted to meet valid legal regulations and implementation regulations as well as to ensure compatibility with new and future technologies.

■ Security-cleared personnel are provided for implementation of measures.

■ Supply, installation, and configuration of systems are provided to allow TSPs to conduct monitoring missions independently.

■ All technical and organizational tasks relating to implementation of monitoring solutions (e.g., coordination meetings with LEAs and regulatory authorities) are supported.

■ Costs are reduced because no investment in GTEN monitoring technology is required; GTEN remains the owner of the equipment.

■ Costs are reduced in that no subject matter experts are needed for maintenance and servicing work or for monitoring missions on behalf of TSPs.

■ A variety of intercepts are implemented simultaneously, resulting in high scalability.

■ Support is provided in the form of assistance in applications for individual licenses granted by the German regulatory authority within the limits of the GTEN concept, as approved by the BMWi.

■ Compliance with legal requirements is achieved, as specified in the appropriate valid legislation.

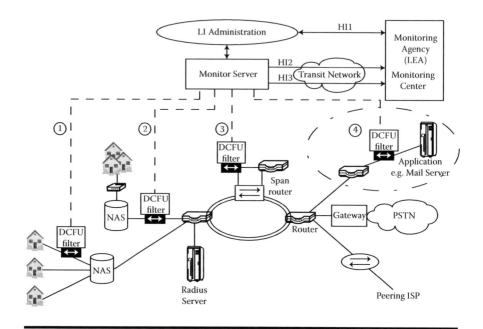

Figure 6.7 Architecture of the GTEN framework. (Legend to the figure: 1. Wire tapping on the access line to the network access router (NAS). 2. Wire tapping on the connection from the NAS to the core router. Listening in to the dynamic allocation of IP addresses by evaluating the dialogue between the NAS and the RADIUS server. 3. In the case of policy routing, the wire tapping takes place on the connection to the span router. 4. Wire tapping on the access line of a mail server or other application server.)

- Planning reliability is guaranteed in that all monitoring systems undergo continuous development to ensure compliance with new legal requirements (e.g., prospective European solutions based on ETSI).
- Support of future LIs is secured by continual implementation and integration of new network technologies and services (e.g., xDSL and VoIP).

In implementing the GTEN solution, there are special requirements for the installed networking equipment due to the fact that this technology intercepts the communications at the access or interconnection lines.

The simplified architecture of the framework is shown in Figure 6.7.

The DCFU/monitor server is temporarily installed in a pool concept as needed and is then connected to the tap on-site. Taps available in the network can also be used.

The LI system can be activated from different locations, depending on the configuration of the existing network infrastructure and the type of investigation needed. The TSP can achieve savings in operating costs due to the fact that the monitoring technology does not need to be implemented on each hub or point of presence (PoP). In addition, the systems can be implemented independently from the topology and configuration of the network without the need for the TSP to make any changes.

If monitoring missions are to be carried out according to guidelines, a number of technical tasks must be dealt with. The most important are as follows:

- Filtering out the telecommunications that need to be monitored
- Interface conversion
- Timing synchronization/resynchronization
- Bit-rate adaptation
- Automatic speed detection
- Automatic protocol detection
- Transfer of data to the LEA
- Simultaneous provisioning for several LEAs
- Authentication of subject matter experts
- Handling of transit networks

The GTEN technology consists of a monitor server/DCFU (installed in the TSP's own network) and a monitor client (installed at the LEA). When in operation, the DCFU is connected to the access line or to the network access point of the network provider that supplies the telecommunication service for the targeted subject of monitoring. The DCFU recognizes the telecommunication to be monitored and generates a copy of it. This copy is then transmitted to the switching monitor server.

The monitor server conveys the telecommunication that is to be monitored over the transit network to the monitor client, which is installed in close proximity to the LEA's recording device. It controls and monitors the calls being set up and completed in the transit network in the case of a dial-up connection. Both a dial-up and a fixed connection are used to monitor the incoming and outgoing data of the target. The monitor server provides support for the different topologies of the transit network. In addition, authentication too is provided.

The monitor client accepts the data transmitted over the transit network by the monitor server and relays it to the LEA on a standard V.11 interface. This integral part of the GTEN solution is always available to the LEA during a monitoring mission.

During a monitoring mission, all transit network connections are included in the closed user group (CUG) on both the monitor server side

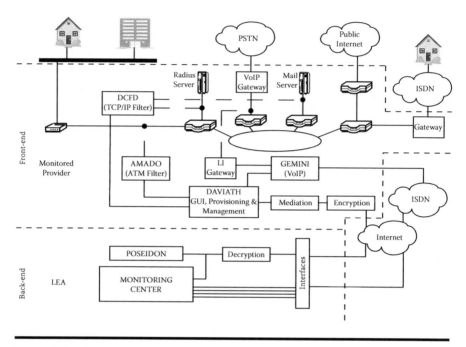

Figure 6.8 GTEN product environment.

and the monitor client side. This feature, along with the checking of calling party numbers, guarantees protection against blockage and transfer of information.

The interfaces supported are fixed connections (V.24, X.21, I.430, E1, and EDSA), packet-transmitted connections (X.25 and frame relay), and integrated services digital network (ISDN)-dialed connections (S_0 and S_2M). Protocols are as follows:

- X.25
- Frame relay
- ATM
- Ethernet
- xDSL
- IP (also includes VoIP)
- All other HDLC-based protocols

The GTEN product portfolio is displayed in Figure 6.8.
The most important front-end products are:

- *Daviath:* The Daviath monitoring system consists of an operator, management, and mediation subsystem and is complemented by network and service-dependent components for data acquisition and filtering. The primary use is for IP, including VoIP and e-mail.

■ *Amado:* This equipment receives xDSL data via ATM lines and converts it to IP flows.

■ *Gemini:* This product converts H.323 voice data into ISDN connections. All data required for the interception are provided by the Daviath manager.

■ *Goliath:* The Goliath monitoring system consists of an operator, management, and delivery subsystem designed to monitor ISDN, X.25/X.75, frame relay, and SDLC networks.

■ *DCFD (data collecting and filtering device):* This hardware device filters data out of IP flows, assuming that the IP address of the target is known. Filtered data is forwarded to the mediation device.

The most important back-end products are Poseidon (in charge of recording and reconstructing IP traffic) and Poseidon Mobile (in charge of intercepting, recording, and reconstructing IP directly at any given network site).

The GTEN framework supports both distributed systems and heterogeneous network capabilities. Figure 6.9 shows the distributed capabilities

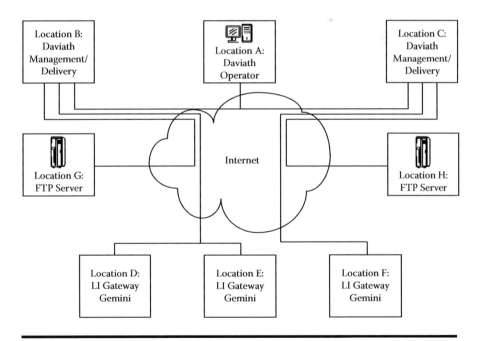

Figure 6.9 Distributed system capabilities.

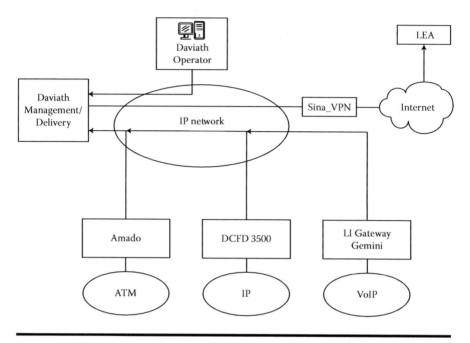

Figure 6.10 Heterogeneous environment network capabilities.

of Gemini and Daviath systems that have been employed at various locations. All locations are securely connected to each other via the Internet.

Figure 6.10 shows an environment with multiple networking technologies, that is, ATM, IP, and VoIP. Each of these technologies requires a different front-end solution: Amado, DCFD, and Gemini, respectively. Daviath operators and managers, as well as LEAs, are connected to each other through a secure IP network.

6.2 Key Products and Players

Different products address different areas of lawful interception. Typically, these products are grouped according to the telecommunications technologies they support. The usual categorization is used here: wireline, wireless, IP, cable, and next-generation infrastructures.

6.2.1 SS8 Networks

Five products based on the Xcipio framework will be described in the following subsections. These products can share the same framework or be deployed individually.

6.2.1.1 Xcipio in Circuit-Switched Networks

Communication intercepts have long been a critical tool assisting LEAs in criminal investigations. As mentioned earlier, the SS8 Xcipio LI platform offers a CSDF that enables service providers to collect real-time communication content or CII from traditional circuit-switched networks and deliver it to LEAs in a standards-compliant format.

The Xcipio CSDF is an off-switch lawful intercept application that supports traditional circuit-switched wireless and wireline networks. The CSDF runs on standard Sun Microsystems servers that include provisioning and intercept capabilities. Once a lawful interception is authorized by a court order, the Xcipio provisioning engine provisions the CSDF with target-identifying information. This information is then used to provision network switches with the target's identity, collect intercepted information from these switches, and deliver this information to the authorized LEAs — all in real-time.

Pertinent call information and voice communications are collected from network switches, and the CSDF platform manages information processing, routing, replication, identification, encapsulation, and delivery to the LEA in a standard format allowing secure access.

The CSDF application utilizes a proprietary switch matrix platform designed to deliver call content to LEAs. A common interface simplifies setup and operation. TSPs can deploy Xcipio to meet the specific needs of LEAs in a secure manner and do so without disrupting their existing voice and data service offerings. Key features of CSDF are as follows:

- It supports multiple switches from a wide range of network equipment vendors.
- It supports simultaneous fan-out of intercept communications information to multiple LEAs.
- Its flexible architecture supports colocated, regional, or centralized deployment models and networks of any size.
- It is rapidly deployable and can adapt to new surveillance requirements quickly.
- It offers scalability that enables TSPs to easily expand LI capabilities throughout their current as well as future networks.
- It offers multiple security features for securing data transport, delivery, and LEA access.
- It uses a proven, field-hardened platform and OA&M features, including ITU-standard MML support, surveillance-provisioning GUI, built-in remote-testing tools, alarm reporting and error logging, automatic software fault recovery, and automatic or manual disk backup.
- It is compliant with CALEA, J-STD-025A, and ETSI standards.

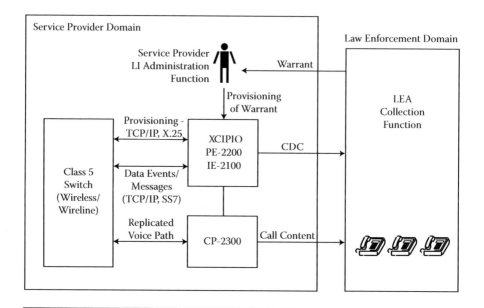

Figure 6.11   Xcipio CSDF architecture.

Figure 6.11 displays the Xcipio CSDF architecture.

6.2.1.2 Use of Xcipio for Intercepting Internet Access

The Internet has brought about significant growth in IP-based communications. E-mail, chat, file transfer, VoIP, and instant messaging applications constitute the bulk of such communications.

Individuals involved in criminal activities increasingly hide behind the Internet's anonymity. New laws require TSPs and ISPs to cooperate with LEAs in providing interception services. Thus, it has become imperative for providers to offer LI solutions that are effective in the dynamic IP environment. The SS8 Xcipio LI platform offers an IADF designed specifically to intercept and deliver IP traffic to LEAs.

Xcipio IADF provides both access and delivery functions that enable ISPs to deliver session-identifying information and communications content to LEAs using standard protocols, transmission media, and delivery standards. The Xcipio IADF runs on standard Sun Microsystems servers and the Xcipio CP-2300-ISP content-processing module. Once an LI is authorized through a court order, the CP-2300-ISP module is provisioned with target-identifying information by the Xcipio provisioning engine. This information is then used to identify data packets belonging to the target subscriber and extract them from the IP network data stream in real-time.

In addition to passive monitoring capabilities, the Xcipio IADF supports dynamic IP addressing, enabling data packets to be extracted in real-time from network switches and aggregation routers. The CP-2300-ISP platform manages information processing, routing, replication, identification, encapsulation, and delivery to LEAs in a standard format for secure access by authorized users.

The IADF application runs on industry-standard servers and packet switches designed for delivering data to LEAs. Multiple CP-2300-ISP platforms can be distributed throughout a network and controlled by a single provisioning engine platform. As new network elements — such as softswitches, aggregation routers, media gateway controllers, call agents, routers, trunking gateways, and CMTSs — are introduced, additional intercept access points are automatically defined. A common interface simplifies setup and operation. TSPs can use Xcipio to meet the specific needs of LEAs without disrupting their existing IP service offerings. Key features of IADF include the following:

- It supports 10/100BaseT and Gigabit Ethernet streams.
- Output can be encrypted for delivery to an LEA.
- The CP-2300-ISP platform can be hidden in the TSP's network to defeat intrusion attempts.
- It supports simultaneous fan-out of intercept communications information to multiple LEAs.
- Its flexible architecture supports colocated, regional, or centralized deployment models and networks.
- It is rapidly deployable and can quickly adapt to new surveillance requirements.
- It offers scalability that enables TSPs to expand LI capabilities throughout their current and future networks.
- It offers multiple security features for securing data transport, delivery, and law enforcement access.
- It uses a proven, field-hardened platform and OA&M features, including ITU-standard MML support, surveillance-provisioning GUI, built-in remote-testing tools, alarm reporting and error logging, automatic software fault recovery, and automatic or manual disk backup.

Figure 6.12 shows the IADF architecture.

6.2.1.3 Xcipio Content-Processing Module

Lawfully authorized electronic surveillance (LAES), also referred to as "wiretapping" or "communications interception," is a critical law enforcement

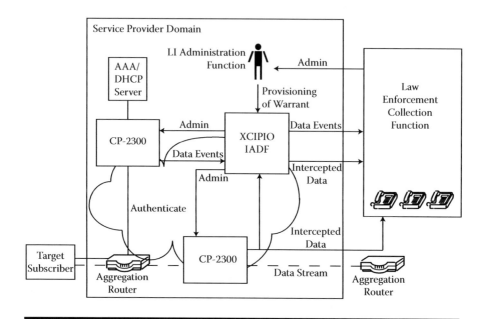

Figure 6.12 Xcipio IADF architecture.

tool that authorized government agencies use to investigate criminal activities. LAES basically involves the collection of communications content or call-identifying information.

LEAs, TSPs, and telecommunication equipment manufacturers have successfully collaborated to develop products and define standards for interception of voice communications. This has enabled wide deployment of interception capabilities in voice-centric, circuit-switched networks. However, with the rapid growth of IP-based networks (such as the Internet) and the now-heavy use of IP-based applications for communications (e-mail, chat, instant messaging, VoIP, FTP, etc.), a clear need has emerged for products and standards that can enable interception of IP-based communications.

The Xcipio CP-2300-ISP content-processing module was designed by SS8 Networks for ISP packet networks. It handles processing, routing, replication, identification, encapsulation, encryption, and delivery of content to LEAs. To perform these tasks, CP-2300-ISP is first provisioned with target-identifying information by the Xcipio PE-2200 provisioning element. This information is then used to identify and filter out packets belonging to the target subscriber. From these packets, "event" messages are identified and sent to the Xcipio IE-2100 intercept engine. The pure content packets are processed by the CP-2300-ISP and delivered to the LEA.

The CP-2300-ISP module precisely extracts application information in real-time from an IP network. This module represents a cost-effective and easy-to-implement solution that meets the specific needs of LEAs without disrupting the data services offered by TSPs. Key benefits are as follows:

- It includes optimal granularity to preserve privacy.
- Its flexible architecture allows for configurations based on country-specific regulations.
- It captures only the traffic to or from the entity listed on the warrant; the privacy of all non-warrant-defined IP traffic is preserved.
- It operates at high speeds without service disruption.
- The high operation speed (measured in Gbps) ensures interception of all IP traffic for a specific warrant-defined suspect.
- Its nonintrusive network connectivity avoids disruption or degradation of customer services.
- Traffic is intercepted in the core of the network, minimizing the number of devices that need to be used and reducing the required investment for IP-interception deployments.

In terms of other key features, CP-2300 ISP:

- Complies with current and emerging standards for IP interception (J-STD-025, TIIT, ETSI, etc.) and meets the interception requirements of various governments (such as CALEA in the United States)
- Connects to the network in a nonintrusive mode
- Collects IP traffic and filters out the exact information requested by a provisioning system
- Filters traffic based on IP address, MAC address, e-mail address (Simple Mail Transfer Protocol [SMTP] and Post Office Protocol 3 [POP3], using to, from, and cc fields), RADIUS log-in name, Dynamic Host Configuration Protocol (DHCP), and universal resource locator (URL)/universal resource identifier [URI] (to and from). Additional filters are planned for future releases.
- Supports provisioning and device management API
- Formats and delivers filtered data to LEAs based on international standards
- Supports both 10Base-T/100Base-TX with two 1000Base-SX port configurations

Figure 6.13 displays the Xcipio CP-2300 ISP architecture.

6.2.1.4 Xcipio in Wireless Data Networks

Data communications are no longer restricted to landline networks. Growing amounts of data are now being sent via wireless devices such as

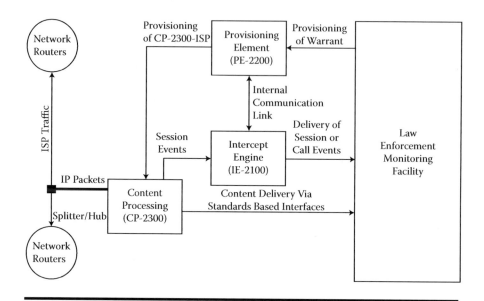

Figure 6.13   Xcipio CP-2300 ISP architecture.

personal digital assistants, laptops, and phone-camera-instant messaging combination platforms. Including the ability to intercept this wireless data is essential if a TSP is to comply with the standards of LEAs. SS8 Networks' Xcipio wireless data delivery function (WDDF) offers TSPs a solution to provision and deliver communication data and content extracted from wireless networks.

The WDDF solution enables TSPs to deliver packet-based wireless data and transmission information to LEAs over standard protocols and media. It runs on standard Sun Microsystems servers, providing LI capabilities for cdma2000 and GPRS networks. In addition to supporting traditional passive monitoring approaches, WDDF can also interface directly with existing network elements such as authorization and accounting (AAA) servers, packet data servicing nodes (PDSNs), serving GPRS support nodes (SGSNs), and gateway GPRS support nodes (GGSN). Direct interfaces eliminate the need for additional hardware, in turn reducing the costs and administration operations associated with provisioning wireless data intercept capabilities.

The Xcipio WDDF application is designed specifically for delivering data to LEAs. Once an LI has been authorized by a court order, the platform is provisioned with target-identifying information by the Xcipio provisioning engine. The provisioning engine's easy-to-use interface enables service providers to provision network elements, such as authentication, AAA, PDSN, and SGSN platforms, across the network.

Target data packets are extracted in real-time and then processed and delivered to the LEA in a standard format with secure access by authorized users. TSPs can use WDDF to meet LEAs' specific needs without disrupting existing wireless service offerings. Designed for maximum flexibility, the Xcipio platform can be deployed by local or regional TSPs, and it can be scaled to meet the needs of large domestic or global carriers. The key features of WDDF include the following:

- It supports both current and next-generation wireless network standards, including cdma2000 and GPRS.
- It interfaces directly with network elements, eliminating the need for intermediate boxes and extra hardware.
- Its flexible architecture supports colocated, regional, or centralized deployment models and networks of any size.
- Its centralized provisioning capabilities and single point of administration simplify deployment and management functions.
- Its distributed system architecture enables presence and reach across the wireless infrastructure.
- It enables centralized operational management of data delivery to LEAs.
- Its simplified deployment and management features reduce administrative costs.
- It offers multiple security features in the areas of data transport, delivery, and access.
- It supports simultaneous fan-out of data to multiple LEAs and filters data to specific agencies.
- It takes advantage of a proven platform and OA&M features (e.g., ITU-standard MML support, built-in remote-testing tools, alarm reporting and error logging).
- It is compliant with J-STD-025B (cdma2000) and 3GPP TS 33.108 (GPRS) standards.

Figure 6.14 displays the WDDF architecture.

6.2.1.5 Xcipio in Next-Generation VoIP Networks

Internet-based communications include more than e-mail and messaging; as mentioned earlier, VoIP calls will soon become as common as traditional circuit-switched voice calls. As a result, TSPs need new LI solutions that can perform effectively in a distributed softswitch environment and meet LI requirements. The SS8 Xcipio softswitch delivery function (SSDF) is designed specifically to provide intercept capabilities for VoIP networks.

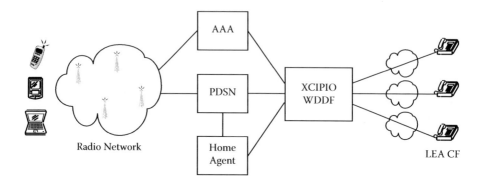

Figure 6.14   Xcipio WDDF architecture.

The Xcipio SSDF enables TSPs to deliver session-identifying VoIP call data and content information to LEAs over standard protocols and transmission media. The SSDF runs on standard Sun Microsystems servers and enables lawful interception of VoIP communications in next-generation networks. Once an LI has been authorized, the Xcipio provisioning engine provisions the platform with target-identifying information. Through its easy-to-use interface, the provisioning engine enables service providers to provision other elements across the network.

The SSDF supports dynamic IP addressing, enabling targeted voice packets to be extracted in real-time from network switches and aggregation routers. The SSDF platform manages information processing, routing, replication, identification, encapsulation, and delivery to LEAs in a standard format for secure access by authorized users.

Compatible with most manufacturers' softswitches, the SSDF's call-agent interface simplifies setup and monitoring. In addition to supporting traditional passive monitoring approaches, the SDDF can also interface directly with existing network routers. Direct interfaces eliminate the need for additional hardware, reducing expenses associated with provisioning intercept capabilities in next-generation networks.

As with other Xcipio features, TSPs can deploy SSDF to meet the specific needs of LEAs and do so without disrupting their existing IP service offerings. SSDF involves several key features:

- It supports a considerable range of network elements, including softswitches, media gateway controllers, call agents, routers, trunking gateways, and CMTS.
- Its flexible architecture supports colocated, regional, or centralized deployment models and networks of any size.
- Its centralized provisioning capabilities and single point of administration simplify deployment and management.

- Its distributed system architecture enables reach across an entire IP network.
- It enables centralized operational management of call-data delivery to LEAs.
- Its simplified deployment and management features reduce administration costs.
- It reinforces network security measures through centralized management of call-data delivery.
- It offers multiple security features for data transport, delivery, and access.
- It supports simultaneous fan-out of specific CDC and CCC messages to multiple LEAs and filters data to specific agencies.
- It takes advantage of a proven platform and OA&M features, including ITU-standard MML support, surveillance-provisioning GUI, and built-in remote-testing tools).
- It is compliant with J-STD-025, PacketCable, CALEA, and ISC standards.

Figure 6.15 displays the SSDF architecture.

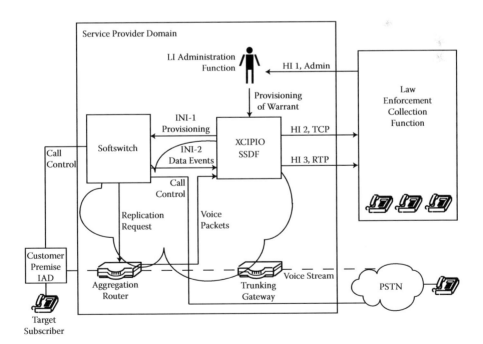

Figure 6.15   Xcipio SSDF architecture.

6.1.2.6 Common Attributes of SS8 Products

The common features are summarized as follows:

6.1.2.6.1 OA&M

The Xcipio OA&M platform has been deployed in more than 50 countries. Xcipio implements a GMOS that is responsible for maintaining and administering delivery functions, configurations, and databases. It also protects intercept controls, intercepted call content, and call-identifying information, consistent with TSPs' security policies and practices.

6.1.2.6.2 Security

A comprehensive range of security features ensures a secure platform and secure access for law enforcement users. Physical access to Xcipio is restricted to network connectivity via the Ethernet card or a direct RS232 port. Authentication, encryption, and security features safeguard data and content. Rule-based user privileges can be tailored to restrict system access to necessary and appropriate users.

6.1.2.6.3 Support of Standards

Compliance with industry and international standards enables LI to take place regardless of geographic borders. Xcipio CSDF supports delivery of call content and call-identifying information in real-time, telco environments in compliance with CALEA. Xcipio also supports J-STD-025A and ETSI requirements.

6.1.2.6.4 Industry Partnerships

SS8 Networks works closely with TSPs and network equipment manufacturers to deliver robust intercept solutions. In addition, SS8 acts as a liaison between equipment vendors, TSPs, and the law enforcement community, exchanging new ideas, supporting existing solutions, and ensuring that future solutions will continue to meet their needs.

Training and knowledge transfer are key elements of SS8 LI solutions. The company provides extensive support to system administrators, operators, and agents who install, maintain, and use the Xcipio platform.

6.2.2 Products from Aqsacom

Based on the ALIS framework, multiple Aqsacom products can share the same framework or be deployed individually.

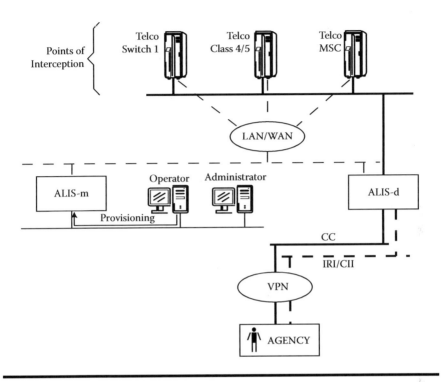

Figure 6.16   ALIS solution for voice lawful interception.

6.2.2.1 Voice Lawful Interception Solutions

Figure 6.16 depicts a classical voice application for both PSTN and PLMN networks. The solution complies with standards such as CALEA J-STD-025, ETSI ES-201-671, and 3GPP 33.107, as well as local law enforcement regulations. The voice mediation capabilities of ALIS allow for voice data to be delivered to the LEA in either TDM/circuit switch mode or voice over packet (VoP) mode (e.g., VoIP).

6.2.2.2 IP Lawful Interception Solutions

The ALIS architecture for IP interception applies to xDSL, dial up, cable modem, satellite, 802.11, fixed, and other IP network access technologies. Interoperability with all major IP networking equipment vendors and conformance to emerging standards (e.g., ETSI DTS 102.232/234) and local law enforcement requirements are essential for effective delivery of interception data to LEAs. Figure 6.17 shows the ALIS solution for IP lawful interception.

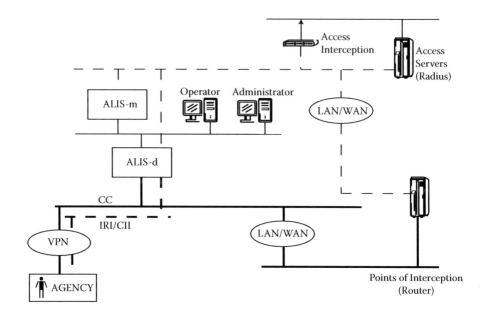

Figure 6.17   ALIS solution for IP lawful interception.

6.2.2.3 E-Mail Lawful Interception Solutions

Given e-mail's role as an essential mode of communication, it is only logical that concerned parties, such as business and residential users, be given the tools to carry out lawful interception of e-mail traffic and be able to fight unwanted bulk e-mails (spam), which now constitute more than half of all e-mail messages.

Equally important with regard to effective delivery of interception data to LEAs is interoperability with all major IP networking equipment vendors and conformance to emerging standards. Figure 6.18 shows the ALIS solution for e-mail lawful interception.

6.2.2.4 VoIP Lawful Interception Solutions

The ALIS architecture, mediation capabilities, and standards support (e.g., TS 102 232, TS 102 233, TS 102 234, etc.) allow lawful interception operations to include VoIP applications. The voice mediation capabilities of ALIS allow voice data to be delivered to LEAs in either TDM/circuit switch mode or VoP mode. Figure 6.19 shows the ALIS solution for VoIP LIs.

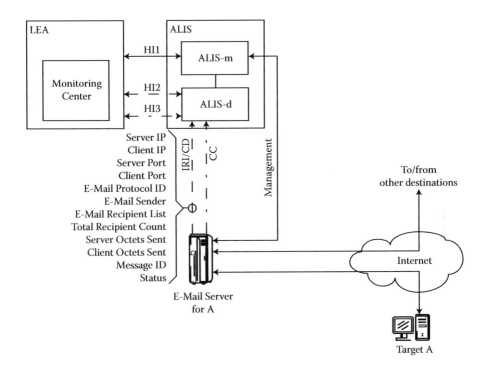

Figure 6.18   ALIS solution for e-mail lawful interception.

6.2.2.5 NGN Lawful Interception Solutions

The ALIS distributed client/server architecture, modularity, and interoperability in terms of current and emerging standards and protocols (e.g., SS7, TCP/IP, H323, RTP, MGCP, MEGACO, SIP, H245) accommodate a multiplicity of interception practices and network architectures, and the voice mediation capabilities of ALIS allow voice data to be delivered to the LEA in TDM/circuit switch or VoP mode. Figure 6.20 shows the ALIS solution for NGN LIs.

6.2.3 GTEN

Multiple products based on the GTEN framework can share the same framework or be deployed individually.

6.2.3.1 Daviath Monitoring System

The Daviath monitoring system is a front-end product that consists of several principal modules, as described in the following subsections.

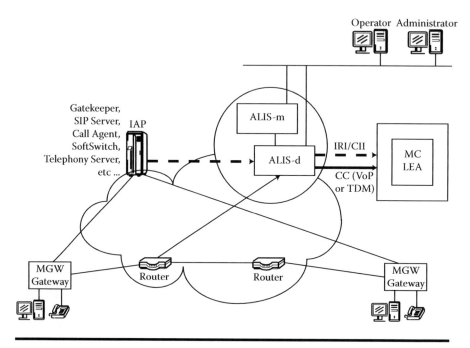

Figure 6.19   ALIS solution for VoIP lawful interception.

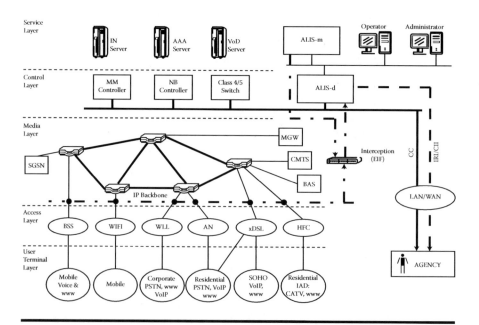

Figure 6.20   ALIS solution for NGN lawful interception.

6.2.3.1.1 Daviath Operator

This is a special application running on a PC under Windows 2000. It is actually the GUI to the Daviath manager. They communicate with each other over the Ethernet interface. For security reasons, no intercept- or user-related data is stored on the operator PC. The operator workstation is responsible for user administration, task control, and rights management.

Users' rights can be derived from allocations to user groups or from the roles users play within their group. Three groups are included in the standard Daviath configuration: (1) administrator responsible for user administration, (2) LI operator responsible for administration of intercepts, and (3) network operator responsible for inventory control of equipment. Each group maintains two roles; those of administrator (with the right to enter, view, change, and delete entries) and assistant (with the right to view entries).

The operator can communicate with a number of Daviath managers over the Ethernet interface deployed at different sites. Communication is supported via IP addresses and the port numbers of the managers.

HI1 administration data may be entered electronically. In such cases, both ASN.1 and XML formats are supported; however, ETSI has recommended use of the ASN.1 format.

6.2.3.1.2 Daviath Manager

The Daviath manager runs on the UNIX operating system and maintains all intercept-critical data and logfiles in a database. It is considered the core controller of all the monitoring systems.

In addition to being responsible for event management and statistics, the Daviath manager is responsible for the configuration of all components of the HI1 information received from LEAs that are part of the surveillance mission. Input can be communicated via the Daviath operator or electronically. The manager is in charge of provisioning and activating the requested components of the network.

6.2.3.1.3 Daviath Mediation Device

The principal task of the mediation device is to sort incoming and available data in accordance with HI2 (IRI records) and HI3 (call-content records). After sorting, data should be delivered to their destinations. As an option, processing and delivery of HI2 data may be integrated into the Daviath manager as an individual subsystem.

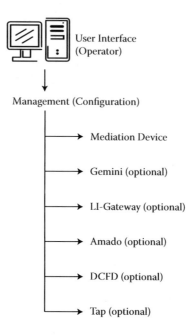

Figure 6.21   Configuration of the Daviath monitoring system.

6.2.3.1.4 Data Collecting and Filtering Device (DCFD)

The DCFD is a hardware component that filters out data from a connection that is monitored in an IP network. A fixed IP address derived from a RSDIUS dialog or e-mail address is absolutely necessary if there is to be unique identification through the filtering process. All filtered data is forwarded to the Daviath mediation device.

On the ingoing side, DCFD supports 10 fast Ethernet or 2 Gigabit Ethernet interfaces. A fast Ethernet interface is available to support the outgoing side. By means of a passive tap (fiber or copper), the data related to connections can be fanned out invisibly, monitored from the network in the form of a data copy, and forwarded to the DCFD input ports. A configuration alternative is shown in Figure 6.21.

6.2.3.2 Poseidon

Poseidon, an IP-recording, database-management, and IP-reconstruction device, collects data communications from various types of interfaces, filters this traffic (if required) according to given criteria, stores the data with a time stamp in raw format in a database, and, if required, reconstructs

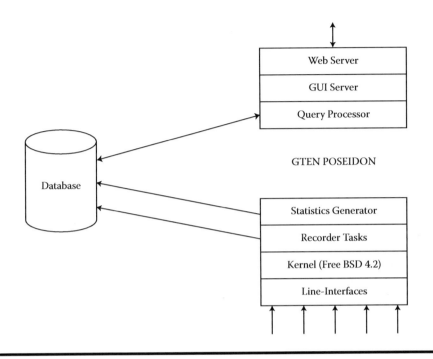

Figure 6.22   Poseidon system configuration.

entire data flows. The Poseidon system is divided into three functional groups (Figure 6.22):

1. Recording of raw data received from various line interfaces
2. Database management with time stamping
3. Reconstruction of IP-based data

6.2.3.2.1 Reconstruction of IP-Based Data

IP data is fed into Poseidon via various line interfaces. All these line interfaces receive but do not transmit, which is why Poseidon is not visible or detectable in a network. The line interfaces operate at full line speed and forward received data to their corresponding recorder task. This recorder task adds time stamps to the raw data and forwards them to the database at wire speed so that they can be stored. In parallel, statistics are generated from the received data and forwarded to the database. The database manages the data, generates statistics from the various line interfaces, and supplies the data according to a query processor (and the GUI server) used in reconstructing IP-based data.

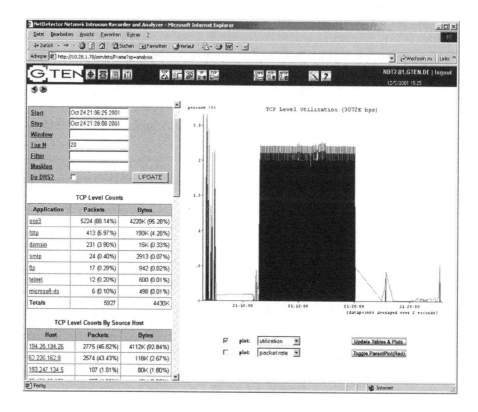

Figure 6.23   TCP application distribution and time graph.

IP-based data are reconstructed by accessing Poseidon with a standard Web browser via the Ethernet management interface. The browser connects to the built-in Web server, which starts the GUI in the browser window. From this GUI, various requests can be sent to the query processor, which extracts the necessary data from the database and forwards them to the GUI server. The server displays the result of the query in the browser window.

One of the key features of Poseidon is its powerful "string-search" functionality. This allows the user to search for any string within the TCP communication, regardless of application data. When the search function is initiated, all recorded TCP data is analyzed. The search results (all TCP applications in which the string was found) are displayed as a list. Selecting the entries begins the reconstruction of these applications. Figure 6.23 shows a time graph and the statistics of recorded data used in reconstructing applications, including the contribution of different applications.

6.2.3.2.2 Functional Description of Poseidon

To receive data from various communication lines or networks, Poseidon is constructed as a modular system. Various receive-only line interface modules can be added to the system. The following network line types are supported:

- 10/100 Ethernet NICs with 1, 2, or 4 ports
- 10/100/1000 copper Ethernet NIC
- Gigabit fiber Ethernet NIC
- T1 NICs for monitoring 2 or 4 FDX links
- E1 NICs for monitoring 2 or 4 FDX links
- FDDI NIC for monitoring 1 FDX UTP or MM fiber link
- V.35 NICs for monitoring 2 or 4 FDX links
- X.21 NICs for monitoring 2 or 4 FDX links
- HSSI NIC for monitoring 1 FDX link
- T3 NIC for monitoring 1 FDX coax link
- E3 NIC for monitoring 1 FDX coax link
- OC-3 NIC for monitoring ATM on MM fiber or SM fiber
- OC-3 NIC for monitoring POS on MM fiber or SM fiber

The network protocols supported are link layer (frame relay, HDLC, CISCO HDLC, PPP, Bay PPP, MLPPP, and 802.3/VLAN) and network layer (IP, ATM and IP, POS and IP, WCP compression, and STAC compression). Poseidon is able to filter or reconstruct data according to these protocols.

The management interface is realized via an onboard Ethernet NIC that supports 10/100 Mbps auto-sensing. It can be connected to a single PC using a standard cross-cable, or it can be connected to an existing LAN infrastructure (i.e., a hub or switch). The basic IP configuration (IP address, subnet mask, default gateway, etc.) can be set up via a serial console port that is built into the system or with a monitor and keyboard directly connected to the system. After Poseidon's IP configuration has been completed and the system connected to the Ethernet, all further configurations can be done via IP-based applications. Access to Poseidon is possible (depending on the configuration of the built-in firewall) for the following applications:

- HTTP or HTTPS (all configuration, reconstruction, and data import/export)
- Telnet (access to operating system when changing line interface modules or shutting down the system)
- FTP (uploading or downloading recorded data files)

The filter mechanism can be applied to the data at two different stages of data processing:

1. *Recording filters:* Filters that check the received data before they are stored in the database. Only data meeting the filter rules are forwarded to the database. Any data not meeting these criteria are not recorded.
2. *Query filters:* Filters that are designed for the query processor only and applied for reconstruction only. For example, all captured data is kept in the database, ready for other queries using different filters, string searches, or other applications.

Poseidon is configured in two steps:

■ *Step 1:* The basic IP configuration has to be set up before Poseidon can be connected to the LAN. This can be done via a serial terminal port that is built into the system or with a monitor and keyboard directly connected to Poseidon.
■ *Step 2:* After a PC with a Web browser has been connected to Poseidon, either through a secure LAN or through an Ethernet cross-over cable, an HTTP session will be established. This configuration includes the following:
  – Adding users who are allowed to access Poseidon
  – Starting or stopping the recording tasks on the line interface modules
  – Applying filters to the recording tasks, if required
  – Defining various alarms triggered by the recorded data, if desired
  – Selecting the firewall rules that apply to the management interface

A wide variety of alarms may be created. If an alarm is triggered, an e-mail may be sent to attract a prosecutor's attention.

6.2.3.2.3 Reconstruction of Recorded Data

Reconstruction of recorded data can be initiated at any of the data communication layers involved in the process:

■ PPP link (displayed as ASCII or HEX) (PAP, IPCP, and LCP)
■ Ethernet link (displayed as ASCII or HEX)
■ IP (displayed as ASCII or HEX) (ICMP, UDP, and TCP)

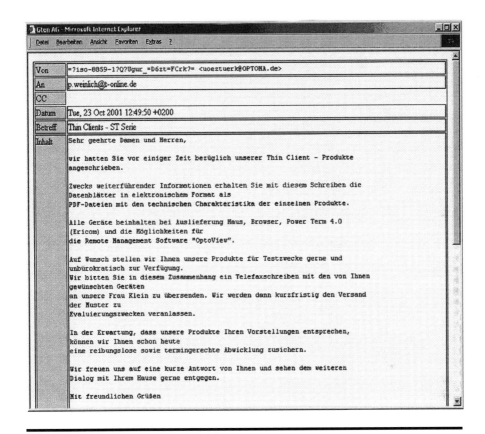

Figure 6.24   Reconstructed e-mail (Session 1) header and content.

■ TCP (displayed as an application; alternatively, it can be displayed in ASCII to allow complete TCP session flows to be seen) (SMTP, POP3, HTTP, IMAP4)

Reconstruction can be completed on any of the applications listed in the preceding text (i.e., SMTP, POP3, HTTP, and IMAP4). The sections that follow provide examples involving e-mail and FTP sessions. All other applications are reconstructed in the same manner and can be viewed in the application or ASCII view mode, as shown in the following text.

6.2.3.2.4 Reconstruction of E-Mail

Figure 6.24, Figure 6.25, Figure 6.26, and Figure 6.27 provide examples on how to view a reconstructed e-mail session. First, lists, including all

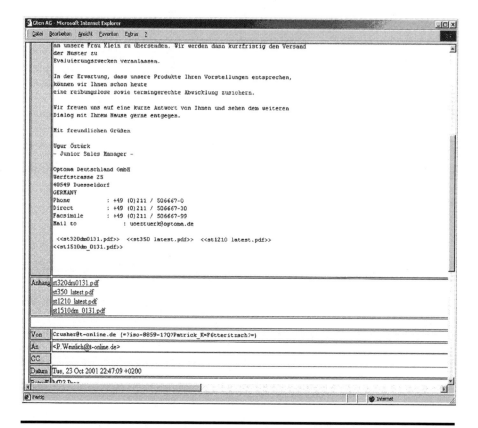

Figure 6.25 Reconstructed e-mail (Session 1) content and list of attachments.

the recorded e-mails (separate lists for incoming [POP3] and outgoing [SMTP] mail), are displayed. All necessary information about the TCP session is included in these lists, that is, IP address of server and client, start and end time of TCP session, TCP port of server and client, and the number of transferred bytes.

One of the entries has to be selected and the "Reconstruct" button activated. The e-mail is reconstructed and displayed as shown in Figure 6.24 to Figure 6.27. E-mail attachments are shown at the end of the reconstructed e-mail. LEAs and other users can click on the attachments shown and open them with the appropriate application (e.g., Acrobat Reader for PDF files).

Another view shows an outgoing (SMTP) e-mail. This e-mail is reconstructed in ASCII to illustrate the complete SMTP session information as well as the content of the e-mail as it was sent from the e-mail client to the e-mail server.

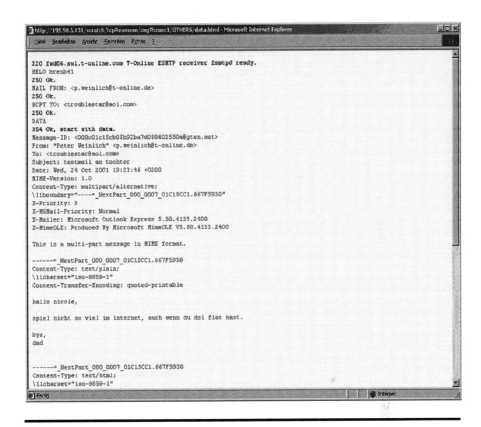

Figure 6.26 Reconstructed e-mail in ASCII, showing complete SMTP session start.

6.2.3.2.5 Reconstruction of FTP Sessions

Character-based applications are reconstructed in ASCII (Figure 6.28). Both the server and client portions of the communication are displayed, allowing the complete session, including all client inputs and server responses, to be followed up. Files transferred during this session with a "Put" or "Get" command are separated from session data. This allows LEAs to reconstruct the transferred files in the same manner as with e-mail attachments.

6.2.4 Utimaco Safeware AG Interception Management System (IMS)

Nearly all countries worldwide engage in wiretapping of certain forms of communications traffic in public networks (mobile, switched, IP, or intelligent networks). Such tapping performed by legal authorities is called

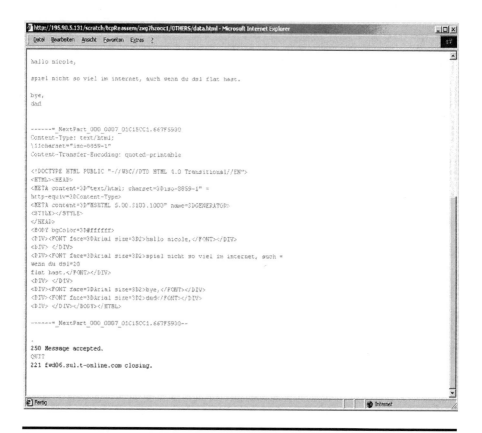

Figure 6.27   Reconstructed e-mail in ASCII, showing complete SMTP session end.

lawful intercept (LI), implying a dependency on international laws and policies (e.g., ETSI, CALEA, and J-STD-25). The interception management system developed by Utimaco Safeware AG is designed to control LI capabilities within different communication networks. It is designed under the aspect of high security requirements to prevent misuse and allow intercepts only in accordance with legal regulations. Figure 6.29 shows the IMS architecture.

The IMS, which is employed in more than 30 installations worldwide, is reliable and easy to use, and it meets the highest levels of security demands. The system consists of the following main modules:

■ *Administration system (AdminSys):* This system is designed to provide assistance with regard to the administration of lawful interception decisions. It collects, stores, and distributes all information needed to carry out lawful interception activities on the relevant network components.

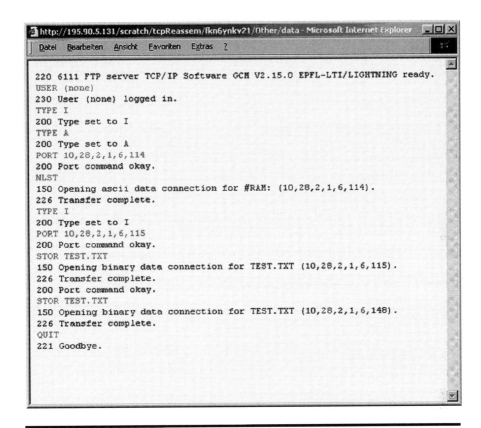

Figure 6.28 Reconstructed FTP session.

- *S-record handler (SRH, Delivery Function 2):* The SRH receives call-related information (S-records) from the network; filters, duplicates, and reencodes this information; and distributes it to the LEA.
- *Communications content handler (CCH, Delivery Function 3):* The CCH is designed for distribution of the intercept data (communications content) in packet-oriented networks. Call content is processed by an external device (DF3 for Call Content, called DF3CC) or transferred directly from network elements to LEAs.
- *Hardware:* Workstations or server systems running on the UNIX operating system serve as the platform for the IMS, and these components are scalable according to the customer's requirements. Different levels of system availability can be achieved via internal or external redundancy, from mirrored hard disks to fully redundant systems in "hot standby."
- *Standard software:* A relational database server is used to store all intercept-related data. Standard products (e.g., communication

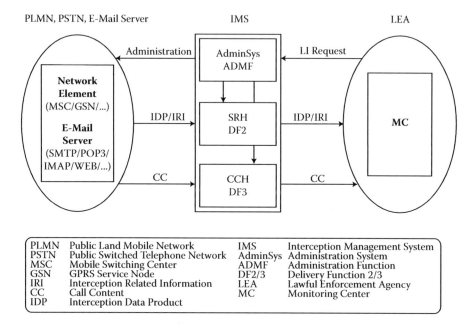

PLMN, PSTN, E-Mail Server   IMS   LEA

PLMN	Public Land Mobile Network	IMS	Interception Management System
PSTN	Public Switched Telephone Network	AdminSys	Administration System
MSC	Mobile Switching Center	ADMF	Administration Function
GSN	GPRS Service Node	DF2/3	Delivery Function 2/3
IRI	Interception Related Information	LEA	Lawful Enforcement Agency
CC	Call Content	MC	Monitoring Center
IDP	Interception Data Product		

Figure 6.29 IMS from Utimaco.

stacks comprising X.25 drivers as well as implementations of OSI and FTAM) are used in communicating with network elements and LEAs.

In addition, the following elements are included:

- Extensive node management with automatic consistency check
- Support of X.25, ISDN, and TCP/IP
- Remote processing
- Logging, alerting, and monitoring
- High security standards (e.g., communication encryption, user access control)

The administration system, S-record handler, and call-content handler modular software architectures allow easy integration of new interfaces. IMS supports multivendor as well as multi-environment networks and can manage separate networks in parallel. In addition, it can be adapted to specific customer requirements (e.g., new interfaces or country-specific regulations).

Originally designed for GSM networks, IMS is now used in different types of networks, including GSM, GPRS, UMTS, fixed, IP, and e-mail.

Interfaces to fixed nodes, GSM nodes (MSCs), GPRS nodes (SGSN and GGSN), UTMS nodes, VoIP/Push-to-talk nodes, softswitches, e-mail servers, voice mail servers, and IP nodes of different vendors and for different releases are available or are under development.

Additional devices for data collection are available for cases in which active interception is not supported by the network nodes.

Key features of IMS are as follows:

- Central management system with heterogeneous networks
- Multivendor capability; one system for GSM, GPRS, UMTS, voice mail, mail server, and others
- Supports ETSI, CALEA/J-STD-0255, TR-TKÜ, and others
- User-friendly GUI
- High availability and high performance by scalable hardware
- Competent professional support services

IMS has been developed in the Transaction Security section of Utimaco Safeware AG in Aachen, Germany. The section realizes innovative customer-specific security solutions in the field of E-payment, gateways, time stamping, and mobile phone–based authentication.

6.2.5 ETI Connect LI Network Connector (LINC)

ETI Connect provides products and solutions enabling TSPs to meet the constantly changing requirements associated with LI activities. The LI network connector is the support component of ETI Connect. It is compliant with worldwide LI standards, such as CALEA and ETSI, and consists of three principal modules:

1. Central management and mediation (CMM)
2. IP box input unit for data acquisition
3. Data retention system

6.2.5.1 CMM

CMM, the core of the LINC concept, is the central component with regard to the management, control, and configuration of the entire system. In addition to the management aspects, this device also performs functions related to mediation and hand over of data to the relevant law enforcement monitoring facility (LEMF).

CMM allows for the configuration of various input sources (routers, ETI input, or third-party units), management of network elements, target setup, distribution to monitoring facilities, integrated auditing, and optional billing of services. The system allows integration with existing monitoring systems because it has been designed to set up target criteria on both ETI and third-party equipment. It accepts streaming input from the IP box input unit and provides interfaces to already-installed systems. Regardless of source and transport media, all data is brought together in a single centralized subsystem for further automated distribution. In addition, CMM simplifies the work of administrators in that it uses the field-proven ETI Control Center central management software.

Data mediation and handover are significant features of LI activities. CMM mediates the data received; that is, it organizes data in a standard output format as per the requirements of individual LEAs or LEMFs. These mediation and organization functions are performed in real-time to ensure nearly immediate delivery to LEAs (and thus maintaining the ability to listen to audio and examine data in real-time). Distribution from the CMM to LEMFs is compliant with ETSI, ATIS/TIA (also known as CALEA), and other standards as required. The unit provides all three handover interfaces, HI1, HI2, and HI3 (authorization channel, CDC, and CCC, respectively), between TSPs and LEAs.

On the basis of identification headers assigned during the acquisition phase, CMM determines which LEMF should receive what data. If data has to be delivered to multiple LEAs, it is copied without delay in the forwarding process. The concept of streaming data from acquisition to LEMF delivery is maintained throughout the system. In addition, the same data can be delivered in different output formats.

6.2.5.2 IP Box Acquisition Device

In the event a TSP's existing network equipment cannot provide the requested IP traffic, ETI Connect's IP box can be used as the input unit. This unit connects passively to IP lines and, based on user-defined criteria, acquires the requested data. Following acquisition, data is forwarded to the CMM, which in turn distributes the required information and intelligence to the targeted recipient. At present, IP box input units interface with LANs (up to 1000 Mbps) and WANs (up to 622 Mbps).

The main task of the IP box input unit is to interface with the various communication lines used in transporting IP traffic and process the layers of data within the communication protocol stack. This allows the requested data to be filtered. Output is forwarded to the CMM. Depending on requirements, the forwarded output of the CMM can be filtered or can simply be the raw intercepted traffic. Management of the IP box input unit is handled by the CMM system. The unit is compatible with the following line types:

- ADSL
- E3/T3/DS3
- STM1-4/OC3-12
- Ethernet 10/100/1000

The IP box is under continuous development. In the future, the unit will support all new types of communication lines and protocols that become available in public networks.

Timely delivery is often a significant requirement faced by TSPs. This requirement can be met by streaming data from the IP box input unit to the CMM and further on to the LEMF, allowing live monitoring of intercepted traffic. Optionally, transport of data from the IP box to the CMM and the LEMF can be protected to meet local security requirements. This can be achieved by securing the transfer with encryption (e.g., IPSec or other customer-specific types of encryption). In addition to protection of data, digital signatures may be added to authenticate and verify data.

6.2.5.3 Data Retention Systems

Data retention is a current focus of various standardization and legislation bodies, and TSPs are faced with existing and, probably, future requirements in terms of retaining data. There is not yet full agreement with regard to the details of these requirements, nor has the time frame for their implementation been established. The function of data retention is basically that of monitoring the activities of a given network without monitoring the actual content of the communications taking place. Therefore, only header information is used for logging of activities, providing a historic as well as current overview of network traffic. All upcoming standards and recommendations will be supported by ETI Connect's data retention solutions.

The company's current solutions include the capability to log and monitor overall network activities, activities associated with specific IP addresses, and traffic based on other user-defined parameters. More specifically, ETI Connect is focusing on four main data categories — ISP data, e-mail data, Web activity, and other services such as instant messaging and P2P — that will be supported in data retention solutions.

The information logged is specific for each of the categories and contains data such as log-on, authenticated username, assigned and used IP addresses, data contained in the from, to, and cc fields of e-mails, URLs visited, and date/time of activity. Time stamping of each activity is very important; hence, the unit must reliably support this aspect of data retention. To ensure accurate time stamps, ETI Connect uses external time stamping (e.g., GPS).

ETI Connect provides a secure and reliable system as part of its overall product strategy, and further services will be implemented as legislation is enacted in different countries. Through such comprehensive statistical analysis and viewing of monitored data, TSPs can identify and track changes in traffic patterns down to individual users. In addition to fulfilling LEA requirements, data retention is a helpful tool for TSPs in monitoring misuse, unauthorized access, or malicious activity, so that steps can be taken to protect their networks.

Key features of the LINC concept are as follows:

■ A high level of data security is maintained throughout the system.
■ Customers' prior investments are protected because input from existing equipment (e.g., routers and switches) is accepted, and there is full integration with existing monitoring systems.
■ The amount of management and data collection necessary is reduced by utilizing a networked solution with central management and mediation, regardless of input source.
■ Timely delivery is facilitated by distributing the monitored data to multiple destinations in real-time, using streaming output.
■ An interface is available with all types of IP communication lines when relevant data is present.
■ A seamless connection is provided between the TSP and LEMF, complying with legal requirements.

In addition to LINC, ETI also develops and supplies complete LEMFs that include tools for meeting the challenges of extensive IP monitoring. The platform is open to multiple data inputs, but results are best when other tools from ETI Connect are also used.

6.2.6 Forensic Explorers NetWitness

For any IT system to be useful, subject matter experts must be trusted to use it. When access is granted to the first user, all best efforts to secure the system can become useless if the user is careless or malicious. After minimizing access as much as possible, the only remaining mitigation technique is to audit and monitor users' actions. Through these actions, misuse can be detected and incidents investigated. NetWitness is designed to provide auditing and monitoring at the one layer that users cannot circumvent: the network layer.

This product audits and monitors all traffic on customers' networks. It creates a holistic log of network activities and, more important, translates these activities to a format that network engineers and management alike can rapidly understand. Investigation time may be reduced from weeks to hours.

NetWitness involves a collection, transformation, correlation, and analysis solution providing insight into various networks. It acts as a video camera focusing on the network, recording all activities and transforming the data volume to a dense, transactional model describing the network, application, and content levels of activities. Advanced analytics enable information security personnel to quickly and effectively check the model for violations of policy and expected behaviors or for pre-event and post-event incident response investigation.

The product "sniffs" the network, reassembles fragments to packets and packets to their TCP/UDP sessions, and then invokes a parser engine that identifies datagram payload against a list of 40 applications. Given the detection of a particular application payload, it exploits the payload to build a transactional model of the events occurring within the session. A dense metadata transactional model is created that includes the IP, TCP/UDP/ICMP, application, and content layers.

In addition, the content of the reassembled datagrams can be saved. These transactional logs, from any number of collection points or third-party application logs transformed into the NetWitness format, can be uploaded to the central database that acts as the back-end to the NetWitness analysis system. Within this system, transactions are summarized and clustered according to end-user requirements. The interface is a Web-based application that creates interactive, dynamic reports on activities from a user's perspective.

Criminals have long realized the value of cyber connections; it is not just the well-trained high-tech professional who takes advantage of it. The Internet knows no boundaries, providing criminals anonymity and a sense of invulnerability as they use it as a tool to plan terrorism, perpetrate frauds, engage in software piracy and corporate espionage, distribute controlled substances, traffic in child pornography, and more.

Without sufficient law enforcement solutions, such criminal activity thrives, resulting in enormous human and financial loss. LEAs need a forensic tool that rapidly and accurately targets violations and provides investigators with the ability to prosecute those who use cyberspace for crime. If the perception of cyberspace as a safe haven is eliminated, those who hide behind the Internet will learn that their crimes will be detected, and that they will be prosecuted.

NetWitness is a network wiretap tool that equips LEAs with a force multiplexer solution in detecting crimes committed in cyberspace. It can be used to analyze all records, including stored records, network pan registers, and network wiretap data. It rapidly summarizes these data into nontechnical evidentiary reports that provide LEAs with accurate leads and tips, profiles of criminal behavior, and additional targets of potential criminal activity — all with a clear chain of custody throughout the network. With this tool, law enforcement officers and prosecutors can clear cases faster, make better use of personnel, and close bigger cases than with manual wiretap-review tools.

For information security officers, those involved in incident response, and IS auditors, gaining comprehensive visibility into network events and determining what is worthy of attention is the major challenge. Insight into network activity can come from any number of applications and host logs, intrusion detection and prevention systems, and network analyzers. However, to be responsive and effective, the network security professional needs all of this information and a tool to quickly process it to determine what is of concern and what is not. Collecting the significant network data is only half the battle. NetWitness also provides extensive analytical tools that can be used to reconstruct activities surrounding an event and answer the question "Who did what, when, and how?"

Unlike a network analyzer, NetWitness does not copy data byte-for-byte off a network and overwhelm analysts with volumes of information of marginal value. Instead, this tool observes bytes, reconstructs them into activities, and abstracts them into dense descriptions of what occurred at all layers of the communication model. In fact, if a customer has invested in a network of sensors or probes, NetWitness can read the collected files from most commercial and open source network analyzers and automate their interpretation. Unlike intrusion detection systems, which provide alerts and respond to recognized attack signatures, this tool collects and retains a record of all activity preceding an "attack," the attack itself, and what happens after the attack.

The most valuable part of NetWitness is its central analysis system. Auditors can use reporting, data mining, and data visualization techniques to uncover suspicious activity, conduct surveillance on suspected hosts or users, reconstruct and replay suspect events, and profile activities that violate laws or corporate policies.

6.2.7 Session Border Control

As TSPs look to creatively reach out to more customers, offer new services, and merge IP networks, an entirely new set of problems arises. Merely connecting two IP networks, whether between customers and TSPs or between two TSPs, creates an entirely new set of security, service assurance, and law enforcement requirements at the network's edge. Those new requirements have isolated today's VoIP networks and have severely limited revenue opportunities for TSPs. There are basically three different applications for deployment of session border control (SBC):

- The first is peering service provider networks. Today, many providers employ managed IP networks with softswitches and gateways to reduce the operational and capital costs of trunking PSTN traffic between central offices. The next step in this network evolution entails connecting these softswitches/gateway islands to expand network reach and minimize PSTN termination costs. SBCs enable these VoIP providers to peer networks for PSTN origination and termination, IP transit, and, ultimately, IP termination and origination.
- The second refers to instances in which facilities-based providers offer IP-interactive communication services, such as voice, video, unified messaging, conferencing, presence and instant calling, multimedia collaboration, gaming, and IP PBX transport, and want to benefit from the use of SBCs.
- The third application takes place at the doorway to the data centers of voice applications service providers. These providers deliver calling card, directory, messaging, and other services to retail providers or directly to users.

Across all these applications, there are critical security, service assurance, and law enforcement requirements that must be satisfied.

An SBC uses the provider's signaling infrastructure to control network access based on layer-5 signaling messages instead of the layer-3 IP addresses utilized by firewalls or routers. When communications are authorized, SBCs allow the media streams to enter by opening and closing firewall pinholes. Most existing firewalls lack the ability to dynamically open and close the multiple ports required.

Concealing network topology is absolutely critical. SBCs perform network address and port translation (NAPT) on all signaling and media packets, including IP addresses embedded in signaling and error messages. As an additional layer of security, SBCs strip all layer-5 routing information to hide network topology and conceal suppliers from customers. The same layer-3 and layer-5 NAPT features can also be used to preserve IP addresses by enabling the use of private addresses for CPEs behind an SBC serving as a network-based firewall.

SBCs also protect against service infrastructure overloads by intelligently limiting incoming signaling messages. In the case of a softswitch that may be capable of handling only 50 calls/s before malfunctioning, an SBC in front of it can reject new call requests above the critical threshold. Another facet of the security problem facing providers is moving traffic through premise-based firewalls. Firewalls allow inbound traffic only if there is a request from the inside.

Whereas NAPT is fine for Web traffic, it presents a roadblock for IP voice or video calls. To overcome this challenge, SBCs support a hosted NAPT traversal feature that does not require any new premise-based hardware or software or firewall configuration changes, thereby preserving existing security policies. This feature exploits periodic registrations by IP phones or other endpoints to keep a signaling port open in the firewall for incoming signaling messages. As registrations pass through the SBC, it maps the firewall IP address to the phone number/username behind the firewall. When an incoming signaling message is received, the SBC sends it to the correct address on the firewall. A similar technique is used for allowing the media through.

SBC technology is critical because as providers move to the next generation, they must address not only security but service assurance issues at session borders. With the use of SBCs, providers can not only guarantee the quality of service-level agreements (SLAs) but also maximize revenues and profits by extending their service reach, delivering innovative services, protecting against service theft, and minimizing expenses. One of the most important SLA assurance challenges involves converging revenue-generating voice, video, and multimedia with data traffic such as Internet, e-mail, instant messaging, and corporate data applications on oversubscribed access networks.

Ensuring session quality requires guiding routers on both ends of the access network to correctly prioritize traffic. Any accepted session must be given top priority. Because the SBC is the destination for all signaling and media flows, access routers and the provider's edge routers can easily prioritize authorized session traffic based on the IP address of the SBC. These mechanisms are also valuable tools for delivering new high-quality, revenue-generating SIP-based services such as instant calling and video conferencing. When an SBC is used as an intermediate source/destination, traffic classification problems are eliminated.

Similar admission control issues are presented with transit links between providers. Because each transit link has a finite capacity, the SBC must actively manage the number of live sessions to prevent additional calls from degrading the quality of all the calls active on the link. For optimal routing across the backbone network, SBCs can explicitly assign QoS markings (ToS bits, DiffServ code points, or MPLS labels), off-loading this task from overworked edge routers. Alternatively, the router can perform this function, because all signaling and media traffic is going to/coming from the SBC.

The explicit QoS marking also insulates networks from QoS theft by removing the need to trust any packet markings originating from another network. When an SBC is used, the only media packets transported with high-quality status across the backbone are those authorized by a provider's signaling infrastructure. SBCs also protect against bandwidth theft by policing bandwidth, ensuring, for example, that a low-bandwidth voice call between two SIP endpoints cannot turn into a high-bandwidth video call without explicit authorization.

In addition to overcoming security and service assurance problems, SBCs also help providers meet legal intercept requirements for IP networks in the same manner required by governments for the PSTN. According to CALEA and ETSI, it must be possible to replicate and route specific calls to multiple LEAs. The demand for packet taps is increasing. This must be done in real-time and be transparent to those under surveillance and all LEAs. SBCs are able to accomplish such real-time transparency because they actively control both signaling messages and media flows. Acme-Packet is one of the leaders in terms of providing support for LIs in packet networks.

Because of their control capabilities, SBCs represent strong business opportunities in areas such as peering between TSPs and delivery of services to enterprise and residential customers by facilities-based providers or voice application service providers.

As networks gradually change their look and feel, new problems always arise. But with the assistance of innovative products such as SBCs, neither the problems nor their associated costs need be near as great for IP networks. SBCs do a skillful job of soothing security, service assurance, and law enforcement woes while simultaneously creating opportunities for revenue-generating, lower cost interactive communication services.

The movement to SBC deployments is especially strong in Asia, where there are many greenfield VoIP networks delivering business and residential services. Throughout the world, peering by all tiers of providers is taking place or being actively planned. As Tier 1 providers, with their typically strong installed base of enterprise customers, begin to realize the capabilities of SBCs and seek to further minimize the amount of circuit switching in their networks, it is likely that they too will begin deployments.

Companies such as AcmePacket have already gained traction with many TSPs, and as the interest in SBCs continues to grow and deployments mount, perceptions will soon change. Perception will now be that revenue can be generated out of IP networks.

6.3 Siemens AG Monitoring Center

The Siemens AG monitoring center (MC) is an advanced and flexible, but complex, collection of software modules and hardware components that interoperate to perform monitoring tasks in an auditable, secure, and reliable manner. It handles intercepts of voice and data in fixed and mobile networks as well as the Internet and other IP networks. Within the two general forms of intercept, voice and data, it manages a range of communications methods.

Installations can vary in size from a few computers with customized hardware to an extensive system comprising many servers and racks of customized DSP components depending on the application. Complexity can range from simple passive connections to a single trunk line to responsibility for monitoring an entire country's fixed, mobile, and Internet networks. Sophisticated user rights and access control mechanisms have been designed to meet the needs of LEAs. Implementation is not rigid, and these mechanisms can be used to suit most organizational structures and variations within and from the ETSI standards. The mechanisms also build upon the Microsoft Windows 2000 environment to offer a secure but flexible application.

The system performs these monitoring and management tasks from a scalable, distributable, and reliable platform with facilities designed to ensure the safety of system and intercepted data. Its architecture is modular, allowing systems to be built and scaled as appropriate to customers' needs.

The MC supports a wide range of fixed and mobile switches, Internet local loop modems and protocols, Internet ISP SPAN and backbone IAPs, and the many variations within facsimile standards. It is currently in use in more than 50 countries.

6.3.1 Architecture of the MC

The architecture of the MC (Figure 6.30) has been vital to its success. It is designed with front-end and back-end components. The front-end components are specific to the target network (e.g., PSTN or GSM networks). Multiple front-end components are used to interface with varying switch manufacturers' needs and to scale appropriately to network sizes. All voice and data received are normalized into a single internal format and passed on to back-end applications.

The back end receives the normalized data from the front-end components and correlates and stores this information in a reliable manner according to the configuration of the system. There are two primary user interfaces. The management station (MS) is used to configure the system according to the requirements of the customer and to perform routine administrative tasks such as adding new users or folders to the system. The unified user station (UUS) is used by operators to perform the day-to-day monitoring operations of viewing, reading, and listening to intercepted transmissions.

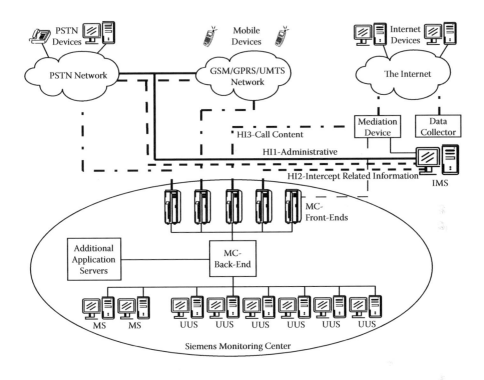

Figure 6.30   MC architecture.

Because of this architecture, as new networks or communication methods achieve more ubiquitous use, and with the consequent need for monitoring, new front ends can be added to the system with minimal changes in terms of management and presentation to the operator. This has many benefits for users: system size increases no more than necessary, there are no "forklift" (total software and hardware replacements) upgrades, and the intuitive handling of the interception, regardless of communication method, remains familiar to the operator. The database of the monitoring center is standard SQL, which allows for add-on applications, either by Siemens (e.g., MC-GIS) or by the customer, to integrate data and existing processes.

6.3.2 Components and Applications

6.3.2.1 Interceptions

The MC manages two general types of intercepts: voice and data. Within these, however, it manages the following more specific types:

- Voice conversations
- Fax transmissions
- Modem transmissions, including local-loop Internet
- DTMF in-band transmissions
- SMS messages
- Call-related information
- Location-based information for mobile networks (GIS)
- Internet sessions

This last item, "Internet sessions," is different from the others because it represents a veritable explosion of communication types, including practically all the other listed items. Currently, most monitoring customers are interested in three main uses of the Internet: Web sessions, e-mail, and chat. These three elements are now managed in the MC, with more types being deployed as their use becomes more prevalent.

6.3.2.2 Networks

Siemens is an innovator in the world communications technology market and a leader in the field of public switched telephone and mobile networks. It has a major presence in all areas of data networks, from transport to IP core routers, and it maintains an MC roadmap that is synchronized to the evolution of telecommunications networks. As an example, the MC is "GPRS/UMTS ready," awaiting the mass deployment of these networks. The MC supports interceptions from the following networks:

- PSTN
- GSM
- GPRS/UMTS
- IP networks (the Internet)

6.3.2.3 Add-On Applications

Siemens is constantly evolving the MC not only with regard to emerging telecommunications trends but also in the direction of applications making further use of available intercepted information. One such application is the monitoring center geographical information system (MC-GIS). In GSM/GPRS/UMTS networks, it is always possible (indeed necessary) for the switch to know the location of a mobile device while it is maintaining an active call. The network knows the location with a certainty equal to the footprint of a mobile cell. This information can be passed to the MC, correlated with other information about the target, and displayed on a geographical map such as a city plan.

Further information can be extrapolated and shown on the map, including the probable direction in which the mobile device user is moving and whether he or she is likely to be walking or driving. Other add-on applications are being considered for development and deployment on the basis of the information contained in the MC database.

6.3.3 Features of the MC

The most important features are summarized as follows.

Principal attributes of the MC include:

- Universal concept for all telecommunication-monitoring requirements
- Network concentrates on fixed-network PSTN (local and international exchanges); mobile-network GSM, GPRS, and UMTS; and IP networks (local loop, ISP, and Internet backbone)
- Automatic correlation of content of communication with intercept-related information
- Mono and stereo, optionally compressed voice recording
- Full-duplex/no-compression recording for data demodulation (fax, Internet, e-mail, etc.)
- Use of customized applications
- Centralized or distributed deployment choices
- Scalable and adaptable to the requirements of the organization
- Joint roadmap for upcoming telecommunication technology

6.3.3.1 Multivendor Capability

The MC is designed for integration with all telecommunication networks (with any type of modern standardized switch following ETSI recommendations, i.e., Siemens, Ericsson, Alcatel, Nokia, Nortel, Lucent, etc.).

6.3.3.2 Use of State-of-the-Art Intercepting Technologies

- Detailed trigger mechanisms enable interception of a "needle in a haystack."
- Filters enable agents to discern the important data from a hub of activity.

■ Hot monitoring alerts agents to the activities of targeted subscribers and allows near-real-time listening, viewing, or reading of communications.

■ A single, unified view of all interception types is presented to the operator.

6.3.3.3 Flexibility

■ Integrates into all existing infrastructures and is applicable to a vast range of monitoring tasks, whether involving fixed, mobile, or satellite-based public networks.

■ Scalable and adaptable on demand to the size of the organization without compromising performance.

■ Capable of handling required features with switch support.

6.3.3.4 Security and Reliability

■ Multiple-level, granular security concept for administrators, agencies, groups, and agents that can be configured to meet customers' differing organizational structures.

■ Built-in reliability from initial interception to transfer to secure media once data is no longer required in the system.

6.3.3.5 Legal Regulations

When required, it is designed with facilities and mechanisms for segregation of data and users and system-imposable intercept inception, completion, and flushing. Designed with ETSI in mind, it is capable of being configured to comply with other legal requirements or country-specific variations as well.

6.4 Selection Criteria

In selecting the correct product for an LI application, several selection criteria are recommended. These criteria can be sorted onto several groups: basic functionality, security features, mediation capabilities, provisioning capabilities, hardware/software requirements, life-cycle support, compliance with standards, price, and vendor reputation.

- Basic functionality:
  - Real-time intercept capabilities
  - Connection to networks (intrusion, nonintrusion)
  - Networking technologies supported (voice, data, wireless, IP, VoIP, etc.)
  - Networking protocols supported
  - Network equipment supported
  - Scalability for higher traffic volumes
  - Ease and speed of deployment
  - Fan-out to multiple LEAs
- Security features:
  - Use of security platforms
  - Use of secure access
  - Use of authentication
  - Use of encryption
- Mediation capabilities:
  - Connectivity to data sources
  - Filtering capabilities
  - Data management capabilities
  - Correlation capabilities
  - Support of rule-based maintenance
  - Support of active mediation
  - Support of real-time mediation
- Provisioning capabilities:
  - Pre-provisioning
  - Testing tools and applications
  - Ad hoc provisioning
  - Use of various deployment models (colocated, regional, and centralized)
- Hardware/software requirements:
  - Receiver applications
  - LEA GUI
- Life-cycle support:
  - Operations support
  - Administration support
  - MML support
  - Management support
- Compliance with standards:
  - J-STD-025A
  - ETSI
  - Country-specific standards

Table 6.1   Product Selection Guidelines

Selection Criterion	Weight (%) (Recommendation)	Scores (Example)	Total (Example)
Basic functionality	30	8	240
Security for hand-over interface	10	9	90
Mediation capabilities	10	6	60
Provisioning capabilities	5	5	25
Hardware/software requirements	5	6	30
Life-cycle support	5	4	20
Compliance with standards	15	8	120
Price	10	5	50
Vendor reputation	10	5	50
Total	100	—	685

Note: 10 = very strong, 1 = very weak.

■ Price:
  − Entry price
  − Maintenance fees
■ Vendor reputation:
  − Financial stability
  − General references
  − Market position for lawful interception

Table 6.1 summarizes these criteria and their recommended weights.

6.5 Summary

The choice of tools used in LI activities is one of the critical success factors associated with these activities. Functions and roles have been addressed, and now it is up to TSPs and LEAs to find the optimal mix of tools that collaborate with their frameworks of choice. This chapter has provided representative examples along with evaluation guidelines, including solutions involving frameworks, best-of-breed products, and the MC concept. If the best possible results are to be achieved, all three of these solutions must complement each other.

We were not able to cover all available tools here. In addition to the tools covered, Alcatel and TopLayer are available for front-end solutions, Atis and DigiTask for back-end solutions, and Syborg and Verint for integrated solutions.

We can mention several new companies: Neturity with the particular strength of intercepting high-speed communications traffic; Netrake with the particular strength of intercepting VoIP traffic; and Mera with the particular strength of intercepting at the Session Border Controller.

Also, several suppliers of routers and switches offer solutions for LIs; Service Independent Intercept (SII) from Cisco and M-Series from Juniper are well-known examples. (Usually, these suppliers partner with one or more tool vendors.)

The Content Services Gateway from Cisco is becoming increasingly significant for lawful interception. The attributes are:

- High performance layer 4-7 packet inspection and reporting platform
- Single-shot line card for Catalyst 6500 or 7600
- Custom network processor-based hardware

The CSG is capable of supporting two methods of lawful intercept for data:

- Data wiretrap by replicating the entire data stream
- Activity reporting with the following capabilities:
  - URLs and hosts visited
  - FTP files downloaded and/or uploaded
  - Server logins (basic TCP/UDP or generic IP session tracking)
  - E-mail correspondence
  - WAP URLs

For integrated solutions, Cisco is working with partners. A well-known example is using CSG as the information source, FusionWorks from Openet as an interception platform, and Central Management and Mediation (CMM) from ETI Connect as a manager for security, administration, and provisioning.

Solution concepts will be introduced in the next chapter, which targets case studies of lawful interceptions involving various telecommunications technologies.

Chapter 7

Case Studies
for ISS Solutions

CONTENTS

Case studies can help provide an understanding of the actual status of lawful interception. In this chapter, we have intentionally selected very different topics for case studies, but all are of practical use. Companies with well-known credentials have contributed, including Lucent, Siemens, Aqsacom, GTEN, and SS8. The case studies address different telecommunications technologies such as traditional voice switching, wireless services, IP solutions, Web activity logging, Voice-over-IP (VoIP), and cable and e-mail interceptions.

7.1 Case Study 1: Wireline Voice Intercept and Surveillance Solutions from Lucent Technologies

Despite new and next-generation technologies, traditional voice still dominates the global market. Lucent addresses this technology with its high-end state-of-the-art voice switches. This technology is mature: lawful intercept (LI) standards do exist, and the legal background is clear and proven. In addition to providing a description of this solution, this study also focuses on handover trade-offs. The two options offered by Lucent help to control the costs of lawful interception activities borne by telecommunications service providers (TSPs).

7.1.1 Network Reference Model

The integrated delivery function of the 5ESS® Communications Assistance for Law Enforcement Act (CALEA) implementation follows the J-STD-025 model. The call content channel (CCC) and call data channel (CDC) can be economically provisioned to law enforcement agencies (LEAs) with a fan-out distribution capability. This model (Figure 7.1) provides a reliable and economical solution without the need for any mediation device.

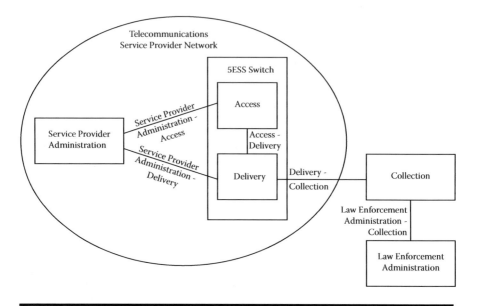

Figure 7.1   5ESS CALEA network reference model.

7.1.2 CALEA Functions

With the network diagram shown in Figure 7.1, it is clear that a TSP should provide the following CALEA functions:

- *Access:* network entity that intercepts a subject's communications and reports call progress data and call content to LEAs
- *Delivery:* network platform that provides the network interface to LEAs for delivery of call content and call data
- *Administration:* capability that establishes and maintains surveillance with a service provider network

7.1.3 Levels of Surveillance (Level I and Level II)

Lucent distinguishes two levels of surveillance:

- *Level I — support of call-related information:* Only call-identifying information (CII) is reported to the law enforcement collection function. Call content is not provided, as level-I surveillance is intended to satisfy pen register and trap and trace court orders.
- *Level II — support of call- and content-related information:* Both CII and call content are provided to the LEA. The intent is to satisfy a Title-III court order.

7.1.4 CALEA Interfaces (SAS, CDC, and CCC)

5ESS can directly interface with the LEA collection box, because the delivery function is integrated within 5ESS to reduce hardware costs. 5ESS uses all existing hardware to support CALEA interfaces. These interfaces include the following:

- *Surveillance administration system (SAS):* The SAS performs subject provisioning using existing 5ESS TTY ports. Although it is recommended by Lucent Technologies that SAS TTYs be ports dedicated specifically for CALEA, they can be shared with existing TTYs used in other activities. Typically, there will be one CALEA terminal for subject provisioning and one CALEA ROP for receiving spontaneous alarms related to CALEA interfaces.
- *CDC:* This network connection reports CII (CDC messages) from the switch to the LEA. Multiple selections are available so that LEAs or TSPs can select the best-fitting interface. The following options are implemented in 5ESS to support the CDC interface:
  - TCP/IP/X.25 (PVC) over BRI, XAT, X.75, or X.75
  - TCP/IP/X.25 (SVC) over BRI, XAT, X.75, or X.75
  - GR-30 CDC
- *CCC:* This connection delivers call content from the switch to the LEA. 5ESS provides a limited number of CCC selections, and for some switches with X.25 packet services, it provides packet data channels used in delivering the call content of the intercepted X.25 packet call. The options implemented in 5ESS to support the CCC interface are (1) dedicated CALEA CCC trunks and (2) dial-out CCC over public switched telephone network (PSTN) lines or trunks.

Figure 7.2 shows CALEA interfaces for high-end compliance, and Figure 7.3 shows simplified interfaces that provide an economical CALEA solution.

7.1.5 Conclusions

The 5ESS CALEA implementation involves some important considerations as well as benefits:

- *J-STD-025 compliance:* The industry standard according to J-STD-025 is to provide "safe harbor" conformance, allowing TSPs to meet their obligations under CALEA.
- *Flexibility:* Different LEAs in different locations may require different CALEA interfaces. Although the high-end solution can provide reliable results in a timely fashion, it may not be appropriate in geographical locations where interception rarely occurs.

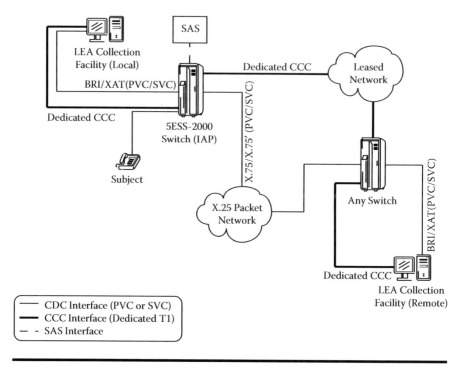

Figure 7.2 CCC and CDC interfaces for high-end compliance.

- *Cost:* The integrated delivery function and dial-out capability have significantly reduced the costs associated with supporting the 5ESS CALEA implementation.
- *Evolution:* The current 5ESS CALEA solution can be adapted to future technologies without affecting the LEA collection box.

7.2 Case Study 2: Lawful Interception in CDMA Wireless IP Networks from SS8 Networks

Existing standards specify that Internet Protocol (IP) access services be available for both simple IP and mobile IP. The CDMA2000 wireless IP architecture is shown in Figure 7.4. The home agent (HA) is not used for simple IPv4 and simple IPv6 access. Considerations relating to simple and mobile access are:

- *Simple IPv4 access:* The user establishes a point-to-point (PPP) link with the packet data serving node (PDSN) and uses a local IP address provided by the PDSN to access the IP network following

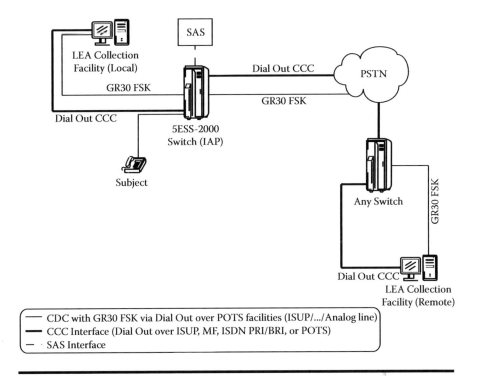

Figure 7.3 Simplified CCC and CDC interfaces.

successful authentication and authorization by the home network. The management station (MS) retains its assigned IP address for the duration of the PPP session. If the user moves to a new PDSN, the MS must initiate a new PPP connection with that PDSN, and the user will not be able to maintain the former IP address.

■ *Mobile IPv4 access:* The user establishes a PPP link with the PDSN and registers with the HA in the home network after successful user authentication and authorization by the home network. The user accesses the IP network via a home IP address. The HA maintains the mobile IP binding information for the MS and forwards data packets to the PDSN in which the MS is currently registered.

According to CALEA, TSPs must provide LEAs with identifying information for communications generated by or destined for the intercept subject, regardless of whether or not those communications are successful. When authorized to do so (and the necessary information is available), the TSP must also provide LEAs with the content of communications

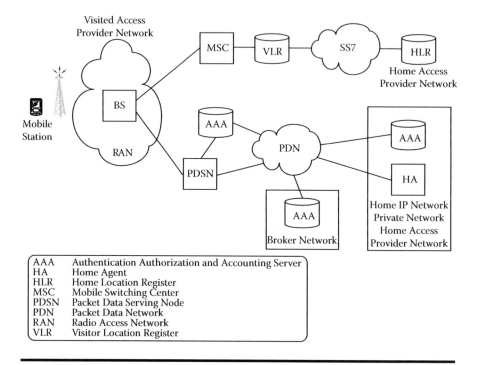

Figure 7.4   CDMA2000 network diagram.

generated by or destined for the intercept subject, including communications that have been redirected or have multiple recipients.

Figure 7.5 shows the basic Xcipio lawful interception model, and the lawful interception function in cdma2000 networks is illustrated in Figure 7.6. Xcipio serves the delivery function (DF) in the cdma2000 network.

The access function (AF), through its constituent intercept access points (IAPs), is responsible for providing access to an intercept subject's communications and CII. The AF typically can:

- Access the intercept subject's CII unobtrusively and make the information available to the DF
- Access intercepted subject call content unobtrusively and make it available to the DF
- Protect (e.g., prevent unauthorized access, manipulation, and disclosure) intercept controls, intercepted call content, and CII consistent with TSPs' security policies and practices

The DF is responsible for delivering intercepted communications and CII to one or more collection functions. The DF typically can:

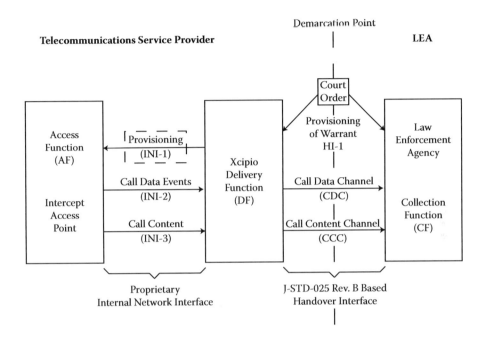

Figure 7.5 Xcipio lawful interception model.

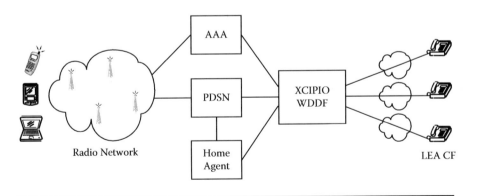

Figure 7.6 Lawful interception in cdma2000 networks.

- Accept call content for each intercept subject from the AFs
- Deliver call content for each intercept subject to the collection functions (CFs)

■ Accept call-identifying or packet mode content information for each intercept subject and deliver it to the CF

■ Ensure that the CII and call content delivered to a CF are authorized for a particular LEA

■ Duplicate and deliver authorized CII and content for the intercept subject to one or more CFs (up to a total of five)

■ Protect (e.g., prevent unauthorized access, manipulation, and disclosure) intercept controls, intercepted call content, and CII consistent with TSPs' security policies and practices

The CF is responsible for collecting lawfully authorized intercepted communications (i.e., call content) and CII for an LEA. The collection function is handled by the LEA.

The AF consists of one or more IAPs. In the cdma2000 packet data network, the IAPs are as follows:

■ AAA (IAP for CII)
■ PDSN (call-content IAP for simple IP)
■ HA (call-content IAP for mobile IP)

Xcipio interfaces with the authentication, authorization, and accounting (AAA) server as an IAP during the process of obtaining CII. Also, it interfaces with PDSN/HAs as an IAP to obtain call content. SS8 Networks is working to develop a common interface for all PDSN/HA vendor equipment.

Several typical call flow scenarios are addressed in this case study:

■ *Scenario 1:* an intercept provisioning scenario in which the target is not involved in a data session when the intercept is provisioned

■ *Scenario 2:* an intercept provisioning scenario in which the target is involved in a data session when the intercept is provisioned

■ *Scenario 3:* data session termination

■ *Scenario 4:* an intercept expiration scenario in which the target is not involved in a data session

■ *Scenario 5:* an intercept expiration scenario in which the target is involved in a data session

7.2.1 Scenario 1: Intercept Provisioning, Target Not Involved in Data Session

Figure 7.7 shows the message flow between the AAA server and the DF when the target is not involved in a data session at the point at which

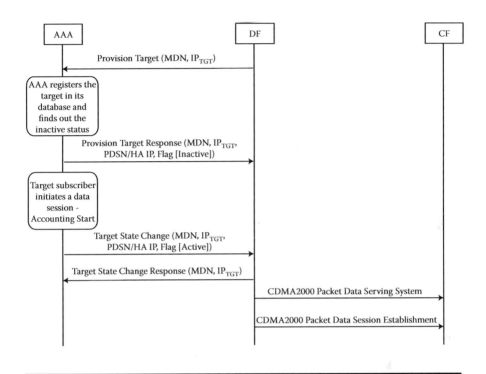

Figure 7.7   Intercept provisioning at AAA (target is inactive).

the intercept is provisioned. Figure 7.8 shows the message flow between the PDSN/HA and the DF when the intercept is provisioned.

7.2.2 Scenario 2: Intercept Provisioning, Target Involved in Data Session

Figure 7.9 shows the message flow between the AAA server and the DF in an instance in which the target is involved in a data session when the intercept is provisioned. Figure 7.10 shows the message flow between the PDSN/HA and the DF when the intercept is provisioned.

7.2.3 Scenario 3: Data Session Termination

Figure 7.11 shows the message flow between the AAA server and PDSN/HA and the DF when the intercepted data session in which the target is involved is terminated.

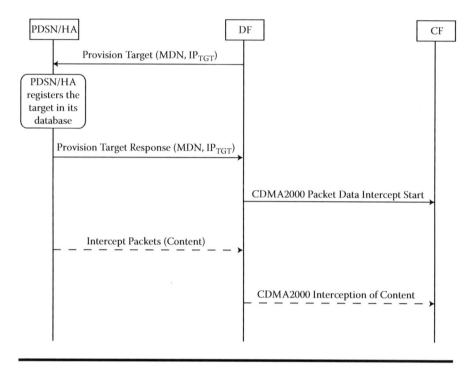

Figure 7.8   Intercept provisioning at PDSN/HA.

7.2.4 Scenario 4: Intercept Expiration, Target Inactive

Figure 7.12 shows the message flow between the AAA server and the DF in deprovisioning the intercept at the AAA server when the court order expires and the target is not involved in a data session.

7.2.5 Scenario 5: Intercept Expiration, Target Active

Figure 7.13 shows the message flow between the AAA server and PDSN/HA and the DF in deprovisioning the intercept when the court order expires and the target is involved in a data session.

The provisioning and message interface between Xcipio and the AAA server is based on eXtensible Markup Language (XML). All messages are intended to be acknowledged. In case of a provisioning failure (due to time-out or other reasons) during the provisioning of the AAA server, Xcipio provides a retry mechanism. The retry mechanism waits for a systemwide configurable time interval before making the next provisioning attempt with the AAA server. The number of provisioning attempts can

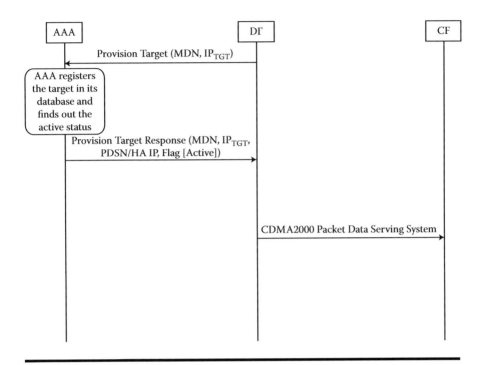

Figure 7.9   Intercept provisioning at AAA (target is active).

be configured according to a systemwide parameter. Xcipio generates alarms in cases in which there are provisioning failures. The AAA server is assumed to have similar time-out and retry mechanisms.

The provisioning interface between the PDSN/HA and Xcipio should be based on scripts running over "ssh." The DF maintains a list of all PDSNs and HAs in the network, with a username and password for remote log-in. Xcipio remotely logs in to the PDSN/HA to provision a target and run the script and then logs out immediately. Each script is designed to return a reason code if there is a failure. There is no retry mechanism for provisioning PDSN/HAs. Xcipio generates alarms upon provisioning failures. PDSN vendors using SS8 networks are expected to provide a common API for the scripts. SS8 works with these vendors closely to develop a common provisioning interface.

The call-content delivery interface between the PDSN/HA and Xcipio is placed over UDP/IP. The PDSN/HA sends the intercepted call content to an IP address and port number on the Xcipio platform. This address and port number are provided to the PDSN/HA on a per-target basis during the provisioning of the target at the PDSN/HA. The PDSN/HA encapsulates the intercepted packets with a UDP header that includes the following information:

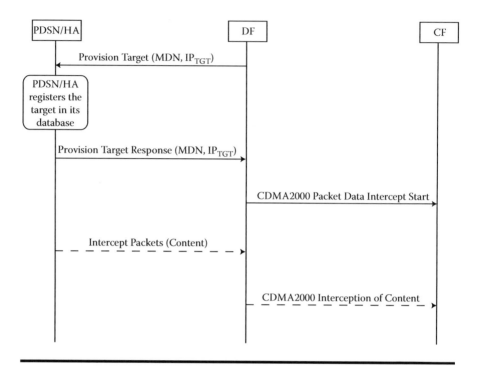

Figure 7.10 Intercept provisioning at PDSN/HA.

- MDN
- IPTGT
- Correlation number (copied from the provision target message)
- Time stamp
- Sequence number
- IP packet direction

Xcipio employs the CDC interface used in the CDC-manager product. This interface is based on the TCP/IP protocol. Xcipio implements cdma2000 call data messages as described in J-STD-025B specifications.

Xcipio also uses a TCP/IP-based CCC interface similar to the CDC interface. Xcipio initiates a TCP/IP connection to the LEA collection function. After the TCP/IP connection has been established, Xcipio uses it to deliver the intercepted call-content packets received from the PDSN/HA to the collection function. Xcipio manages the connection and reinitiation of the TCP/IP connection if there is a failure. As described in J-STD-025B, the interface between the DF and CF is a unidirectional one; there is no acknowledgment mechanism from the CF to the DF. Therefore, Xcipio relies on events and signals from the TCP layer of the Solaris operating system to determine the status of the TCP/IP connection.

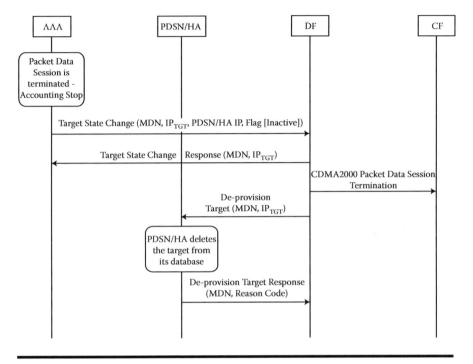

Figure 7.11 Data session termination.

7.2.6 Push to Talk over Cellular (PoC)

There are two basic ways to support lawful intercepts for PoC:

■ cdma 2000 wireless data networks and
■ GPRS wireless data networks

Potential events required for PoC interception include:

■ Registration with the network
■ De-registration from the network
■ Presence or availability information
■ Buddy or group list update
■ PoC call invitation or invite to call
■ Party join/drop
■ Release of a PoC call

Solutions differentiate two ways to intercept PoC communications:

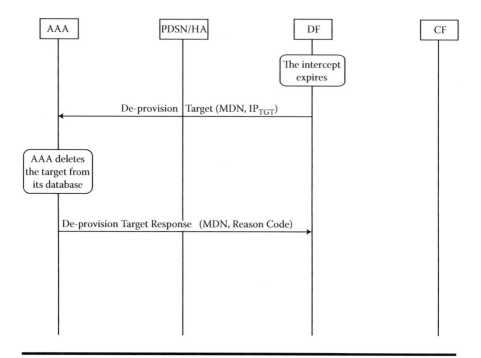

Figure 7.12 Intercept expiration (target is inactive).

- *Passive mode:* Passively monitoring the traffic at the PoC application and buddy list database. This provides a generic solution without depending on the PoC application's capabilities. However, the capabilities of this solution may be limited because it is hard to know the changes in the database in real-time and also join and drop of associates is difficult to determine externally.
- *Active mode:* Using the PoC application as an Intercept Access Point (IAP). This provides a more capable and simple solution because certain events within the PoC application can be made available to law enforcement.

7.3 Case Study 3: LIs for 3G Networks Using ALIS

Although 3G networks promise a number of new applications, TSPs are expected to provision the technology for LIs. IAPs are available in network equipment of 3G architectures, but their volume may increase costs for both TSPs and LEAs. With specific applications, the Aqsacom's lawful interception management solution (ALIS) framework offers an affordable solution for 3G networks.

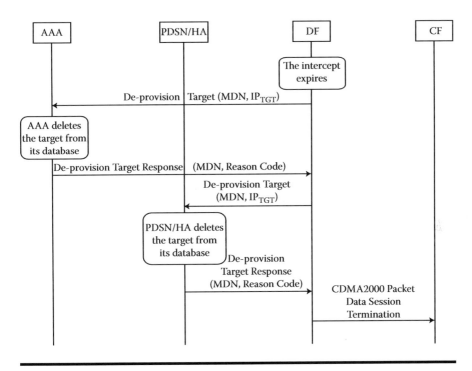

Figure 7.13 Intercept expiration (target is active).

7.3.1 Uses of 3G Technology and Implications for Lawful Interception

First we evaluate a number of typical 3G applications:

■ *Voice:* Although 3G networks are often associated with "killer" applications such as video e-mail and high-speed Internet connectivity, from the operator's point of view voice will likely remain the dominant application operating over 3G networks for the foreseeable future. As users migrate from wireline to wireless services, voice traffic moving over wireless systems and the number of users making voice calls will continue to grow. The increased amount of voice traffic over wireless networks has already had implications for lawful interception activities, in that an increasing proportion of LI requests from LEAs have targeted mobile telephones and their users. For example, according to the U.S. Department of Justice, approximately 70 percent of lawful interception requests during the year 2002 involved cellular phone taps. Trends have been similar in other countries and will probably continue.

■ *Short message services (SMSs):* This application will also continue to grow, especially as the proportion of younger users increases in the overall user population. Although it is not a 3G service in itself, 3G networks will nevertheless have to support this service and its growing usage (now amounting to hundreds of millions of users worldwide). Likewise, lawful interception will have to address the growing use of the service among interception targets, who also take advantage of mobility in their communications.

■ *General Internet connectivity:* Here law enforcement officials are faced with the same set of challenges they face in regard to interception of information on IP networks, namely, assignment of information flow to the targeted accounts from which IP packets originate and terminate. Of course, in the case of 3G mobile networks, there is the added complication of the mobility of the target. As in the case of voice, criminals will probably find mobile Internet connections a "safer" and more convenient means to communicate. Thus, the proportion of Internet communications over mobile networks subject to lawful interception will likely grow in proportion to that of fixed networks. Another factor that will drive the growth of Internet over mobile networks is the variety of devices with which to communicate, including notebook computers (equipped with 2.5/3G modem cards), PDAs, and phones with alphanumeric entry and display.

■ *High-speed photo and video clip upload and download:* Many operators are now offering such services, even over 2.5G networks. As phones with built-in cameras proliferate and improve in image quality, privacy concerns will become a growing issue. Gross abuse of such services for the purpose of outright privacy invasion can have legal implications; therefore, LEAs need to be prepared to intercept video and still imagery in preparing cases against such abusers.

■ *Multimedia games:* As handsets become more sophisticated in their support of downloadable and networked games, lawful interception issues related to games may arise. Clearly, lawful interception has a role in tracking users and sources of games involving illicit thematic material such as child pornography, gambling, and hate targeting.

■ *VoIP:* This application will have slow uptake, as data services may not be sufficiently robust to support the continuous data flow that VoIP requires, and nationwide flat-rate calling plans make the economics of direct voice calls overwhelmingly compelling. Nevertheless, VoIP-capable handsets are now under development, and notebook computers can serve as suitable VoIP interfaces. Thus, as robust 2.5/3G networks become more widely deployed, increases in the use of VoIP will probably be seen among mobile users. Clearly, lawful interception of VoIP traffic raises a number of technical and legal issues that cannot be ignored by LEAs and network operators (NWOs).

7.3.2 Overview of 3G Architectures

Before we discuss specifics regarding the application of lawful interception to 3G networks, it is instructive to review the overall network topologies of UMTS and cdma2000 mobile networks. These technologies represent the bulk of the 3G networks now being deployed worldwide. In a general sense, networks based on UMTS and CDMA are quite similar. Both interconnect a group of BTS units to a single BSC. From the BSC, circuit-switched and packet data are sent, respectively, to a mobile switching center (MSC) and a packet manipulation system (PDSN for cdma2000 or SGSN for UMTS). There is also some level of overlap in terms of signaling and database functions. It is not necessary for each network device to be a separate physical entity, and many of the network elements can be combined into a single unit. Figure 7.14 and Figure 7.15 offer generalized descriptions of UMTS and cdma2000 networks. Slight variations can occur depending on choice of vendors and desired features.

The diagram shown in Figure 7.14 corresponds to the current UMTS specification. Configuration is nominal and varies according to the vendor providing the equipment. Some functions may be combined into a single network entity. The diagram in Figure 7.15 corresponds to the current cdma2000 specification. Again, configuration is nominal and varies according to vendor, and some functions may be combined into a single network entity.

7.3.3 Lawful Interception in 3G Networks

Given the network topology of each type of network (cdma2000 and UMTS) and the ETSI framework for lawful interception, users can visualize where to capture call data (i.e., interception-related information [IRI]) and call content and where LI management functions flow (Figure 7.16 and Figure 7.17). The notions of *content of communications* (also known as *call content*) and *call data* (IRI) may seem somewhat inappropriate for characterizing packet data. Nevertheless, these terms have well-defined meanings in the context of packet (including IP) data: call content represents the bulk data intercepted from the target, whereas call data represents information used to set up and tear down data transmit/receive

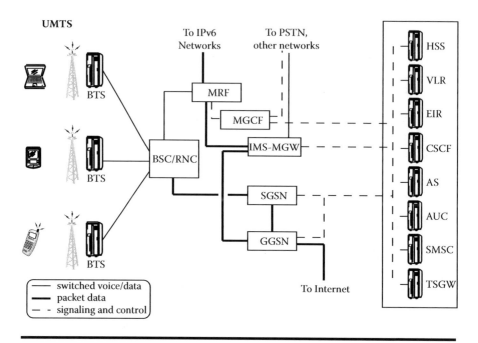

Figure 7.14   Generalized view of a mobile 3G network based on UMTS.

sessions between the mobile device and network. CDMA network interception is formalized in the updated J-STD-025B standard.

Although CDMA and UMTS are generally very similar in their lawful interception implementations, there are slight differences. For example, UMTS target identifiers apply the subscriber identity module (or SIM card) ID of the target's mobile device, whereas CDMA phones do not use these cards. Likewise, interception session setup can differ given the at times subtle differences in equipment functions between the two networks. We emphasize that the diagrams — Figure 7.14 and Figure 7.15 — are mainly conceptual and that many of the network elements can be combined into a single piece of equipment. Likewise, the flow of LI information does not consider the underlying network transport technology, which can be based on IP, asynchronous transfer mode (ATM), or other means. Interception functions (illustrated by magnifying glasses in Figure 7.16 and Figure 7.17) may be internal to the equipment (circuit-switched equipment, in particular) or may be incorporated through database interrogation or equipment installed for interception information collection (routers and probes).

The network elements and network points designated in Figure 7.16 and Figure 7.17 denote possible points for intercepting data. Usually, only one to three of these points need to be intercepted, depending on equipment design, access, and other factors.

CDMA2000

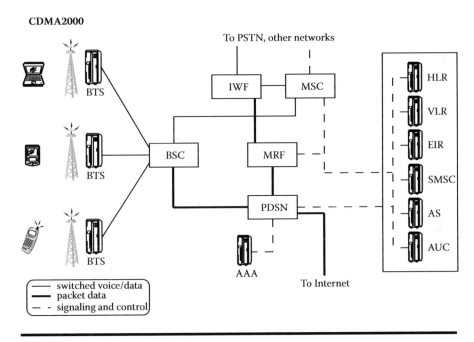

Figure 7.15   **General overview of a typical 3G mobile network based on cdma2000 technology.**

Figure 7.18 provides a closer view of the interception topology expected to be found in 3G networks, in this case for circuit-switched network operations. This depiction (based on that published by 3GPP) is sufficiently general to include cdma2000. In summary, it shows that:

- LI management commands are conveyed between the administrative function (ADMF) and other network elements via the X1 interface.
- Intercepted call data (IRI) are conveyed via the X2 interface.
- Intercepted call content is gathered via the X3 interface.

X3 can convey both bulk content (bearer) and signaling information, which are ultimately relayed to the LEA via handover HI3. The shaded boxes represent functions performed by Aqsacom's core product, the ALIS mediation platform. A similar diagram pertaining to packet data services is shown in Figure 7.19. It is important to understand from Figure 7.18 and Figure 7.19 that it is not the definition of another interface, but rather the separation of the LEA and data-gathering functions within the NWO's domain that is important. Ths solution is supported via a mediation function. It is this separation that enables LEAs and TSPs to configure

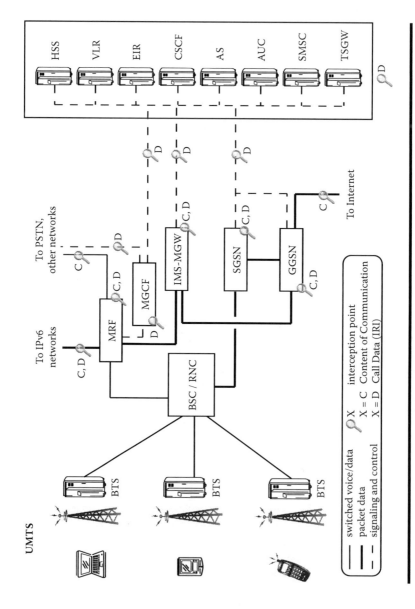

Figure 7.16 Overview of interception points for a UMTS network.

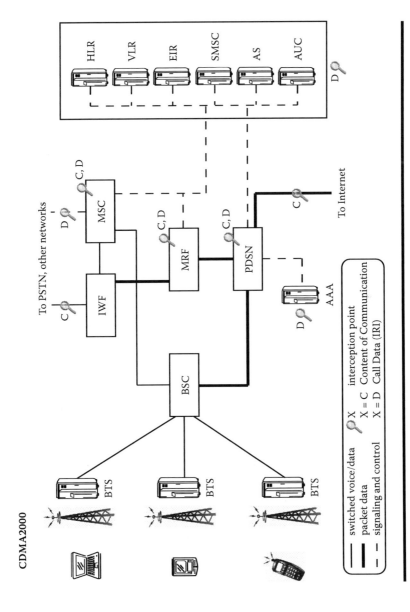

Figure 7.17 Overview of interception points for a cdma2000 network.

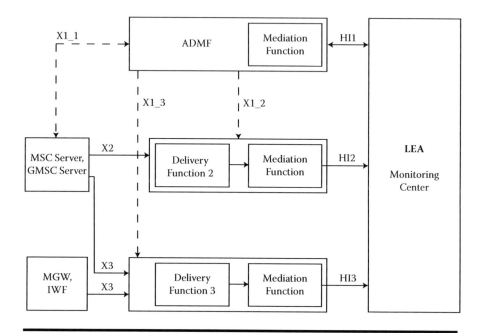

Figure 7.18   Interception interfaces for circuit-switched services within a 3G mobile network.

interception systems in a generalized manner that covers a wide range of services and technologies, including wireline voice, wireless voice, wired and wireless data, and emerging services such as VoIP.

The issue of location of the interception target may come into play for two reasons: to simply track the location of the target or to restrict lawful interception, as authorized by a given LEA, to the geographical territory representing the jurisdiction of the LEA. Execution in terms of simple tracking of location remains rather vague in that no formal standards have been introduced to formally track the movement of a target for lawful interception purposes, as useful as this information may seem to be. One reason is that the target may cross boundaries controlled by different LEAs, not all of whom may have authorized the interception. Another reason is that the required accuracy, typically to within the range of the nearest base station, may not be adequate to pinpoint the location of the target. Technical means, such as global positioning satellites, triangulation methods applying multiple towers, and statistical methods that track the motion of the target, are generally available to enhance accuracy in regard to position determination. Nevertheless, formal LI procedures incorporating these methods have yet to be introduced.

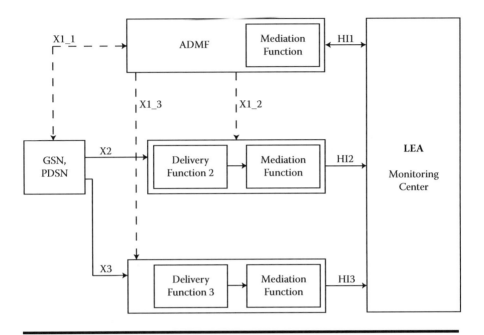

Figure 7.19 Interception interfaces for packet data services (including IP) within a 3G mobile network.

In the second case, a given base station controller (BSC) may traverse many different interception areas (IAs), with each area defined by a set of BTS cells within the BSC. As mentioned, these IAs may correspond to different jurisdictions. Therefore, when the intent is to intercept a moving target's communications, a check must be made to ensure that the corresponding LEA initiating the interception can in fact receive intercepted information from the IA where the target is located at a given point in time. Checks for valid IAs, when they are called for, are performed by the DFs and other network elements (e.g., MSC, GMSC, CSCF, and IWF).

Also, the notion of geographic versus identity-driven interception should be mentioned. The former refers to instances in which all subjects at a given location become targets of a LI procedure. This technique can be useful in tracking the presence of targets in sparsely populated (subscriber-wise) zones. In the case of identity-driven LI, the more common form, targets are identified according to specific identity information (e.g., the SIM card's international mobile subscriber identity [IMSI] or the handset's international mobile equipment identity [IMEI]). In both cases, novel target-detection methods must be used to incorporate the notion of location in the surveillance activities.

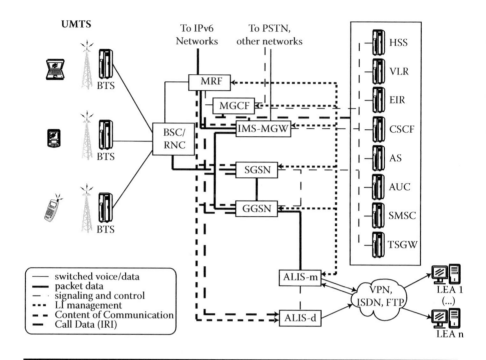

Figure 7.20 Role of ALIS in the interception of UMTS 3G mobile networks.

7.3.4 ALIS in 3G Networks

Figure 7.20 depicts the implementation of ALIS as a mediation platform in a UMTS network. This network configuration follows the generalized views introduced earlier in this case study. Important are the call data, call content, and LI management paths leading from ALIS-D and ALIS-M to the appropriate network elements and functions. Figure 7.21 provides a comparable diagram for cdma2000, where the LI network configuration is quite similar. In both diagrams, a number of different possibilities are identified as to where ALIS-D can receive interception data; not all the connections to ALIS specified in these figures need to be implemented.

7.3.5 Conclusions

This case study has presented an overview of the technical processes and challenges involved in lawful interception of targets subscribing to 3G mobile services. The processes are delineated by architectures, such as those specified by ETSI, 3GPP, ANSI, and other standards bodies, that facilitate systematic implementations and provisioning of lawful interception systems.

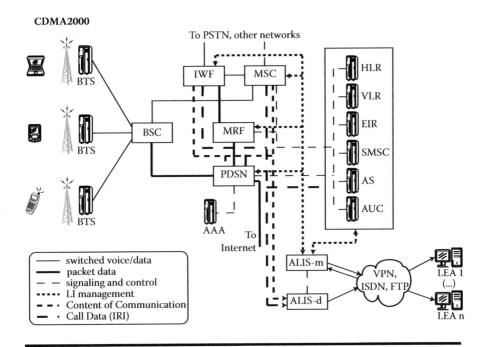

CDMA2000

To PSTN, other networks

IWF — MSC
HLR
VLR
EIR
BSC — MRF
SMSC
PDSN
AS
AUC
AAA
To Internet
ALIS-m
VPN, ISDN, FTP
LEA 1 (...)
ALIS-d
LEA n

BTS
BTS
BTS

—— switched voice/data
━━ packet data
– – signaling and control
····· LI management
– ·· – Content of Communication
— · Call Data (IRI)

Figure 7.21   Role of ALIS in the interception of CDMA 3G mobile networks.

However, challenges to lawful interception remain, including the need to support a diversity of services, vendor technologies, wireless networking technologies, voice, and a multiplicity of high-speed data services.

7.4 Case Study 4: Lawful Interception for IP Networks Using ALIS

For several reasons, interception of Internet traffic involves many additional complications:

- Target source and destination identities of the information flow are embedded within the overall flow of data and must be carefully extracted to avoid detection by the target.
- Target and nontarget data are tightly intermingled at numerous IP circuits and network elements throughout the Internet. In addition, the circuits making up the Internet are not always well designed, rarely regulated, and often deployed in an *ad hoc* manner. Therefore, privacy concerns arise, because nontarget data can erroneously be captured.

- Many parties are typically involved in transporting data over the Internet, including access providers at each end of the communication, transport operators, core NWOs, and service providers. Furthermore, and unlike traditional telephony, these parties are unregulated and subject only to their own business practices.

- In many countries, current laws on how to handle Internet interception are not clear. Interception efforts are often blocked by Internet service providers (ISPs) in the interest of protecting their customers or simply because it is easier not to cooperate.

- Separation of applications and relevant data from the overall data stream is not a trivial matter and requires significant software development and computing power, along with considerable trial and error.

- There is a lack of standards implementations, and most attempts at IP interception are carried out by esoteric organizations within government agencies. Although efforts are now under way to make the processes of data interception and delivery to LEAs more routine, tools for analyzing IP data remain limited to a few suppliers.

7.4.1 Issues in IP Interception

In the case of lawful interception, it is important to distinguish between network access and network services because the two are somewhat different by convention. For the purposes of this case study, network access is typically managed by the network access provider (AP), whose infrastructure often relies on that of the NWO, for example, the incumbent telecom operator, local cable TV service, or wireless services operator. Access operates at all levels of the OSI model, from authorization to session transport to overall public use of the Internet.

In contrast, network services (e-mail, chat, VoIP, etc.) may be provided by the NWO or by a third-party service organization. For example, popular e-mail services such as Hotmail and Yahoo! Mail, as well as instant messaging services such as MSN Messenger and AOL Instant Messenger, are offered by service organizations — and not by NWOs or access providers. Figure 7.22 represents an attempt to illustrate the distinction between service providers and AP/NWOs. In the context of lawful interception, LEAs often must interact with both network access and network services to intercept target data.

The NWO can be a telecom operator (e.g., supplying DSL services over existing local loop copper), cable TV operator, or another type of operator. Core Internet or managed intranet functions are managed by a NWO that may or may not also provide network access.

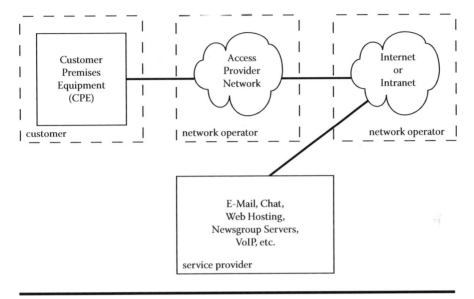

Figure 7.22 Separation of network access, core network, and service provider functions.

7.4.2 IP Interception Examples

Three examples are provided that require different interception solutions.

7.4.2.1 Internet Access

Figure 7.23a to Figure 7.23d depicts typical access configurations for xDSL, dial up, cable modem, and Wi-Fi. All access methods perform the overall function of network access, connecting the subscriber or user to the public Internet, various network-based services (e.g., e-mail and chat), or private networks based on IP or other technologies. The access function is typically performed along with the sequence of AAA. Authentication confirms that users are who they say they are (e.g., through a password, a physical token device such as a smart card, or biometrics data). The authorization function controls what users can do once they are authenticated (e.g., connecting to the network and accessing e-mail). Accounting refers to the process of checking users' subscriber records to ensure that their account is paid up and they are billed for services rendered. Likewise, accounting can debit prepaid accounts as network services are consumed (e.g., in VoIP). AAA functions are typically managed by the NWO through a RADIUS server and its associated protocol.

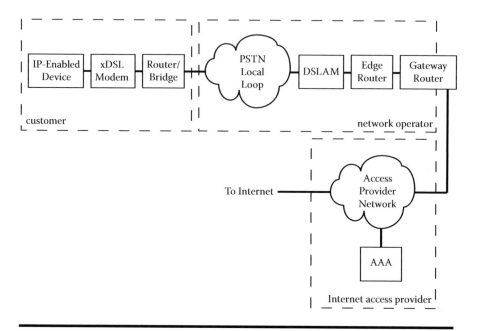

Figure 7.23a   Typical configurations for xDSL Internet access.

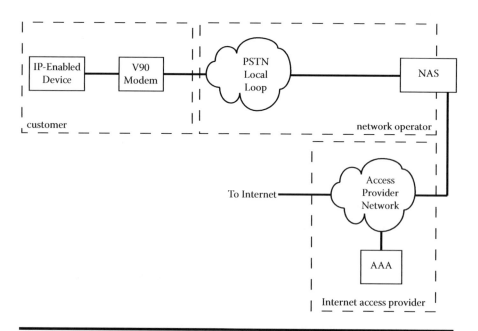

Figure 7.23b   Typical configurations for dial-up Internet access.

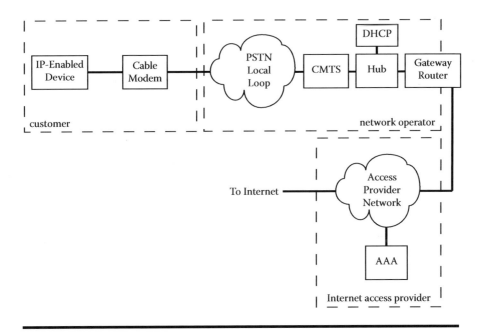

Figure 7.23c   Typical configurations for cable modem Internet access.

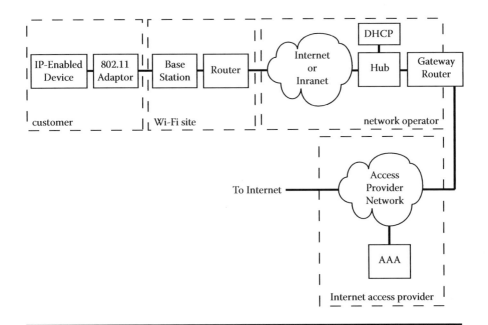

Figure 7.23d   Typical configurations for Wi-Fi Internet access.

7.4.2.1.1 Internet Access Target Identification

Lawful interception of packet-based data flows begins with the specification of the target. However, unlike traditional voice interception, wherein the target can be identified via a telephone number, a process needs to be invoked that matches the target's assigned IP address or other unique identifier. The IP address assignment may be dynamic as in dial up, as well as consumer/small-business-oriented xDSL, cable modem, and more recently, Wi-Fi access services; therefore, the LEA must conduct coordinated internal interception activities in conjunction with the NWO. IP addresses are typically assigned through the use of Dynamic Host Configuration Protocol (DHCP), in conjunction with the AAA functions of the RADIUS server. Here the RADIUS server aids the LEA in identifying the target, while the DHCP process provides the LEA with the target's corresponding IP address. Interception occurs between assignment and deassignment of the targeted user's IP address.

Public Internet access services oriented toward business customers usually make use of fixed IP addresses assigned to customers. The associated access technologies are typically dedicated T1 or fractional T1 line, xDSL, and, to a lesser but growing extent, cable modem. In these cases, the LEA relies on a set of permanent IP addresses provided by the NWO. Other target identifiers include:

- Username and network access identifier
- Ethernet address (layer 2)
- Dial-in calling number identity
- Cable modem identifier
- Other unique identifiers agreed upon between the network provider and LEA

The Ethernet and cable modem identifier are related to the physical devices of the user, which must be linked to an authorization process if they are to remain effective as spoof-free identifiers — in other words, targets should not be allowed to hide their connection to the network by using a stolen or tampered-with cable modem that is connected to their usual cable TV wiring.

7.4.2.1.2 Collected Data

Call data (IRI) sent to the LEA over the HI2 handover interface (HI) includes the following:

- Identity of target (using, for example, one or more of the preceding target identifiers)
- Services and access privileges of the target
- Time of network access attempt by target
- Time network access is successfully achieved or denied
- Change in network status
- Change in network access location

In terms of content of communication (conveyed via the content CCC under CALEA), relevant interception data delivered to the LEA via the HI3 HI includes the datagrams of targeted data, for example, source and destination IP addresses (even though these addresses, technically, are also considered call data).

It is important that LEAs not become the victim of IP address spoofing, such as when a target's IP address replaces another party's source or destination address. This results in the LEA mistakenly believing that it is intercepting data to or from the target when the data is actually associated with another nontargeted party. Such spoofing can be reasonably easy to prevent in packets originating from the target, by probing the appropriate internal network points. These points in theory should not allow for IP datagram modification. However, packets falsely destined for the target from outside the target's immediate network are more difficult to validate. Here the LEA may have to resort to route tracing, gateway analysis, and possibly lower-level OSI layer analysis to ascertain the origin of such packets. The same holds for determining the origin of parties who attempt to spoof their origination addresses and send IP data to the target.

7.4.2.1.3 Lawful Interception Configurations for Network Access

The diagrams shown in Figure 7.23a to Figure 7.23d are updated in Figure 7.24a to Figure 7.24d to indicate the many interception points available to the NWO and LEA. These interception points are represented only as suggestions; only one or two would need to be put to use, depending on network element availability, cost, and other factors. All interception points route their call data (D) and content data (C) to a mediation platform that in turn routes this data to the LEA via the HI2 and HI3 HIs. All indicated interception points implement internal interception by applying probes or networking interfaces to local networks, access loops, routers, gateways, AAA functions, and so forth. External interception is indicated at the level of the public Internet, beyond the immediate access network.

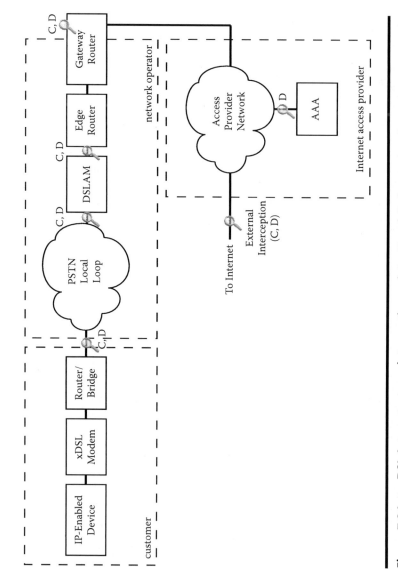

Figure 7.24a xDSL Internet access interception points. C and D denote intercepted content and session-related data, respectively.

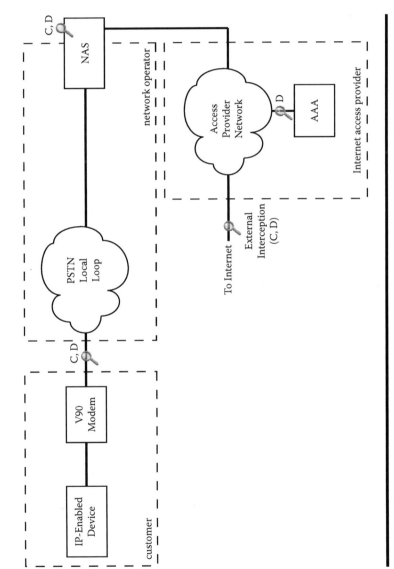

Figure 7.24b Dial-up Internet access interception points. C and D denote intercepted content and session-related data, respectively.

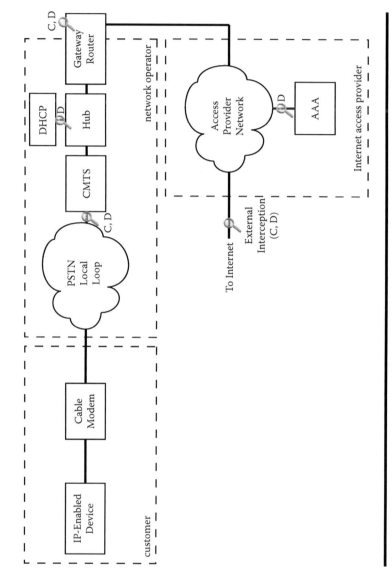

Figure 7.24c Cable modem Internet access interception points. C and D denote intercepted content and session-related data, respectively.

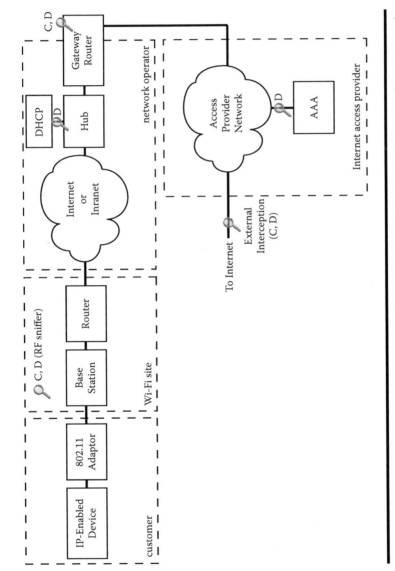

Figure 7.24d **Wi-Fi Internet access interception points. C and D denote intercepted content and session-related data, respectively.**

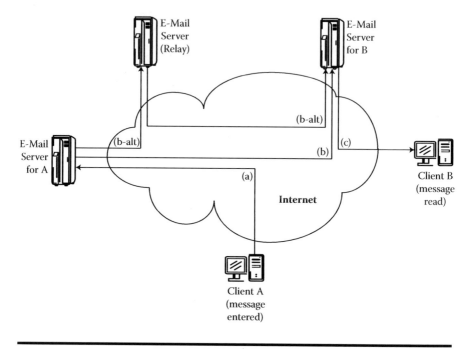

Figure 7.25 The process of sending an e-mail message via SMTP protocol (and similar other protocols).

7.4.2.2 E-Mail

Given e-mail's role as an essential mode of communication, it is only logical that LEAs and ISPs be given the tools necessary to carry out lawful interception of e-mail traffic. Of equal interest is the growing problem of unwanted bulk e-mails (spam), which now constitute more than half of all e-mail messages. Here, lawful interception can play a crucial role in detecting, tracking, and limiting this menace. E-mail interception for lawful purposes can be understood by first looking at the typical steps undertaken by the Simple Mail Transfer Protocol (SMTP) to convey an e-mail message (other e-mail protocols follow a similar process). The following description (see also Figure 7.25) is highly simplified and omits details regarding message exchanges within the protocol:

1. User A enters a message for user B via his or her e-mail client on a personal computer, portable device, or within a Web site. The e-mail client then forwards the message, via SMTP, to the designated server (known as a mail transfer agent, or MTA) that handles all outgoing e-mail from that user.

2. Client A's server routes the e-mail to the destination server that handles user B's incoming e-mail. Routing is determined through a domain name system (DNS) lookup that matches the destination's e-mail domain name to an IP address. Alternatively, the message can be routed through one or more intermediate "relay" servers (see path "b-alt" in Figure 7.25) for the purposes of network traffic routing (e.g., gateways) or in an attempt to hide the identity and location of user A.

3. Client B typically extracts the incoming e-mail from its assigned server via the POP3 or IMAP protocol. POP3 and IMAP manage the process of downloading the e-mail to client B for access by its user.

It is not necessary to detail all the processes involved with SMTP, IMAP, and POP3; it is sufficient to say that there is considerable information embedded within the headers of e-mail messages based on these protocols. This information includes the following:

- Server IP
- Client IP
- Server port
- Client port
- E-mail protocol ID
- E-mail sender
- E-mail recipient list
- Total recipient count
- Server octets sent
- Client octets sent
- Message ID
- Status

All the preceding information represents IRI data intended to be made available to the LEA.

Internal interception, in theory, can take place in the context of any e-mail server in the paths described earlier to identify targeted e-mail traffic and route the corresponding call data (CD) information to the mediation platform (Figure 7.26). Through appropriate parsing either within or outside of e-mail servers, e-mail content can also be directly extracted from these servers. Of course, if the content is encrypted by the user or e-mail service, additional efforts will be necessary to decrypt the message. Generally, ETSI and other standards involve the following requirements:

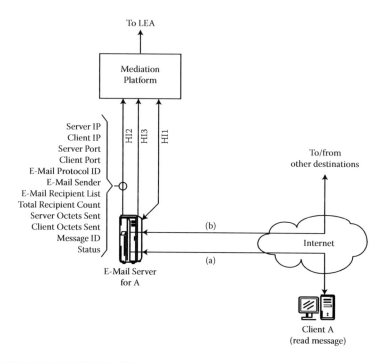

Figure 7.26 Interception of e-mail.

- When a TSP encrypts e-mail data, it is the responsibility of the NWO or TSP to decipher this information before sending it to the LEA.
- When the subscriber encrypts e-mail data, it is the responsibility of the NWO or TSP to send the ciphered data to the LEA. It is then the responsibility of the LEA to decipher the data.

On the other hand, many e-mail servers do not allow for separate interception ports. Thus, TSPs are expected to equip their operation with updated servers that support LEAs. These providers will also have to maintain the servers and ensure their security against intrusion.

One might ask: Why not simply augment e-mail messages with a blind copy to the LEA? This method is not recommended for the following reasons:

- It acts only on the server originating the e-mail (when multiple servers in the e-mail chain might be intercepted).
- It is prone to operator error, whereas LI methods that are well engineered are more resistant to operator error.

- The blind copy would not necessarily be secure during relay to the LEA.
- Addition of a blind copy constitutes e-mail tampering on the part of the authorities, resulting in risk of exposure or violation of law.

Thus, interception should be performed in a manner detached from manipulation of the e-mail message.

LEAs as well must deal with spam. For example, LEAs must ensure that their own interception operations are not affected as a result of modifications to headers in the target e-mail information they receive. LEAs can play a role in detecting spam and in seeking its perpetrators.

LEAs' interception operations can be impacted as a result of weaknesses in SMTP and other common e-mail protocols. Users often can easily modify From mailbox addresses and Reply To addresses at the level of the e-mail client. Therefore, reliance on From and Reply To fields is hardly a good means of identifying the sender of a targeted e-mail; the interception target could falsely be specified as the source, or targets may attempt to hide themselves as the source. A more reliable approach is to make use of the target's assigned IP address as an identifier of the e-mail while performing interception at the level of the target e-mail server, which is confirmed to be free of viruses. Nevertheless, even this latter approach is not fail-safe in that rogue e-mail servers (including those hijacked by viruses) can create false message-origination IP addresses.

At present, a number of initiatives are under way to block spam sent with falsified headers. One group of methods attempts to authenticate the origination of an e-mail by matching the From domain name with the originating IP address range through a reverse DNS lookup (e.g., the sender policy framework and Microsoft's caller ID for e-mail). LEAs should use reverse DNS lookup practices now while leveraging standardized approaches as they become available. Another means of confirming authenticity of e-mail origination is through the use of consistency checks of header information corresponding to e-mail threads. Unfortunately, headers are not always preserved in message threads, thus making this method of limited value.

Finally, LEAs should subscribe to the e-mail blacklists that are compiled and disseminated regularly by nonprofit and commercial spam-prevention services. By maintaining updated information on spam-origination addresses, subject headings, and other data broadcast to e-mail servers and filtering appliances, these lists provide LEAs with an additional weapon in the fight against spam. This battle cannot be won through any single method; spam is best controlled through a mix of measures.

7.4.2.3 VoIP

VoIP represents a specific technology falling under the broader Voice-over-Packet (VoP) category. However, given the popularity of the term VoIP, it is perhaps recognized more as a type of telephone service than as a facilitating technology. VoIP originally drew interest as a means of bypassing traditional telephone networks for the placement of international calls, especially calls made between Western nations and developing countries; the latter are known to impose high long-distance and international tariffs. However, deployment of broadband access, improvements in codec technology, converging standards, and increased enterprise interest in the technology have transformed VoIP into a mainstream technology for placing both local and long-distance voice calls. VoIP calls can take place over a variety of network topologies and among a variety of user groups. In the following, we describe representative examples of these topologies and users.

7.4.2.3.1 Phone to Phone for Consumer and Small Business

This group consists of services that, for a fee (and sometimes without one), enable customers to place calls over IP networks. These networks employ soft switches, account management platforms (i.e., gatekeepers), and gateways that control the placement of voice calls between the traditional telephone network and IP networks. Phone-to-phone dialing may occur with the traditional PSTN acting as transport between user telephones and gateways to the IP networks. Likewise, phone to phone can be supported via direct IP access, wherein users have at their premises a VoIP interface that connects to their broadband Internet access service (typically xDSL, cable modem, a dedicated line, or Wi-Fi service). Such a device allows users to bypass the PSTN, at least at their end. Companies such as Vonage and, notably, cable TV operators are offering this form of VoIP service. In some cases, the VoIP interface is built into the cable modem box. The IP network may consist of (1) privately managed IP networks designed to ensure quality of service (QoS), as implemented by the cable operators; (2) the public Internet, in which quality is difficult to ensure but reach is ubiquitous; or (3) a combination of these two networks.

7.4.2.3.2 PC to PC

This is perhaps the original form of VoIP. In this case, PC users connect their PCs to well-functioning higher speed dial-up modems, broadband Internet connections, or fixed LANs. Calls are then placed through the PC to another, distant PC. All codec transformations are performed within the software operating on the users' PCs. Connections are typically managed from a central server that maps user names to current IP address locations.

7.4.2.3.3 Corporate

VoIP enables corporations to leverage existing IP networking, which typically rides over lower layer Ethernet, ATM, frame relay, or other technologies. Connectivity to traditional corporate voice networks or the PSTN occurs through gateways managed by the company. VoIP is recognized, at least in theory, as a means of consolidating the enterprise's voice and data networks into a single network, thereby creating cost savings. VoIP system vendors also claim that configuring the features and locations of terminals is much simpler than with traditional PBX-based systems.

7.4.2.3.4 Protocols

In past years, the H.323 specification was the driving force behind how voice calls were transported and managed over IP networks. More recently, however, a competing protocol labeled Session Initiation Protocol (SIP) has been gaining favor among operators of VoIP services, with further support through the IETF. SIP has the added advantage of managing the "presence" of a user throughout a network. Presence enables one user to readily know whether a distant user is online, how he or she is connected, and in some cases where he or she is connected. Of course, all this information would be of considerable interest to LEAs in the context of targeted intercept activities.

VoP IRI/CD messaging does not correspond precisely to TIA/CALEA J-STD-025 standards. For example, there is no definition of the SIP INVITE message under J-STD-025. This is overcome by mapping VOP IRI messages to messages recognized by the standard or through direct signal response. The latter is useful in implementing LI in newly built VoP systems not dependent on legacy voice installations. SIP message bodies are treated as call content, with headers and other information describing these bodies as call data.

7.4.2.3.5 Interception

Figure 7.27 provides a generalized, conceptual interception framework. The network functions represented by each box may be physically combined or may be carried out by various pieces of equipment.

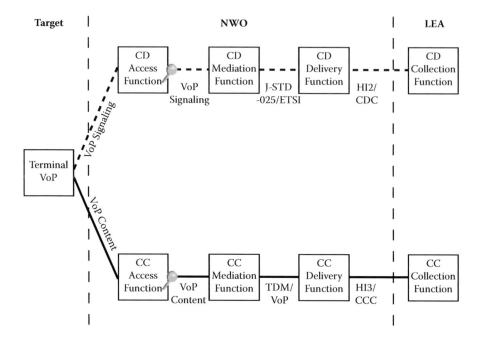

Figure 7.27 Conceptual view of interception for packet networks.

Call data is associated with *surveillance events* related to the placement and dropping of a VoP call. Many of the parameters of these events are similar to those found in traditional voice interception. The first group of surveillance events is referred to as *call control events*, which include the following:

- *Answer:* The target answers an incoming VoP call or the distant party answers a call placed by the target.
- *Origination:* The target originated the call.
- *Release:* A completed or attempted VoP call has been released.
- *Termination attempt:* A VoP call session termination attempt in regard to the target has been detected.

Signaling events are another form of call data associated with diverse network functions carried out during the placement or manipulation of a call:

- *Dialed digit extraction (DDE):* This refers to the capture of the extra digits that a target dials after a call is connected (e.g., resulting from the entry of a calling card number, line extension, or destination phone number to be dialed from an intermediate gateway). DDE remains a point of contention in the standards community. Some advocate that it be considered part of call content and therefore under the responsibility of the LEA in regard to interception activities; others claim that the NWO should furnish DDE digits to the LEA.

■ *Direct signal reporting:* A signaling message is sent between the subject and the VoP network, or the VoP network sends or receives a signal on behalf of the subject.

■ *Network signal:* Activity on the network that produces CII — busy, ringing, alerting, etc. — is initiated or sent by a network element to the network facilities that are serving the target and are under surveillance.

■ *Subject signal:* This refers to instances in which facilities under surveillance are used by the subject to initiate control features such as call forwarding, call waiting, and call hold.

Feature use events involve signaling associated with conference calling, call transfer, and other call features. Finally, *registration events* occur when the target, or the target's network facilities or equipment, provides address information to the VoP network, such as contact information, street address, and so forth, upon sign-up for a service or termination. As in the case of traditional telephony interception, all call data must be presented to the LEA with a time stamp to ensure synchronization with call content.

At present, VoP technologies do not attempt to identify the physical locations of targets. This contrasts with traditional wireline telephony, in which the location of a target is usually implied by virtue of the target's telephone number. However, even traditional voice line identification can be obliterated through attempts to call through a gateway (such as with prepaid calling cards), and mobile telephony is fraught with technical challenges in regard to determining locations. Of course (and by default), locations of cable modem and xDSL services can be locked down by tying equipment ID numbers to specific cable modem termination system (CMTS) or digital subscriber line access multiplex (DSLAM) circuits. The termination location of these circuits would be known — and hence the location of the user (unless the equipment has been tampered with, which is not a trivial concern). Depending on system design, emerging VoIP services that make use of gateways and switches may lose call-originating information. In fact, preservation of call data and the ability of TSPs to furnish this data to LEAs is a controversial topic among VoIP operators, the FCC, the U.S. Justice Department, and various state agencies in the United States.

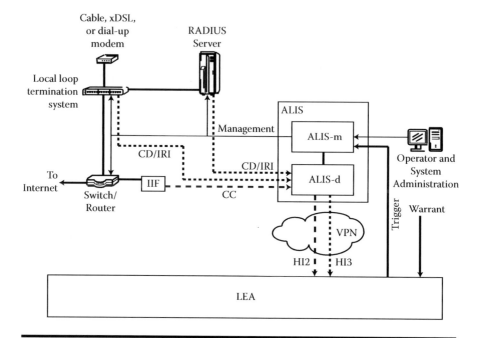

Figure 7.28 Application of the ALIS platform in the interception of a target's access to a network.

7.4.3 ALIS for IP

ALIS is a mediation system facilitating lawful interception activities in the areas of Internet access, e-mail, and VoIP networks. Figure 7.28 illustrates the ALIS Internet access (cable modem, xDSL, or dial up) application. Here, an example of internal interception is shown wherein target call data information is extracted from the RADIUS server and access termination point (CMTS, DSLAM, or modem pool). An internal intercept function (IIF) in a router replicates call content to and from the target and sends this data to ALIS-D.

Figure 7.29 illustrates the function of ALIS as the mediation platform for lawful interception of e-mail. Relevant e-mail header information and other protocol information are captured directly from the e-mail server as call data and routed to ALIS-D for reformatting and delivery to the LEA. The contents of the e-mail messages are routed to ALIS-D as call content.

VoIP calling is illustrated in Figure 7.30. ALIS-M sets triggering events within relevant network equipment, including the call agent (gatekeeper, SIP server, gateway, etc.) and routers assigned to capture data flow. Call data and call content are then extracted from the network elements by

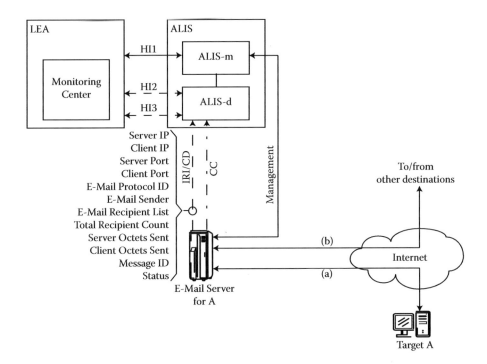

Figure 7.29   Example of e-mail interception.

means of internal interception. External interception of the data would be executed at points within the Internet cloud but would be distinct from the network elements shown in the figure.

In general, the indicated access method could be cable modem, xDSL, or dial up. The customer termination system and RADIUS server supply call data to ALIS-D. The IIF in the router replicates and routes content to ALIS-D as well. ALIS-M takes on the function of network device management for the interception session. In this example, call data and call content are delivered to the LEA through a VPN.

In the example provided, internal interception acts directly on the e-mail servers handling outgoing and incoming messages to and from the target. Further interception can be carried out through external means both within and outside the Internet.

Call data information is extracted from the gatekeeper (or a similar device) via internal interception and sent to ALIS-D for processing. Provisioning of pertinent network elements is carried out by ALIS-M. An IIF within a router replicates call content to be intercepted according to the IP address of the originating or destination target.

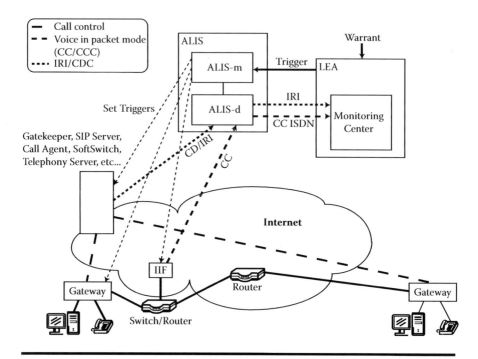

Figure 7.30 Application of the ALIS platform in the interception of VoIP.

7.4.4 Conclusions

The ALIS framework, with its mediation function, supports LI in the areas of accessing of Internet functions and services, e-mail, and VoIP services and networks. The Aqsacom Internet access functionality supports xDSL, dial up, cable modem, and Wi-Fi.

LI e-mail support offers a large number of data sources for the ALIS mediation function. In addition, Aqsacom solutions help reduce volumes of unsolicited e-mails.

Finally, IP-based voice solutions target phone-to-phone, PC-to-PC, and corporate solutions for LIs with mediation and delivery functions. Cable-based VoIP solutions are supported by the delivery and administrative functions.

7.5 Case Study 5: Lawful Intercepts for Cable VoIP Networks from SS8 Networks

In view of the potential importance of multiple systems operators (MSOs) in the offering of public telephony services, CableLabs has published a specification regarding lawful surveillance for voice services operating over PacketCable networks (Rosenfeld, 2003). PacketCable is a set of specifications issued by CableLabs defining how IP data services are to be implemented over cable networks; among these services is voice telephony. PacketCable rides over CableLab's underlying DOCSIS (data over cable service interface specifications). The specification just mentioned serves as the basis of the IPCablecom standard, as submitted by the Society of Cable Television Engineers (SCTE) to ANSI for formal standardization. The goal of this specification is to make cable-based voice telephony CALEA compliant through safe-harbor provisions.

The need for a PacketCable-based surveillance standard arose because the TIA CALEA standard (STD-0275), which focused mainly on traditional telephony, did not address the inherent technologies underlying Packet-Cable. In the United States, the FBI, the Department of Justice, and the Drug Enforcement Agency submitted a petition to the FCC in March 2004 encouraging that agency to immediately push forward directives that would extend CALEA to broadband packet networks.

The modified version of the Xcipio framework for cable applications is displayed in Figure 7.31.

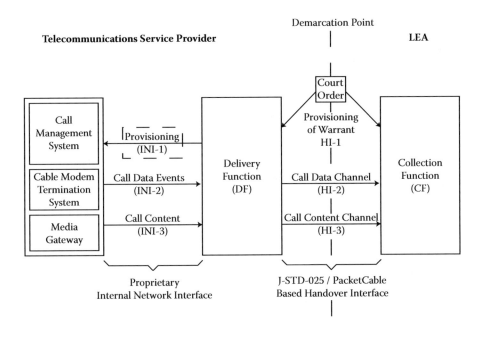

Figure 7.31   Generic view of the LI architecture for cable-based services.

The standardized core functions of LIs can be defined as follows:

- *AF:* network elements (CO switches, MSC, HLR, AAA, PDSN, SGSN/GGSN, routers, trunking gateways, softswitches, and CMTS) that provide access points to and replication of intercepted traffic
- *DF:* database of target and warrant information; provisioning interface; proprietary interfaces to the AF; standards-based (e.g., PacketCable) delivery of intercepted traffic to CFs
- *CF:* collects and records lawfully authorized intercepted communications (e.g., call content and CII) for delivery to LEAs

VoIP over cable, as well as over other access technologies, poses an interesting problem for lawful interception activities because, in some cases, portions of the intelligence used to control call sessions are placed at the edge of the network, within equipment located at the customer's premises. This equipment usually consists of a cable modem with a built-in or detached VoIP interface adaptor that connects to a typical telephone through an RJ-11 connector. Because the equipment is within the reach of the customer, and in some cases owned by the customer, it is subject to tampering, especially when users attempt to obtain free services. In addition, it is highly unlikely that users will facilitate any LI session that requires physical or even remote access to their premises. Therefore, LI activities must proceed within a network that supports these edge devices.

The model proposed by CableLabs clearly has implications for cable-based VoIP services. The principal components are:

- *CMTS:* This system aggregates the physical connections and data flow from a distribution of subscriber cable modems and other customer terminal equipment (e.g., VoIP adaptors). Call content packet streams are captured and replicated, typically via a router, and then relayed to the DF. Call content includes embedded IP header information associated with the calling and called parties. In summary, the CMTS controls the set of cable modems attached to the shared medium of the DOCSIS network.
- *Call management system (CMS):* This system supports the specific service provided to the subscriber, in this case telephony. In effect, the CMS captures and interprets call-routing information to set up the call with the distant party for outgoing and incoming calls. It is an important source of call data information such as originating telephone number, other ID parameters, time at which a call was placed, time at which a call was attempted, destination of call forwarding, and third-party conference call identifiers. Call data

delivered to the mediation system also includes the media-stream encryption key and an identifier for the encryption algorithm, both of which must be conveyed to the LEA for eventual processing. The key information can be issued from the RADIUS server. The CMTS communicates with the CMS via the Common Open Policy Service Protocol (COPSP), a (C/S) protocol that exchanges QoS signaling and resource management. In summary, the CMS is responsible for intercepting CII.

■ *Media gateway (MG):* The MG serves as the bridge between the PSTN and the IP network of the cable operator, thereby enabling the user to accept calls from parties connected to the PSTN or dial out to such parties. This can provide call content conforming to standardized fixed-line LIs. Cable operators may situate gateways at large distances from the immediate cable infrastructure affecting the interception target, and they rely on such remotely placed gateways to provide dial tones for long-distance and even local calls. Thus, interception may have to take place at remotely located PSTN facilities far removed from the local calling area of the target. The ubiquity of IP networking removes geographic barriers to locations of network functions. In summary, the MG can be designated as an IAP.

■ *Media gateway controller (MGC):* The MGC captures signaling information on the SS7 network to set up calls between the cable VoIP user and a PSTN party. This device can also perform subscriber-dialing authorization and usage metering, and it supplies call data information. In summary, the MGC is responsible for interworking with signaling systems.

Issues associated with LIs in the area of cable VoIP networks can be summarized as follows:

■ Existing J-STD-025 and ETSI standards were designated with TDM switching in mind. The only standard for VoIP interception available today is PacketCable.
■ PacketCable specifications have evolved to support certain punchlist items.
■ Technology is evolving every day, and LI standards are not currently available to meet legal mandates.
■ Different VoIP architectures require different implementations.
■ CF technology is available but is still a work in progress.
■ There is confusion over the concepts of VoIP and voice-over-Internet.

- There is as yet no clear information regarding requirements associated with voice-over-Internet LIs.
- Call forwarding to a distant phone number within a cable network, or a distant network that might be different from the cable network, is difficult to follow in the case of LIs.
- Secure communications between the CMTS and customer terminal equipment require encryption. LEAs require decryption of the necessary keys by the code operator.
- Systems are complex as a result of the distributed nature of VoIP networks.

In addition, current technical realities must be kept in mind. For example:

- The centralized DF is feasible and preferable.
- Administrative overheads are significant.
- Problem resolution in VoIP environments is not yet mature.
- There is very little time to build a knowledge base around common issues and solutions.

Two basic examples in the area of lawful voice intercepts are the use of edge routers (Figure 7.32) and the use of the MG (Figure 7.33). If edge routers are PacketCable-compliant, they use COPS or SGCP/MGCP for provisioning of intercepted packets. Cisco typically uses SNMPv3 for this purpose. In both cases, copies of all intercepted RTP packets are sent to and from the target's IP address to the mediation device.

Typical call data events are:

- *Answer:* A two-way connection has been established in a call under surveillance.
- *CC change:* A change occurs in the content delivery description of an intercepted call.
- *CC close:* This signals the end of content delivery for an intercepted call.
- *CC open:* This signals the beginning of content delivery for an intercepted call.
- *Network signal:* The PC/TSP network requests that a signal be directed toward the surveillance subject.
- *Origination:* The IAP detects that the surveillance subject is attempting to originate a call.
- *Redirection:* A call under surveillance is redirected (e.g., via terminal special service processing or a call transfer).

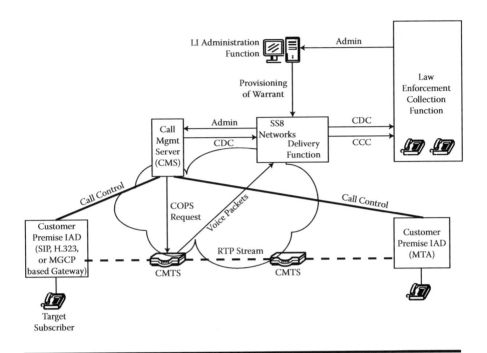

Figure 7.32 PacketCable voice intercept — use of edge routers.

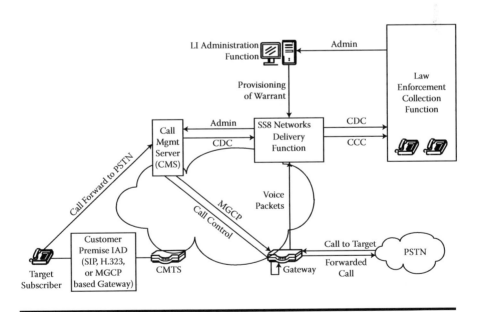

Figure 7.33 PacketCable intercept — use of MG.

- *Release:* The resources used in a call under surveillance have been released.
- *Subject signal:* The surveillance subject sends dialing or signaling information to the PC/TSP network to control a feature or service.
- *Termination attempt:* The IAP detects a call attempt to a surveillance subject.

In summary, the technical challenges of conducting LIs involving cable-based VoIP services include the following:

- The only potential safe-harbor architecture is PacketCable based and requires DQoS. Call-content interception cannot be performed if the CMTS does not support DQoS. This situation has created new and different architectures requiring that delivery functions play an active role in call-content interception.
- Most network elements (call management system, gatekeepers, MGs, aggregation routers, CMTS, etc.) need to support this feature within the distributed IP environment.
- The CMS subscriber-provisioning interface does not address lawful interception provisioning. Target provisioning requires proprietary interfaces.
- It is extremely difficult to capture CII and call content in certain call features, specifically those implemented within IADs located at the customer's premises.

Alternative solutions are use of edge routers (Figure 7.34), MGs (Figure 7.35), or data intercepts via passive monitoring (Figure 7.36). Most routers involve a proprietary means of conducting intercepts. As mentioned, Cisco uses SNMPv3 to provision the target's IP address at the router, after which all packets (data and voice) to and from that IP address are relayed to the mediation device.

As a network element, the DF should include the following attributes to facilitate successful LI activities:

- Built-in test tools for remote testing
- Standard MML and remote graphical user interface (GUI) support
- Alarm reporting and error logging
- Automatic software fault recovery
- Automatic or manual disk backup
- SNMP support
- Support for SAS functionality

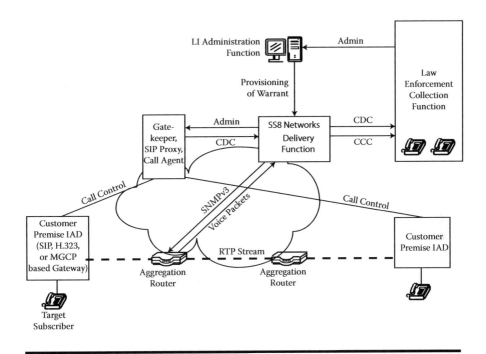

Figure 7.34 Alternative solution with edge routers.

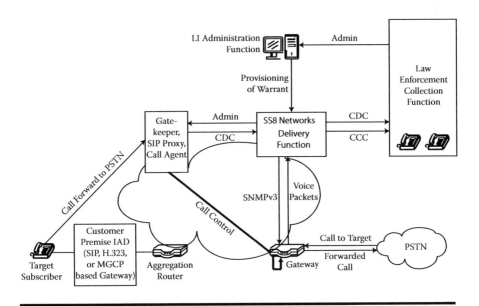

Figure 7.35 Alternative solution with MGs.

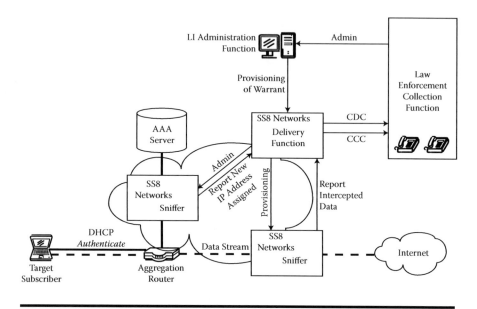

Figure 7.36 Data intercept via passive monitoring.

Several conclusions can be drawn from this case study:

■ The Xcipio framework and related SS8 products can support most core LI functions.
■ SS8 solutions principally target support of the DF.
■ If required, SS8 cooperates with other vendors; for example, if passive monitoring is required.
■ If required, SS8 will target more functionality in future solutions, particularly support for pre-provisioning and rapid provisioning.

7.6 Case Study 6: Monitoring and Logging Web Activities

In general, three features of monitoring and logging tools may provide assistance in terms of conducting LIs:

■ Site-usage analysis: provides an understanding of how site visitors (potential targets of surveillance) interact with Web sites
■ Site-user analysis: targets particular messages to increase the like-lihood that site visitors (potential targets of surveillance) will be interested in the information that sites provide

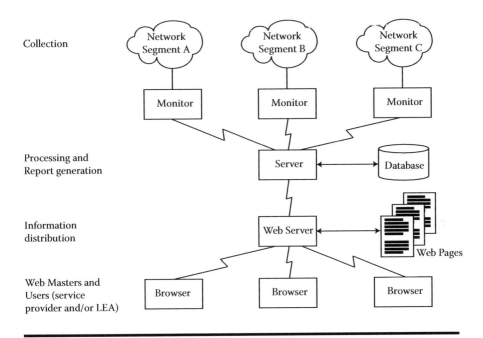

Figure 7.37   Generic product architecture for processing traffic measurement data.

■ Site-content analysis: analyzes the content and structure of Web sites that may help indirectly with recognizing usage patterns

7.6.1 Features and Attributes of Monitoring and Logging Tools

The architectures of particular products such as Web-log analyzers, traffic sniffers, load balancers, traffic shapers, and probes answer the question of whether or not they can support a distributed architecture. Distribution may mean that collecting, processing, reporting, and distributing data can be supported in various processors and at different locations. Figure 7.37 shows these functions in the case of a solution in which special monitoring devices are used at distributed locations.

The monitors shown are passively measuring the traffic in the network segments. They are actually microcomputers with ever-increasing amounts of intelligence, and their operating systems are either proprietary or based on UNIX or, more likely, Windows NT. Usually, they are programmed to interpret many protocols. TCP/IP, UDP/IP, and HTTP are high on the priority lists of vendors.

The technique used to capture data is an essential element of traffic measurement tools. Measurement probes are attached to the digital interface of the communication channels. They can reside directly on the

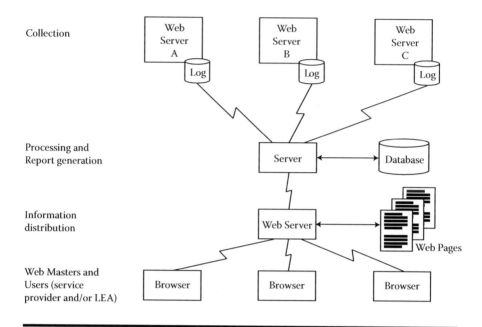

Figure 7.38 Generic product architecture for log-file analysis.

network (stand-alone probes) or be colocated with networking equipment. In this case, the probe is used as a plug-in. Even software probes can be implemented in networking components or end-user devices. Hardware or software probes usually include event scheduling (determining polling cycles and time periods when downloading of measurement data is intended). Transmission should be scheduled for low-traffic periods. Probes are intended to deal with large data volumes. These volumes depend, to a large degree, on visitor traffic in networking segments. Probes have limited storage capabilities; implementation examples have shown capabilities of up to 24 hours. When this limit is exceeded, measurement data is overwritten by new data.

The data-capturing technique is also very important in the case of log-file analyzers. The first question to be asked is where the logs are located. Figure 7.38 shows that these logs are located in the Web servers. However, more accurate information is required in this case study regarding the following items (Terplan, 1999):

- What memory area is used?
- What auxiliary storage area is used?
- What is the size of this area?
- What types of log files are supported?

If log files are processed in real-time or near real-time, it is important to know where they are stored until they are downloaded for processing by the DF. Log-file analysis deals with very large data volumes, which depend on visitor traffic.

Many vendors place a great degree of emphasis on how quickly a log analyzer can scan data. The speed issue is not really what it appears to be. Most products can process multiple megabytes per minute under ideal conditions. In the real world, however, initial log-read speed is often a factor of the speed of disk drives and not that of the log-analyzer program, because much of the work involves reading huge amounts of data off the drive. Benchmark results show excellent numbers with preresolved domain names. Most vendor benchmarks do not perform reverse DNS lookup on IP addresses. Under typical conditions, it takes time for a Web server to resolve domain names. Optimal processing speed may drop in lookup and DNS conversion cases by a factor of up to 50.

Usually, measurement data and log files are downloaded for further processing. It is important to know how downloads are organized and how rapidly they can be executed. If wide area networks are involved, they may exhibit bandwidth limitations. Bandwidth is usually shared with other applications, potentially producing traffic congestion. Bandwidth-on-demand solutions are rare with measurement probes. When transmission is arranged for low-traffic periods, measurement results may suffer. In such cases, local storage requirements increase, and processing, report generation, and information distribution are delayed by several hours or even by days.

Two solutions may help. The first is using intelligent filtering during and shortly after data collection by monitors. Redundant data is removed from captured packets during collection. Data volumes decrease, along with local storage requirements, but the processing requirements of the probes increase. In the case of logging, intelligent profiling at the source of data collection is very helpful. Redundant data is removed in this early phase. Here as well, Web server processing requirements may increase significantly. The second solution in both cases is to use data compression or data compaction; results and effects will be similar to those observed with the first solution.

Overhead is a critical issue with large data volumes. Data capturing is expected not to introduce any overhead in case of hardware-based probes, and overhead is minimal with software-based probes. It is assumed that measurement data will be stored away immediately after collection. If local processing is taking place, overhead must be carefully quantified. If resource demand is high, probes must be upgraded properly.

Data capturing for logs is expected to introduce little overhead when logs are stored immediately. Again, if local processing is taking place, overhead must be quantified; if resource demand is high, the performance of Web servers may be affected. Data transmission overhead can be heavy in instances in which everything is transmitted to the site where processing takes place. Dedicated bandwidth would be too expensive for measurement and management purposes only. If bandwidth is shared with other applications, priorities must be set higher for business applications than for transmitting measurement or logged data. In the case of LIs, surveillance data may become the highest priority.

It is absolutely necessary that all data necessary in conducting a detailed Web-site analysis of visitors or groups of visitors be captured, including:

- Who is the visitor?
- What is the purpose of the visit?
- Where is the visitor coming from?
- When did the visit take place?
- What key words brought the visitor to the site?
- What search machines helped to access the site?
- How long was the visit?

When different products are compared against the same logging data, results may be different. The reason is that different tools make different assumptions during log analysis. One problem occurs when there is a unique visitor — a potential surveillance target. Without cookies, log files do not record data on people or machines; rather, they record IP addresses only. If a user is browsing from behind a firewall, the program records the IP address of the proxy server. By assuming that one IP address equals one user, these programs risk underreporting visitors if more than one person accesses a site through the same proxy server.

There is also the question of how log-file analyzers define a visit or session. Because HTTP is a stateless protocol, analyzers cannot determine when a user has left a site, which makes it difficult to determine visitation lengths. How much inactivity signals the end of a visit? Default settings vary from vendor to vendor. In terms of LI activities, the fact that a visit took place is more important than the eventual length of the visit.

Data losses cannot be completely avoided. Logging functions in Web servers, storage devices, probes, monitors, networking devices, user workstations, or transmission equipment may fail; in such cases, there will be gaps in the sequence of events. Backup capabilities may be investigated, but IT budgets usually do not allow for extensive resources to be used in backing up large volumes of log-file data. In the worst case, certain time windows are missing in reporting and in statistics. These gaps may be filled with extrapolated data for strategic surveillance. However, targeted surveillance cannot tolerate data losses.

Management of log files is very important. One of the functions in this area is automatic log cycling. Multiple logs are expected to be used to avoid data loss. When one of the logs is full, another seamlessly takes over. A second function is translation of DNS. In this case, speed is absolutely critical for real-time information distribution to LEAs. To generate more meaningful reports, results produced by log-file analyzers must be correlated with other data, which may be maintained in other databases. In order to facilitate this correlation process, *ad hoc* database links should be established and maintained. Management of the logs of any log-file analyzer can be taken over by the Web-server operating system. Basic services in this area are supported today, and additional services may follow.

In cases of server farms or of many individual Web servers, coordination of log transfers and processing is not a trivial task. An event scheduler may help in this respect. Cookie support is important to speed up work initiated by visitors. The connection between Web sites and browsers is logical; a persistent identification code is assigned to a user, and this code allows the user to be tracked across several visits.

Similar to the processing-speed issue is the question of how large a log file a product can handle. Log-file size is dictated more by the amount of RAM or disk space available than anything else. If a product is using a memory-based log-file analysis program to crunch a gigabit-level log, its performance may depend on the quality of the server's operating system. Vendors prefer to use databases to store log-file data.

Due to considerable data volumes, databases should be considered for maintenance of raw or processed data from both log files and monitored traffic. Database managers would then offer a number of built-in features to maintain data. Visitors may be clustered on the basis of various perspectives, such as geography, common applications, common interests on home pages, data, and time of visit. Here automatic log cycling can also be supported by database managers. Open Database Connectivity (ODBC) support assists the exchange of data between different databases and correlation of data from various databases. In addition to measurement data, other data sources can be maintained in the same data warehouse. Also, in addition to routine log-file analysis with concrete targeted reports, a special type of analysis — data mining — may occasionally be conducted. Data mining can reveal traffic patterns and user/visitor behavior. Both are important in sizing systems and networking resources.

The downside of using a database for maintaining log files is that loading the database with data can be a time-consuming procedure. Straight memory-based log-file analysis tools will perform more effectively than database tools on the first pass, but these memory-based tools require a complete reread of the file to run a new query. In cases of significant amounts of logged data, the database method is the only way to go, and this should help service providers and LEAs in regard to the size issue. In order to lower disk space requirements and reduce query times, most products dump certain portions of the log-file data from the database. Despite such steps, log files are usually large. If users want to save and be able to run queries for a longer period of time, a data warehouse with data-mining capabilities is the most promising solution.

One of the most important questions is that of how measurement data analysis performs when data volumes increase. A volume increase can result from more pages being offered on more Web servers, as well as from more visitors, longer visits, and extensive use of page links. In any case, collection and processing capabilities must be estimated and quantified before a decision is made regarding procedures and products.

To reduce the processing and transmission load of measurement and log-file data, redundant data should be filtered out as close as possible to data-capturing locations. Filters can help avoid storing redundant data. They can also be very useful in the report generation process. Again, unnecessary data must not be processed for reports. Powerful filters help to streamline reporting.

Not everything can be automated in measurement and log-file data analysis. The user interface is still one of the most important product selection criteria. GUIs are a likely option, but simple products still use textual interfaces. When measurement and log-file data are integrated with management platforms, this integrated request is automatically met by management platforms.

Reporting is the tool that distributes the results of measurement data and log-file analyses. Predefined reports and report elements, as well as templates, help to speed up the report-design and generation process. Periodic reports can be automatically generated and distributed for both single Web servers and Web-server farms. In cases involving many Web servers, report generation must be carefully synchronized and scheduled. Flexible formatting helps to customize reports to special user needs.

There are many alternatives in terms of report output. Frequently used solutions include Word, Excel, HTML, and ASCII. There are also multiple choices in the area of report distribution:

- Reports may be stored on Web servers and accessed by authorized users equipped with universal browsers.
- Reports can be uploaded into special servers or even pushed to selected users.
- Reports can be distributed as attachments to e-mail messages.
- Reports can be generated at remote sites, which may conserve bandwidth when preprocessed data rather than completely formatted reports are sent to certain remote locations.

Documentation may take various forms. For immediate answers, an integrated online manual would be helpful. Paper-based manuals are still useful in providing detailed answers and analyses. This role, however, will soon be taken over by Web-based documentation systems. In critical cases, hotlines can provide assistance with operational problems.

Measurement and log-file data analysis is actually another management application. If management platforms are used, this application can be integrated into the management platform. There are many ways to complete such an integration; most likely a command line interface (CLI) will be deployed.

7.6.2 IP Monitoring System from GTEN AG

The modular GTEN IP monitoring system (IMS) solution was specially created to undertake assignments on behalf of LEAs. The IMS records all logged data included in data packages. It guarantees system-integrated security procedures, thus eliminating the possibility of data manipulation or mix-ups.

The smallest version is an all-in-one solution using Poseidon. With Poseidon, prosecutors can directly intercept the lines at any given Web site and record, store, and analyze the data immediately. However, in the case of continuous, network-wide monitoring, a complete IMS consisting of three subsystems — data collection and filtering, mass storage, and data re-creation and analysis — is recommended. Figure 7.39 shows a typical IMS architecture.

The components of the subsystems just mentioned can be connected by means of completely separate, secure LANs with 10/100BaseT Ethernet connections or VPNs situated across the Internet. The VPN can be offered as a separate option using SINA (Secure Inter Network Architecture) VPN routers.

The IMS, which has been used successfully by numerous criminal prosecution authorities worldwide, can be extended in increments as a response to the demands of LEAs and in view of the extent of data-monitoring requirements.

7.6.2.1 Data Collection and Filtering Subsystem

The data collection and filtering subsystem is deployed in the field at strategic locations (e.g., ISP or carrier). It passively reads all data from a wide variety of communication lines (such as 10/100/100BaseT Ethernet, GigE, ATM, E1, E3, and STM-1). To avoid flooding the database with unnecessary data, recording filters can be applied. All data meeting filter

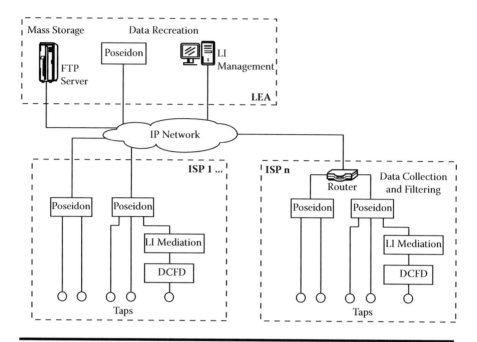

Figure 7.39   Typical example of an IMS system.

criteria are stored at wire speed in a database with an accurate time/date stamp. These recording filters can be based on IP address, TCP port, protocol, e-mail address, or RADIUS log-in ID.

LI mediation and data collection and filtering device (DCFD) are required for application of target monitoring based on log-in identification in conjunction with dynamic IP address assignment. DCFD will be configured and used as a prefilter, as well as for RADIUS. In cases of RADIUS snooping, the DCFD will continuously read all RADIUS traffic and trigger upon a user log-in ID. Up to 250 different target IDs can be handled by a single DCFD.

The recorded data can already be viewed by Poseidon during system setup; Poseidon acts as a data-collecting and storage subsystem to verify the proper operations of complex filters. This setup may be accomplished locally, with a direct connection to an Ethernet crossover cable, or through secure LANs from one or more central locations.

7.6.2.2 Mass Storage Subsystem

In a modular distributed IMS configuration, a central mass storage system will store all collected data. The file server acting as the mass storage system may be sized in accordance with the amount of data recorded and the required archiving duration. Upload of the prefiltered data from the data collection and filter subsystem to the file server can be activated manually or triggered as an automatic process. One or multiple LEAs can retrieve the collected data from the file server for simple viewing, additional postfiltering, and data correlation or other analyses.

7.6.2.3 Data Re-Creation and Analysis Subsystem

Using the Poseidon tool, the LEA can view the recorded data by means of a standard browser; that is, an e-mail is displayed in e-mail format and an Internet page is displayed as an Internet page. The IMS data re-creation and analysis subsystem manages the following applications:

- *WWW sessions:* All target activities can be traced and reconstructed using an Internet browser.
- *FTP transfer:* All data transfers, both uploads and downloads, are traced.
- *E-mails:* All transmitted and received e-mails are recorded.
- *Chat:* All target conversations and chat rooms visited are recorded.
- *Radius:* Data communications associated with an ISP account are recorded.
- *All other IP application data:* These are recorded for offline processing.
- *VoIP:* VoIP sessions are audibly replayed.

7.6.2.4 Typical Monitoring Applications

7.6.2.4.1 Web-Site Monitoring

The purpose of Web-site monitoring is to collect all traffic moving to and from a particular Web site (e.g., Web-mail server). To provision Web-site monitoring in the network, data-monitoring Poseidon units are connected with taps at the lines to the Internet. If a proxy is used inside the network, the taps are usually in front of the proxy. At this point within the network, the source address of the user is detectable and can be correlated with the data recorded at the RADIUS server, which authenticates all user information.

Another Poseidon is connected with taps on the fast Ethernet, which connects the RADIUS server of the ISP. This Poseidon records all authentication dialogs that serve as sources of correlation of user IDs and IP addresses.

Using FTP, the recorded data from the two Poseidons is automatically exported (every 15 minutes, every hour, every day, etc.) to a file server. This file server stores the data (data recorded at the proxy and authentication recorded at the RADIUS server) in a directory structure that must be defined during the installation phase. Both types of data can be imported from the file server to Poseidon units at the LEA for data analysis purposes.

All recorded data is examined at analysis stations (standard PCs with browsers) connected to a specific analysis Poseidon. These analysis stations manage the import of recorded data from the file server to the analysis Poseidon. Because analysis stations have access to the recorded data at the proxy and to the recorded RADIUS data, the recorded IP address and authenticated user information can be correlated.

7.6.2.4.2 Target Monitoring

If all the data traffic of a specific target is to be monitored, the unique ID of the target must be known. This ID can be a fixed IP address or the user identification (log-on ID) during the authentication process with the RADIUS server. The GTEN IMS can incorporate either type of ID. In the case of user authentication via a RADIUS server, the intercepting tap must be connected to the network at a point where the authentication dialog and the data for a specific target can be seen. This does not have to be the same link; one of the DCFD monitoring ports can be connected to a link carrying the data, and the other port can be connected to a link intercepting the RADIUS traffic.

The GTEN DCFD sniffs the entire authentication dialog. If a specific target (previously configured in the management system) is authenticated, the DCFD retrieves the assigned IP address from the RADIUS authentication or accounting messages. Afterward, all data moving to and from this IP address is monitored and sent to a mediation device for further processing. The mediation device replaces the dynamically assigned IP address in the mirrored IP packets with a unique address entered into the configuration during addition of the target to the system; also, it forwards the packets to Poseidon for recording purposes.

All the data from a specific target is exported via FTP from the collecting Poseidon to the file server and target-specific directories. From these directories, data may be imported to the data re-creation Poseidon and viewed via a Web browser running on a standard PC. No correlation has to be made, because the data of a specific target is marked with a unique address. The re-creation Poseidon can be the same as that used for Web-site monitoring.

7.7 Case Study 7: Lawful Interception of VoIP by NetCentrex and GTEN AG

VoIP is a challenging media in regard to legal interception. Many users are concerned that because voice is transmitted "on the Internet," it is not as safe as voice transported over the traditional dedicated telecom network. However, the reverse is true:

- VoIP is often compressed using highly sophisticated media encoders. The only way to access the original voice information is to implement a range of coders in use in a given network. There is no way to simply clip a probe to a pair of wires to listen to a conversation.
- Whereas traditional voice is processed by telecom switches, VoIP softswitches process only call signaling; voice flows directly between the end-user devices (or the VoIP gateways in the case of hybrid VoIP/TDM networks). Thus, it is very easy to access and duplicate the voice media for the HI3 interface from a traditional ISDN switch but very complex in the case of a softswitch, because the softswitch normally does not access the media stream.

In traditional telephony, lawful interception is frequently implemented through an external, independent box situated in one of the voice trunks reaching the central office, which analyzes the call signaling independently and intercepts calls. Because of the difficulties involved in identifying, locating, and accessing the media stream, the softswitch must be an active component in the interception of VoIP calls.

The softswitch must detect those calls that are subject to lawful interception and take appropriate actions to ensure that the media stream is accessible to the media interception function. This requires that the softswitch be notified by various information segments included in the warrant transmitted through the interface HI1. The softswitch must also communicate with the device implementing the HI2 and HI3 interfaces to transmit the essential signaling information required for HI2, as well as the media-stream parameters required for HI3.

7.7.1 Architecture of the Solution

Recognizing the need of all VoIP service providers to comply with regulations, NetCentrex and GTEN have worked together to provide a seamless, turnkey solution for LIs of VoIP calls. In conducting lawful interception, the NetCentrex softswitch (CCS) and the GTEN lawful interception system (Daviath) operate together as follows:

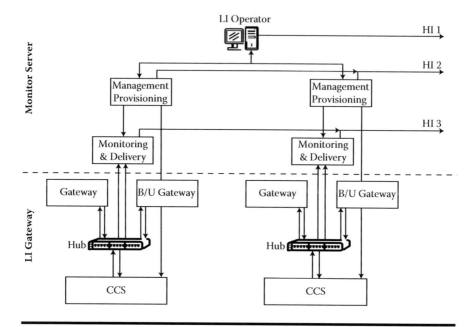

Figure 7.40 Architecture of the GTEN VoIP solution.

■ GTEN Daviath notifies NetCentrex CCS in regard to calls to be
   intercepted using the H1 warrant information.
■ CCS is responsible for identifying the relevant calls (direct calls to
   an intercepted party, calls from the intercepted party, and calls
   forwarded by the intercepted party) and making all the signaling
   and media information accessible to the GTEN Daviath probes.

The system is modular, allowing for distributed deployment. An integrated DCF77 receiver is used to synchronize the internal clock to a high-
precision, international official timing signal. Alternatively, time synchronization may be achieved via a GPS receiver. It is important to receive
the most reliable RF signals at the installation site. The architecture is
shown in Figure 7.40.

The GTEN operator interface to the LI management function uses an
advanced GUI. Access to the management subsystem is controlled by user
IDs and passwords. Each user must be assigned to a user group. Access
rights are controlled, at several levels, by at least one of the following
groups:

■ *System administrator:* configuration of the Daviath system and
   maintenance of user accounts
■ *Network administrator:* configuration of the network interface in
   a distributed environment

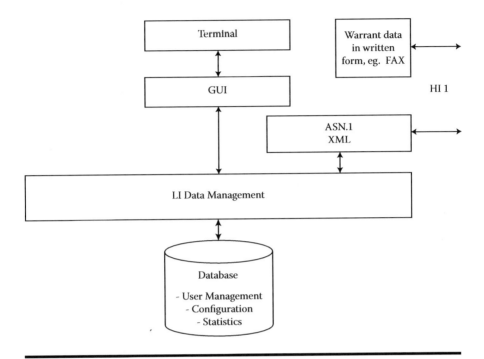

Figure 7.41 HI1 (operator) interface.

- *LI administrator:* entry of warrant data
- *LI operator:* HI1 reporting

A single operator interface may control several geographically distributed management subsystems. The HI1 interface is shown in Figure 7.41.

The HI1 interface may also be connected fully electronically, using an ASN.1 or eXtensible Markup Languge (XML) parser. The ETSI standard involves the use of ASN.1-coded data structures. In order to integrate GTEN Daviath into an existing management system, the HI1 interface may be XML based as well, using a Secure Sockets Layer (SSL) connection.

Provisioning the CCS softswitch on the basis of interception information is supported directly by GTEN Daviath using native CCS provisioning interfaces, and thus this provisioning process does not require that a typical CCS administrator be aware of warrants. In fact, telephony service administrators in general should not be informed of any warrant-related information.

The management and provisioning subsystem maintains all data in an SQL server. The database contains statistics and logs in addition to warrant data. All relevant actions are logged. The provisioning function is responsible for conversion of data into the internal format that will be used to control the LI gateway and the delivery subsystem. This subsystem is also responsible for generation and submission of IRI records.

The monitoring and delivery subsystem is responsible for monitoring of the H.323 protocol and for generating call-related data and relaying this data to the provisioning subsystem, which is required in IRI generation. The contents of all communications are relayed to the HI3 port. Two versions of such ports are available: ISDN BRI or PRI, and HI3 delivery via H.323.

7.7.1.1 HI3 Delivery via ISDN

The NetCentrex CCS softswitch (Figure 7.42) is responsible for VoIP call control and services for established IP networks. The GTEN LI solution provides lawful interception on VoIP networks; in addition, it supports filtering, mediation and offers a HI to the LEA's law enforcement monitoring facility (LEMF), including LI management at the network site.

The VCMI1 interface (100BaseT full-duplex SSL connection) is used to exchange management information between the LI management function in the monitor server and the user management function of the softswitch (Lightweight Directory Access Protocol [LDAP] database). SSL support between the LI monitor server and the LDAP database is not required with a private LAN architecture.

Any calls to and from users identified by an LI tag in the LDAP database are routed through the VoIP LI gateway. Thus, all these calls are automatically routed to the VoIP LI gateway just as they would in the case of any other (e.g., international) gateway. The gateway returns the call with exactly the same Q.931, H.225 parameters. For instance, the VoIP LI gateway acts as a transparent transit form in the communication path between the calling user and the called user. The gateway interface is a 100BaseT full-duplex IP interface extending across the IP network for both the signaling and RTP flow of intercepted VoIP connections.

7.7.1.2 HI3 Delivery via H.323

As an option, the gateway to the PSTN may be used to connect the HI3 port to the LEMF (Figure 7.43). However, there are two major functional requirements that must be met:

1. The gateway must support ISDN closed user group (CVG) facilities.
2. The gateway must support called-party subaddresses and calling-party subaddresses with 20 transparent characters each.

Two HI3 port connections are established as the intercepted call is established, one for the received content and one for the transmitted content. This mode is called stereo mode.

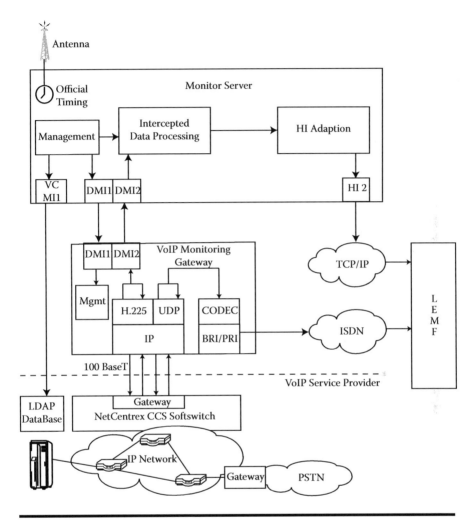

Figure 7.42   System overview using ISDN as HI3 interface.

The LI gateway terminates incoming calls and returns calls with exactly the same Q.931, H.225 parameters. For instance, the VoIP LI gateway acts as a transparent form of transit in the communication path between the calling and called parties.

7.7.2 Description of the Interfaces

7.7.2.1 LEA Interface

The generic handover LEA interface involves a three-port structure such that administrative information (HI1), intercept-related information (HI2),

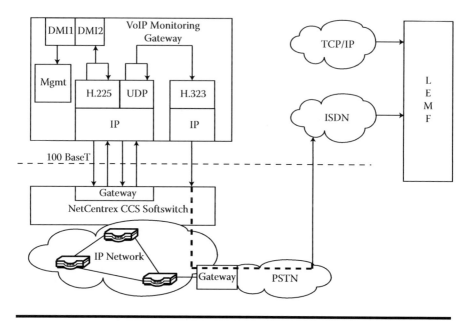

Figure 7.43 HI3 port option H.323.

and communication content (HI3) are logically separated. ETSI Standard ETSI ES 201 158 defines the lawful interception requirements for network functions, and Standard ETSI ES 201 671 defines the HI for lawful interception of telecommunications traffic.

Figure 3.5 (see Chapter 3) shows a block diagram with the relevant domains. The outer circle represents the NWO/AP/SvP domain where the LI monitor server system resides. It contains the network internal functions, the internal network interface (INI), the AF, and the mediation functions for IRI and CC. The inner circle contains the internal functions of the network (e.g., switching, routing, and handling of communications). Within the network internal function, interception results (IRI and CC) are generated in the internal interception function (IIF).

The IIFs provide the content of communication and IRI at the INI. In the case of both kinds of information, mediation functions may be used, which provide the final representation of the standardized HIs at the NWO/AP/SvP domain boundary. Within the NWO/AP/SvP administration center (Daviath LI management subsystem), interception-related tasks, as received via interface HI1, are translated into man–machine commands for the NWO/AP/SvP equipment.

7.7.2.1.1 HI Port 1 (HI1)

HI port 1 transports various kinds of administrative information from and to the LEA and the NWO/AP/SvP organization. This interface may be manual; that is, the data may be entered into the system manually, via a GUI, or electronically, via XML or the ASN.1 coding standard. The HI1 interface may cross borders between countries.

A complete separation is required between the administrative part (HI1) and the technical part (INI) of the interface. The LEMF has no direct access to the switching function. Only the NWO/AP/SvP can activate, deactivate, or modify an interception in the switching function. As an option, some HI1-related information (e.g., fault reporting) may be delivered directly to the LEA using the HI2 mechanism.

The interface HI1 is typically bidirectional. It is used to hand over requests for lawful interception to the NWO/AP/SvP, including orders for activation, deactivation and modification and corresponding notifications, and to send other information to the LEA. The LEA/LEMF has no direct control over the NWO/AP/SvP's equipment.

If the LEA requests lawful interception, the LI management system needs a minimum set of information to activate interception activities in the network. The following information should be supplied by the LEA to activate LI actions:

- Identification of interception subject
- Agreed-upon lawful interception identifier (LIID)
- Start and end (or duration) of interception
- Further specification regarding type of interception (i.e., kind of information to be provided: IRI, CC, or both)
- HI2 destination address of the LEMF to which IRI records will be sent (if applicable)
- HI3 destination address of the LEMF to which the communication content will be sent (if applicable)
- Other network-dependent parameters (e.g., location information and delivery mechanisms used for HI2 and HI3)
- Reference for authorization of the interception
- Technical contact for issues relating to setup and execution of the interception (e.g., solution of problems involving communication links to the LEMF)
- Other information as required

LI management notifications will be sent to the LEMF in the following cases:

- After activation of the lawful interception
- After deactivation of the lawful interception
- After modification of an active lawful interception
- In instances involving certain exceptional situations

If the HI1 is designed as a manual interface, it will normally consist of paper documents. The request for lawful interception may be sent via letter or fax to the NWO/AP/SvP administration center. Administration center personnel will activate the request in the network element (activation of interception). After the interception specified in the lawful authorization is activated, the LEA will be informed. From this point on, the LEA will be prepared to receive IRI via HI2 and CC via HI3.

An alternative solution is to electronically transmit the lawful interception. Information content can be provided, with an XML code, to authorized personnel of the NWO/AP/SvP. This information is electronically imported in the database to reduce the probability of errors.

7.7.2.1.2 HI Port 2 (HI2)

HI port 2 will transport the IRI from the provisioning unit to the LEMF. Delivery takes place, via FTP, across a secured TCP/IP network connection. The individual IRI parameters are coded using ASN.1 and the basic encoding rules (BER). If possible, the format of the parameters' information content is based on existing telecommunications standards.

IRI parameters are sent to the LEMF at least once. The IRI records will contain information available through normal network or service operating procedures. In addition, these records will include information for identification and control purposes as specifically required by the HI2 port. Examples of such information are:

- IRI-BEGIN record at the initiation of a communication attempt, opening the IRI transaction
- IRI-END record at the end of a communication or communication attempt, closing the IRI transaction
- IRI-CONTINUE record at any time during a communication or communication attempt within the IRI transaction
- IRI-REPORT record generally used for non-communication-related events

7.7.2.1.3 HI Port 3 (HI3)

HI port HI3 transports the content of the communication of the intercepted telecommunication service from the delivery unit to the LEMF. The content of communication will be presented as a transparent *en-clair* copy of the information flow during an established, frequently bidirectional, communication of the interception subject. It may contain either voice or data (e.g., from a modulation source such as fax). A target call has two associated directions of transmission: to the target and from the target.

Two communication channels to the LEMF are needed for transmission of communication content (i.e., stereo transmission). The GTEN monitor server system does not record or store communication content.

7.7.2.2 Interface to the Database

The VoIP database is accessed directly from the LI management system of the monitor server through an SSL connection using LDAP. SSL support between the LI monitor server and the LDAP database is not required if there is a private LAN architecture. The following parameters need to be interchanged:

- Target ID: the unique identifier of the target to be intercepted in the VoIP network (a specific number expressed in the pivot format defined by the administrator in CCS)
- LI virtual trunk tag: the unique name that enables routing of the call to either a single LI-GW IP address or several LI-GW IP addresses for redundancy purposes

Two different implementations of the LDAP dialog are provided corresponding to NetCentrex softswitch versions V3.3 and V3.5.

7.7.2.3 Interface between CCS and VoIP LI Gateway

All intercepted connections are routed through the VoIP LI gateway. Basically, this gateway acts as a VoIP bridge. It receives only those setups configured by the provisioning interface. The signaling protocol is terminated according to the H.323 protocol. Figure 7.44 shows a typical example of the protocol process. The RTP flow passes transparently through the VoIP LI gateway.

One VoIP LI gateway can handle 8 interceptions simultaneously. For instance, it can receive 8 simultaneous setups and issue 8 corresponding outgoing setups, and it can handle 16 RTP flow ports, 8 receiving and 8 sending. The data rate and 100BaseT interface will be less than 3 Mbps depending on whether compression (and what type of compression) is used.

NetCentrex information is provided in the incoming setup to the LI gateway. NCX extensions are provided in the nonstandard parameter as an ASN.1 buffer (PER encoding). These extensions are always provided in incoming SETUPs to the LI gateway (Table 7.1). In the same way, they are provided — without modification — in outgoing SETUPs from the LI gateway.

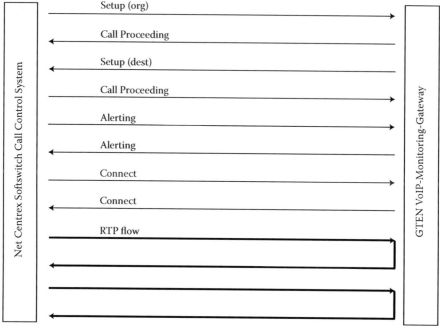

Figure 7.44 Typical protocol flow.

7.7.3 Deployment of the Solution

Many existing VoIP networks have been built on peer-to-peer architectures without any real softswitches for routing of calls. Such networks do not have a "class 4" layer; the VoIP gateways are responsible for routing calls directly. In most cases, these networks are used for transit and toll bypass applications and should not be subject to LI requirements. However, these networks are frequently expanded to support other services, for instance, prepaid calling cards. Many TSPs then overlook the need to revise their network architecture, and they encounter problems when they realize they need to comply with lawful interception requirements.

The NetCentrex-GTEN solution can be deployed relatively easily in such networks, provided that they support a standard such as H.323 or SIP for VoIP call transit. The CCS must be deployed between the users or applications requiring LIs and the remainder of the network. The advanced call-routing functions of CCS can accommodate almost all configurations, allowing them to remain as transparent as possible in regard to existing VoIP applications while providing lawful interception. Figure 7.45 displays the deployment of GTEN Davliath.

Table 7.1 Setup Parameters for NetCentrex

Intercepted	ENUM Either **callingParty** when intercepted call applies to caller or **calledParty** when it applies to receiver of call
CallingPartyPivot	STRING Target ID (if intercepted is **callingParty**); in any case, caller E164 alias expressed in pivot format
CalledPartyPivot	STRING Target ID (if intercepted is **calledParty**); in any case, caller E164 alias expressed in pivot format
RedirectedPartyPivot	STRING FFS
SourceCallSignal-Address	STRING Original source call signal address (as received from caller)
ReplyAddress	STRUCT CCS address where the outgoing SETUPs from the LI-GW must be sent (can change for each intercepted call)
FrameCounter	INTEGER Frame counter (does not decrease)
NonStandardParameters	OCTET BUFFER Original nonstandard information (as received from caller)

In new VoIP networks, TSPs typically are looking for the following applications:

- Residential telephony for primary-line or secondary-line applications: NetCentrex MyCall is a proven solution for such requirements, one used by TSPs such as FastWeb. MyCall seamlessly integrates with the GTEN LI solution.
- Multiservice virtual private networks (VPN) and hosted business telephony, as provided by the NetCentrex IPCentrex solution: Calls from the PSTN to the VPN and from the VPN to the PSTN are subject to LI in some countries. The IPCentrex solution can be integrated with the GTEN LI solution.

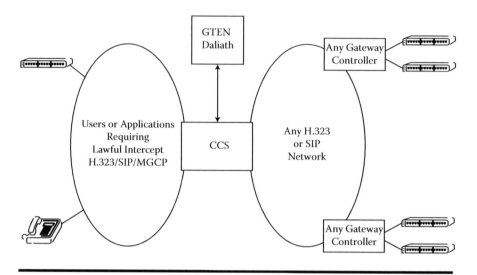

Figure 7.45 Deployment of the GTEN Daliath.

■ Prepaid telephony from IP phones or through VoIP gateways: NetCentrex provides prepackaged, prepaid applications along with its media control server (MCS). The LI feature can be incorporated seamlessly at any time by the addition of GTEN Daviath to the CCS softswitch.

In most cases, the NetCentrex-GTEN solution will be preinstalled and preconfigured at the TSP's premises, and administrators will be trained for the LI function and, in some cases, the warrant activation (if no automated interface is provided to the interception authority). In some cases, however, the solution can be deployed on demand on existing CCS-based VoIP networks following a warrant request from a legal authority. This is possible only in countries where laws allow for a sufficient delay between warrant request and warrant activation, and it requires an initial audit from GTEN experts as well as a service contract.

The current NetCentrex-GTEN solution covers the needs of most TSPs under current regulations. NetCentrex and GTEN are preparing to meet the challenges of future regulations and tougher privacy constraints on LI activities. The main areas of solution development are:

■ Implementation of the Europe-wide lawful interception directive ES 201 671 (telecommunications security, lawful interception, HOI for lawful interception of telecommunications traffic), as well as local variants and profiles (e.g., TR TKÜV in Germany)

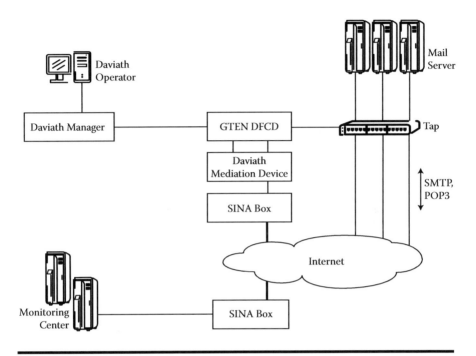

Figure 7.46 Passive filtering in SMTP and POP3 protocols.

- Interface with new router software features that will enable the LI probe to request media packets directly from the router without accessing it directly
- Enhanced reconstruction capabilities for new media types beyond voice

7.8 Case Study 8: Lawful Interception for E-Mail Server Providers by GTEN AG

E-mail has become a key communication, workflow, and collaboration tool for both business and residential users. Four solution alternatives are discussed in this case study.

7.8.1 Passive Filtering in SMTP and POP3 Protocols

Figure 7.46 shows the configuration of the passive-filtering solution. Using a passive tap, all data to and from a mail server are intercepted in front of the mail server. Data is forwarded to DCFD of the Daviath monitoring

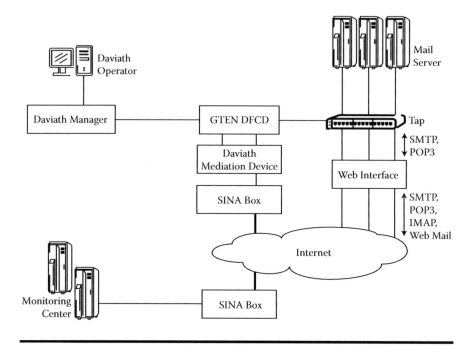

Figure 7.47   Passive filtering with a Web interface.

system. On DCFD, one or more filters are configured for one or more e-mail addresses using the Daviath manager and Daviath operator.

Filtered DCFD data is forwarded to the Daviath mediation device, which packs the data in HI2 and HI3 formats in accordance with valid standards and forwards them to the SINA box. There the data is encrypted and transmitted to the LEA via an Internet tunnel. Data can be reconstructed and evaluated on the other side of the tunnel by the LEA, for instance, by using monitoring center (MC) applications. (At present, this solution is applicable only for the POP3 and SMTP protocols. It cannot as yet be utilized with Web mail or IMAP.)

7.8.2 Passive Filtering with a Web Interface

Figure 7.47 shows the configuration of this solution. The passive tap is provisioned between the mail server and the Web interface. Data flowing to and from the mail server is forwarded to DCFD. Between the two entities, POP3 and SMTP protocols are in use; between the Web interface and the Internet, other protocols, such as HTTP or IMAP, might be in use.

Again, filtered DCFD data is forwarded to the Daviath mediation device. This devices packs the filtered data in HI2 and HI3 formats in accordance

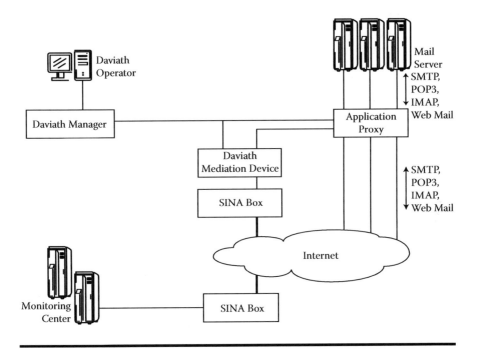

Figure 7.48   Filtering using an application proxy.

with valid standards and forwards it to the SINA box, where it is encrypted and transmitted to the LEA via an Internet tunnel. The data can be reconstructed and evaluated on the other side of the tunnel by the LEA. (At present, this solution can only be used with an existing Web interface. However, all important protocols, for example, POP3, SMTP, IMAP, and Web mail, including SSL, are supported.)

7.8.3 Active Filtering Using an Application Proxy

Figure 7.48 shows the configuration of this alternative. The task of the MG located in front of the mail server is to terminate the connection to the Internet and to hand over the protocol in use to the mail server. On the MG, one or more filters are configured for one or more e-mail addresses using the Daviath manager and Daviath operator.

As in the previous examples, filtered DCFD data is forwarded to the Daviath mediation device, which packs it in HI2 and HI3 formats and forwards it to the SINA box. There, data is encrypted and transmitted to the LEA through an Internet tunnel. Data can be reconstructed and evaluated on the other side of the tunnel by the LEA. (This solution

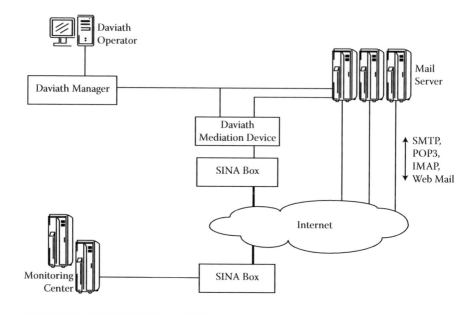

Figure 7.49 Modification of the mail server software.

supports all relevant protocols, including POP3, SMTP, IMAP, and Web mail, with SSL. Considerable changes may be necessary if new Web-mail versions are deployed in the future.)

7.8.4 Modification of Mail Server Software

Figure 7.49 shows the configuration of this alternative. The software of the mail server is modified in such a way that a separate interface forwards the data of the connection to be monitored directly to the Daviath mediation device. Customization of the mail server will be requested at the mail server manufacturer by the mail server operator. The mail server obtains the necessary information about the nature of the data to be intercepted and collected via the Daviath operator and the responsible Daviath manager.

The mediation device packs the filtered data in HI2 and HI3 formats in accordance with valid standards and forwards them to the SINA box, where they are encrypted and transmitted to the LEA through an Internet tunnel. Data can be reconstructed and evaluated on the other side of the tunnel by the LEA. (This solution supports the following protocols: POP3, SMTP, IMAP, and Web mail, including SSL. Modified versions are available for Postfix, Qmail, Exim, and Sendmail.)

In summary, the following conclusions can be drawn regarding e-mail interception:

- Various e-mail intercept solutions are available.
- Emphasis must be placed on dealing with data volumes, given that both IRI and content must be maintained.
- Powerful analytical applications are needed to reduce the volumes of intercepted data.

7.9 Case Study 9: MC Case Examples from Siemens AG

The MC is a flexible but complex collection of software modules and hardware components that interoperate to perform the tasks associated with monitoring. It handles intercepts of voice and data in fixed and mobile networks as well as the Internet and other IP networks.

7.9.1 Fixed Network — PSTN

This case example looks more closely at the MC application for lawful interception in PSTN networks. Three main entities in this application scenario are addressed by the ETSI standards for lawful interception: network, interception management system (IMS), and monitoring system.

Target subscribers are "marked" in the PSTN network by the IMS application upon request by an external entity such as an LEA. When the target subscriber uses his or her mobile device to make or receive a call, this information is relayed to the IMS, along with all subsequent call-related data (called number, call duration, cell identifier, etc.). The content of the call (i.e., voice or data content) is passed by the network switch directly to the MC associated with the requesting LEA. The call-related data relayed to the IMS is then distributed by the IMS to the (one or more) MCs associated with the respective requesting LEAs.

These two sets of information, which may arrive at the MC at different times, are eventually correlated with a single intercept and made available in the folders in which they are "triggered" and made visible to users with the appropriate approval. Figure 7.50 shows the role of the MC in fixed network intercepts.

7.9.1.1 Network Protocols

The MC supports E1 interfaces to network switches and the EDSS1 line protocol.

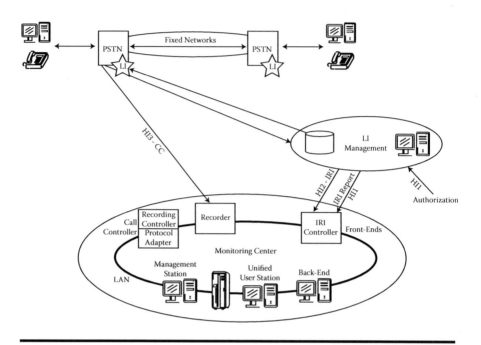

Figure 7.50 MC for LI in fixed networks.

7.9.1.2 Network Switches

The MC can receive intercepts from any manufacturer switch that adheres to the ETSI standard for lawful interception. In particular, it has been deployed with the Siemens, Ericsson, Alcatel, and Nokia switches.

7.9.1.3 Interception and Recording Modes

Several modes of operation are used in receiving and recording intercepts. The MC can be set up to receive stereo intercepts wherein one channel is used for each direction of the call. Each direction of the call can then be played back, either together or separately. If stereo recording is not required, mono mode can be used, with resultant savings in terms of interface lines.

Also, several manually configurable compression modes can be used for voice recording and can result in great disk space savings. One automatic mode is controlled in the front end. When the initiation of a fax or modem transmission is detected in the call content, the current recording mode is terminated and "high-quality" or full-line-speed recording is initiated. The goal is to ensure that none of the transmission is lost, as this would render later demodulation attempts useless.

7.9.1.4 Types of Interception

The MC supports the following types of interception from PSTN networks:

- Voice conversations
- Call-related information
- DTMF in-band transmissions
- SMS messages
- Fax transmissions (with optional add-on system)
- Modem transmissions, including local loop Internet (with optional add-on system)

7.9.1.5 Interception Management Systems

The MC supports any IMS that adheres to the ETSI standard for lawful interception. In particular, it has been deployed with Siemens LIOS, Utimaco IMS, Ericsson IMS, and Alcatel IMS.

7.9.1.6 Add-On Systems

The MC supports demodulation and decoding of fax transmissions and modem transmissions, including local loop Internet, by integrating third-party systems. The modes of third-party integration offered to customers vary according to customers' requirements. However, no matter what the integration option, operators are offered a single unified view of the resulting information via the unified user station (UUS).

With a PSTN fixed-line network, the LEA can, in most cases, determine the physical address of the target subscriber based on the telephone number used. The TSP can match the subscriber number to a switch and then identify the address of the line connected to the subscriber.

7.9.1.7 General Interception Management Features

A primary strength of the MC is that, whatever the target-network type (fixed, mobile, or Internet) and the interception type (voice, fax, call-related data, DTMF tones, SMS message, local loop Internet or ISP, or core-level Internet), users are offered a single unified set of interception management features.

7.9.1.8 Feature Highlights

The following table (Table 7.2) summarizes the principal intercept management features.

Table 7.2 Principle Intercept Management Feature Highlights for Fixed Networks

Feature	Highlights
Intercepts	View in list or as individual intercepts, filter list view
	Copy, paste, delete from list
	Configure associated information columns as desired
	View all associated attachments in list format
Attachments	View in list or as individual attachments, filter list view
	Copy, paste, delete from intercept
	Add, edit, delete transcription attachments
Playbacks	Real-time and variable-speed playback of voice recordings
	Multiple marking of recording for annotation or looping
	Hot-key control of playback from within transcription editor
	Multiple- or single-channel synchronized playback
Fax viewing	View, zoom, rotate, negative viewing, print
Internet local loop	Launch viewer on Internet attachment and navigate entire sessions from modem signaling to Web pages viewed; any FTP transmissions or e-mail sent and received may be monitored as well
DTMF tones	Playback as voice recording or read detected tones in attachment
	View visually marked tones in voice-recording playback
SMS messages	Read plaintext of transmitted SMS message
Location	View current and previous locations of mobile device (with add-on MC-GIS)
Call-related data	View, delete, print all call-related records associated with an intercept
Trigger management	Configure triggers to direct flow of intercepts to appropriate folders (dossiers)
Folder management	Configure folders into filters (triggers) directing intercepts
	Automate folder initiation, completion, and flushing times
Archiving	Archive data to a variety of media types, including MOD, DVD-RAM, and hard disk; produce labels to mark media; restore from archived media

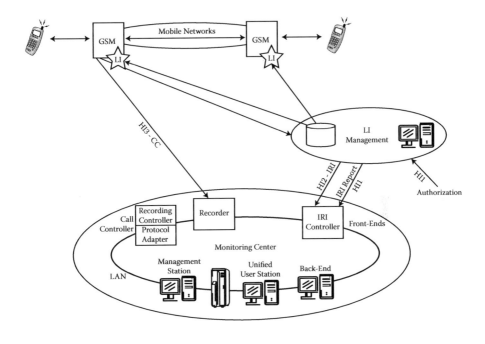

Figure 7.51 MC for LI in GSM networks.

7.9.2 Mobile Network — GSM

This case example highlights the MC application for lawful interception in GSM networks. Three main entities (networks, interception management system and MC) in this application scenario are addressed by the ETSI standards for lawful interception.

Also, GSM networks make additional information available to the MC. The identifier of the GSM call from which the mobile device is receiving a signal is passed to the IMS, and hence to the MC, as call-related data. Figure 7.51 shows the role of the MC in GSM network interceptions.

7.9.2.1 Add-On Systems

With a PSTN fixed line, the network physical address of the target subscriber device is known. In the case of GSM mobile devices, this information is not as easy to gather. However, the location of the mobile cell is known, and it can be passed to the MC geographical information system (MC-GIS) to track the locations of active calls. Feature highlights are identical to those associated with intercepting fixed networks.

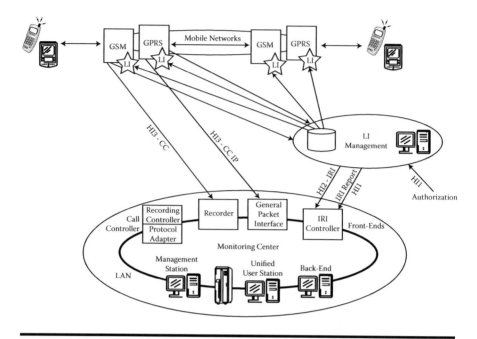

Figure 7.52   MC for LI in GPRS/UTMS networks.

7.9.3 Mobile Networks — GPRS/UMTS

This case example concentrates on the new generation of networks. The General Packet Radio Service (GPRS)/Universal Mobile Telecommunications System (UMTS) third-generation mobile networks are different in at least one respect from the GSM networks: they involve both circuit-switched and packet-oriented features. The MC addresses interception needs related to both types of traffic. This study assesses the MC lawful interception application in the case of circuit-switched elements of GPRS/UMTS networks.

GPRS networks have not been widely deployed to date, and UMTS networks have only been piloted. The MC was developed and tested in advance of wide deployment of these networks. Figure 7.52 shows the role of the MC in intercepting GPRS and UMTS networks.

Some additional information is available to the MC from GPRS/UMTS networks: the identifier of the cell in which the mobile device is receiving a signal is passed to the IMS and the MC as call-related data.

7.9.3.1 Network Protocols

The MC supports E1 interfaces to network switches and the EDSS1 line protocol.

7.9.3.2 Network Switches

The MC can accept interception from any manufacturer switch that adheres to the ETSI standard for lawful interception.

7.9.3.3 Interception Types

To the interception types reviewed in the earlier case examples of Siemens, IP traffic on the packet-switch part of the network is added.

7.9.3.4 Add-On Systems

Due to the mobility of the device used in GPRS/UMTS systems, location information is not available to the TSP. What is available, however, is a discrete cell identifier from which the mobile device receives its signal. Using the MC-GIS add-on application, this information can be transposed to a physical map showing the current location of the mobile device. Further extrapolations to the incoming information can indicate the direction of travel of the device. This add-on has been discussed in more detail in Chapter 5.

7.9.3.5 Feature Highlights

In addition to the feature highlights discussed earlier, IP traffic is under consideration, with the following attributes: read, view, navigate entire Web, e-mail, FTP, and chat sessions.

7.9.4 Internet Monitoring

The MC supports IP traffic monitoring with interfaces to GPRS and UMTS networks as well as ISP and Internet backbone points. Unlike with fixed- and mobile-network technology, there has to date been no standardization regarding Internet lawful interception activities.

The MC offers passive Internet monitoring. It also supports lawful interception of IP packet data on GPRS and UMTS networks.

Figure 7.53 shows the role of the MC in dealing with Internet and IP network intercepts.

7.9.4.1 Data Collectors

The MC uses a variety of data collectors to connect points on the Internet to intercept data. These different data collectors offer varied interface and throughput alternatives such that solutions can be tailored to customers'

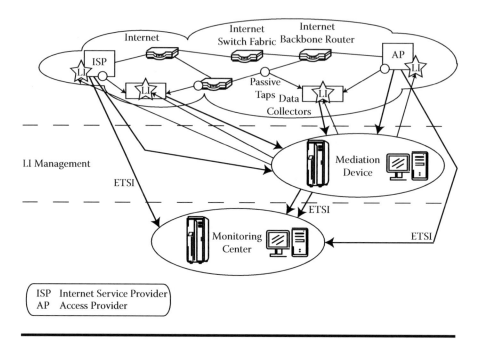

Figure 7.53   MC for LI in Internet and IP networks.

needs. Differences in data collector interfaces are mediated via the MC's mediation device. The MC administrator operator can apply sophisticated filters to the data collectors to refine the data they capture. In the case of GPRS, all available IP data is collected by the GPRS GPI, as the lawful interception elements of the GPRS switches have completed the filtering process.

Several data collectors can be used in parallel in instances in which many Internet connection points are required or in which there are large amounts of IP traffic. The data collectors are managed by a mediation device, and captured data is sent to the decoder. There, data is normalized into the MC internal format and passed further to the back end. In the back end, data is handled in a manner similar to circuit-switched intercepts. IP data interceptions benefit from all the system capabilities and interception-handling features of the MC.

7.9.4.2 Internet Applications

The Internet uses IP, the Internet protocol, to universally transport control and data information packets. Different application protocols on top of IP are used for different Internet facilities such as Web pages, e-mail, FTP, and so forth. The MC can intercept and record all IP traffic. It directly supports decoding, interception management, and visual display of the following (other IP application decoders can be applied to the remaining recorded IP traffic if required):

- Web sessions
- E-mail (SMTP, POP3, and Web mail)
- Internet relay channels (IRC and chat)

7.9.4.3 Internet Access Points

The MC can apply data collectors to any IP source. These source points are usually GPRS switches, ISP SPAN ports, Internet backbone links, or Internet core computers.

7.9.4.4 Physical Interfaces

The MC data collectors support many physical interfaces. The most common three are Ethernet 100 Mbps, Ethernet 1000 Mbps, and OC3.

7.9.4.5 Filtering

Large amounts of IP data are handled by even the smallest ISP every day. Typically, through the use of filters, the MC is required to target only a small amount of that traffic. The operator sets a filter that contains information about the target user, such as e-mail address, Web-site address (URL), or even an IP address itself. The filter is applied by the MC mediation device to the appropriate data collector. It filters all the IP data it receives, looking for matches. This action leads to significant reductions in the amount of data that must be further managed and eases the task of the operator.

7.9.4.6 Back-End Internet Applications

In the MC UUS, the operator is presented with the captured Internet information in a manner appropriate to the Internet application. If this is a Web session, the operator can replay the Web sites visited and the Web pages viewed by the target user. If the captured data consists of e-mails, operators are offered a viewer that provides three means of viewing the e-mail:

1. A simple view of the e-mail as if they had received it themselves
2. A more detailed view of the e-mail showing its structure and the "where, when, and from-whom" details and route traveled
3. A detailed view including raw content and all normally hidden details

This is typical of the approach taken in the MC to offer operators a level of detail appropriate to the task at hand. The simple view can be used to quickly scan through all e-mails first. If the operator needs to study an e-mail more closely, he or she can use the more detailed views to fully dissect the messages. Viewers with similar levels of viewing are offered for Web and IRC sessions.

7.9.4.7 Interception Management Features

As mentioned, a primary strength of the MC is that no matter what the target-network type or interception type, the user is offered a single unified set of interception management features. Most of the features summarized in the following table (Table 7.3) are subject to the appropriate permissions being allocated to a user.

7.9.5 Conclusions

Siemens concentrates on complete end-to-end solutions, emphasizing collaboration between front-end and back-end products. The MC is a high-tech solution on its own. In addition, it represents an entry for outsourcing lawful interception. The MC is actually the peering point between TSPs and LEAs.

7.10 Summary

Case studies, in addition to the necessary level of awareness regarding product features, can help provide an understanding of how to deal with practical solutions. This chapter has addressed nine different cases — with some overlaps — that represent actual telecommunications services and products. These case studies, e.g., for wireless networks, packet data applications and VoIP, show that there are no technological barriers to lawful interception activities. Operational issues and cost considerations will be addressed in the next chapter.

Table 7.3   Principal Intercept Management Feature Highlights for Internet Monitoring

Feature	Highlights
Intercepts	View in list or as individual intercepts, filter list view
	Copy, paste, delete from list
	Configure associated information columns as desired
	View all associated attachments in list format
Attachments	View in list or as individual attachments, filter list view
	Copy, paste, delete from intercept
	Add, edit, delete transcription attachments
Playbacks	Real-time and variable-speed playback of voice recordings
	Multiple marking of recording for annotation or looping
	Hot-key control of playback from within transcription editor
	Multiple- or single-channel synchronized playback
IP traffic	Read, view, navigate entire Web, e-mail, FTP, chat sessions
	Simple or detailed views of IP applications
Filter management	Configure filters (triggers) to intercept target users' Internet communications and direct them to the appropriate folders (dossiers)
Folder management	Configure folders into appropriate filters (triggers) directing the intercept
	Automate folder initiation, completion, and flushing times
Archiving	Archive data to a variety of media types, including MOD, DVD-RAM, and hard disk; produce labels to mark media; restore from archived media

Chapter 8

Operating Lawful Intercepts

CONTENTS

Operational efficiency is a key success factor in lawful interception. After summarizing operational requirements, here we address elements and prerequisites of conducting lawful intercept (LI) activities in the United States, Europe, and Japan. From a practical perspective, special emphasis is placed on the execution process involved in lawful interceptions. A role-based model allows clear identification of all players, including telecommunications service providers (TSPs), law enforcement agencies (LEAs), and outsourcers, along with their responsibilities and typical job profiles. Administration and management are key in terms of minimizing the human resource demands associated with lawful interception activities.

More automation is targeted for inventory management, order processing, provisioning, and performance management. Security solutions for the LEA handover interface (HI) are addressed in detail. Finally, headcount estimates are included as an aid in quantifying budgets for lawful interception activities.

8.1 Operational Requirements

In a typical operation, a lawfully authorized surveillance request arrives for a specified intercept subject. Authorized personnel provision the intercept, which may focus on content only, IRI only, or both. Once the intercept is provisioned, the interception access points (IAPs) send the intercept-related information (IRI) or content to the mediation device (MD), which formats the information for delivery to the LEA. Some of the operational issues that need to be considered are as follows (Baker, 2003):

- *Location and address information for content intercepts:* In some cases in which location or address information for the intercept is not known until the subject registers (or, in the case of voice, makes a call), the IRI may provide the information necessary to conduct the content tap (e.g., IP address and port for content streams).
- *Content encryption:* If the intercept content is encrypted and the service provider has access to the encryption keys (e.g., receives the keys in Session Description Protocol for Voice-over-IP [VoIP]), the keys can be sent via IRI. It is, however, possible for end users to exchange keys by some other means without the knowledge of the service provider, in which case the service provider will not be able to provide the keys. In any event, MD content formatting should not modify the original intercepted information in a way that the LEA is unable to decipher it. This is why, in the case of VoIP intercepts, for example, it is recommended that the original voice packets be sent to the LEA rather than attempting to convert them to some other format (e.g., TDM).
- *Detection by the intercept subject:* One of the most important requirements is to ensure that intercept subjects are unable to detect that they are being intercepted. Subjects can check IP addresses and use trace routes to determine whether any unusual signaling is taking place on their customer premises equipment (CPE) and to detect degradation or interruptions in service. Thus, the intercept mechanism must not involve requests to the CPE, rerouting of packets, or end-to-end changes in IP addresses, and content must be intercepted on a device situated along the normal content path (i.e., no rerouting is involved) on the service provider's

(rather than the customer's) network. A convenient content IAP is a router or switch at the edge of the service provider's network to which the intercept subject connects. An alternative is to place a special device along the path that provides content IAP capabilities.

■ *Unauthorized creation and detection:* Another concern is prevention of unauthorized creation and detection of intercepts. This is particularly important when a network element such as a router is used as a content IAP. Routers that have the necessary capability must be carefully controlled, with only authorized personnel having access to intercept capability and information. The recommended approach is that the MD be situated in a controlled environment and the intercept request to the content IAP be made over an encrypted link. In addition, logging and auditing must be used to detect unauthorized attempts to access the intercept capability.

■ *Maintenance and management:* The LI solution selected should involve only minimal interference with normal maintenance and management procedures.

■ *Capacity:* Support for LI activities results in additional consumption of resources in terms of network equipment capacity. Therefore, support for LI requires capacity planning and engineering to ensure that revenue-producing services are not adversely affected.

8.2 Prerequisites of Lawful Interception in the United States, Europe, and Japan

This section addresses conditions associated with LIs. Both the parties involved — LEAs and TSPs — are expected to be aware of the rules that are specific and relevant to the geographical area under consideration.

8.2.1 United States

U.S. laws and regulations are very clear, and justification of LIs is taken very seriously. Details of LI activities involving national security are usually not made public.

8.2.1.1 When Is Surveillance Justified?

The basis for surveillance is "probable cause" as defined by the Fifth Amendment of the U.S. Constitution. Wiretapping is warranted in situations involving the following:

- Drug trafficking
- Gambling
- Blackmailing
- Manslaughter and murder
- Armed robbery
- Debt crime and racketeering
- Bribery
- Kidnapping

The U.S. Patriot Act adds the following crimes to this list:

- Use of chemical weapons and weapons of mass destruction
- Global terrorism
- Financial transactions supporting terrorism
- Financial support of terrorists and terrorist organizations

Wiretapping does have some limitations for probable cause. The pen/trap and trace statute is not limited to particular categories of crimes.

8.2.1.2 Approval for Surveillance

Each surveillance action (e.g., Title III or pen/trap statute) must be granted approval by a U.S. federal or state judge. In addition, other associated legal processes may include:

- An administrative subpoena authorized through a federal or state statute
- A subpoena issued by a federal or state grand jury
- A trial subpoena
- A specific and articulable facts order signed by a judge or magistrate
- A search warrant
- Proof of customer consent (but not for call to destinations)

(Note that the government cannot use a subpoena to obtain e-mail addresses, Web-site communications, or IP addresses of Web sites visited.) General requirements in the area of warrants are as follows:

- Prosecutors must establish probable cause that one or more serious felonies are being committed; they must also establish the parties responsible for the felonies and determine that the target phone is being used to conduct communications related to these crimes.
- The government must show that it has exhausted alternative investigative means and that eavesdropping is necessary.

- The government must ensure that procedures are in place to minimize the number of conversations intercepted.
- The order's duration must be 30 days or less.
- The court must supervise the execution of the order.

At present, binding recommendations are not in place, or guidelines are unclear, in certain circumstances related to mail and communication content. The current situation can be summarized as follows in regard to voice mail, e-mail, and text messages:

- Under federal law, a search warrant can be used to obtain access to unopened voice mail, e-mail, and text messages.
- It is unclear whether a search warrant is needed to gain access to opened voice mail, e-mail, and text messages.
- Most states appear to still require a warrant for eavesdropping activities.
- Proof of customer consent is sufficient to grant access.
- Preservation of content is often the most significant problem.

Real-time interception of telephone conversations, real-time interception of e-mail and text messages, and accessing of unopened voice mail (in most states) require Title III eavesdropping warrants.

8.2.1.3 Duration of Surveillance

Typically, wiretap warrants are in force for 30 days; in certain cases, they may be extended by another 30 days. The usual duration for pen/trap orders is 60 days, with 60-day extensions in some cases.

8.2.1.4 Checking Warrants

Appropriate personnel are expected to check warrants and legal documentation. The "good faith reliance defense" protects them against criminal charges.

8.2.2 Europe

Laws and regulations in Europe are very clear. Legal bodies in all countries take the area of justification of LIs very seriously. Regulations in cases of national security emergencies differ in various countries.

8.2.2.1 France

The process in France is similar to that in other countries; however, additional emphasis is placed on the protection of economy and science.

8.2.2.1.1 When Is Surveillance Justified?

Ècoutes judiciares can be issued for serious crimes (i.e., those in which the expected sentence exceeds two years). Also, preventive surveillance warrants can be issued in the following cases:

- National security and national defense
- Organized terrorism or crime
- Protection of science and economy

As of yet, however, there are no regulations in the area of data retention.

8.2.2.1.2 Approval of Surveillance

Ècoutes judiciares must be signed by a judge as part of either crime control or the trial process. These signed warrants are forwarded to TSPs directly. TSPs are expected to distribute them to the sites that will be responsible for the intercepts.

Preventive surveillance is authorized by the prime minister subsequent to surveillance applications submitted by the minister of interior, minister of defense, or the minister in charge of customs. In such instances, applications have been reviewed by the *Groupe Interministeriel de control* (GIC) and *Controle des Interceptions Securite* (CNCIS).

8.2.2.1.3 Duration of Surveillance

Four months is the typical duration granted for surveillance activities, and this period may be extended by another four months. In addition, there are no upper limits in terms of such extensions. The duration specified for data retention is one year.

8.2.2.1.4 Checking Warrants

There is no legal guidance in terms of reviewing warrants. However, TSPs face sanctions if they reveal information about their customers without a valid legal order. The content and legality of warrants and search orders should always be assessed.

8.2.2.2 United Kingdom

The process is very similar to that in other countries, with additional regulations in place for public health emergencies.

8.2.2.2.1 When Is Surveillance Justified?

According to Regulation of Investigatory Power Act (RIPA) regulations, valid justifications for surveillance are national security, protection against and prosecution of serious crime, and economic protection of the United Kingdom. Data retention guidelines and rules are regulated by RIPA as well. Valid reasons for data retention are as follows:

- National security concerns
- Protection against and prosecution of serious crime
- Economic protection of the United Kingdom
- Public safety
- Public health
- Collection of taxes and customs

8.2.2.2.2 Approval of Surveillance

Applications to conduct surveillance activities must be signed by the home secretary or by the Scottish representative. The following individuals are responsible for submitting applications:

- Director general of secret services
- Chief of secret services
- Director of government communications headquarters
- Director general of the National Criminal Intelligence Service
- Commissioner of police of the metropolis
- Chief constable of the Royal Ulster Constabulary
- Chief constable (or representative) of the Scottish police
- Commissioners of customs and excise
- Chief of defense intelligence
- Other internationally accredited personnel

The reasons why surveillance is necessary must be clearly stated (e.g., no other investigative alternatives are available or all other alternatives have been exhausted).

8.2.2.2.3 Duration of Surveillance

According to RIPA regulations, surveillance activities can continue for up to three months. This mandate may be extended by another three months (in the case of serious criminal activities) or by six months (in the case of national security and protection of the economy).

8.2.2.2.4 Checking Warrants

There are no guidelines in place in regard to checking the legitimacy of warrants. However, TSPs typically engage in this practice to avoid violating privacy laws. There have been past cases in which fraudulent warrants have been issued by private investigators.

8.2.3 Japan

There is a need for more clarification in terms of guidelines surrounding LIs. However, Japan's regulations differ from those of other countries in that more of an emphasis is placed on illegal immigration.

8.2.3.1 When Is Surveillance Justified?

In Japan, LIs are justified in cases involving drug trafficking, illegal arms commerce, organized murder, and illegal immigration.

8.2.3.2 Approval of Surveillance

Surveillance activities are based on warrants issued by district court judges or higher ranked police officers. Applications are submitted by prosecutors. Typically, approval is granted in cases involving criminal activity and criminal activity supported by electronic communications, as well as those in which other investigative alternatives are not feasible. Also, approval is usually granted in instances in which the surveillance actions to be undertaken are very accurately specified.

8.2.3.3 Duration of Surveillance

The typical surveillance duration is 10 days; this period may be extended up to a maximum of 30 days.

8.2.3.4 Checking Warrants

There is no need for checking warrants; surveillance actions are executed by LEAs.

8.3 Executing LI Missions in the United States, Europe, and Japan

In this section, guidelines for executing LI activities are addressed, with an emphasis on technical procedures and capabilities, data maintenance, and handover of data to LEAs.

8.3.1 United States

As a result of substantial experience with LI technology, U.S. guidelines are rich in regard to details.

8.3.1.1 Required Specifications for Targets

Targets must be clearly identified by particular means, such as name, address, phone number, fax number, e-mail address, or other technical attributes that determine clearly the surveillance action. However, this does not mean that all types of records maintained by TSPs must be handed over to LEAs. Such records are limited to the following (see 18 USC § 2703(c)(2)):

- Customer name and address
- Local and long-distance connection records and records of session times and durations
- Length of service (including initiation date) and types of services used
- Telephone or instrument number or other subscriber number or identity
- Means and source of payment for service (including any credit card or bank account numbers)
- Numbers from which the target phone was called (calls-to-destination reports)

8.3.1.2 What Is Subject to Surveillance?

In the case of wiretaps, complete surveillance records and communications-related information and content must be forwarded to LEAs. In instances involving Internet communications, the nature of the warrant determines the type of surveillance action. If a Title III warrant has been issued, all communications must be forwarded; if a pen/trap statute is in place, communications-related data, but not content, must be made available to LEAs. In the case of e-mail, the fact that an e-mail exchange has occurred (send or receive) is recorded without the "reference" line (pen/trap), or the full content is intercepted and forwarded to the LEA (Title III).

8.3.1.3 Handover to LEAs

Wiretap warrants involve an expectation of real-time handover. This is a real "interception" in accordance with Title III. The public switched network is used in handovers of voice to LEAs; VPNs are typically used in data handovers. By the law, emergency operators always represent the highest priority.

In instances in which a public emergency assistance number, such as 911 or *CG (Coast Guard), is called, the subscriber's name, phone number, contact number, billing address, and cell-site location can be provided to the following:

- Public-safety answering point
- 911 operator
- Emergency medical services provider
- Emergency dispatch provider
- Public safety agency (e.g., Coast Guard)
- Fire service
- Law enforcement official
- Hospital emergency or trauma care facility

The preceding does not apply to private crisis and suicide hotlines.

TSPs are granted approval to store data in instances in which LEAs are to receive information or intelligence in correspondence with pen/trap statutes. This data is usually burned onto CD-ROMs and sent to the LEA. Stored communications may be confiscated by LEAs on the basis of ECPA 18 USC 270 3(a).

8.3.1.4 Technical Equipment Requirements

Wiretap and pen/trap, and trace activities require specific and usually different technical equipment (monitors, sniffers, and logging applications), as well as different organizational processes.

8.3.1.5 Real-Time Surveillance or Storing Data

Supervised and intercepted content is forwarded immediately to LEAs. Data storage is considered occasionally for communications-related data and stored communications such as e-mail. The usual storage duration is 14 days. Stored communications are subject to search warrants.

8.3.2 Europe

European countries have experience in regard to the technical aspects of LIs but still must find a common denominator for EU-wide standards.

8.3.2.1 France

Detailed guidelines are available, and requirements can be categorized in regard to both real-time and data retention actions.

8.3.2.1.1 Required Target Specifications

Warrants should contain the following target information in writing: clear identification of connections (name of owner, number, address, and other attributes), clear identification of the crime, and duration of intended surveillance. The name of the targeted person, however, must not be disclosed.

8.3.2.1.2 What Areas Are Subject to Surveillance?

All telecommunications services — that is, all forms of "correspondence" — are subject to surveillance.

8.3.2.1.3 Handover to LEAs

Handover can, but must not, be supported in real-time. Intercepted information can be relayed to LEAs either online or offline. Decisions regarding handover protocols depend on the technical capabilities of TSPs and LEAs.

8.3.2.1.4 Technical Equipment Requirements

There are strong guidelines differentiating *ècoutes judiciares* (individual surveillance) from *interceptions de securitè* (preventive surveillance). Among others, separate rooms are required for these two different types of operations. In addition, the results of a single surveillance action cannot be shared with multiple LEAs. However, there are no requirements for TSPs in terms of the technical solutions deployed in individual and preventive surveillance activities.

8.3.2.1.5 Real-Time Surveillance and Data Storage

Intercepted voice traffic is forwarded to LEAs in real-time. Handover of Internet traffic depends on the technical capabilities of LEAs. The following rules must be followed in regard to data retention:

- Access providers record log-ins of users, addresses, and dates and times of initiations and terminations of communications (typical duration: three months).
- Proxy-server providers store data regarding IP addresses of users, identifications of connected servers, identifications of targeted documents, dates, and times (typical duration: three to five days).
- Hosting providers record log-ins of users, IP addresses, and dates and times of initiations and terminations of communications (typical duration: three months).

If so requested, this data can be handed over to LEAs within the retention time frame.

8.3.2.2 United Kingdom

No binding guidelines are available at present. Coordination between the National Technical Assistance Centre (NTAC) and the data controller is key to successful LI operations.

8.3.2.2.1 Required Target Specifications

The following items are included in warrants:

- Copy of the order issued by the minister of the interior
- Important surveillance data such as names, addresses, and other IDs
- Additional surveillance and handover details

This information is collected by the targeted TSP.

8.3.2.2.2 What Is Subject to Surveillance?

Ongoing telecommunications activities are targeted, and content and communications-related information are buffered and stored. All types of telecommunications services are subject to surveillance.

8.3.2.2.3 Handover to LEAs

Intercepted information is initially handed over to the NTAC; LEAs receive the information or intelligence required from this single point of contact (SPOC). Sharing of information on the same target on the part of different LEAs is not permitted.

8.3.2.2.4 Technical Equipment Requirements

At present, no specific guidelines are available. It is expected by LEAs that RIPA would not disclose such guidelines. It is further assumed by TSPs that individual and strategic surveillance activities will require different types of technical equipment.

Moreover, no guidelines are in place for data retention. The Data Protection Act 1998 regulates general access to data. A so-called data controller can, with cause, gain access to the stored data of TSPs; prerequisites are as follows:

- The requested data is available.
- The data can assist LEAs in solving concrete cases.
- LEAs have exhausted other investigative alternatives.

8.3.2.2.5 Real-Time Surveillance and Data Storage

RIPA requires that intercepted data be forwarded in real-time. However, the Crime and Security Act 2001 permits buffering and storing of data for further use by LEAs. The storage interval, typically between six and twelve months, depends on the nature of the data. Seven years is under consideration as a guideline in regard to archiving data.

8.3.3 Japan

A limited number of regulations are in place in regard to real-time surveillance. No centralized guidelines have been issued in the area of equipment; types of equipment used are subject to negotiations between the government and TSPs.

8.3.3.1 Required Target Specifications

Targets must be clearly identified according to name, address, phone number, fax number, e-mail address, or other technical attributes that determine clearly the surveillance action.

8.3.3.2 What Is Subject to Surveillance?

All telecommunications services are subject to surveillance.

8.3.3.3 Handover to LEAs

According to regulations, only real-time communications can be intercepted. Interception is acted upon in the physical presence of LEAs at sites established by TSPs. No handover is required.

8.3.3.4 Technical Equipment Requirements

On the basis of the CI Act, Article 11, TSPs must support LEAs during surveillance actions by making existing technical equipment and technology available. New equipment, however, is outside the scope of such required cooperation.

8.3.3.5 Real-Time Surveillance and Data Storage

Article 2 of the CI Act regulates surveillance by means of "spot monitoring." If this sampling does not indicate the expected results, surveillance activities must be terminated. Search warrants are issued in cases of e-mail interception, and e-mail may be confiscated by LEAs. Using "temporary mailboxes," e-mail may be intercepted on-site.

8.4 Functional Role Model

To reiterate from earlier chapters, "LI" refers to lawfully authorized interception and monitoring of communications. In a number of countries worldwide, TSPs are being asked to meet legal and regulatory requirements for the interception of voice, data, and video communications in various networks.

There are various aspects of interception. National laws describe under what conditions, and with what restrictions, interception is allowed. If an LEA wishes to use lawful interception as a tool, it will request lawful authorization (e.g., a warrant) from a prosecuting judge or other responsible body. If granted, the LEA will present the lawful authorization to the NWO/AP/SvP via an administrative interface or procedure (interface port HI1). When the lawful interception is authorized, the IRI and the content of communication (CC) are delivered to the law enforcement monitoring agency (interface ports HI2 and HI3).

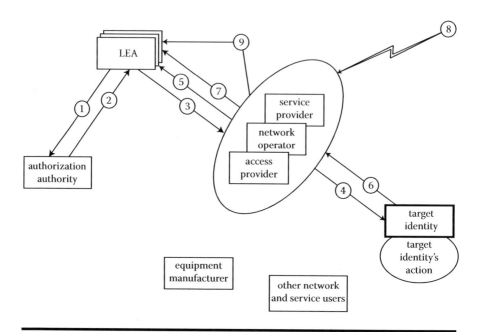

Figure 8.1 Functional role model.

A lawful authorization may describe the IRI and CC that are permitted to be delivered to the LEA, investigation, time period, and interception subject in question. In the case of different LEAs and different investigations, different constraints can apply that further limit the general borders set by laws. Also, the interception subject may be described in different ways (e.g., subscriber address, physical address, and services).

A lawful authorization or multiple lawful authorizations will be issued to one or more NWO/AP/SvPs (labeled TSPs in this book). This will depend on the subscribed services and networks that could be used by the interception subject.

A single subject may be the target of interception activities initiated by different LEAs in different investigations. It might be necessary to strictly separate these investigations and LEAs. Thus, more than one lawful authorization (each based on a specific application) may be issued relating to the same interception subject, and they may contain different constraints in regard to IRI and CC. These various lawful interception activities could fall under different laws.

Figure 8.1 shows the functional role model (ETSI, 2001), and process steps are numbered and displayed in more detail in Figure 8.2, using a flowchart. The most important players are identified in Table 8.1 (ETSI, 2001).

Process
steps

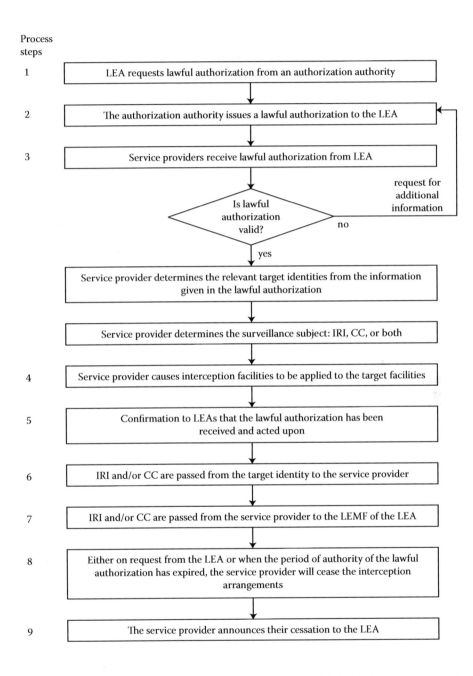

Figure 8.2   Flowchart of operations.

Table 8.1   Players in the Role Model

Player	Role
Player	*Role*
Authorization authority	A judicial or administrative authority authorizing the LEA to engage in interception activities
LEA	The LEA requests an NWO/AP/SvP to intercept communications according to a lawful authorization. The LEA receives, through an LEMF, the interception results (CC and IRI) relating to a target identity. Several LEAs may request interception of the same target identity at the same time
NWO	An NWO operates the telecommunication network on which services are connected. The operator is responsible for providing interception to LEAs via the HI. Several NWOs might be involved in interception activities with the same LEAs
SvP	An SvP provides services, additional to those provided by the network itself, to users of a network. An SvP may use and administer various (target) identities that are, of themselves, unknown to the network. The SvP is responsible for making arrangements, which may involve an NWO, for the lawful interception of communications. The SvP may be the same organization as the NWO. Interception may be required for several SvPs using the same telecommunication network
AP	The AP provides a user of the network with access from the user's terminal to the network. The AP may be the same organization as the NWO. Several APs may provide access to the same network
Target identity	The target identity corresponds to the identity of a given interception subject who is a user of a given service offered by an NWO/AP/SvP. Neither the interception subjects nor the other parties involved in their communications should be able to detect that interception is taking place
Other network and service users	When an interception facility is set up, or interception is taking place in a network, no other users of any telecommunications service should be able, by any means, to detect that any interception facility has been added or removed or that interception is taking place. The communications of other network or service users must not be intercepted unless those communications involve a target identity

Table 8.1   Players in the Role Model (continued)

Player	Role
Manufacturers	Manufacturers provide equipment that is deployed and operated by an NWO/AP/SvP. Pieces of equipment from different manufacturers may be integrated in a common telecommunications infrastructure

The process described in the preceding text is as an example. In specific countries, processes are based on various national laws and circumstances.

The authorization authority requires, through the LEA, interception of the target when the latter uses a service via the telecommunications network. The LEA receives the communications involving the identity (or identities) that the NWO/AP/SvP, singly or severally, has associated with the interception subject. Referring to the functional role model (and assuming that the lawful authorization is to be assigned to an NWO/AP/SvP), relevant actions are shown in Table 8.2.

To perform interception actions, an administrator typically requires the following special command parameters:

- Target identity
- Target identification
- Law enforcement monitoring function (LEMF) address for CC
- LEMF address for IRI
- Address parameters for LEMF (e.g., for authentication and security)
- Alarm routing
- NWO/AP/SvP identity
- The syntax of the necessary commands, which may be different in various systems

8.5 Administration and Management

TSPs usually follow a dual path in terms of administration and management. First, traditional service fulfillment and service assurance processes target the infrastructure components that serve as the basis for customer services. Inventory management, provisioning, and fault and performance management represent the support for this group.

Second, systems management and administration functions are targeting internal networks (e.g., data communications network [DCN]) and the internal infrastructures of TSPs. The surveillance administration system (SAS) can be used to unify the two groups.

Table 8.2 Functional Role Model Process Actions

Reference (See Figure 8.1)	Action
1	An LEA requests lawful authorization from an authorization authority, which may be a court of law
2	The authorization authority issues a lawful authorization to the LEA
3	The LEA passes the lawful authorization to the NWO/AP/SvP. The NWO/AP/SvP determines the relevant target identities from the information provided in the lawful authorization
4	The NWO/AP/SvP applies interception facilities to the relevant target identities
5	The NWO/AP/SvP informs the LEA that the lawful authorization has been received and acted upon. Information relating to target identities and target identification may be passed along
6	IRI and CC are passed from the target identity to the NWO/AP/SvP
7	IRI and CC are passed from the NWO/AP/SvP to the LEMF of the LEA
8	Either on request from the LEA or when the period of authority of the lawful authorization has expired, the NWO/AP/SvP will terminate interception arrangements
9	The NWO/AP/SvP announces this cessation to the LEA

The security infrastructure targets LEA HIs. This infrastructure will be detailed in the following section.

8.5.1 Inventory Management Processes

Inventory management processes involve the management of network inventory, both physical and logical. Methods of operation may be characterized as follows.

At present, carrier processes involved in maintaining inventory have two primary characteristics: excessive inventory and capacity are required to overcome system and process limitations, and it is difficult to keep documented inventory up-to-date, regardless of how and where it is stored. The result is additional work required upon service provisioning.

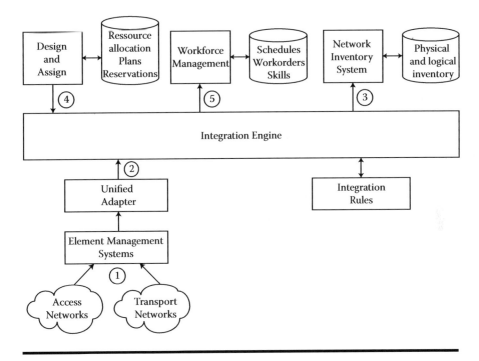

Figure 8.3 Automated process flow for inventory management.

The principal reason for this situation is that tools and procedures have not yet been synchronized with each other. Surveillance-related inventory must be maintained very carefully. When authorized orders arrive, there is little time to clean up and align inventory. LIs require additional inventory. These additional items may be maintained in securely partitioned segments or as part of the master inventory.

Also, managing spare and faulty parts is an extremely important task of TSPs in supporting LIs. Depending on the size of the service provider, special logistics should be considered. For example, geographical range should be assessed in the process of determining optimal provisioning solutions. Pre-provisioning is always a viable solution. Figure 8.3 shows an enhanced structure with a number of automation options.

The information flows shown in Figure 8.3 can be summarized as follows:

1. The source for the inventory update flow is either the network element or the element management system (EMS).
2. In either case, the EMS generates one of several CORBA notifications in Interface Definition Language (IDL), including object creation, object deletion, attribute value change, state change, and protection switch.

3. These notifications are converted to the appropriate add, update, and delete transactions at the boundary with the inventory management system.

4. The inventory-threshold crossing flow does not directly affect the EMS northbound interface, but it does lead to automated inventory synchronization flow when the field technician adds (or removes) physical inventory. In this flow, a low-inventory-threshold crossing event is generated by the design and assign system when the underlying inventory drops to a predefined level at which new capacity must be added to the network.

5. In this case, the message will be transformed into a work order destined for the workforce management systems (WMSs), with subsequent dispatch of field personnel to update the network and rectify the inventory shortfall.

Inventory management is extremely important in terms of compliance with LIs. All related managed objects should be maintained using standard management information bases (MIBs). These contain all the mandatory and optional attributes to be maintained.

8.5.2 Problem Management and Repair Processes

At present, methods of operation in the area of problem management and repair can be characterized as follows:

■ These processes involve a variety of systems, including EMS, fault management, diagnostics, ticketing, and workforce management.
■ Manual correlation is used to identify root causes of problems.
■ Trouble tickets are created via a ticketing-system user interface.
■ Separate WMSs are used to deal with interfacing problems.
■ The tools used are typically effective, but there is a lack of integration.

Figure 8.4 shows an enhanced structure with a number of automation options.

Information flows are as follows: A typical flow is initiated by the generation of a trap or alarm from the network element or the EMS (1). These alarms can take the form of actual status alarms (such as a hardware failure), threshold-crossing alarms (TCA) for performance thresholds (such as BER), or protection switch notifications describing the affected protection groups and paths. Each of these alarms carries enough information to precisely identify source, date/time, alarm type, and severity. In some

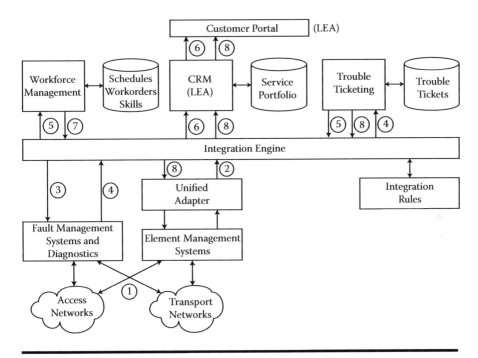

Figure 8.4   Automated process flow for problem management.

cases, additional diagnostic information might be sent along with the alarm. However, it is usually the role of the EMS to perform alarm correlation, filtering, and root-cause analysis. Manual root-cause analyses are frequently performed, supported by third-party diagnostic tools. These tools should be integrated into the process flow as well.

In the automated process flow, the EMS (or third-party FMS) would receive the raw alarms from the network and filter (based on time-based filtering rules, filtering on thresholds, suppression of specific alarm types, and suppression of alarms from specific network elements [NEs]). The EMS often performs root-cause analyses to identify symptomatic relationships between alarms and their root causes. Finally, the EMS may determine when capacity thresholds have been exceeded. Once the EMS determines the root cause and performs the necessary filtering, a notification is generated for the alarm (2).

Third-party systems may be used for the additional diagnostics required to create a trouble ticket. These systems would subscribe to alarm notifications (3), as transmitted by the EMS across the message bus. Based on alarm type, severity, or originating NE, appropriate scripts can be executed to pull additional performance, alarm, or logging information out of the network. These scripts typically take the form of sequences of

Simple Network Management Protocol (SNMP), Transaction Language 1 (TL1), or proprietary protocol commands. The collected diagnostic information, along with the original alarm information, is formatted into a trouble-ticket creation message shown on the message bus and received by the ticketing system (4).

The ticketing system creates the trouble ticket in its database, enters the ticket into the appropriate workflow, and routes the ticket to appropriate personnel. If the fault can be rectified by actions in the network operating center (NOC), the ticket workflow typically remains contained within the ticketing system. However, if a field technician must be dispatched to fix a physical network problem, the ticketing system can generate a dispatch request message received by the WMS (5); a work order is created to schedule and dispatch the appropriate personnel.

In some cases, TSPs may opt to identify or notify customers affected by an outage. The ticketing system can create a customer outage message that is received by the customer relationship management (CRM) system, which in turn can notify affected customers (in this case, LEAs) (6). As long as the CRM system has access to the underlying network resources assigned to a particular customer's service (interaction with design/assign and inventory systems may be requested), the system can determine whether that customer is affected by a fault generated on those network resources. It is critical that customer notification rules be conservative; the main reason TSPs would want to notify customers of outages is to proactively avoid heavy inbound customer care call volumes. In other words, customers should not be notified of every fault occurring on the network, even if they are affected to some extent. If necessary, customers can be notified via the customer portal, through outbound call lists, blast fax lists, or automated pager notifications.

Once the network problem is eliminated, the ticket must be cleared, and a ticket-clear event is shown on the message bus (9) and received by the CRM system (to send the clear notification to previously notified customers) and the EMS and FMS systems (to clear the originating alarm). In cases requiring field repair, the WMS may initiate the ticket clearing by sending a message to the ticketing system (7), which will propagate the ticket-clearing event to the other interested systems. In some cases, eliminating the problem in the network will result in an automated alarm-clearing event from the network elements. In these situations, the clear message is propagated to all interested systems, and the ticket is cleared.

Most situations involve no fundamental changes in this process and its information flows, and LI-related managed objects are treated in the same manner as any managed object. However, there are certain cases in which LI-related managed objects receive expedited fault-resolution support.

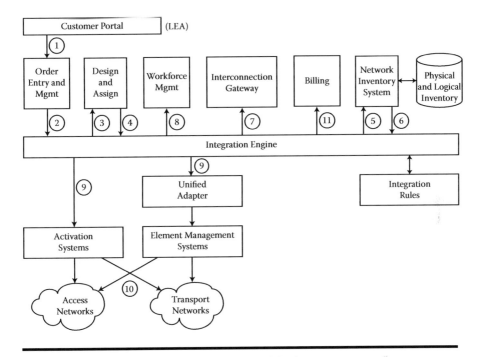

Figure 8.5   Automated process flow for provisioning.

8.5.3 Provisioning Processes

Automated provisioning is vital to the scalability of all services offered and supported by TSPs. The current situation in this area can be characterized as follows:

- Scalability is critical in access networks.
- Provisioning is very expensive in transport networks.
- Order backlogs are usually high, and thus customer waiting times are long.
- The level of automation is low; paper-based systems are still in use.
- Flow-through-provisioning solutions are beginning to be implemented.
- There are many interfaces (e.g., to WMS, EMS, and TT) without standards.
- Mediation devices have not yet taken an active role in provisioning.

Figure 8.5 shows an enhanced structure with a number of automation options.

Information flows are as follows: Nominal provisioning flows are originated via customer service requests or change requests (1). An order is either entered by the customer via the customer portal or by a sales representative using a sales force automation (SFA) tool. Either way, the order moves into an order-management workflow via an order-management system, which is responsible for validating the order. Once the order is validated, it is shown on the message bus (2) and sent to the design and assign system (3).

Traditionally, the design and assign system has been the least likely to be automated. However, with the advent of intelligent network path/circuit creation/optimization protocols, there are good automation options for SDH and WDWM, ATM, and IP. Whether this step is manual or automated, the circuit must be designed at some level, and inventory resources must be assigned to the designed circuit (4, 5). Once these tasks are completed, the designed circuit is shown on the message bus (6), often in the form of a circuit layout record (CLR) that can be sent to activation systems, interconnection gateways, and WMSs. The recipients of the designed and validated circuit message are the network-facing activation systems and EMSs, interconnection gateways, and WMSs.

The first step in provisioning a circuit or path is the ordering of interconnections from trading partners (7), unless the entire circuit resides in a private domain. Circuit design details are transmitted to the appropriate trading partners via interconnection gateway systems in the form of loop service requests (LSRs) for transport providers and access service requests (ASRs) for access providers. In addition, order and circuit information may be used to obtain third-party services. There are two main reasons why interconnection provisioning should be the first step in the provisioning process (once a circuit is designed). First, it is the longest step, and second, details of the interconnection are typically required in the activation process — specifically, the termination parameters at the interconnection points.

In advance of the service "turn up" date, the circuit design information must be received by the WMS in the form of a work order (8). This data should specify the remote configuration requirements for the CPE, as well as field inventory and scheduling requirements.

Network-facing service activation systems are also recipients of the circuit design (9). In many cases, these designs will be transformed to the appropriate sequence of activation commands in a standardized EMS interface. In other cases, third-party activation systems are sent the information required to map these commands to the appropriate primitive element directives (10). In the former case, the transformation rules are housed externally in the transformation metadata. In the latter case, the third-party activation system is responsible for performing these transformations.

Once the circuit/path has been activated, trading partner interconnections — including connections to outsourcers and LEAs — have been installed and tested, and any field deployment and configuration is complete, the circuit is considered fully provisioned, and the order that generated the service request is sent to the billing system indicating that the service is installed (11). Subsequent orders involving changes to the service will follow the same provisioning flow.

Provisioning is key to supporting LIs. Once authorized orders arrive at TSPs, they are expected to be acted upon rapidly. Assuming that resources are available (and, in most cases, even pre-provisioned), rapid actions should concentrate on activation and on-the-fly testing of all equipment and communication paths involved.

8.5.4 Service-Level Management (SLM) Processes

The broader topic of service management includes all activities involved in the processes of provisioning, monitoring, and billing for customer services and circuits. In the area of performance monitoring, TSPs can differentiate their offerings by providing stronger service-level agreements (SLAs). Present SLM solutions can be characterized as follows:

- The metrics used in SLAs are network or service dependent.
- Most standard SLAs involve collection, aggregation, and reporting of statistics from underlying network elements.
- *Ad hoc* reports are generated, but there is a lack of long-term observation.
- Network elements involve different reporting capabilities.
- Frequently used technologies, such as ATM, offer a number of good performance metrics.
- Operations support systems (OSSs)/ business support systems (BSSs) and network management systems (NMSs) do not offer much in regard to SLM.

Figure 8.6 shows an enhanced structure with a number of automation options.

The customer portal is used as the interface for reporting SLA performance to customers. The first step in any SLM process is to collect statistics from the network elements, either through periodic autonomous messages reporting statistics to an EMS or mediation device or via periodic statistics polls (1). The statistics polled are related to hardware, termination points, cross-connects, and logical services. Performance statistics are almost always collected asynchronously with other processes involving the use of these statistics (e.g., service-performance reporting).

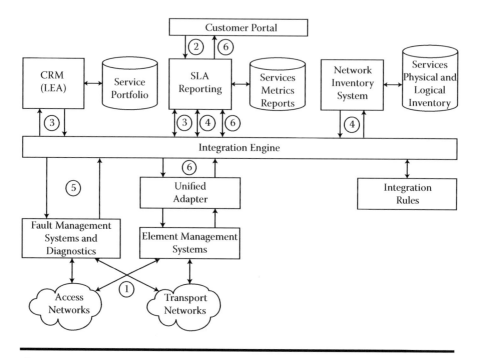

Figure 8.6 Automated process flow for service-level management.

Existing customers make a request via the customer portal (2) to view the performance of their service, as well as information on this performance against the SLA associated with their purchased service level. The main system with which the customer portal interacts is the SLA-reporting system. Once that system receives the request, it solicits the customer's service definition from the CRM or billing system via a service definition request (SDR) (3) that includes information on the service package and the purchased SLA. Once the SDR is made, the inventory system is queried to identify the network elements traversed by the customer's service (4).

When the SLA-reporting system has identified the service level and the underlying network inventory, it queries the network regarding performance statistics for these elements, either through a performance management mediation device or through one or more EMSs. Once the SLA-reporting engine has collected all the raw data related to the service, it aggregates this data to provide summary reports and graphs to the customer via the customer portal (6). Successful SLM depends heavily on the integrity of the network and circuit inventory data, as well as the inventory synchronization process with the network.

Processes such as those just described are not the highest priority in the case of LIs. Service providers are expected to maintain an agreed-upon service level with their customers. Continuous attention is required to ensure that LI actions do not affect the quality of the services provided to customers.

8.5.5 Systems Management and Administration

Systems management and administration may be limited to infrastructure components of LIs, or it may be unified with other unrelated infrastructure components. In the former case, components used include probes, databases, management stations, analysis software, servers, and storage area networks. In the latter case, all these components, along with all components of the TSP's internal infrastructure, are included.

8.6 Security Considerations

Service providers rely on a variety of security products, including firewalls, intrusion detection systems, vulnerability assessment tools, anti-virus applications, Web applications, operating systems, and networking devices, to monitor, investigate, and report on the many types of security issues experienced each day. These devices are offered by many vendors, and organizations seek best-of-breed products. However, each type of device and each vendor has its own message, log, and console format; thus, as the security infrastructure is built up, it becomes increasingly difficult to understand, interpret, and correlate the output of individual devices or groups of devices and obtain a complete view of threat profiles.

If maximum value is to be obtained from these heterogeneous devices, they must be assembled into a framework that provides the necessary intelligence and tools to deal with a large number of messages, events, alarms, and alerts on a daily basis. Security management frameworks provide a consolidated component set that collects security data from the network, organizes them into a common format, stores them in a database, and executes a range of analysis, display, response, and reporting tasks (Lunetta, 2003).

A security management framework consists of software agents, server-based managers, and consoles. Agents can be deployed on the security devices, network devices, and applications that report security events at aggregation points or as listening posts for SNMP broadcasts. The agents forward the data to server-based managers that consolidate, filter, and cross-correlate the events using a rules engine and a central database. These managers report relevant information to consoles used by security experts to monitor events, receive notifications, and perform incident investigation and response management functions. Consoles are available as applications for dedicated workstations or via a browser-based interface allowing remote access.

Because of the need, in some cases, to automatically examine and analyze millions of events per day, real-time correlation is the key element in an effective security management framework. The system works by reading the original event, alarm, or alert; parsing it for its individual fields; and organizing these fields into a common format or schema. These messages, which are forwarded by the collection component, are then assigned a proper priority level. Real-time correlation combines the threats that the firewall or intrusion detection system identifies with information about the targets or assets. The correlation system contains a rule set that scores threats according to the following:

- What else has occurred?
- Is the asset vulnerable?
- How valuable is the asset?

Because the point is to take the right action at the right time, TSPs can set up policies to govern automated responses and responses acted on by subject matter experts. These rules may separate LI-related events, alarms, and alerts and assign them the highest priority. In other words, assets involving LI functions will be assigned the highest value.

Framework products may be labeled differently, for example, security event management (SEM) or security information management (SIM). Key players in this area are ArcSight, e-Security, netForensics, Tenable Lightning, Network Intelligence Corp, and Secopia.

In most cases, choices of connections between LEAs, LI outsourcers, and TSPs include the following:

- Dial-up connections
- Private dedicated leased lines
- ISDN
- Secure circuits over a public network
- Public networks involving no security
- 3G wireless services
- Partner-ready connectivity

Attributes that should be sought in making decisions regarding security solutions for these connections include authentication, confidentiality, integrity, and non-repudiation. Technically speaking, there are multiple alternatives, including the use of IPSec gateways, SSL, and various encryption techniques.

The TSP's demilitarized zone (DMZ) should contain the following managed objects:

- Specific servers
- Firewalls
- Storage area networks
- Database servers

DMZs may become integral parts of LEMFs. Recommended security solutions for the HI were summarized in Chapter 5.

8.7 Human Resources

Human resources management provides the human infrastructure used by an enterprise to fulfill its objectives in supporting LIs. Management processes in this area should provide salary structures by level, coordinate performance appraisal and compensation guidelines, and set policies in relation to people management, employee-benefit programs, labor relations, safety program development and communication, employee review policies, training programs, employee acquisition and release processes, retirement processes, resource planning, and workplace operating policies.

8.7.1 Building a Team

Workforce strategy processes can define the requirements for competency modeling, application of profiling, overall job design, approach to meet employee needs, and employee satisfaction. These processes create the strategies needed to ensure that the required numbers of suitable employees will be available in the right locations to complete future necessary tasks for TSPs and LEAs. Such factors complicate the hiring process by making it very difficult to write job descriptions and analyze candidates' backgrounds. The following is a list of recommended criteria for use in the hiring of human resources to support LI activities:

1. *Identify team members:* The earlier chapters of this book provided an overview of principal LI functions. Depending on the size of the network, human resources demand can be computed. Demand on new hires can be quantified by subtracting available staff resources from the total demand in each functional area.
2. *Recruit candidates:* Advertisements, conferences, headhunters, and individual contacts with colleges, universities, and other companies can assist in the process of identifying candidates to be interviewed.

3. *Establish interview criteria:* Guidelines and evaluation criteria must be set prior to starting the interview process. To keep the investment of both parties low, written applications must be filtered carefully. Occasional phone conversations may fill existing gaps.

4. *Hire properly qualified candidates:* A decision to hire must be to the mutual benefit of both parties and not simply to fill an opening. In this manner, future turnover can be avoided. Indicate the organization's interest in a long-range relationship of not less than three years.

5. *Assign or reassign responsibilities:* Static job descriptions should serve as a guideline only. Within this framework, more dynamic descriptions are necessary with rotations in mind.

6. *Institute performance evaluations:* Periodic reviews are the most widely used type of evaluation. If possible, upward performance appraisals should be agreed upon as early as possible in the team-building phase.

7. *Promote openness and handle complaints:* To emphasize team spirit, opinions and even complaints must be encouraged. Employees must have the feeling that their comments and suggestions are handled at the earliest convenience of managers.

8. *Resolve personnel problems quickly:* To avoid tensions within the organization, problems must be resolved as rapidly as possible, and the reward system must provide opportunities to do so. In many cases, problems can be resolved almost automatically if there is general awareness of how the reward system works.

9. *Institute systematic training and development programs:* Systematic education should include training in the areas of LI functions, surveillance tools, and personal skills. A curriculum instituted in coordination with vendors and educational institutions would facilitate employee satisfaction.

10. *Ensure regular interface between staff and LEAs:* To promote mutual understanding of working conditions and problems, both parties should exchange views and opinions. The level of formality may vary from very informal to very formal; the latter case would involve written SLAs.

11. *Evaluate new technologies:* As part of the motivation process, renovation opportunities in regard to LI technology must be evaluated continuously. This process includes new management and security platforms, new distribution technologies, feasibility of new and existing solutions, new monitors, changes in *de facto* and open standards, simplification of surveillance processes, changes in the offerings of leading manufacturers, and monitoring the needs of users.

8.7.2 Retaining the Team

Workforce development processes focus on developing employees to meet needs related to LI activities. These processes include competency modeling, skill assessment, job and employee strength profiling, succession planning, training development and delivery, career development, work design, and employee recruitment. The following list provides a sequence of priorities for keeping the network management team together:

1. *Compensation:* Although organizations attempt to use a number of person-based or skill-based compensation techniques, compensation is still the most important motivating factor. Compensation is a matter involving perceptions and values that often generates conflict.

2. *Benefits:* Depending on the type of business involved, benefits can take the form of a company car, life insurance, lower interest rates, or housing. Costs of benefits can be as high as 35 to 45 percent of wages.

3. *Job security:* Ensuring job security is a valuable management practice, particularly when the economy is stressed. Job security policies include retirement plans, options for early retirement, and nonlayoff agreements. Job security packages are more advanced in Europe and Japan than in the United States.

4. *Recognition:* Recognition may come from the organization or from fellow employees. One periodic form of recognition is performance appraisals conducted by supervisors. So-called upward appraisals, in which subordinates evaluate managers, represent a relatively new form of recognition in which subordinates can communicate criticisms as well as ideas for improvement. However, such evaluations can result in problems in that most managers do not want to be evaluated by their subordinates.

5. *Career path and creation of dual ladders:* To keep motivation high, managerial and technical assignments must be compensated equally. Promoting technically interested individuals to managerial positions may not have the desired results; such individuals are usually high in affiliation motivation and low in power motivation. Helpful activities include career counseling and exploration, increased provision of company career-opportunity information, improving career feedback, and enrichment of lower-level jobs with more challenges.

6. *Effective training:* This type of motivation helps to ensure that both the specific and generic knowledge of employees remain at the most advanced level. Three to six weeks of training and education

each year is considered adequate in the dynamically changing surveillance technology environment.

7. *Quality of assignments:* Job descriptions are expected to represent the framework in regard to expectations. However, dynamic job descriptions may help to avoid monotony and promote job rotation. Client contact points, systems administration, and change control may be rotated periodically.

8. *Use of adequate tools:* Better-instrumented surveillance environments facilitate the jobs of LI staff, increase the quality of service (QoS) delivered to LEAs, and improve the image of the organization. At the same time, people working with advanced tools are proud of their special knowledge and of their employer, and they typically are highly motivated to continue with the company.

9. *Realistic performance goals:* As part of dynamic job descriptions and rotations, realistic performance expectations may help to stabilize the position of the LI support team. Management must find the balance between quantifiable and nonquantifiable goals. Average time spent on trouble calls, response time to problems, time spent on repair, and end-user satisfaction or dissatisfaction are examples of both types of goals.

10. *Quality of environment:* This is more or less a generic term expressing the mix of LI-related tools, a pleasant working atmosphere, comfortable furniture, adequate legroom, easy access to filing cabinets or hypermedia, acceptance of opinions on shortcomings, and team spirit.

11. *Employee control:* Individuals need certain levels of control that can be determined only via managerial skills. Depending on the individual in question, positive or negative motivation, or a combination of both, may be most effective.

In constructing this list, we attempted to focus only on key motivation alternatives. There are many more possibilities. To determine optimal combinations in individual installations, a human resource management audit is recommended.

8.7.3 Job Profiles

Successful operations require a well-educated management team with adequate skill levels. To simplify the hiring and cross-education processes, the most important team profiles should be well prepared and well maintained. These job descriptions serve as a basis for evaluating the comprehensiveness of existing descriptions and documents regarding managers and

Table 8.3 Allocation of Job Profiles to Service Providers and LEAs

Service Providers, Access Providers, and Network Operators	Law Enforcement Agencies
Network operations manager	Contact manager
Call center operator	Manager of law enforcement monitoring center
Network infrastructure operator	Security analyst
Service technician	Legal counsel
Security analyst	
Database administrator	
Legal counsel	

subject matter experts, as well as LEAs and LI outsourcers. Job profiles should contain the following information:

- Responsibilities
- External job contacts
- Qualifying experiences
- Required education
- Personal attributes
- Salary range (highly dependent on internal organizational structures)

To assist TSPs, LEAs, and LI outsourcers in preparing job profiles, we provide a few examples here. Allocations of jobs in two categories — service providers, access providers, and network operators; and LEAs — are shown in Table 8.3. LI outsourcers can identify relevant human resources in both groups.

8.7.3.1 Profile: Operations Manager for LIs

Responsibilities:

1. Supervises and monitors the quality of LIs
2. Estimates cost and resource requirements
3. Reviews and approves processes and tools
4. Plans and schedules product implementation
5. Develops, implements, and enforces procedural and security standards

6. Evaluates performance of processes, instruments, and people, and reports results to management
7. Plans and directs acquisitions, training, and development projects
8. Creates and supervises SLAs in collaboration with LEAs
9. Defines and selects QoS metrics
10. Manages outsourcers

External job contacts:

1. Management-level LEA personnel
2. Other information systems managers
3. Surveillance-tool vendors
4. External consulting company personnel

Qualifying experience and attributes:

1. Prior experience in statistics, surveillance technologies, accounting, legal procedures, telecommunications, or equivalent
2. Training in advanced practices, skills and concepts, administrative management, supervisory techniques, resource management, and budgeting and planning
3. Excellent communication, negotiation, and managerial skills

8.7.3.2 Profile: Call Center Operator for LEA Inquiries and Complaints

Responsibilities:

1. Network supervision: implements first-level problem-determination procedures and maintains documentation to assist customers in terminal operations
2. Problem logging: uses procedure guide for opening trouble tickets and reviews change-activities log
3. Problem delegation: determines problem areas, assigns priorities, and distributes information
4. Additional duties when call center activity is low: performs data entry for configuration and inventory, summarizes active problems for problem coordinator, enters change information for change coordinator, monitors security, and generates management and technical reports
5. Recommendation of procedure modifications

External job contacts:

1. Representatives of LEAs
2. Vendor representatives
3. Problem and change managers
4. Network operation and technical support personnel
5. Network administrator for trouble tickets
6. QoS and SLA managers

Qualifying experience and attributes:

1. Familiarity with functional applications and client equipment
2. Training in personal relationships
3. Clerical rather than technical background, data-entry skills, and problem determination know-how
4. Sensitivity to and understanding of the needs of LEAs, pleasant telephone voice, and language know-how

8.7.3.3 Profile: Network Infrastructure Operator

Responsibilities:

1. Observes ongoing operations and performance to identify problems
2. Initiates corrective action, where required, within scope of knowledge and authority
3. Interprets console messages from network software or applications programs and performs required actions
4. Assists with network-oriented problem determination
5. Implements backup procedures
6. Implements bypass and recovery procedures for system/network problems
7. Fulfills administrative-reporting requirements with network problems
8. Maintains communications with systems control
9. Understands monitoring technologies supporting LIs
10. Monitors all network activities
11. Uses and invokes network diagnostic aids and tools
12. Uses and provides input to database for problem and inventory control
13. Determines second-level problems

14. Conducts network startup and shutdown
15. Schedules network activities such as testing and maintenance
16. Understands LI-related standards
17. Identifies intercept access points in the networking infrastructure

External job contacts:

1. Technical support staff
2. Configuration and inventory function personnel
3. Network administration problem and change coordinators
4. Customer education and customer support desk personnel
5. Vendor representatives
6. Network administrators

Qualifying experience and attributes:

1. Training in concepts of network infrastructure operations
2. At least one year of network experience with access and transport networks; lines, clusters, and terminal types; and service levels
3. Alert, intelligent, strives for efficiency
4. Can execute bypass/recovery procedures
5. Can perform authorized network alterations
6. Understands escalation procedures, operating of problem and change management, and reporting requirements and procedures
7. Possesses communication skills
8. Can use various surveillance tools

8.7.3.4 Profile: Service Technician

Responsibilities:

1. Provides in-depth problem determination (third level) as necessary
2. Provides technical interfaces with vendors as necessary
3. Designs and maintains up-to-date problem determination, bypass, and recovery procedures
4. Provides technical interfaces, as necessary, with application and system programmers
5. Uses inventory-control database
6. Ensures valid run procedures
7. Assists in network configuration/reconfiguration
8. Activates/deactivates live monitoring
9. Starts and evaluates special-purpose diagnostics
10. Evaluates QoS metrics

External job contacts:

1. Change managers
2. Problem managers
3. Call center operators
4. Vendor technical personnel
5. Application and system programmers
6. Network infrastructure operators
7. Inventory managers

Qualifying experience and attributes:

1. Several years of experience with a broad range of communications equipment and the tools and aids necessary to maintain the network, including network operation, network-control programs, access and transport networks, network equipment, and configuration/reconfiguration procedures
2. Aptitude for communicating with people
3. Can use diagnostic tools
4. Understands vendor standards and procedures
5. Exhibits patience in pursuing problems

8.7.3.5 Profile: Security Analyst

Responsibilities:

1. Defines monitoring and surveillance functions
2. Evaluates and selects security management frameworks and services to support HIs
3. Evaluates performance effects of security techniques
4. Constructs threat matrix and assesses vulnerabilities
5. Recommends tools for intrusion detection and prevention, firewalls, and anti-virus procedures
6. Determines policies regarding tools
7. Customizes passwords and access authorization
8. Supervises deployment of tools
9. Establishes procedures for securing surveillance systems

External job contacts:

1. Security officers of TSPs
2. Security officers of LEAs
3. Representatives of security-related-tool vendors

4. Security auditors
5. Other internal users

Qualifying experience and attributes:

1. Has superior security record
2. Has in-depth knowledge of surveillance technologies
3. Has in-depth knowledge of security management services and tools
4. Possesses technical skills necessary to customize surveillance products
5. Possesses necessary skills for communicating with LEAs and vendors

8.7.3.6 Profile: Database Administrator

Responsibilities:

1. Defines database and data retention functions and procedures
2. Estimates data volumes
3. Determines hierarchical layers for data archiving
4. Supervises all data archiving-related processes
5. Selects, deploys, and maintains tools
6. Keeps in contact with regulatory bodies
7. Audits compliance with regulations
8. Supervises format translations
9. Prepares evidence
10. Uses intelligent analysis tools
11. Formulates escalation procedures
12. Determines criteria for business continuity, backup, and restoration

External job contacts:

1. LEA personnel
2. Security analysts
3. Legal counsel
4. Representatives of regulatory bodies

Qualifying experience and attributes:

1. Has extensive database and data warehousing know-how
2. Has above-average product know-how
3. Has technical skills necessary to customize products

4. Possesses skills necessary to communicate with LEAs and vendors
5. Has superior security record

8.7.3.7 Profile: Legal Counsel

Responsibilities:

1. Investigates lawfulness of LEA requests
2. Approves surveillance activities from legal perspective
3. Maintains contacts with peers at LEAs
4. Evaluates and follows precedence cases
5. Differentiates targets of interception (call-related data, content, or both)
6. Differentiates between telecommunications and information services
7. Interprets law for TSPs
8. Prepares evidence
9. Uses intelligent analysis tools
10. Protects privacy of customers

External job contacts:

1. LEA legal personnel
2. Security analysts and officers
3. Supervisors of LIs
4. Representatives of regulatory bodies
5. Court personnel, judges, and representatives of police departments

Qualifying experience and attributes:

1. Has superior security record
2. Has legal background
3. Has extensive knowledge of LIs and their authorization
4. Possesses skills necessary to communicate with peers

8.7.3.8 Profile: Contract Administrator

Responsibilities:

1. Understands legal basis of LIs
2. Monitors compliance with regulations
3. Differentiates between intercept-related and content-related warrants

4. Differentiates between communications and information services
5. Supervises handover of raw data or intelligence
6. Initiates intelligent analysis
7. Assists in preparing court evidence
8. Participates (occasionally) on-site in surveillance actions
9. Selects tools used in intelligent analysis

External job contacts:

1. Representatives of LEAs
2. Representatives of TSPs
3. Access providers
4. Network operators
5. Outsourcers
6. Legal counsel

Qualifying experience and attributes:

1. Has superior security clearance
2. Has legal background
3. Understands procedures associated with warrants
4. Is well informed regarding regulations
5. Has basic networking background
6. Possesses know-how regarding LI standards
7. Possesses managerial skills

8.7.3.9 Profile: Manager of LEMF

Responsibilities:

1. Supervises all LEMF processes
2. Supervises handover of raw data and intelligence
3. Maintains data
4. Distributes data to other LEAs
5. Supervises security measures
6. Determines priorities in cases of multiple requests from other LEAs

External job contacts:

1. Representatives of LEAs
2. Representatives of service providers

3. Access providers
4. Network operators
5. Outsourcers
6. Legal counsel

Qualifying experience and attributes

1. Has superior security clearance
2. Has legal background
3. Understands procedures associated with warrants
4. Has basic networking background
5. Possesses know-how regarding LI standards
6. Possesses know-how regarding data retention technologies
7. Has experience with data center operations

8.7.4 Head Counts

Depending on the services offered by TSPs, LEAs, and LI outsourcers, a full position refers to a certain number of hours that must be staffed annually:

5×8 = 2080 hr/year

5×16 = 4160 hr/year

5×24 = 6240 hr/year

7×8 = 2920 hr/year

7×16 = 5840 hr/year

7×24 = 8760 hr/year

An average person can work approximately 1600 hours a year, considering vacations, holidays, training, and illnesses. To calculate the real number of personnel required to fill a certain position, the total hours required for the function should be divided by 1600.

On the basis of the experiences of the service provider or outsourcer in question, total human resources demand should be fine-tuned using the following weighting factors:

■ Complexity and number of managed objects
■ Speed of technology change

Table 8.4   Head-Count-Impacting Factors

Factor	Category A	Category B	Category C
Complexity and number of managed objects and IAPs	High	Medium	Low
Speed of technology change	High	Medium	Low
Technology and age of managed objects	State-of-the-art	Average age	Past prime
Geographical distribution of managed objects	Highly distributed	Moderately distributed	Limited to a few locations
Diversity of network architectures	High	Medium	Low
Diversity of surveillance devices	Many	Some	Few
Number of trouble tickets generated for managed objects	High	Medium	Low
Education level and skills of subject matter experts	Medium	Medium	Medium
Quality of support, documentation, and management tools	Medium	Medium	Medium
Number of LEAs expected to be supported	Many	Some	Few

- Technology and age of managed objects
- Geographical distribution of managed objects
- Diversity of network architectures
- Diversity of surveillance devices
- Number of trouble tickets generated for managed objects
- Educational level and skills of subject matter experts
- Quality of support, documentation, and management tools
- Number of LEAs expected to be supported

In accordance with these factors, three categories of alternatives can be devised. Table 8.4 shows these alternatives.

Table 8.5   Head-Count Example

	Category A	Category B	Category C
Job profiles:			
A. Service providers			
Network operations manager	1	1	1
Call center operator	3	2	1
Network infrastructure operator	3	2	1
Service technician	1	1	1
Database administrator	1	1	1
Security analyst	1	1	1
Legal counsel	1	1	1
Total	11	9	7
B. Law enforcement agencies			
Contact administrator	1	1	1
Manager of LEMF	3	2	1
Security analyst	1	1	1
Legal counsel	3	2	1
Total	8	6	4

Human resources are the dominating expense factor in operating communication networks. Hardware, software, and physical infrastructures are less expensive than human resources. Table 8.5 shows head-count examples for both service providers and LEAs.

The numbers in Table 8.5 relate to one shift only. If more shifts must be supported, the numbers will increase.

8.8 Summary

All parties involved in the process of operating LI technologies and tools play an important role. The best way to organize collaboration among TSPs, LI outsourcers, and LEAs is to deploy workflow concepts and tools. These concepts and tools concentrate on access, delivery, collection, and distribution of raw data or intelligence.

Support of LIs must seamlessly integrate into TSPs' existing business and technical processes. Basic operations include inventory, incident and problem management, and provisioning and service-level management. In this chapter, we have identified peering points of LIs with these principal processes.

Finally, human resources are a key element in terms of collaboration among TSPs, LI outsourcers, and LEAs. Here we have outlined realistic head counts and typical job descriptions to facilitate decisions in the area of human resources. TSPs, as a result of economic considerations or shortages of subject matter experts, may consider the alternative of outsourcing; more details on outsourcing options will be provided in Chapter 10.

Chapter 9

Costs and Reimbursement of Expenses for Telecommunications Service Providers

CONTENTS

The governments of many countries mandate support of lawful interception activities. Telecommunications service providers (TSPs) are in agreement with such mandates in general, but they are still careful in making additional investments. Having a powerful intelligence support system (ISS) with lawful intercept (LI) features is, of course, in the public interest, but as is the case with E-911 and local number portability mandates, TSPs must make substantial investments with practically no return.

Because criminals rely a great deal on telecommunications networks to engage in their various unlawful acts, there is a societal need for service providers to include ISSs in their infrastructure. Three specific ISS needs (Lucas, 2003f) require a special focus:

1. *Lawful interception mandates:* Coverage is improving across the globe, with LI activities producing remarkable results.
2. *IP technology:* This technology is now extremely complex, including such features as temporary addresses, intermixed voice and data packets, and identity theft and hidden identity functions.
3. *High traffic volumes:* For intelligence to be gathered, monitored traffic must be stored, processed, and analyzed, which requires substantial computing, networking, and human resources.

In summary, TSPs that invest in ISSs will not have a clear idea whether they will be reimbursed or will achieve a return on their investment.

9.1 Cost Components

Two principal categories of costs can be analyzed: one-time costs and recurring costs. The former cover service providers' initial investments, whereas the latter include ongoing expenses incurred. After analysis and quantification of costs, average prices for legal requests can be calculated.

9.1.1 One-Time Costs

The following one-time-cost categories are important to consider:

■ *Hardware upgrades of networking equipment:* To support lawful interception, principal networking equipment requires hardware extensions such as CPUs, buffers, storage, ports, and counters.

- *Software upgrades of networking equipment:* To support interception, networking equipment requires software extensions such as filters, rules-based control applications, and data processors.
- *Distributed probes:* Hardware, software, or a combination of both are necessary to collect and process data on-site. Prices vary depending on the capabilities of the probes.
- *Management station for controlling probes:* To control probes, management stations are necessary to download configurations, rules, and policies and upload intercepted data.
- *Storage media for surveillance data:* Storage requirements are expected to be significant. Long data retention periods require significant storage capacity. DAS-, NAS-, and SAN-based solutions are possible options depending on the volumes to be maintained. Related data may be stored in storage device areas or maintained completely separately from other data.
- *Pre-provisioning and deployment:* Lawful interception pre-provisioning is very helpful in ensuring immediate actions when real-time surveillance warrants arrive. Pre-provisioning estimates the most likely configuration and reserves resource for lawful interception.
- *Tests:* Interception functions are assessed with a test database of customers and services or with real customers if feasible.
- *Preparation of procedures:* The entire lawful interception procedure should be carefully prepared in both legal and technological sense. Roles should be defined and described clearly. Escalation steps must be included, along with time limits and names of responsible individuals.
- *Security solutions (framework, event analyzer) for handover interface (HI) between service providers and the law enforcement agency (LEA):* HIs should be protected by various security solutions such as firewalls, encryption, IPSec gateways, and so forth. These solutions will typically be coordinated by a security framework.
- *Software for analyzing surveillance data:* In most cases, COTS (component of the shelf) — as far as they are available — are considered for acquisition and deployment.
- *Support system modification:* In most cases, existing support systems, such as OSSs, BSSs, inventory management tools, provisioning processes, fault notification solutions, element and network managers, mediation devices, and documentation systems, must be slightly modified to support lawful interception.
- *Human resources:* In addition to hardware and software demands, levels of human involvement are expected to be high in terms of preparatory work, deployment, and tests. In many countries, human resources represent a substantial cost factor.

9.1.2 Operating Costs

Categories of recurring operating costs include the following:

- *Training of subject matter experts:* Turnover of human resources is expected to be lower than average due to a more careful team-building process. However, subject matter experts should be continuously educated in regard to legal procedures, new mandates, and new technology.
- *Human resources:* In addition to hardware and software, human involvement is expected to be high in regard to supervision, control, provisioning, analysis, and handover functions.
- *Facilities and supplies:* Substantial ongoing expenditures are required in the case of either stand-alone buildings or colocation of equipment (or demilitarized zones [DMZs]).
- *Hardware maintenance:* Continuous hardware maintenance is required, particularly in the case of parts directly used in lawful interception activities. Examples include probes, management stations, and security frameworks.
- *Software maintenance:* Continuous software maintenance is required as well, again including probes, management stations, and security frameworks.
- *Ad hoc provisioning:* If pre-provisioning is in place, then only activation of networking elements and data paths is required. Costs will be incurred for the use of network equipment and for data transmission.
- *Change management:* The networking infrastructure of service providers is in a permanent state of change. Lawful interception tools must be kept up-to-date and must incorporate mainline technological changes.
- *Intelligent analysis of data:* Specific data searches, correlation of data, data mining, and forensics fall under this category.
- *Overhead (indirect equipment costs due to reduced payload processing and performance effects):* In cases involving internal data collection, overhead levels associated with support of LI activities must be estimated as at least five percent.
- *Handover of data to LEAs:* Independent from the services selected, facilities should be in place for physical handover of data to monitoring centers or directly to LEA servers.
- *Costs of testimony at trials, hearings, and depositions:* Investments are required for human resources time, along with work replacement and traveling expenses.
- *Activities of the legal department:* Legal departments will face a substantial workload as a result of the need for analysis and interpretation of legal requests on behalf of LEAs.

9.1.3 Cost Analysis

As a means of demonstrating how cost components can be quantified and analyzed, we present a case study of a Tier-2 TSP. Eleven assumptions are made in this case study:

1. The TSP operates 50 traditional voice switches.
2. The TSP operates 50 routers.
3. The TSP is using 25 intelligent probes to collect intercept-related data from the network.
4. The probes are administered by one management station.
5. The TSP has provisioned five pairs of firewalls to secure the TSP–LEA connections.
6. The firewalls are administered by one security management station.
7. The TSP has provisioned one T1 connection for handing over intercept-related data to LEAs; its bandwidth may be subdivided into various services.
8. The TSP operates an OSS for billing and provisioning; a lean BSS; element, documentation, and network management systems; and an inventory management tool.
9. The loaded salary for subject matter experts is $200,000.
10. On the basis of the criteria described in Chapter 8, the (Tier 2) TSP needs nine subject matter experts to support LI activities.
11. LEAs and government estimates in a sample country 500 warrants annually; $50,000 is budgeted for each warrant with the result of $25,000,000 to be reimbursed to the TSP.

Table 9.1 presents further assumptions and comments regarding each of the cost components.

Table 9.2 illustrates a simple way of calculating costs associated with legal demands.

Final results can be calculated by dividing net costs with annual legal demands. This is a good basis for estimating costs when estimated reimbursement budgets have to be modified. The following conclusions can be derived:

■ Human resource expenses dominate the recurring cost category. If LEA human resources are added, the impact of such expenses is even larger.
■ One-time costs are surprisingly low.
■ Costs in both categories can be reduced if expenditures are shared among multiple ISS applications.
■ The reimbursement magnitude in this example is too optimistic.

Table 9.1   Case-Study Cost Components

Cost Components	Assumptions and Comments
One-Time Costs	
1. Hardware upgrades of networking equipment	Switch prices are between $300,000 (minimum) and $600,000 (maximum) Router prices are between $50,000 (minimum) and $90,000 (maximum) Extension magnitude is estimated as between 2% (minimum) and 5% (maximum)
2. Software upgrades of networking equipment	Extension magnitude is estimated as between 4% (minimum) and 10% (maximum) related to the hardware prices in Component 1
3. Distributed probes	Prices are between $30,000 (minimum) and $50,000 (maximum)
4. Management station for controlling probes	Estimated price is $50,000
5. Storage media for surveillance data	Prices are between $100,000 (minimum) and $200,000 (maximum)
6. Pre-provisioning and deployment	Estimated price of equipment and software is $50,000
7. Tests	Equipment and software prices are between $10,000 (minimum) and $20,000 (maximum)
8. Preparation of procedures	Human resources costs are $200,000 (minimum) to $300,000 (maximum)
9. Security solutions	Firewall prices are between $40,000 (minimum) and $60,000 (maximum); management station price is between $30,000 (minimum) and $80,000 (maximum)
10. Software for analyzing surveillance data	Price is between $50,000 (minimum) and $80,000 (maximum)
11. Support system modifications	Assuming a value of $2 million, extension magnitude is estimated as between 5% (minimum) and 10% (maximum)
12. Human resources for preparatory tasks, deployment, and tests	Estimated cost of human resources for supporting Components 6 and 7 is $100,000 (minimum) to $200,000 (maximum)

Table 9.1   Case-Study Cost Components (continued)

Cost Components	Assumptions and Comments
Recurring Costs	
1. Training of subject matter experts	9 persons are involved for a period of between 4 weeks (minimum) and 6 weeks (maximum)
2. Human resources to execute tasks	9 persons support LI activities
3. Facilities and supplies	Estimated price is between $1 million and $2 million
4. Hardware maintenance	Extension magnitude is estimated as between 10% (minimum) and 15% (maximum) of the one-time-cost components 3, 4, 5, and 8
5. Software maintenance	Extension magnitude is estimated as between 15% (minimum) and 20% (maximum) of the one-time-cost components 3, 4, 8, and 10
6. *Ad hoc* provisioning of resources	No expense incurred if pre-provisioning is supported; if not, activation is not expected to require substantial resources
7. Change management	Extension magnitude is estimated as between 10% (minimum) and 15% (maximum) of the one-time-cost components 3, 4, and 9
8. Intelligent analysis of data	In addition to Component 2, costs are between $200,000 (minimum) and $300,000 (maximum)
9. Overhead	Extension magnitude is estimated as between 3% (minimum) and 5% (maximum) related to the original costs of switches; 5% (minimum) and 10% (maximum) for storage devices; 15% (minimum) and 25% (maximum) for routers
10. Handover of data to LEAs	T1 price is between $1,500 (minimum) and $3,500 (maximum) per month
11. Cost of testimony	Estimated cost is between $200,000 (minimum) and $300,000 (maximum)
12. Activities of the legal department	Estimated cost is between $200,000 (minimum) and $300,000 (maximum)

Table 9.2 Calculation of Legal Demand Costs

Cost Component	Cost (in $)	
One-Time Costs	Minimum	Maximum
1. Hardware upgrades of networking equipment	350,000	1,725,000
2. Software upgrades of networking equipment	700,000	3,450,000
3. Distributed probes	750,000	1,250,000
4. Management station for controlling probes	50,000	50,000
5. Storage media for surveillance data	100,000	200,000
6. Pre-provisioning and deployment	50,000	50,000
7. Tests	10,000	20,000
8. Preparation of procedures	200,000	300,000
9. Security solutions	230,000	380,000
10. Software for analyzing surveillance data	50,000	80,000
11. Support system modifications	100,000	200,000
12. Human resources for preparatory tasks, deployment, and tests	100,000	200,000
Total one-time costs	**2,690,000**	**7,905,000**
Position 1: Aggressive reimbursement (1 year)	2,690,000	7,905,000
Position 2: Moderate reimbursement (2 years)	1,345,000	3,952,500
Position 3: Opportunistic reimbursement (3 years)	896,667	2,635,000
Recurring Costs		
1. Training of subject matter experts	1,800,000	2,900,000
2. Human resources to execute tasks	21,600,000	21,600,000
3. Facilities and supplies	1,000,000	2,000,000
4. Hardware maintenance	113,000	282,000
5. Software maintenance	199,500	376,000
6. Ad hoc provisioning of resources	0	0
7. Change management	85,000	207,000
8. Intelligent analysis of data	200,000	300,000
9. Overhead	830,000	2,645,000

Table 9.2 Calculation of Legal Demand Costs (continued)

Cost Component	Cost (in $)	
One-Time Costs	Minimum	Maximum
10. Handover of data to LEAs	18,000	42,000
11. Cost of testimony	200,000	300,000
12. Activities of the legal department	200,000	300,000
Total annual recurring costs	**26,245,500**	**30,752,000**
Total annual costs (1 year)	**28,935,500**	**38,657,000**
Total annual costs (2 years)	**27,590,500**	**34,704,500**
Total annual costs (3 years)	**27,142,167**	**33,387,000**
Total payments and reimbursements	**25,000,000**	**25,000,000**
Net costs (1 year)	**3,935,500**	**13,657,000**
Net costs (2 years)	**2,590,500**	**9,704,500**
Net costs (3 years)	**2,142,167**	**8,387,000**

9.2 Quantification of Costs and Reimbursement Strategies

In this section, we discuss cost policies and strategies in use in the United States, the European Community, and Japan. The basic issues are similar but, as a result of different interpretations of written agreements, not identical. In addition, reimbursement philosophies differ in different countries. Patriotism and business on behalf of TSPs are at the extreme poles in terms of reimbursement expectations. The few reimbursement alternatives available from LEAs and governments are not overwhelming. In best-case scenarios, TSPs will not lose money if they faithfully support lawful interception activities.

9.2.1 United States

The general rule in the United States is as follows: providers of electronic communication services that furnish facilities or technical assistance in connection with lawful electronic surveillance are entitled to compensation from the law enforcement agencies they assist for reasonable expenses incurred in providing such facilities or assistance.

9.2.1.1 Estimating and Quantifying Expenses

As described, TSPs must consider both one-time costs and recurring costs in their profitability calculations. The reimbursement system in place in the United States has produced a minimal number of protests on the part of TSPs. Reimbursement levels differ according to levels of the Communications Assistance for Law Enforcement Act (CALEA) support and generic criminal code support. The generic rules of compensation apply to production of stored information (e.g., customer records and content of communications in electronic storage) and real-time monitoring of communications (e.g., tracing and interception of communication content).

9.2.1.2 Reimbursement Strategies

The U.S. Congress has agreed to pay considerable amounts to TSPs that comply with CALEA regulations in their technological solutions. Section 109 of CALEA sets forth the conditions under which the attorney general may agree to reimburse a service provider, through the Telecommunications Carrier Compliance Fund (TCCF), for reasonable costs associated with modifications needed to adhere to CALEA's capability and capacity requirements. The TCCF is funded by various entities.

The Department of Justice is responsible for periodically submitting reports to Congress regarding policies associated with reimbursement. The general opinion is that funding of LI activities is — and will continue to be — hopelessly low.

The FBI has been assigned responsibility for distributing funds to manufacturers and TSPs. To date, the following manufacturers have received such reimbursements:

- Lucent Technologies
- Nortel Networks
- Motorola
- Siemens
- AG Communications

Similarly, specific agreements are in place with a number of TSPs, including:

- Bell Atlantic (Verizon)
- GTE Communications Systems
- Nextel
- Loretto Telephone Company
- Farmers Telephone Company

These are examples only. It is important that "right-to-use" (RTU) licenses are distributed by the FBI for certain products. The basic rule is: "Any provider of wire and electronic communication service, landlord, custodian, or other person furnishing such facilities or technical assistance shall be compensated therefor by the applicant for reasonable expenses incurred in providing such facilities or assistance." The following types of costs can be recovered (Cividanes, 2003):

- Direct costs associated with developing the modifications necessary to comply with capability or capacity requirements
- Costs of training personnel in the use of the required capability or capacity functions
- Direct costs associated with deploying or installing the required capability or capacity

The government entity obtaining the requested (stored) information is mandated to reimburse the service provider assembling or providing such information for such costs as are reasonably necessary and that have been directly incurred in searching for, assembling, reproducing, or otherwise providing information. Such reimbursements include any costs due to necessary disruptions in the normal operations of the electronic communication services through which such information may be stored.

In most cases, amounts are mutually agreed upon by the government entity involved and the entity providing the information. In the absence of such an agreement, amounts are determined by the court that issued the order in question. However, the following costs cannot be recovered or compensated (Warren, 2003a):

- General and administration costs (management, financial, and other expenditures incurred by or allocated to a business unit as a whole)
- Customer service costs (marketing, sales, product management, and advertising)
- Plant costs not directly associated with CALEA modifications
- Costs already recovered from governmental or nongovernmental entities
- Costs that cannot be directly assigned or allocated
- Additional costs due to the failure of the service provider to comply with CALEA regulations in the agreed-upon time frame
- Costs associated with modifications to equipment installed and deployed after January 1, 1995, that the FCC deems reasonably achievable
- Nonrecoverable costs that — in typical accounting practices — are grouped with recoverable costs for the purpose of calculating standard or otherwise allowable costs

The FBI defines "significant upgrade and modification" as "any fundamental or substantial change in the network architecture or any change that fundamentally alters the nature or type of the existing telecommunications equipment, facility or service that impedes law enforcement's ability to conduct lawfully authorized electronic surveillance." In addition, courts may order payment if it is determined that the information required is unusually voluminous in nature or otherwise causes an undue burden for the provider.

TSPs and manufacturers invoice the LEAs requesting surveillance services. They will be compensated for reasonable costs of deployment and modifications in the case of wiretaps and pen/trap and trace support. Invoices should detail actual investments, maintenance fees, and human resources expenses.

According to CALEA Section 109(e)(3), service providers must submit claims for reimbursement along with "such information as the Attorney General may require." The FBI claims procedure includes the following steps:

- Request for proposal
- Submission of cost estimates
- Execution of a cooperative agreement
- Submission of a request for payment
- Audits of the service provider's submissions
- Adjustments to the agreement estimate
- Agency payment to service provider for modifications

In general, LEA reimbursements to TSPs and manufacturers are relatively low in comparison with the overall costs related to LIs.

9.2.2 Europe

The general rule in the European Community is as follows: Providers of electronic communication services that furnish facilities or technical assistance in connection with lawful electronic surveillance and interception are entitled to be compensated, by the law enforcement agencies they assist, for reasonable expenses incurred in providing such facilities or assistance. However, significant differences exist between countries.

In Europe, there has long been an emphasis on protecting state-owned and state-supported monopolies. The processes of privatization and liberalization in the telecommunications sector are not yet complete. Due to the incubatory preferences of governments, TSPs (at least Tier-1 providers) are expected to fully and unconditionally support lawful interception activities.

9.2.2.1 France

In general, France's reimbursement levels are higher than those of other countries. Guidelines on responsibilities, roles, and compensation structures in regard to interception activities are in place, and there are separate compensation policies for targeted and strategic surveillance activities.

9.2.2.1.1 Estimating and Quantifying Expenses

Because of the country's reasonable compensation strategies, protests on the part of TSPs are infrequent. Actual costs are compensated, and full payment is expected for all data transferred to the Groupe Interministeriel de Controle (GIC). Investments are compensated as well. Amounts are subject to negotiations between LEAs and TSPs.

9.2.2.1.2 Reimbursement Strategies

The Department of Justice is in charge of compensating all network-related surveillance activities. The Department of Police is responsible for compensating preventive and strategic surveillance activities. In the respective cases, the same entities are in charge of compensation for all transfer of data to the GIC.

9.2.2.2 United Kingdom

The United Kingdom seems to be gradually increasing the levels of compensation provided to TSPs. However, due to the lack of clear structures and procedures, TSPs are not awarded reasonable compensation as of yet. Typically, Tier-2 and Tier-3 providers and ISPs are very much interested in signing mutually acceptable agreements with the home office. These providers need fundings due to their reduced revenues in comparison to Tier 1 providers. Compensation is a key factor of these agreements.

9.2.2.2.1 Estimating and Quantifying Expenses

There are significant costs, particularly in the case of ISPs, involved in supporting LI and data retention activities. There have been many discussions regarding whether RIPA is having an adverse effect on the business health of TSPs. However, due to the lack of specifications published in handbooks or codes of practice, there are no simple answers to this question. The Internet Service Providers' Association (ISPA) is negotiating with the home office regarding mutually acceptable agreements. Solutions reached on a volunteer basis do not seem to be a viable option.

9.2.2.2.2 Reimbursement Strategies

The home office is mandated to compensate providers for LI activities. Compensation levels in regard to hardware, software, and human resources seem to be adequate. The most appropriate compensation level is provided for wireline voice surveillance activities. Wireline voice is best understood for determining the right price range for compensation. The home office wants to avoid situations in which TSPs profit from conducting LI activities.

9.2.3 Japan

The general rule in Japan is as follows: Providers of electronic communication services that furnish facilities or technical assistance in connection with lawful electronic surveillance are entitled to be compensated by the law enforcement agencies they assist for reasonable expenses incurred in providing such facilities or assistance. However, this rule is not stipulated in any particular legislation. There continues to be a need for individual agreements between government agencies and TSPs.

9.2.3.1 Estimating and Quantifying Expenses

Representatives of the industry — manufacturers and TSPs — do not publicly criticize the requirements in force in the area of LIs. However, TSPs consider the requirement that a subject matter expert be present during surveillance activities as producing excessive expenses. LEAs are working on a reimbursement strategy, but the outcomes of this process are not known at present.

9.2.3.2 Reimbursement Strategies

The government is willing to compensate providers for special development efforts. For example, the National Police Agency and the Ministry of Justice have provided compensation for the "temporary mailbox" used by the police to analyze e-mails. However, national laws do not mention requirements for reimbursement. Discussions are still under way regarding reasonable costs in situations in which technical requirements do not match the capabilities of or technology deployed by TSPs.

Reimbursement is considered for significant business risks stemming from LI activities. TSPs consider reimbursement a better choice than noncompliance or lack of cooperation.

9.2.4 Reimbursement Strategies at Large

In review, global reimbursement strategies in regard to LI activities can be summarized as follows:

- TSPs and manufacturers can recover costs but not raise revenues or profits.
- All costs considered to represent additional expenses incurred in providing assistance to LEAs can be recovered.
- In most cases, capital or other expenses incurred, regardless of specific requests for assistance by LEAs, cannot be recovered.

9.3 Return on Investment (ROI)

ROI is one of the most important metrics for evaluating the profitability of investments. Because ISS represents more than supporting lawful interception, support for ISS cannot be judged exclusively on the basis of ROI.

9.3.1 Considerations Other Than ROI

The following considerations are important in decisions regarding lawful interception:

- *Total cost of ownership (TCO) over long time periods:* Successful investments guarantee a low TCO with well-controlled operating costs.
- *Value of the lawful interception initiative:* A viable business without noncompliance penalties as a result of complying with lawful interception mandates is a measurable value to all TSPs.
- *Technological feasibility:* Many innovations in the underlying infrastructure of TSPs could be combined with ISS requirements, such as mediation, traffic analysis, and fraud protection.
- *Risks related to investing in (or not investing in) ISS:* Not supporting lawful interception and not complying with surveillance mandates may mean that TSPs cannot do business with government agencies or cannot do business in certain geographic areas.
- *Overall governance model:* Visibility of compliance, control of processes, and rectifications when necessary with leadership capabilities will ensure the successful support of lawful interception and is more valuable than short-range revenues or even profits from lawful interception ventures.

9.3.2 ISS Cost Justification

ISS is not only the support vehicle for lawful interception. Other areas must be considered in justifying the cost of ISS investments.

All ISS-based processes must ultimately provide comprehensive surveillance in a lawful manner. This includes gathering comprehensive information from any network (e.g., wireline, wireless, access, transport, and broadband) and on any scale. The ISS-based process should provide comprehensive information on a real-time basis (i.e., proactive intelligence).

Proactive intelligence requires that, nationwide, even global networks be instrumented in such a manner that all communications can be monitored on a grand scale allowing identification of potential targets with summary intelligence while respecting privacy laws. Once targets have been identified, further monitoring can be conducted and intelligence obtained as authorization is granted.

An ISS that provides this level of information needs to capture all key summary information in a manner that is lawful and protects the rights of individuals. In particular, a well-designed and deployed ISS can satisfy business (customer and partner relationship management), operational (billing and portfolio management), security (infrastructure protection and fraud avoidance), and surveillance (lawful interception) needs. A powerful mediation system should be in place between data sources and applications.

9.3.3 ISS Profitability Trends

Several factors have an influence in terms of whether ISSs can be cost-effective (Lucas, 2003f). First, criminal acts are not a remote possibility. However, LEAs as a group see TSPs as not being sufficiently cooperative, and they will single them out in case of noncompliance and point the finger at the telecommunications industry and their service providers given the opportunity. Also, they would have such an opportunity should a criminal act with serious consequences occur.

Another factor in regard to ISS profitability, a geographic one, is that Western Europe is far ahead of North America in terms of lawful interception standards and the issue of law enforcement ownership of the ISS infrastructure, including colocation of ISSs in operators' facilities. It is expected that, in the near future, both Western Europe and North America will institute a policy in which TSPs will face two choices: either they implement ISS or LEAs will do it for them, under LEA control. In most countries, sufficient budgets are already in place to make such a scenario a reality. Losing opportunities with their own ISSs would heavily impact profitability.

Also, the largest new markets for telecommunications equipment are in the Asia–Pacific region, and governments in this region interpret privacy differently from North America and Europe. Suppliers will not be able to sell to this high-value government market without ISSs that support lawful or other kinds of intercepts.

In terms of voice and data convergence, the idea that a service provider is going to offer a public IP service that cannot support lawful interception is unrealistic. A model in which a provider will not implement CALEA or other mandates and support other LI mandates might not be viable. Convergent services require ISSs.

Finally, the U.S. government spends billions per year on telecommunications services, and it will continue spending significant amounts for E-government initiatives requiring precise authentication. TSPs considering business with the U.S. government should have ISSs in place.

9.4 Summary

Experience shows that, for several reasons, TSPs typically have no economic interest in setting up a monitoring facility. For example:

- Development and operation of a solution complying with legal requirements results in intense use of financial and personnel resources.
- System-integrated solutions require high investments, and ongoing development of networks, introduction of new services, and alterations in legal requirements offer no protection whatsoever for the investments made.
- In some cases, system-integrated solutions have negative effects on network performance.
- System-integrated, permanently installed facilities may have negative effects in terms of the trust unsuspecting customers place in communication confidentiality.

Thus, TSPs face costs and investments that represent no profit benefit to them. However, TSPs must rethink their positions. Support for lawful interception is neither a revenue generator nor a profit maker. However, in most cases the ROI for ISSs cannot be quantified with hard numbers, and, considering their overall functionality (powerful mediation capabilities, infrastructure protection, and fraud avoidance), they can be cost justified. Although the reimbursement process is typically slow and cumbersome, reasonable costs will be reimbursed in most countries.

On the positive side, TSPs that are supporting lawful interception and are in compliance with surveillance mandates will derive viable business benefits over the long term, can do business with governments, and can innovate their public IP service portfolio.

Outsourcing lawful interception functions is being considered by both TSPs and LEAs. It is a viable option in regard to streamlining processes, reducing costs, and better controlling expenditures for both parties. Details on outsourcing are provided in the next chapter.

Chapter 10

Outsourcing Lawful Interception Functions

CONTENTS

Law enforcement agencies (LEAs) make four fundamental types of requests in regard to electronic surveillance: access to past billing and statistical traffic records, access to contents of computer long-term storage, access to current billing and statistical records of communications, and access to current content. In the case of each request, three functions can be differentiated: the access function (AF), the delivery function (DF), and the collection function (CF).

When telecommunications service providers (TSPs) are interested in outsourcing lawful intercept (LI) activities because of a shortage of skilled human resources, technical limitations, cost, or a combination of these elements, they typically consider the following options:

- Other telecommunications service providers (TSPs)
- Mainframe vendors
- Database vendors
- System integrators
- LEAs
- Consultants
- LI-monitoring centers

The decision of whether or not to outsource can be simplified by assessing the following four areas:

1. *End-to-end costs:* development, rollout, integration, and change-management expenses
2. *Availability of the necessary skilled human resources:* subject matter experts, business analysts, and software developers
3. *Uniqueness of the required solution:* most likely a "no outsourcing" answer to this item because of existing standards and streamlined access, delivery, and collection functions
4. *Timeline requirements:* most likely a "yes outsourcing" answer to this item because of existing LI frameworks and scalable devices that can be customized to the networking technology of TSPs

10.1 Forces Driving Outsourcing

Several principal forces drive the outsourcing of LI functions (Warren, 2003b):

- In-house provisioning, administration, and security surveillance have become too expensive; in particular, personnel costs are increasing rapidly.
- There is a chronic shortage of skilled personnel.
- TSPs must comply with LEA requirements, and legal interpretations must be clear and quick in today's changing legal environment.
- Supporting LIs in-house may result in a loss of focus on strategic issues that help increase revenue and generate profit.

- Service expectations may be defined and supervised more effectively with an outsourcer than in the case of an insourced solution.

TSPs must contend with several other issues as well:

- Technology has simplified access to network elements and information.
- LEAs are now demanding access to digital storage of customer-related information.
- LEAs are demanding Communications Assistance for Law Enforcement Act (CALEA) and ETSI compliance.
- Most ISPs do not have the personnel or business support systems (BSSs) in place to handle broad record production searches and electronic surveillance demands.

Another important factor to consider is the increasing personnel burden and high costs involved in support of LEAs' demands for records and technical assistance. For example, growing workloads increase the potential for mistakes. Also, as workloads increase and backlogs grow, there are greater legal risks stemming from the possibility of errors, thus potentially leading to greater risk of damage to a TSP's public image.

Finally, in terms of business challenges, more is being demanded of TSPs, and business realities show that the LI function is not a revenue-generating one. In addition, today's economic conditions require cost reductions on the part of TSPs. TSPs must weigh two fundamental options:

1. Building an internal infrastructure: obtaining legal assistance in developing policies and procedures, hiring and training personnel with expertise in legal matters, implementing compliance programs and audit procedures, and investing in technology to support operations
2. Outsourcing surveillance-related activities: using an outside law firm for deploying policies and procedures and implementing an end-to-end solution with a service bureau

Before deciding for or against outsourcing, TSPs should carefully evaluate the following criteria:

- *Present or expected end-to-end costs of supporting LIs:* All effects should be quantified in terms of both capital and operational expenses.
- *Efficiency of existing processes, tools, and human resources:* This area is essential in determining which functions, if any, to outsource.

- *Extent of dependence on speed:* The real-time requests of LEAs must be met.
- *Grade of service and applications required:* These needs may dictate the type of outsourcing used.
- *Level of security* for the handover interface (HI) between SPs and LEAs.
- *Cost effectiveness:* Is it more cost-effective to concentrate on the provider's core business than to build a full infrastructure to support lawful interception.
- *Capital investment required:* If the company must invest substantial amounts in lawful interception, it should favor outsourcing; if not, outsourcing may still be considered but should receive lower priority.
- *Current and future need for skilled personnel:* The most sophisticated LI technology will be useless if the company cannot find employees to run it.
- *Potential acquisitions, mergers, sales of business units, as well as changes in service portfolio:* These elements should be carefully evaluated, given that each may affect contracts with outsourcers.
- *Whether it is possible to negotiate acceptable outsourcing contracts:* Contract terms are of paramount importance considering the long durations of contracts in this sensitive area.
- *Careful evaluation:* Determination of all services and functions offered by the outsourcer, as well as knowledge levels and experience.
- *Careful review of the proposed transitioning warranty:* This must be done on behalf of the outsourcer.

10.2 The LEA Model

In this case, LEAs take full responsibility for all principal functions. If required, they initiate all necessary processes including on-the-fly provisioning of networking equipment and facilities. TSPs are expected to provide physical access to equipment and facilities. Occasionally, the physical presence of subject matter experts of TSPs is required during surveillance.

In addition to obvious benefits in the area of legal expertise, benefits of this model are LEAs' extensive knowledge regarding the targets of and reasons for surveillance, their high motivation to prosecute criminals, and the possibility of enhanced collection results. Disadvantages included limited technical know-how in regard to networking technologies, the limited (and most likely obsolete) surveillance tools available, lack of experience with the access and delivery functions (AF and DF), and shortages in terms of human resources.

10.3 The ASP Model

In this case, application service providers (ASPs) take full responsibility for providing the application software necessary to support all principal surveillance functions. ASPs are represented by TSPs or third parties. Benefits of this model include the following:

■ Good scalability of solutions
■ Usage-based billing
■ Lower number of personnel required
■ Flexibility in instances in which networking technology changes are required

Disadvantages include:

■ Security risks due to shared applications
■ Dependence on the ASP
■ Contractual risks
■ Limited legal background of the ASP

10.4 The Service Bureau Model

The requirements associated with this model can be summarized as follows:

■ The service bureau must provide comprehensive record production.
■ It must adhere to professional legal and service standards.
■ It must support effective coordination with LEAs.
■ It should provide technology that is trusted by both SPs and LEAs.
■ It must ensure high scalability for increasing data volumes.
■ It must minimize legal risks in both civil and criminal terms.
■ It must protect the public image of the SP.
■ It must represent a cost-effective alternative to an SP internal structure.
■ It is expected to be staffed by subject domain experts with extensive field experience.

The benefits of the service bureau model are:

■ Focus on core business opportunities
■ Reductions in operating costs
■ Conservation of capital; risk and up-front investments in personnel and surveillance technology assumed by service bureau
■ Support of future-proof services
■ No concern about operations for TSPs

Disadvantages include:

■ Legal dependency on outsourcer
■ Technological dependency on outsourcer
■ Security risks with HI
■ Possible internal resistance
■ Potential loss of subject matter experts
■ Need for minimal (critical) mass of staff as backup
■ Need for continuous supervision of contracts
■ Possible lack of cost savings
■ Transitional problems
■ Risk of losing control over LI-related information
■ Risk of outsourcer not representing the interests of the SP

Supporting the Service Bureau Model, Trusted Third Parties (TTP) are gaining a lot of attention these days.

The value proposition of TTP includes the following items:

■ Independence is key to trust by enhancing privacy with Calea and Etsi
■ TTP has freedom to employ a range of architectures, such as internal, external, and adjunct
■ TTP can generally follow safe harbor standards
■ TTP offers value-added services, such as authentication of trust systems, legal analysis and verification of orders, proof of performance, and subpoena processing

Comparing costs, outsourcing most likely outperforms self-deployment of lawful intercept technologies from year one.

Outsourcing of lawful intercept in service bureau form offers the following additional values to LEAs and TSPs:

■ Reduces operations expenses including staffing needs
■ Minimizes capital expenditures for future network services

- Minimizes LEA-related network interference
- Alleviates risk of stranded investment in rapidly changing network infrastructure
- Most cost-effective way to meet LEA needs at the right time
- Faster time to market, easier entrance to new markets, generates compliance rapidly
- Allows carriers to focus on their core business

Table 10.1 shows options in the functions for outsourcing supporting LI activities.

Outsourcers should be rated according to the following criteria, among others:

- Financial strength and stability over a long period
- Excellent security record and clearance for highly sensitive assignments
- Outstanding business reputation
- Outstanding legal background
- Demonstrated ability to support lawful interceptions
- Number of employees, along with their clearance level and level of experience in supporting lawful interception
- History of using and implementing state-of-the-art technology, frameworks, and tools
- Ability to customize tools to networking technologies

The strengths and weaknesses of each category of outsourcers are summarized in Table 10.2.

It is recommended that the following items be included in contracts between TSPs and outsourcers:

- *Names, addresses, and contact numbers of contracting parties:* All parties to the agreement should be listed, especially when multiple LEAs are involved. Each party defined as a contracting party should sign the contract.
- *Terms of the agreement:* The period for which the agreement is to be in place should be specified. Also, details on procedures relating to changes and modifications must be included.
- *Service description (on the basis of Table 10.1):* This should include the supported AFs, DFs, and CFs for each of the targeted areas such as postbilling records, long-term storage, intercept-related information (IRI), and current content of communications (CC).
- *Service-level indicators:* Service offer (e.g., 7 × 24 × 365), service performance metrics, definition of outages and nonavailability of

Table 10.1   Outsourcing Options

Request and Functions	Past Billing Records			Long-Term Storage			Intercept-Related Information			Current Content of Communications		
	AF	DF	CF	AF	DF	CF	AF	DF	CF	AF	DF	CF
Principal outsourcer												
Other TSPs												
Mainframe vendors												
Database vendors												
System integrators												
LEAs												
Consultants												
LI-monitoring centers												

Note: AF = access function; DF = delivery function; CF = collection function.

services, help-desk and hotline support, and many other parameters should be defined and quantified by the contracting partners.

■ *Commitments and duties of TSPs:* Written confirmation that TSPs will ensure physical access to LI resources and assist in outage detection and problem resolution must be provided.

■ *Reviews and reporting periods:* Reports supported by contract-monitoring tools should be defined and created. Also, guidelines should be formulated in regard to frequency of reviews and reporting, access to reports, and availability of real-time data and reports. It is highly recommended that Web services be used for information exchanges between the contracting partners.

■ *Cost and chargeback policies:* Prices charged for services should be detailed and billing periods determined. In addition, details regarding escalation procedures must be determined.

■ *Penalties for noncompliance:* The contract should include regulations for nonperformance indicating that service-level metrics have been violated by the outsourcer.

■ *Rules regarding employee transitions:* If required, subject matter experts may be transferred permanently or for a certain period of time from TSPs to the outsourcer. Terms of employment, salary, and benefits must be clarified in writing prior to any such transfer.

10.5 Sourcing Governance

With the rise in outsourcing, the types and complexity of sourcing arrangements have exploded. An IT organization can now source almost every facet of its operations — from application development and maintenance to service delivery and assets — to an external provider.

Mission-critical activities, once deemed too risky to vest control in an outsider, are now routinely transferred to SPs. Multiple vendors often participate in sourcing arrangements, adding to the overhead of managing these relationships. Business users — the consumers of sourced services — frequently reside in dispersed locations, complicating delivery of services. Because geographically distributed sourcing teams increasingly interface with one another and directly with business customers, facilitating and coordinating these interactions becomes more of a challenge.

As comfort and sophistication levels increase, organizations naturally desire greater control over their sourcing arrangements. In particular, they typically see the need to do the following (Haynes, 2003):

■ Monitor and adjust service-level performance
■ Oversee contract compliance more closely

Table 10.2 Outsourcer Strengths and Weaknesses

Category of Outsourcer	Strengths	Weaknesses
Other TSP	Can specialize in supporting LI activities	May be a competitor
	Possibility of increased number of surveillance tools	Lack of access or control over surveillance tools
	Increased networking know-how	
Mainframe vendor	Hardware, software, and database know-how	Expertise in the area of LIs cannot be guaranteed
		Possible lack of networking and legal know-how
Database vendor	Database, data warehousing, and data mining and processing know-how	Possible lack of know-how regarding LI activities and networking
	Probable support of forensics	
	Extensive understanding of storage concepts and maintenance	
System integrator	Broad knowledge of technologies, products, and services	Locked-in status for long periods due to dependability on the same integrator
	Knowledge regarding tools	Eventual preference for certain suppliers by the integrator
	Effective collaboration with multiple suppliers	

	Strengths	Weaknesses
LEA	Excellent legal background High motivation to prosecute criminals	Absence of specialized networking skills
Consultant	Broad knowledge of technologies, products, and services Knowledge regarding tools Effective collaboration with multiple suppliers Unbiased evaluation of suppliers and their solutions	Locked-in status for long periods due to dependability on the same consultant Eventual preference for certain suppliers by the consultant Legal background may not be sufficient Possible insufficient motivation to prosecute criminals
LI-monitoring center	Excellent equipment and facilities State-of-the-art technology Highly skilled subject matter experts	Need for long-range commitments Resource-sharing concerns

- Track, control, and adjust work assignments and tasks
- Coordinate the activities of on-site and off-site teams
- Coordinate work flow among multiple vendors
- Effectively share work products among sourcing teams and end users
- Identify and resolve problems promptly
- Facilitate the use of outsourced services, helping end users know which services are available and how to use them

Where there is a need, products and tools will emerge to fill the void. Today, new sets of tools and processes are helping IT organizations meet their sourcing needs and better manage their sourcing arrangements. In most cases, enterprises use a variety of such tools to:

- Reduce the costs and overhead involved in managing sourcing relationships
- Improve performance quality
- Maintain alignment with corporate goals
- Identify issues for quick resolution
- Improve overall returns
- Enhance productivity

When automating the management of sourcing arrangements, there is no one-size-fits-all solution that works for every company and situation. Moreover, no solution available today will result in automation of all aspects of the sourcing relationship.

Figure 10.1 shows a model for automating sourcing arrangements (Haynes, 2003). A complete yet simple view of a sourcing arrangement is provided. The areas considered fall into two categories: relationship management and delivery management.

Relationship management tools address facets of the sourcing arrangement that affect the relationships among the parties (i.e., TSPs and LEAs). The stakeholders most directly affected by relationship management issues are outsourcers and TSPs. Tools may focus on contract terms, covered services, or fostering of collaboration among the stakeholders. They may assist in monitoring and adjusting contract terms and conditions, creating new work orders, publishing and following operating principles, and elevating issues that are not suitable to be dispatched through delivery management channels.

10.5.1 Contract Management

A single sourcing arrangement of moderate complexity and scope may result in a contract several hundred pages in length. However, depending

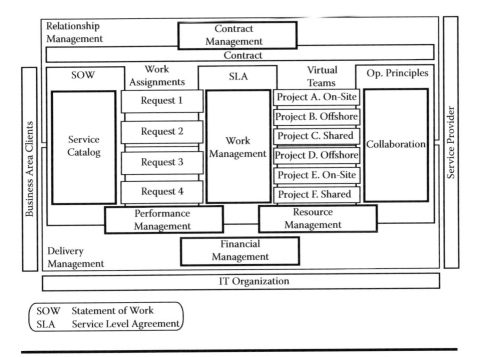

Figure 10.1 Model for automating sourcing arrangements.

on the preferences and organizational capabilities of the negotiating parties, contract documents may be well structured and easy to follow. In the past, the client manager most likely would have locked the contract away in a drawer, taking it out only when a problem arose. Even if the manager desired greater day-to-day control and oversight of the terms, obligations, and promises made in the contract, virtually no commercial tools were available to provide assistance in this effort.

Today's contract management tools, which are still evolving, work with and are driven by the various terms and conditions specified in the contract. The simpler the contract is to understand and the simpler it is to find important terms and information, the easier it is to use an automated contract management tool. Ideally, a contract will consist of several documents, improving understanding and easing administration.

10.5.1.1 Key Components of Contract Management

Figure 10.2 illustrates a typical (and recommended) contract structure, the documents involved, and the relationships between them. Documents used include the following (Haynes, 2003):

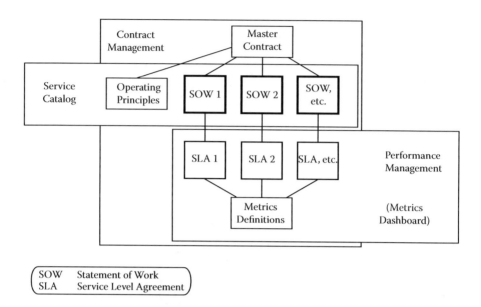

Figure 10.2   Documents composing a sourcing contract.

- *Master contract:* This is a legal document that specifies the rules by which the outsourcer and TSP will operate. Normally, one master contract governs the relationship, containing financial terms and standard legal protections and covering such topics as issue resolution, work changes, and exit clauses — all from a legal perspective. The contract refrains from specifying the details of the work to be sourced, instead referring to attachments (described in the following text); this structure makes it easier to change service-related work without modifying the master contract.

- *Statement of work (SOW):* These form the core of any sourcing arrangement, defining the scope of the service to be provided or the work to be performed. They specify the assets or functions that the outsourcer will support, the types of work that will be performed, the inputs required, the deliverables created, and each party's roles in the arrangement. Multiple SOWs tend to be easier to administer and adjust than one extremely large SOW, with the actual number of SOWs depending on how many discrete projects, functions, or efforts will be transferred to the SP. Depending on their construction, SOWs may relate directly to a service contained in the service catalog. For example, they may cover maintenance of monitoring services, installation of probes, database updates, and other functions.

■ *Service-level agreements (SLAs):* These define the parameters by which the work identified in the SOW will be performed and judged. For example, they define performance criteria such as the volume of work that should be performed in a given time frame, system availability, acceptable response times, quality requirements, and efficiency measures. These commitments may be applicable to both parties, describing the obligations of the TSP as well as the outsourcer. SLA performance criteria are described using metrics. Generally, a separate metric is used for each attribute measured. For example, when a help-desk function is outsourced, work volume may be specified according to the number of calls handled per month, and responsiveness may be defined as average time to call back. SLAs appear in dashboards to give managers a quick view of vendors' performance.

■ *Metrics definitions:* To avoid confusion or misinterpretation, each metric used in an SLA must have a definition. This definition will include a name, description, objective, measurement method, rules of initialization, and responsibility or roles for collection and interpretation. For most sourcing arrangements, a subset of metrics will suffice, and metrics generally are centralized in one definition document. The rules by which a metric is calculated and the data sources are items typically entered into a performance management tool.

■ *Operating principles:* These define how the TSP and outsourcer will work together on a daily basis, with special attention paid to logistics and handoffs between provider and client. Reporting relationships, governance procedures, and processes associated with such activities as submitting work requests, turning completed work over to production, obtaining sign-offs, and raising problems are covered by the operating-principles document. This document is an important source of information for creating a service catalog.

10.5.1.2 Benefits of Contract Management Tools

Contract management tools offer significant benefits over manual, occasional oversight. The tools manage either a single, complex contract or many smaller contracts. Their benefits include the following:

■ *Ability to actively manage the contract throughout its life cycle:* By capturing all relevant contractual terms and obligations (i.e., SOWs, SLA metrics, and payments), important dates and procedures (i.e., operating principles and notice provisions), and interested parties, these tools automate contract administration, relieving managers of the burden of wading through pages of detail.

■ *Ability to manage changes to contract documents:* Contracts will inevitably change as new services are added, existing services are terminated, service levels are adjusted, or the parties involved want to modify terms and conditions. Because tools integrate all the contract's components, they can assist in the change-management process by allowing the parties to assess the effects of changes before they are rolled out. Once changes are approved, tools can help propagate them through all components and documents. This way, tools serve as a central means of routing and tracking change requests and assist in formalizing otherwise *ad hoc* change requests.

■ *Ability to log contract changes and notify affected parties:* Once contract changes are approved, tools can maintain a log of modifications so that all parties have a current view of the contract and associated terms (e.g., changes in SLAs). Tools also can send alerts or notices to parties affected by selected modifications for legal compliance purposes and to enable them to prepare for changes in services, price, responsiveness, hours of operation, or other terms.

■ *Ability to automate the approval process:* In addition to contract changes, various other terms and services will inevitably change during the course of an engagement. The operating principles in force typically specify the approval processes used and the parties involved in approving changes. Tools also can help automate the approval process by ensuring that appropriate individuals are notified, that changes are captured and forwarded without falling through the cracks or languishing on someone's desk, and that sign-offs are obtained in the correct order and from the right people.

■ *Ability to complete initial setup and definition of SLAs and metrics:* Tools are an ideal means of defining metrics and service levels. Using predefined templates, wizards, lists of formulas, and calculations, tools allow companies to translate SLA and metrics definitions from the paper contract to a format that can be used to collect performance data automatically.

■ *Ability to support issue elevation and resolution:* The operating principles involved usually include a description of the process used to raise issues that affect the relationship (as opposed to project or application-type issues that are resolved as part of project management). When issues rise to a certain level — whether a noticeable trend, a failure, or a predicted failure — tools can automate the process described in the operating principles to alert stakeholders, forward relevant data, and monitor the elevation process to completion. In cases of a contract breach or application of a penalty, tools can integrate with other systems to ensure that the correct follow-on activities occur, such as adding credits to an invoice. Tools can even trigger a round of contract changes and the associated approval process.

10.5.1.3 Selection and Setup Issues and Concerns

When automating contract management, a few important caveats apply. The ability to "map" the contract documents and terms into a tool depends greatly on the quality and structure of the documents and the degree of detail in their terms. If the contract is so large that it defies understanding, is confusing, or uses ambiguous terminology, then translating it into tool-friendly form will be challenging. Tools force definitions, and thus it is helpful if the contract is clear and precise from the outset. Even with a well-laid-out contract, taking the information from the contract and entering it into a tool can be a time-consuming effort affected by the number of documents involved and the number of sourcing contracts administered.

Tools can help ease the contract process based on the quality of their interfaces, but considerable setup time is still the norm. On the bright side, this initial investment is quickly recovered via improvements in contract administration throughout the life of the outsourcing engagement. Furthermore, the data entered from SOWs, SLAs, and metrics for contract management purposes are also used for setting up service catalogs and performance measures; thus, once entered, they can be reused for multiple purposes. A sample of contract management vendors and tools is listed in Table 10.3.

Software offerings in this category take information from many sources, but the prime source of input is the contract itself. Users of relationship management tools include executives and IT, purchasing, legal, and contract managers.

Table 10.3   Sample Contract Management Vendors and Tools

Vendor	Product
DiCarta	Contracts
Digital Fuel	ServiceFlow
Upside Software	Upside contract

10.5.2 Delivery Management

Delivery management tools address aspects of the sourcing arrangement that cover day-to-day delivery of services and operations. The parties most involved in delivery management are business area clients such as the LEAs and TSPs that consume services, the outsourcers that deliver the services, and the IT organizations that facilitate the flow of services between the two. Delivery management tools have a wide range of capabilities, with some more robust than others. IT and technical personnel may be familiar with tools in this category, including the following examples.

10.5.2.1 Service Catalog

A service catalog is aimed at business area clients such as LEAs and TSPs to alert them to the services available and how to make use of a particular service. It describes the various types of services that the outsourcer will provide under the terms of the engagement and can guide business area clients in subscribing to a service. Managers also may use the catalog to initiate a service and approve or reject service requests submitted by subordinates. Service catalogs are quite useful in terms of setting expectations (e.g., alerting end users to hours of operations, responsiveness, or price) and maintaining alignment between the parties.

10.5.2.2 Work Management

At a strategic level, work management focuses on selecting and sourcing the right projects from the entire portfolio, i.e., those projects that advance corporate goals and provide an attractive return on investment (ROI). At a tactical level, work management focuses on executing the tasks and activities that constitute a particular project or support an ongoing function, which form the bulk of the work performed under the sourcing contract.

10.5.2.3 Collaboration

Representing one of the latest entrants into the sourcing space, collaboration tools are key to creating a seamless work environment for geographically distributed teams. With a collaborative environment, team members who are geographically dispersed can effectively communicate, exchange information, coordinate their work, and collaborate on various types of projects. The prime users of collaboration tools are working team members and managers in the client and SP organizations, along with technical and business area personnel.

10.5.2.4 Performance Management

The tools of greatest interest to both outsourcers and TSPs are performance management tools. These tools are used to assess a vendor's performance in regard to service-level commitments. In addition, they track and audit compliance with SLAs and provide reports describing results. Dashboards, a popular method of illustrating vendors' compliance and performance status, are used by IT and business area managers to assess whether vendors are living up to their promises.

10.5.2.5 Resource Management

Resource management tools cover two aspects of the sourcing arrangement: the human resources used to accomplish the work and, if appropriate, the "hard" assets involved such as computing equipment and networking devices. Outsourcers are the primary users of these tools, but LEAs and TSPs may use them as well, especially when drawing personnel from multiple sources. Some of the earlier resource management tools were custom-developed by TSPs to monitor their own staff. Today, many commercial packages are available.

10.5.2.6 Financial Management

A favorite of CFOs and business managers, financial management tools are used to assess the performance of the sourcing engagement from an economic perspective. These tools monitor, for example, budget expenditures, commitments, chargebacks, invoice amounts, and credits or penalties. They may also measure larger factors such as ROI or internal rate of return (IRR) and may assist in developing forecasts or scenarios. Through insight into financial metrics, client organizations can better set task and project priorities and allocate resources. Both client and vendor managers use these tools but separately and for different purposes.

10.6 Who Are the Principal Players?

Because of the sensitivity of LIs, participating entities are careful about sharing responsibilities with external companies. As a result, outsourcing trends are not yet visible. If they so desire, professional outsourcers in the telecommunications field can extend their services toward LI activities. Also, outsourcers from the legal side can offer services in regard to at least the collection function. This section considers a few early examples of outsourcing options:

- *LEAs:* Typical example is the FBI in the United States
- *ASPs:* Forensics Explorer
- *Service bureau providers:* VeriSign
- *LI-monitoring centers:* Siemens solution with a number of add-on functions, in cooperation with GTEN, Datakom, and Utimaco
- *System integrators:* VeriSign and GTEN
- *Consulting companies:* Neustar/Fiducianet, Inc., in the United States

It is expected that this short list will grow rapidly in the near future.

10.7 Summary

TSPs must give serious consideration to the decision of whether to outsource LI-related functions such as delivery of data and information and collection of information and intelligence by LEAs. However, outsourcers must be guaranteed access to the networks and network equipment necessary for LIs. This is an issue of mutual trust and good security. Outsourcers should have the highest possible security clearance so that they can be trusted with intelligence data.

By using outsourcing, TSPs can streamline and better control their expenditures. In conducting intercept-related activities, outsourcers would most likely work with multiple TSPs and LEAs. Thus, a client-safe LI infrastructure is necessary, with TSPs and LEAs physically and logically separated from each other. The monitoring center model outlined in earlier chapters comes closest to meeting this requirement. Such a monitoring center would be equipped with state-of-the-art hardware and software supported by highly qualified subject matter experts who have been cleared for the highest security level. Resource and expert sharing for multiple clients are not visible to clients represented by TSPs and LEAs. But, offshoring of any of LI functions and activities to third countries is out of the question.

Chapter 11

Summary and Trends

Lawful interception can play an important role in the operations of telecommunications service providers (TSPs). TSPs are expected to honestly support lawful interception activities whether or not such activities generate additional revenue. Combining lawful interception with powerful intelligence support systems (ISSs) represents the optimal path to be followed by TSPs. In addition to providing the basic functionality for lawful interception, an ISS can support other important functions such as real-time and usage-based billing, fraud avoidance, churn avoidance, provision of data, and real-time traffic control. Assuming a certain level of government reimbursement, cost recovery can be achieved.

The critical success factors in conducting lawful interception activities are process, products, and people:

- *Process:* the functional steps of lawful interception, including interception requests and provisioning of resources; access, delivery, collection, and maintenance of data; and conversion of data into intelligence by TSPs, law enforcement agencies (LEAs), and outsourcers
- *Products:* all existing and future applications supporting process steps, including active and passive hardware or software probes, built-in intercept access points (IAP), management software, in-band or out-of-band data communication networks, receiver applications, forensics, evidence collection, and court replays
- *People:* necessary skills and experiences of subject matter experts working with TSPs, LEAs, and outsourcers to support the process steps and available lawful intercept (LI) products and tools

Lawful interception, also labeled *wiretapping* and *communications interception*, refers to identification, isolation, delivery, and collection of communication sessions (voice, e-mail, packet data, etc.) for use by LEAs. This critical law enforcement tool is employed by many authorized government agencies to investigate criminal activities. LEAs, TSPs, and equipment manufacturers continuously work together to develop products and define technical standards for LIs in the quest to aid LEAs in their role of protecting the public.

At present, LI operating principles can be summarized as follows:

- The technology needed to intercept virtually any telecommunications service is available, but the price tag may be high in such cases as SMS, MMS, VPNs, VoIP, and encrypted traffic.
- Existing laws usually pertain to telephone systems and for the most part are not feasible in the case of Internet-based voice, data, and video technologies; there continue to be disputes regarding the border between "information" and "communications" services.
- There are practically no laws, rules, or guidelines in place in the area of data retention, resulting in problems in instances involving large volumes of stored e-mails, intercepted voice communications, video teleconferences, and other communications-related applications.
- Only a few examples exist of direct dialogues between LEAs, outsourcers, and TSPs addressing technical, economic, and privacy challenges.
- Currently, most TSPs do not deploy ISSs, and thus segmented applications exist around otherwise powerful mediation solutions.
- The handover process between LEAs and TSPs is not supported by the latest technology, with the result that state-of-the-art security solutions cannot be fully implemented to protect sensitive data and intelligence.
- Educational work is needed to separate and integrate lawful interception, security, and forensic solutions; although these areas are very different, there can and should be collaboration among them.
- Data management is a key component of the operations of TSPs; not only lawful interception requests, but also other information requests by LEAs and other government agencies, can be met through querying of internal and external databases.
- Technological challenges remain in the areas of targeting prepaid customers, location tracking, identity management, searches, IPv4 migration toward IPv6, and emerging new products and services; TSPs and network equipment manufacturers are advised to embed interception access points (IAPs) into their equipment.

International and domestic lawful interception standards for IRI, content, and handover are not expected to exhibit significant changes in the near future. Thus, support of the access, delivery, and collection functions remains mandatory. In terms of the access function, expectations for the future can be summarized as follows:

- More embedded IAPs
- Flexible provisioning IAPs
- Simplified physical and logical configurations of probes
- Collaboration in regard to strategic and targeted surveillance techniques
- Easier target identification via IPv6-based addressing mechanisms
- Resolution of dynamic identifiers (IP addresses) with static identifiers (MSID)
- Correlation of data flows from multiple network nodes
- Collection of data on activity at all nodes in voice, data, or video networks
- Informed network routers streaming specific flows to session or packet reconstructors
- Flagging of specific users on content gateways and servers

In terms of the delivery function, future expectations include:

- Mediation systems playing the role of coordinator for receiving data from all kinds of IAPs
- Mediation systems taking responsibility for distributing data to LEAs and other ISS applications
- Flexible conversion of mediated data into intelligence
- State-of-the-art peering with monitoring centers, outsourcers, and LEAs
- Filtering of data in real-time based on intercept warrants
- Provision of reports on all types of filtered usage (real-time or batch)
- Dynamic provision of alarms for layer-7 (HTTP) access of targeted Web sites or bulletin boards, or access by restricted users

Finally, in regard to the collection function, expectations for the future include the following:

- State-of-the-art connections between LEAs, outsourcers, and TSPs
- Flexible collaboration between LEAs, outsourcers, and TSPs
- More secure handover solutions
- New applications for back-office functions

- Unified, simplified user interfaces designed to allow LEAs easy access to intelligence from multiple TSPs and outsourcers

The administration function should see improvements as well, with the arrival of new features. Examples are as follows:

- Secure local or remote access to intercept rules base and data sets
- Dynamic deployment of rules base and data sets to collectors and correlators
- Automated addition of target subjects to watch lists
- Capacity to query external databases as required

In addition, several points must be considered in regard to real-time, active mediation associated with LI activities:

- *Lawful interception is a regulatory mandate, not a profit generator:* An appropriate active mediation deployment can provide a solution for many of the regulators within a software component used for other profitable purposes.
- *Mediation is already established in the network:* Most likely, the mediation solution already communicates with all network nodes as part of its existing functions.
- *There should be restricted user group access:* The mediation solution should include a security subsystem ensuring that access is granted only to those users who are authorized to view the rules base.
- *There should be extensible rules base:* It should be relatively simple to add intercept rules and target data sets (cell number, IP address, and username) to the system.
- *There should be dynamic deployment rules:* Rule deployment should be dynamic, eliminating the need to take the system offline to update data sets.
- *Mediation should support active data warehousing:* It should support real-time and near-real-time data-mining capabilities.

New technologies and new TSPs will be subject to LI regulations. According to one of the latest rulings of the U.S. Federal Communications Commission, communications services offered over broadband pipes, including VoIP, are subject to Communications Assistance for Law Enforcement Act (CALEA) requirements in regard to compliance with LEA requests for IRI and content surveillance. These tentative rules would also cover managed communications services offered over broadband connections, including managed instant message or video services. Nonmanaged peer-to-peer services, including consumer-grade instant-messaging and noncommercial VoIP services, probably would not be subject to CALEA regulations under the proposed order.

New applications regarding dynamic surveillance rules, correlations between intelligence sources, and use of external databases will help to improve activities relating to targeting and identification of criminals and terrorists. If they are to be "future proof," LI strategies need to incorporate the following attributes:

- Seamless operation in PSTN, IP, next-generation, converged, and hybrid networks
- Maximum flexibility in regard to defining rules for multiple data sources: enhancing capabilities to dynamically search live data, handling location attributes, and recognizing multiple identification trace points
- Powerful correlation capabilities: collecting data from multiple sources, and combining and correlating data
- Integration with new data sources and feeding of additional downstream systems
- Cost-effective implementation leveraging a revenue-generating platform
- State-of-the-art technology, beginning with a core platform
- Capability for authorized operators to actively manage warrants
- Coordination of secure delivery functions between carrier network and LEAs
- Indirect provisioning of core network element for Level-1 or Level-2 surveillance
- Use of secure Web services frameworks with information exchange
- Provision of secure tunnels for transmitting CDC and CCC to LEAs

In most democratic countries, the lawfulness of surveillance activities is constantly supervised by human rights and privacy organizations. As a result, the number of illegal interceptions has been reduced to a reasonable minimum. True anonymity during the use of telecommunications products and services remains very important (Rapoza, 2004). For example, individuals engaged in politics and living under oppressive regimes can pursue political activities without fear of revealing their identity. However, factions such as the entertainment industry see anonymity as an obstacle to the protection of digital rights, tracking of violations, and collection of due revenues. Another fact to be considered is that anonymity can protect criminals and terrorists who violate the law. LEAs, groups advocating protection of privacy, organizations investing in surveillance technologies, and emerging TSPs need to engage in continuing dialogue regarding surveillance activities so that optimal compromises can be reached.

Appendix A

Glossary

Access protocol: A defined set of procedures that is adopted at an interface at a specified reference point between a user and a network to enable the user to employ the services or facilities of that network.

Access provider (AP): Provides a user of some network with access from the user's terminal to that network. This definition applies specifically for the present document. In a particular case, the AP and network operator (NWO) may be a common commercial entity.

Accounting: The process of apportioning charges between the home environment, serving network, and user.

Accuracy: A performance criterion that describes the degree of correctness with which a function is performed.

Application: A service enabler deployed by service providers, manufacturers, or users. Individual applications will often be enablers for a wide range of services.

Authentication: A property by which the correct identity of an entity or party is established with a required assurance. The party being authenticated could be a user, subscriber, home environment, or serving network.

Best-effort QoS: The lowest of all QoS traffic classes. If the guaranteed QoS cannot be delivered, the bearer network delivers the QoS, which is called best-effort QoS.

Best-effort service: A service model that provides minimal performance guarantees, allowing an unspecified variance in the measured performance criteria.

Billing: A function whereby CDRs generated by the charging function are transformed into bills requiring payment.

Buffer: Temporary storing of information in case the necessary telecommunication connection to transport information to the law enforcement monitoring facility (LEMF) is temporarily unavailable.

Call: Any connection (fixed or temporary) capable of transferring information between two or more users of a telecommunications system. In this context, a user may be a person or a machine. It is used for transmission of the content of communication. This term refers to circuit-switched calls only.

Call-identifying information (CII): Dialing or signaling information that identifies the origin, direction, destination or termination of each communication generated by means of any equipment, facility, service, or a telecommunications carrier.

Charging data record (CDR): A formatted collection of information about a chargeable event (e.g., time of call set-up, duration of the call, amount of data transferred, etc.) for use in billing and accounting. For each party to be charged for parts of or all the charges of a chargeable event, a separate CDR shall be generated, i.e., more than one CDR may be generated for a single chargeable event, e.g., because of its long duration or because more than one charged party is to be charged.

Communication: Information transfer according to agreed conventions.

Confidentiality: The avoidance of disclosure of information without the permission of its owner.

Connected mode: The state of user equipment switched on and an RRC connection established.

Connection: A communication channel between two or more endpoints (e.g., terminal, server, etc.).

Content of communication (CC): Information exchanged between two or more users of a telecommunications service, excluding intercept related information (IRI). This includes information which may, as part of some telecommunications service, be stored by one user for subsequent retrieval by another.

Content of communication link: A communication channel for HI3 information between a mediation function and an LEMF.

Dependability: A performance criterion that describes the degree of certainty (or surety) with which a function is performed regardless of speed or accuracy, but within a given observational interval.

Element management functions: A set of functions for management of network elements on an individual basis. These are basically the same functions as those supported by the corresponding local terminals.

Element manager: Provides a package of end-user functions for management of a set of closely related types of network elements.

Framework: Defines a set of application programming interface (API) classes for developing applications and for providing system services to those applications.

Guaranteed service: A service model that provides highly reliable performance with little or no variance in the measured performance criteria.

Handover interface: A physical and logical interface across which the interception measures are requested from the NWO/AP/service provider, and the results of interception are delivered from a NWO/AP/service provider (SvP) to an LEMF.

Identity: A technical label that may represent the origin or destination of any telecommunications traffic, as a rule clearly identified by a physical telecommunications identity number (such as a telephone number), or the logical or virtual telecommunications identity number (such as a personal number), which the subscriber can assign to a physical access on a case-by-case basis.

Information: Intelligence or knowledge capable of being represented in forms suitable for communication, storage, or processing. Information may be represented, for example, by signs, symbols, pictures, or sounds.

Information services: The offering of a capability for generating, storing, transforming, retrieving, utilizing, or making available information via telecommunications, and includes electronic publishing but does not include the use of such capability for the management, control, or operation of a telecommunications system or the management of a telecommunications service.

Integrity: In the context of security, the avoidance of unauthorized modification of information.

Interception: Action (based on the law) performed by an NWO/AP/SvP, of making available certain information and providing that information to an LEMF. Usually, this term is not used to describe the action of observing communications directly by an LEA.

Interception interface: Physical and logical locations within the NWO/AP/SvP telecommunications facilities where access to the CC and

IRI is provided. The interception interface is not necessarily a single fixed point.

Interception measure: A technical measure that facilitates the interception of telecommunications traffic pursuant to the relevant national laws and regulations.

Interception subject: A person or persons, specified in a lawful authorization, whose telecommunications are to be intercepted.

Intercept-related information: Collection of information or data associated with telecommunications services involving the target identity, specifically communication-associated information or data (including unsuccessful communication attempts), service-associated information or data (e.g., service-profile management by subscriber), and location information.

Internal network interface: Network's internal interface between the internal intercepting function and a mediation function.

Law enforcement agency (LEA): Organization authorized by a lawful authorization based on a national law to receive the results of telecommunications interceptions.

Law enforcement monitoring facility (LEMF): Law enforcement facility designated as the transmission destination for the results of interception relating to a particular interception subject.

Lawful authorization: Permission granted to an LEA under certain conditions to intercept specified telecommunications and requiring cooperation from an NWO/AP/SvP. Typically, this refers to a warrant or order issued by a lawfully authorized body.

Lawful interception or intercept: See Interception.

Location information: Information relating to the geographical, physical, or logical location of an identity relating to an interception subject.

Mediation function: A mechanism that passes information between an NWO, an AP or an SvP, and a handover interface, and information between the internal network interface and the handover interface.

Messaging service: An interactive service that offers user-to-user communication between individual users via storage units with store-and-forward, and mailbox or message handling functions (e.g., information editing, processing, and conversion).

Network element: A component of the network structure such as a local exchange, higher-order switch, or service-control processor.

Network manager: Provides a package of end-user functions with the responsibility for the management of a network, mainly as supported by the EMs, but it may also involve direct access to the network elements. All communication with the network is based on open and well-standardized interfaces supporting management of multivendor and multi-technology network elements.

Network operator (NWO): Operator of a public telecommunications infrastructure that permits the conveyance of signals between defined network termination points by wire, microwave, optical means, or other electromagnetic means.

Performance: The ability to track service and resource usage levels and to provide feedback on the responsiveness and reliability of the network.

Postpay billing: Billing arrangement between the customer and operator/SvP in which the customer periodically receives a bill for service usage in the past period.

Prepay billing: Billing arrangement between the customer and operator/SvP in which the customer deposits an amount of money in advance, which is subsequently used to pay for service usage.

Quality of Service (QoS): Quality specification of a telecommunications channel, system, virtual channel, and computer-telecommunications session. QoS may be measured, for example, in terms of signal-to-noise ratio, bit error rate, message throughput rate or call-blocking probability. It is the collective effect of service performances that determine the degree of satisfaction of a user of a service. It is characterized by the combined aspects of performance factors applicable to all services, such as service operability performance, service accessibility performance, service retainability performance, service integrity performance, and other factors specific to each service.

Reference configuration: A combination of functional groups and reference points that shows possible network arrangements.

Reliability: The probability that a system or service will perform in a satisfactory manner for a given period of time when used under specific operating conditions.

Result of interception: Information relating to a target service, including the CC and IRI, which is passed by an NWO/AP/SvP to an LEA. IRI shall be provided whether or not call activity is taking place.

Security: The ability to prevent fraud as well as ensure the protection of information availability, integrity, and confidentiality.

Service: A component of the portfolio of choices offered by SvPs to a user, a functionality offered to a user.

Service control: The ability of the user, home environment, or serving environment to determine what a particular service does, for a specific invocation of that service, within the limitations of that service.

Service information: Information used by the telecommunications infrastructure in the establishment and operation of a network-related service or services. The information may be established by an NWO/AP/SvP or a network user.

Service provider (SvP): A natural or legal person providing one or more public telecommunications services whose provision consists wholly or partly in the transmission and routing of signals on a telecommunications network. SvPs do not necessarily have to run their own networks.

Signaling: The exchange of information specifically concerned with the establishment and control of connections, and with management, in a telecommunications network.

Subscriber: An entity (associated with one or more users) that is engaged in a subscription with a telecommunications service provider (TSP). The subscriber is allowed to subscribe to and unsubscribe from services, to register a user or a list of users authorized to enjoy these services, and also to set the limits relative to the use that associated users make of these services.

Target identification: Identity that relates to a specific lawful authorization as such. This may be a serial number or a combination of characters and numbers. It is not related to the denoted interception subject or subjects.

Target identity: The identity associated with a target service used by the interception subject.

Target service: Telecommunications service associated with an interception subject and usually specified in a lawful authorization for interception. There may be more than one target service associated with a single interception subject.

Telecommunication: Any transfer of signs, signals, writing images, sounds, data, or intelligence of any nature transmitted in whole or in part by a wire, radio, electromagnetic, photoelectronic or photo-optical system.

Telecommunications: The transmission, between or among points specified by the user, of information of the user's choosing, without change in the form or content of the information as sent and received.

Telecommunications carrier: An entity engaged in the transmission or switching of wire or electronic communications as a common carrier for hire that:

- Includes commercial mobile radio service
- Includes an entity engaged in the transmission or switching of wire or electronic communications to the extent that the commission finds that such service is a replacement for a substantial portion of the local telephone exchange service and that it is in the public interest to deem it to be a telecommunications carrier for these purposes
- Does not include entities insofar as they are engaged in providing information services

Telecommunications service: The offering of telecommunications for a fee directly to the public or to such classes of users as to be effectively available directly to the public, regardless of the facilities used.

Telecommunications service provider (TSP): Umbrella term for APs, SPs, SvPs, and NWOs.

Appendix B

Acronyms

3Pty	Third-Party Service
AAA	Authentication, Authorization, and Accounting
ACD	Automated Call Distributor
ACSA	Antiterrorism Crime and Security Act
ADMF	ADMinistration Function
AF	Access Function
AIN	Advanced Intelligent Network
ALIS	Aqsacom's Lawful Interception Management Solution
ANI	Automatic Number Identification
AO	Administrative Office
AP	Access Provider
AS	Application Server
ASN.1	Abstract Syntax Notation, Version 1
ASP	Applications Service Provider
ATIS	Alliance for Telecommunications Industry Solutions
ATM	Asynchronous Transfer Mode
AUC	Authentication Center
BER	Basic Encoding Rules
BI	Business Intelligence
BML	Business Management Layer
BRI	Basic Rate Interface
BSC	Base Station Controller
BSS	Business Support System
BTS	Base Transceiver Station
CALEA	Communications Assistance for Law Enforcement Act

CAP	Competitive Access Provider
CB	Collection Box
CC	Content of Communication
CCC	Call Content Channel
CCLID	CC Link Identifier
CCP	Code of Criminal Procedure
CD	Call Data
CDC	Call Data Channel
CDDF	Call Data Delivery Function
CDF	Channel Definition Format
CDMA	Code Division Multiple Access
CDPD	Cellular Digital Packet Data
CDR	Call Detail Record
CES	Circuit Emulation Switching
CF	Collection Function
CGI	Common Gateway Interface
CII	Call-Identifying Information
CIN	Call Identity Number
CLEC	Competitive Local Exchange Carrier
CLI	Calling-Line Identity (Calling-Party Number)
CM	Cable Modem
CMCD	Centralized Management and Centralized Delivery
CMDD	Centralized Management and Distributed Delivery
CMIP	Common Management Information Protocol
CMS	Call Management System
CMTS	Cable Modem Termination System
COL	Connected Line Identity
CORBA	Common Object Request Broker Architecture
COTS	Commercial Off-The-Shelf
CPE	Customer Premises Equipment
CRM	Customer Relationship Management
CSCF	Call Session Control Function
CSDF	Circuit Switch Delivery Function
CSP	Cable Services Provider; Content Services Provider
CSS	Cascading Style Sheet
CUG	Closed User Group
DAS	Direct Attached Storage
DCF	Data Communications Function
DCFD	Data Collecting and Filtering Device
DCN	Data Communications Network
DDE	Dialed Digit Extraction
DEA	Drug Enforcement Agency
DF	Delivery Function

DHCP	Dynamic Host Configuration Protocol
DHTML	Dynamic HyperText Markup Language
DMTF	Desktop Management Task Force
DMS	Document Management Strategy
DMZ	Demilitarized Zone
DN	Directory Number
DNS	Domain Name System
DOCSIS	Data-Over-Cable Service Interface Specifications
DOM	Document Object Model
DSL	Digital Subscriber Line
DSLAM	Digital Subscriber Line Access Multiplexer
DSML	Directory Services Markup Language
DSS	Decision Support System
DSS1	Digital Subscriber Signaling System, No. 1
DSSSL	Document Style and Semantics Specification Language
DTD	Document Type Definition
DTMF	Dual Tone Multi-Frequency
DWDN	Dense Wave Division Multiplexing (DWDM)
EBPP	Electronic Bill Presentment and Payment
ECPA	Electronic Communications Privacy Act
EDGE	Enhanced Data Rates for Global Evolution
EDI	Electronic Data Interchange
EDSA	Extensible Directory Service Agent
EDSS	Equipment Deployment and Storage System
EIF	External Interception Function
EIR	Equipment Identity Register
EML	Element Management Layer
EMS	Element Management System
ENUM	Electronic NUMbering
ERP	Enterprise Resource Planning
ESP	Enterprise Service Provider
ESTS	Electronic Surveillance Technology Section
ETOM	Enhanced Telecommunications Operations Map
ETSI	European Telecommunications Standard Institute
FAB	Fulfillment, Assurance, and Billing
FCAPS	Fault, Configuration, Accounting, Performance, Security
FCC	Federal Communication Committee
FDM	Frequency Division Multiplexing
FDN	Foreign Directory Number
FISA	Foreign Intelligence Surveillance Act
FMS	Fault Management System
FoIP	Fax-over-IP
FPLMTS	Future Public Land Mobile Telecommunications System

FR	Frame Relay
FTP	File Transfer Protocol
GCP	Gateway Control Protocol
GGSN	Gateway GPRS Support Node
GIS	Geographical Information System
GMOS	Generic Managed Object Server
GMSC	Gateway Mobile Switching Center
GPRS	General Packet Radio Service
GPS	Global Positioning System
GSM	Global System for Mobile Communication
GSN	GPRS Service Node
GTP	GPRS Tunneling Protocol
GUI	Graphical User Interface
HA	Home Agent
HDTV	High-Definition TV
HFC	Hybrid Fiber Coax
HI	Handover Interface
HI1	Handover Interface Port 1 (Administrative Information)
HI2	Handover Interface Port 2 (Intercept-Related Information)
HI3	Handover Interface Port 3 (Content of Information)
HLR	Home Location Register
HO	Home Office
HSS	Home Subscriber Server
HTML	HyperText Markup Language
HTTP	HyperText Transmission Protocol
HUR	Home Location Register
IA	Interception Area
IAD	Internet Access Device
IADF	Internet or Intercept Access Delivery Function
IAP	Interception or Intercept Access Point
ICC	Interception of Communication Commissioner
ICP	Integration Communications Provider
IDL	Interface Definition Language
IETF	Internet Engineering Task Force
IEX	Inter EXchange Carrier
IF	Intercepting Function
IIF	Internal Interception Function
ILEC	Incumbent Local Exchange Carrier
IM	Instant Messaging
IMAP	Internet Message Access Protocol
IMEI	International Mobile station Equipment Identity
IMS	Interception Management System; Internet Monitoring System

IMSI	International Mobile Subscriber Identity
IMS-MGW	IP Multimedia Subsystem – Media Gateway
IN	Intelligent Network
INI	Internal Network Interface
IOCA	Interception of Communications Act
IP	Internet Protocol
IPSec	IP Security
IPT	Investigatory Powers Tribunal
IPTGT	IP Target
IRC	Internet Relay Chat
IRI	Intercept-Related Information
ISC	International Softswitch Consortium
ISCSI	Internet Small Computer Systems Interface
ISDN	Integrated Services Digital Network
ISP	Internet Service Provider
ISS	Intelligence Support System
ITI	Intercept Target Identity
ITSP	Internet Telephony Service Provider
IVR	Interactive Voice Response
IWF	InterWorking Function
IXC	IntereXchange Carrier
LAN	Local Area Network
LCN	Logical Channel Number
LD	Long Distance
LDAP	Lightweight Directory Access Protocol
LEA	Law Enforcement Agency
LEMF	Law Enforcement Monitoring Facility
LES	Law Enforcement System
LI	Lawful Intercept or Interception
LIID	Lawful Interception IDentifier
LIOS	Lawful Interception Operation System
LMDS	Local Multipoint Distribution Service
MC	Monitoring Center
MD	Mediation Device
MDN	Messaging Disposition Notification
MF	Mediation Function
MG	Media Gateway
MGC	Media Gateway Controller
MGCF	Media Gateway Control Function
MIB	Management Information Base
MIME	Multipurpose Internet Mail Extensions
MMDS	Multichannel Multipoint Distribution Service
MML	Man Machine Language

MMS	Multimedia Message Service
MPLS	Multi-Protocol Label Switching
MRF	Media Resource Function
MS	Management Station
MSC	Mobile Switching Center
MSISDN	Mobile Subscriber ISDN Number
MSN	Multiple Subscriber Number
MSO	Mobile Switching Office; Multiple Systems Operator
MSS	Mobile Satellite System; Marketing Support System
MTA	Multiple Terminal Adapter
NAP	Network Access Point
NAS	Network-Attached Storage
NAT	Network Address Translation
NC	Network Connector
NEL	Network Element Layer
NGN	Next-Generation Network
NGOSS	Next-Generation OSS
NIC	Network Interface Card
NML	Network Management Layer
NMS	Network Management System
NOC	Network Operations Center
NSP	Network Service Provider
NTAC	National Technical Assistance Centre
NWO	Network Operator
OA&M	Operations, Administration, and Management
OASIS	Organization for the Advancement of Structured Information Standards
ODBC	Open Database Connectivity
ONA	Open Network Architecture
OSD	Open Software Description
OSF	Operations Systems Function
OSI	Open Systems Interconnection
OSS	Operations Support System
PBX	Private Branch Exchange
PC	Personal Computer
PCS	Personal Communication Services
PDA	Personal Digital Assistant
PDN	Packet Data Network
PDSN	Packet Data Serving Node
PDU	Protocol Data Unit
PKI	Public-Key Infrastructure
PLMN	Public Land Mobile Network
PoP	Point of Presence

POTS	Plain Old Telephone Services
PPP	Point-to-Point Protocol
PRM	Partner Relationship Management
PSAP	Public-Safety Answering Point
PSTN	Public Switched Telephone Network
PVC	Permanent Virtual Circuit
QAF	Q Adapter Function
QoS	Quality of Service
RADIUS	Remote Authentication Dial-In User Service
RAN	Radio Access Network
RAS	Remote Access Server
RDF	Resource Definition Language
RIPA	Regulation of Investigatory Power Act
RNC	Radio Network Controller
ROSE	Remote Operation Service Element
RSU	Remote Serving Unit
RTP	Real-Time Protocol
SAML	Security Assurance Markup Language
SAN	Storage Area Network
SAP	Service Access Point
SAS	Surveillance Administration System
SBC	Session Border Control
SCP	Switching Control Point; Service Control Point
SCTE	Society of Cable Television Engineers
SFA	Sales Force Automation
SGML	Standard Generalized Markup Language
SGSN	Serving GPRS Support Node
SINA	Secure InterNetwork Architecture
SIP	Session Initialization Protocol
SLA	Service-Level Agreement
SMIL	Synchronized Multimedia Integration Language
SML	Service Management Layer
SMS	Short Message Service
SMTP	Simple Mail Transfer Protocol
SNMP	Simple Network Management Protocol
SOHO	Small Office/Home Office
SOW	Statement of Work
SP	Service Provider
SPML	Service Provisioning Markup Language
SPVC	Semi Permanent Virtual Circuit
SS&I	Systems Security and Integrity
SS7	Common Channel Signaling System
SSDF	Softswitch Delivery Function

SSL	Secure Sockets Layer
STDM	Statistical Time Division Multiplexing
STP	Switching Transmission Point
SVC	Switched Virtual Circuit
SvP	Service Provider
SWT	Standard Widget Toolkit
TAB	Technical Advisory Board
TC	Technology Connector
TCP	Transmission Control Protocol
TDM	Time Division Multiplexing
TDMA	Time Division Multiple Access
TE	Test Equipment
TETRA	Trans European Trunked Radio
TIA	Telecommunications Industry Association
TMF	TeleManagement Forum
TMN	Telecommunications Management Network
TSGW	Transport Signaling Gateway
TSP	Telecommunications Service Provider
TTI	Test-Target Identity
UDP	User Datagram Protocol
UDWDM	Ultra Dense Wave Division Multiplexing
UM	Unified Messaging
UMTS	Universal Mobile Telecommunications System
UPC	Universal Personal Communication
URI	Universal Resource Identifier
URL	Universal Resource Locator
USA PATRIOT Act	Uniting and Strengthening America by Providing Appropriate Tools Required to Intercept and Obstruct Terrorism Act of 2001
UUS	Unified User Station; User-to-User Signaling
VCI	Virtual Circuit Identifier
VCMI	Virtual Circuit Messaging Interface
VLR	Visitor Location Register
VoIP	Voice-over-IP
VoP	Voice over Packet
VPN	Virtual Private Network
VSAT	Very Small Aperture Satellite System
W3C	World Wide Web Consortium
WAN	Wide Area Network
WDDF	Wireless Data Delivery Function
WDM	Wavelength Division Multiplexing
WLL	Wireless Local Loop
WMS	Workforce Management System

WSF	Work Station Function
WUS	Wake-Up Service
WWW	World Wide Web
XDR	XML Data Reduced
xGSN	SGSN or GGSN
XLL	eXtensible Linking Language
XML	eXtensible Markup Language
XSL	eXtensible Style Language

Appendix C

References

ANSI: Lawfully Authorized Electronic Surveillance (LAES) for Voice over Packet Technologies in Wireline Telecommunications Networks, TI.678, 2003.

Axland, J.: Keep Your Eyes Open, ISS World Conference, Washington, D.C., May 2004.

Baker, F.: Cisco Support for Lawful Intercept in IP Networks, Internet Engineering Task Force, 2003.

Carragher, O.: Basic Requirements of LEAs, Tutorial, ISS Conference, Washington, D.C., November 2003.

Cividanes, E.W.: What Costs Related to Assisting Law Enforcement are Reimbursable? ISS Conference, Washington, D.C., November 2003.

Cohen, O.: Internet Surveillance via an Intelligence Support System, *Narus White Paper*, Palo Alto, CA, USA, 2003-12-24.

CTL: PacketCable Electronic Surveillance Specification, PKT-SP-ESP-Io3-040113, Cable Television Laboratories Inc., January 2004.

ETSI: Handover Interface for the Lawful Interception of Telecommunications Traffic, ETSI ES-201-671, Telecommunications Security, 2001.

ETSI ES 201 158: Telecommunications Security; Lawful Interceptions (LI) Requirements for Network Functions, 2002.

ETSI ES 201 671 Edition 2 Draft 13: Telecommunication Security; Lawful Interception (LI); Handover Interface for Lawful Interception of Telecommunication Traffic, 2003.

ETSI: ETSI TS 102 233 Service Specific Details for E-Mail Services, Technical Specification, Telecommunications Security, Lawful Interception, Version 1.1.1, 2004a.

ETSI: ETSI TS 102 234 Service Specific Details for Internet Access Services, Technical Specification, Telecommunications Security, Lawful Interception, Version 1.1.1, 2004b.

443

ETSI: Handover Specification for IP Delivery, ETSI TS-102-232, Telecommunications Security, 2004c.

Fransen, F.: Lawful Interception of Internet in the Netherlands, ISS Conference, Washington, D.C., November 2003.

Gartner Group: Combine CobiT and ITIL for Powerful IT Governance, TG-16-1849, Research Note, June 10, 2002.

Greenfield, D.: Location-Aware Networking. We Know Where You Are, *Network Magazine*, March 2005, pp. 46–51.

Haynes, I.: Using Tools to Manage Sourcing, Cutter Consortium Advisory Service Executive Report, 2003, USA.

Hochmuth, P.: Users Tap Network Monitoring Technology, *Network World*, February 16, 2004, pp. 17, 18.

ITU: Recommendation X.690, Information Technology: ASN.1 Encoding Rules: Specification of Basic Encoding Rules (BER), Canonial Encoding Rules (CER), and Distinguished Encoding Rules (DER), July 2002.

Lucas, J.: Circuit Switched Voice and VoIP Basics, Tutorial, ISS World Conference, Washington, D.C., November 2003a.

Lucas, J.: Internet Technology Basics, Tutorial, ISS Conference, Washington, D.C., November 2003b.

Lucas, J.: Introduction to Wireless Networks, Tutorial, ISS Conference, Washington, D.C., November 2003c.

Lucas, J.: Lawful Interception for Cable/VoIP Networks, Tutorial, ISS Conference, Washington, D.C., November 2003d.

Lucas, J.: ISS ROI Revisited, *Billing World and OSS Today*, December 2003e, pp. 6, 43.

Lucas, J.: Making Money with ISS, *Billing World and OSS Today*, July 2003f, pp. 4, 5.

Lunetta, L.: Frameworks Coordinate Security, *Network World*, November 24, 2003, p. 31.

McCollum, D.: Electronic Surveillance Law, Tutorial, ISS Conference, Washington, D.C., November 2003.

Packet Cable: PacketCable Electronic Surveillance Specification, PKT-SP-ESP-I03-040113, Cable Television Laboratories, Inc., 2004.

Pellero, B.: Lawful Interception Requirements for Communications Satellite Operators, *ISS World*, Fall 2004, McLean, VA, USA.

Petersen, J.K.: *Understanding Surveillance Technologies: Spy Devices, Their Origins & Applications*, Handbook, CRC Press, Boca Raton, FL, USA, 2001.

Rapoza, J.: Who Am I — Net Anonymity, Technical Directions, *eWeek*, August 16, 2004.

Rosenfeld, E.: Lawful Intercept Challenges for VoIP, ISS Conference, Washington, D.C., November 2003

Rutkowsky, T.: Handover Interfaces and Standards, ISS Conference, Washington, D.C., 2003.

SCTE: IPCableComm Electronic Surveillance Standard, ANSI/SCTE 24-13, May 2001, Society of Cable Television Engineers.

Terplan K.: *Intranet Performance Management*, CRC Press, Boca Raton, FL, USA, 1999.

Terplan, K.: *OSS Essentials — Support System Solutions for Service Providers*, John Wiley & Sons, New York, USA, 2001.

Terplan, K.: *Electronic Bill Presentment and Payment*, CRC Press, Boca Raton, FL, USA, 2003.

Warren, H.M.: CALEA Cost Recovery, ISS Conference, Washington, D.C., November 2003a.

Warren, H.M.: Outsourcing: An Option for Law Enforcement Support Services, ISS Conference, Washington, D.C., November 2003b.

Index

Note: Italicized page numbers refer to tables and illustrations.